Discover

Contents

Australia

Throughout this book, we use these icons to highlight special recommendations:

The Best...
Lists for everything from bars to wildlife – to make sure you don't miss out

Don't Miss
A must-see – don't go home until you've been there

Local Knowledge Local experts reveal their top picks and secret highlights

Detour
Special places a little off the beaten track

If you like...
Lesser-known alternatives to world-famous attractions

These icons help you quickly identify reviews in the text and on the map:

Sights

Eating

Drinking

Sleeping

Information

This edition written and researched by

Charles Rawlings-Way,
Brett Atkinson, Jayne D'Arcy, Peter Dragicevich,
Sarah Gilbert, Paul Harding, Catherine Le Nevez,
Virginia Maxwell, Miriam Raphael, Regis St Louis,
Steve Waters, Penny Watson, Meg Worby

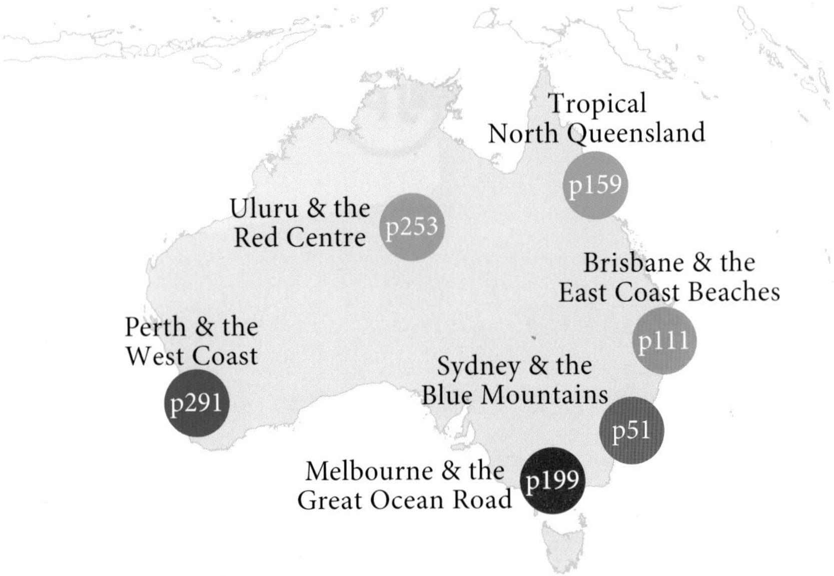

Tropical
North Queensland
p159

Uluru & the
Red Centre
p253

Brisbane & the
East Coast Beaches
p111

Perth & the
West Coast
p291

Sydney & the
Blue Mountains
p51

Melbourne & the
Great Ocean Road
p199

Contents

Plan Your Trip On the Road

Contents

On the Road

This is Australia

Island, country, continent...Australia is a big 'un whichever way you spin it. The essence of the place is diversity:
deserts, coral reefs, tall forests, snow-cloaked mountains
and multicultural melting-pot cities.

Most Australians live along the coast, and most of these folks live in cities.

In fact, Australia is the 18th-most urbanised
country in the world, with around 70% of Australians
living in the 10 largest towns. It follows that cities here
are a whole lotta fun! Sydney, the sun-kissed Harbour
City, is a glamorous collusion of beaches, boutiques
and bars. Melbourne is all arts, alleyways and Australian Rules football. Brisbane is a subtropical town on the
way up; boomtown Perth breathes west-coast optimism.
But whichever city you're wheeling into, you'll never
go wanting for a decent coffee, a live band, art-gallery
opening or music festival mosh-pit.

Hungry?

Australia's multicultural chefs fuse together
European techniques and fresh Pacific Rim ingredients.
'Mod Oz' (or Modern Australian) is what the locals call it.
Seafood plays a starring role: from succulent Moreton
Bay bugs to delicate King George whiting, there's a lot
of variety in the ocean's bounty. And of course, beer in
hand, you'll still find beef, lamb and chicken at traditional
Aussie barbecues. Don't drink beer? From Barossa Valley
Shiraz to Hunter Valley Semillon, Australian wines are
world-beaters. Need a caffeine hit? These days there are
coffee machines in pubs and petrol stations, and baristas
stationed at downtown coffee carts – you're never far
from a double-shot, day or night.

There's a heckuva lot of tarmac across this wide brown land.

The temp-
tation is to 'Get your motor runnin'...Head out on the
highway...', as Steppenwolf cry in 'Born To Be Wild'. But
remember that Australia is really big! An intrepid outback road trip will require some serious planning. On the
other hand, state capitals and regional centres are well
connected by airlines: with a little groundwork you can
cover a good chunk of the country in just a few weeks.

> 66
> 'Mod Oz'
> (or Modern
> Australian)
> is what the
> locals call it.
> 99

Sydney Opera House (p65)

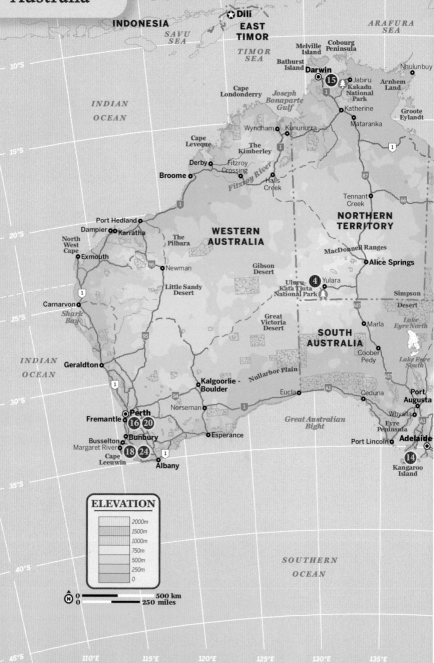

Australia

INDONESIA

★ Dili

EAST
TIMOR

*SAVU
SEA*

*TIMOR
SEA*

*ARAFURA
SEA*

Melville
Island

Cobourg
Peninsula

Bathurst
Island

Darwin ⊙ ❶⑮ ◦ Jabiru
Kakadu
National
Park

Nhulunbuy

Arnhem
Land

Groote
Eylandt

*INDIAN

OCEAN*

Cape
Londonderry

*Joseph
Bonaparte
Gulf*

Wyndham ◦ Kununurra

Katherine

Mataranka

Cape
Leveque

**The
Kimberley**

Derby ◦ Fitzroy
Crossing

Fitzroy River

Broome ◦

Halls
Creek

NORTHERN
TERRITORY

Tennant
Creek

Port Hedland ◦
Dampier ◦◦ Karratha

North
West
Cape

**WESTERN
AUSTRALIA**

The
Pilbara

MacDonnell Ranges

Alice Springs

◦ Exmouth

Newman

Gibson
Desert

Uluru-
Kata Tjuta
National Park

❹ Yulara

Simpson

Carnarvon ◦

*Shark
Bay*

Little Sandy
Desert

Great
Victoria
Desert

**SOUTH
AUSTRALIA**

Desert

Marla

*Lake
Eyre North*

*INDIAN

OCEAN*

Geraldton ◦

Kalgoorlie -
Boulder

Nullarbor Plain

Coober
Pedy

*Lake
Eyre
South*

Norseman ◦

Eucla

Ceduna

Port
Augusta

Fremantle ⊙ Perth

⑯ ⑳

Esperance ◦

*Great Australian
Bight*

Whyalla ◦

*Eyre
Peninsula*

Port
Augusta

Busselton ◦◦ Bunbury
Margaret River

⑱ ⑭

Cape
Leeuwin

Albany ◦

Port Lincoln ◦

Adelaide ◦

❶⑭

Kangaroo
Island

ELEVATION

	2000m
	1500m
	1000m
	750m
	500m
	250m
	0

▲
N

0   500 km
0   250 miles

*SOUTHERN

OCEAN*

25
Top Experiences

25 Australia's Top Experiences

Sydney Opera House

The magnificent opera house (p65) on Sydney Harbour is a headline act in itself. An exercise in architectural lyricism, Jørn Utzon's building on Bennelong Point holds its own amid the visual feast of the harbour's attention-grabbing bridge, shimmering blue waters and jaunty green ferries. Best of all is the fact that everyone can attend – its restaurant, bars, daily tours and regular performance schedule make sure of that.

RICHARD I'ANSON/LONELY PLANET IMAGES ©

(2)

Great Barrier Reef

Stretching more than 2000km up Queensland's coast, the Great Barrier Reef (p172) is one of the world's great wonders. Among the best ways to experience it: donning a mask and fins and delving into the undersea kingdom for a close-up view of coral, sharks and tropical fish... or exploring the reef by sailboat, taking a scenic flight, gazing at marine life through a glass-bottomed semisubmersible and lingering in a resort (or camp) on a coral-fringed island.

Melbourne

Head down bluestone-lined laneways in Melbourne's city centre (p212) to find the outstanding hidden restaurants and bold street art that encapsulates the alternative vibe here. Take your place on a milk crate in Degraves St or Centre Place and let a local barista change the way you think about coffee, then window shop for quirky 'only in Melbourne' craft and clothes. Watch evening's arrival by the Yarra River, then head up some stairs or down to the very end of a graffiti-covered lane to find a smooth drinking establishment serving up quality Victorian wine, beer and music. Centre Place

The Best...
Big-City Coffee Spots

FRATELLI PARADISO
Fab espresso and sexy staff: Rome ain't so far away... (p85)

PELLEGRINI'S ESPRESSO BAR
Melbourne's original (and still the best) espresso bar has serious cred. (p230)

BLEEDING HEART GALLERY
Art, architecture, concerts...oh, and central Brisbane's best coffee! (p138)

LITTLE WILLY'S
Our pick for a quick-fire caffeine hit in Perth. (p308)

The Best...
Museums

MUSEUM OF OLD & NEW ART (MONA)
Architecturally astonishing new museum just north of Hobart (...and the art's not bad either!). (p339)

WESTERN AUSTRALIAN MUSEUM – MARITIME
A whole lot of boats have floated into Fremantle over the years. (p313)

MUSEUM & ART GALLERY OF THE NORTHERN TERRITORY
Cyclone Tracy, Indigenous art, maritime history and Sweetheart, the 5m crocodile. (p266)

SURF WORLD MUSEUM
Surfing history on the Great Ocean Road. (p243)

MUSEUM OF BRISBANE
Digging up the dirt on Brisbane's history. (p133)

4 Uluru-Kata Tjuta National Park

With its remote desert location, deep cultural significance and spectacular natural beauty, Uluru is a pilgrimage well worth the many hundreds of kilometres it takes to get there. But Uluru-Kata Tjuta National Park (p286) offers much more than the chance to see the Rock. Along with the equally captivating Kata Tjuta (the Olgas), there are mystical walks, sunsets and ancient desert cultures to encounter.

Uluru (Ayers Rock)

5 Museum of Old and New Art (MONA)

A ferry ride from Hobart's harbour, the Museum of Old and New Art (p339) is a world-class institution. Designed by architect Nonda Katsalidis, MONA's three levels of underground galleries showcase hundreds of controversial artworks. Owner, philanthropist David Walsh, describes it as a 'subversive adult Disneyland'. Intense conversation is guaranteed after viewing this unique arts experience.

 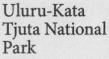

Daintree Rainforest

Fan palms, ferns and man-groves are just some of the 3000-plus plant species in the World Heritage–listed Daintree Rainforest (p189), which is alive with a chorus of birds, insects and frogs. Guided day walks, wildlife-spotting night tours, horse riding, croc-spotting cruises, kayaking...there are many ways to experience one of the most extraordinary ecosystems on the planet.

PAUL DYMOND/LONELY PLANET IMAGES ©

CHRISTOPHER GROENHOUT/LONELY PLANET IMAGES ©

Byron Bay

Vibrant, laidback and offbeat are words often used to describe this small-time, big-hearted, beachside destination. At first encounter, it might seem too touristy, too packed – but no matter how many bronzed shoulders you rub up against, Byron Bay (p122) tends to soften even the hardest critic. Long lazy stretches of beach and a cute undeveloped town centre help; so too does the eclectic food scene, where cheap, cheerful takeaway joints sit comfort-ably next to hip bars and restaurants. The town's infectious, up-beat vibe puts a smile on your dial, no matter where you hail from. Cape Byron lighthouse

Great Ocean Road

The Twelve Apostles – rock formations jutting out of wild waters – are one of Victoria's most vivid sights, but it's the road trip there that doubles their impact. Take it slow while driving beside Bass Strait beaches, then whip slightly inland through rainforests with small towns and big trees. The secrets of the Great Ocean Road (p242) don't stop here; further along is maritime treasure Port Fairy and hidden Cape Bridgewater. For the ultimate in slow travel, walk the Great Ocean Walk from Apollo Bay to the Apostles. Lookout, Twelve Apostles (p247)

8

The Best...
Beaches

BONDI BEACH
Big, wide and handsome, Bondi is Australia's most famous beach. (p75)

AVALON
The pick of Sydney's Northern Beaches: a dreamy arc of orange sand with solid surf. (p77)

COTTESLOE BEACH
Perth's best beach is a good time waiting to happen. (p311)

LITTLE WATEGOS
A Byron Bay gem: mainland Australia's most easterly beach. (p122)

BELLS BEACH
A wild Southern Ocean beach with brilliant (but unreliable) surf: the Rip Curl Pro surf competition happens here every Easter. (p244)

The Whitsundays

Sailing across the shimmering blue water of the Coral Sea, lounging beside the pool in a luxury island resort, playing castaway on a secluded beach...there are so many ways to enjoy the beautiful Whitsunday Islands (p173). One of the best is from the deck of a sailing boat, basking in the warm sunshine and balmy sea air, savouring the dramatic tropical sunsets and star-studded night skies. Sailing through this island paradise brings the romance of the sea to life.

Hamilton Island (p179)

The Best...
Markets

PADDINGTON MARKET
Big crowds mill around 250 stalls in superhip Paddo: clothes, food, music, massage...(p74)

CENTRAL MARKETS
Adelaide's multicultural foodie heaven is a South Australian must-see. (p336)

ORIGINAL KURANDA RAINFOREST MARKETS
Head for the hills behind Cairns on an historic train to this famous hippie market. (p190)

MINDIL BEACH SUNSET MARKET
A hyperactive market behind the Darwin dunes, with Asian eats and beaut buskers. (p267)

SALAMANCA MARKET
Every Saturday morning along Hobart's happening waterfront. (p339)

Bridge Climbing

Got a good head for heights? Vertigo not an issue? Make a beeline for Sydney's iconic Harbour Bridge or Brisbane's Storey Bridge and climb above it all. Sydney's BridgeClimb (p80) has been sending intrepid visitors over the grand arch for more than a decade: the views from the top are predictably sublime. Storey Bridge Adventure Climb (p136) is a newer experience but no less mesmerising. And it's not just about views – the bridges themselves are amazing structures! Sydney Harbour BridgeClimb

Gold Coast Surf Carnivals

They're the bronzed gods of the surf, the beefcakes of the sea and the uberfit icons of Australia's beach-crazed culture. From the first appearance of a surf belt in 1907, Australia's surf-lifesavers have evolved into superfit and superbuff athletes, pitting their skills against each other in seasonal surf carnivals on the Gold Coast (p127) – gruelling events involving ocean swimming, beach running and surf boat racing. It's hard work but makes for an extraordinary – and sensorily pleasing – spectator sport for the rest of us limp squids.

12

Canberra

If there's one thing Canberra's got going for it, it's museums. Whether your passion is art, history, film or big guns, you'll find it in spades in the bush capital. Highlights include the National Gallery of Australia (p334), with its magnificent collection of Aboriginal and Torres Strait Islander, Australian and Asian art; the National Museum of Australia (p334), whose imaginative exhibits provide insights into the Australian heart and soul; and the War Memorial (p334) with its moving Hall of Memory and fascinating displays. Australian War Memorial

13 ## Wilsons Promontory

For sheer natural beauty, Wilsons Promontory (p249) has it all. Jutting into Bass Strait, this national park boasts ocean beaches and some of the best wilderness hiking and camping in coastal Australia. The overnight walk from Tidal River to Sealer's Cove and back is a great way to get started. Serious hikers should tackle the three-day Great Prom Walk, staying a night in the gloriously isolated lighthouse keepers' cottage. Tidal River

Kangaroo Island

'KI' (p338), as South Australians call it, is a big place –
150km long and 57km wide. Plenty of room for the local
wildlife to run amok! You'll see kangaroos (of course),
plus wallabies, bandicoots, possums, koalas, platypuses,
cockatoos... Echidnas, goannas and tiger snakes mooch
around in the undergrowth, while offshore there are
dolphins, whales, penguins and seals. After you're done
wildlife spotting, there are country pubs, wineries and
seafood shacks to keep you fed and watered.

The Best...
Eat Streets

BRUNSWICK ST, MELBOURNE
Wall-to-wall cafes and
restaurants in inner-city
Fitzroy. There are some
great pubs around here
too! (p231)

CHINATOWN, SYDNEY
Pan-Asian delights for just a
few dollars. (p85)

LYGON ST, MELBOURNE
Italian restaurants and
Lygon St go together like
spaghetti and bolognaise
sauce. (p231)

MITCHELL ST, DARWIN
Backpacker bars and
crowded street terraces
overflow with edibles.
(p272)

The Best...
Indigenous Cultural Experiences

INDIGENOUS ART GALLERIES, DARWIN
Close to the source, Darwin's commercial art galleries sell gorgeous Indigenous art. (p267)

ANANGU TOURS, ULURU
Tour the remarkable rock with the people who know it best. (p286)

KAKADU ROCK ART
Check out the amazing rock art galleries at Ubirr and Nourlangie in Kakadu National Park. (p277)

ALICE SPRINGS
Explore 'The Alice' and the nearby MacDonnell Ranges with a local Warlpiri guide. (p281)

15

Darwin & Kakadu National Park

Levelled by WWII bombs and then Cyclone Tracy, Darwin (p266) knows a thing or two about reinvention. This frontier city, closer to Bali than Sydney, has emerged from the tropical steam to become a multicultural, hedonistic hotspot: the launch pad for trips into some of Australia's most remarkable wilderness. A couple of hours southeast, Kakadu National Park (p277) is the place to see Indigenous rock art under escarpments and waterholes at the base of plummeting waterfalls. Saltwater crocodiles and birdlife are guaranteed highlights. (left) Jim Jim Falls, Kakadu; (above) Indigenous rock art at Nourlangie Rock, Kakadu

(ABOVE) HOLGER LEUE; (LEFT) RICHARD I'ANSON/LONELY PLANET IMAGES ©

Perth & Fremantle

Perth (p302) may be isolated but it's far from being a backwater. Sophisticated restaurants offer modern Australian cuisine, while a new crop of cocktail bars lurks down laneways. In contrast to the flashy face that Perth presents to the Swan River, charmingly grungy inner suburbs echo with the thrum of guitars and the sizzle of woks. Just down the river, the lively port of Fremantle (p313) has a pub on every corner that doesn't already have a hostel on it, and a wealth of colonial buildings. Little Creatures (p316), Fremantle

Learning to Surf

When the swell is working, Australia's beaches fill with flotillas of rubber-suited people, bobbing around in the surf. Learning to surf is an Australian rite of passage – if you feel like joining in, Byron Bay (p123) in northern NSW has a few good learn-to-surf schools. You can also learn some skills at Noosa in Queensland, Bondi and Manly beaches in Sydney, and Anglesea on Victoria's Great Ocean Road. Bondi Beach (p75)

ANDREW WATSON/LONELY PLANET IMAGES ©

Margaret River

The joy of drifting from winery to winery along country roads shaded by tall gum trees is only one of the delights of Margaret River in Western Australia's southwest (p320). There are also caves to explore, historic towns to visit and spring wildflowers to admire. Surfers flock to world-class breaks around 'Margs', but it's not unusual to find yourself on a brilliant white-sand beach and nobody else in sight. In late winter and early spring, look offshore and chances are you'll spot whales cruising on the coast-hugging 'Humpback Highway'.

18

The Best...
Live Music Venues

ESPLANADE HOTEL
Melbourne's 'Espy' is still rockin', despite developers' wrecking balls casting shadows every few years. (p236)

BASEMENT
Subterranean jazz joint near Sydney's Circular Quay, with big-name touring acts. (p92)

ZOO
Go animal at Brisbane's best independent music venue, a real breeding ground for local talent. (p140)

BENNETTS LANE
Hip, jazzy hotspot down a central Melbourne laneway. (p236)

ANNANDALE HOTEL
This rude rock room in Sydney's inner west is a sure-fire bet for something loud, fast and funky. (p92)

AFL Grand Final

19

AFL Grand Final day in Melbourne (p217) on the last Saturday of September is the perfect time to head to your local pub (or make it your local for the day) and get rowdy with footy supporters. In 2010 Melburnians loved it so much there were two grand finals: the first one was a draw, so they had to replay it the following week – another excuse to go to the pub! The regular season lasts the entire length of winter, so expect colourful beanies and scarves bobbing around the state as a sign of devotion.

© THE SLATTERY MEDIA GROUP

The Best...
Shopping

QUEEN VICTORIA BUILDING
Wow, what a beauty! Downtown Sydney's Victorian shopping masterpiece. (p94)

QUEEN VICTORIA MARKET
Melbourne's freshest fish, meat and fruit 'n' veg, plus a fab night market on Wednesdays in summer. (p237)

PADDINGTON & WOOLLAHRA
Dandy designer duds along Sydney's Oxford St, Glenmore Rd and Queen St. (p93)

SYDNEY FISH MARKET
It's not just fabulous fresh fish! The world's second-largest fish market also has restaurants, sushi bars, florists, guided tours...(p73)

SYDNEY'S WEEKEND MARKETS
Hit the market stalls and bag yourself an unexpected bargain. (p73)

GRANT DIXON/LONELY PLANET IMAGES ©

20 Indigenous Art in WA

Around 59,000 Aboriginal people call Western Australia home, comprising many different Indigenous peoples, speaking distinct languages. The Art Gallery of Western Australia (p302) is a treasure trove of Indigenous art. To the north, the art of the Kimberley is like no other. Encompassing the powerful Wandjina, the prolific Gwion Gwion (Bradshaw) images, bright tropical coastal colours, subtle and sombre ochres of the bush and the abundance where desert meets river, every work sings a story about country. Indigenous rock art, The Kimberley

East Coast Wildlife

Furry, cuddly, ferocious – you can find all this and more on a wildlife-watching journey along Australia's magnificent east coast. Head south to Victoria's Phillip Island (p239) for Little Penguins and fur seals, and to Far North Queensland for cassowaries (p179) and crocodiles. In between, you'll find a panoply of extraordinary animals: koalas, kangaroos, wombats and platypuses.

Cradle Mountain

A precipitous comb of rock carved out by millennia of ice and wind, crescent-shaped Cradle Mountain (p340) is Tasmania's most recognisable – and spectacular – mountain peak. It's an all-day walk (and boulder scramble) to the summit and back, for unbelievable panoramas over Tasmania's alpine heart. Or you can stand in awe below and fill your camera with the perfect views across Dove Lake to the mountain. If the peak has disappeared in clouds or snow, warm yourself by the fire in one of the nearby lodges...and come back tomorrow.

Fraser Island

Fraser Island (p151) is an ecological wonderland created by drifting sand, where wild dogs roam free and lush rainforest grows on sand. It's a primal island utopia, home to a profusion of wildlife including the purest strain of dingo in Australia. The best way to explore the island is in a 4WD – cruising up the seemingly endless Seventy-Five Mile Beach and bouncing along sandy inland tracks. Tropical rainforest, pristine freshwater pools, and beach camping under the stars will bring you back to nature. Seventy-Five Mile Beach

23

The Best...
Wildlife Spotting

GREAT BARRIER REEF
Turtles, dolphins, whales, dugongs and fish, fish, fish... A trip to the reef is a submarine spectacular! (p172)

KAKADU NATIONAL PARK
Spot a croc and more birds than you've had feather pillows. (p277)

ROYAL NATIONAL PARK
Just south of Sydney, Royal National Park is a haven for native birds and 43 mammal species. (p98)

THE OTWAYS
Look for koalas in the Otway forests along Victoria's Great Ocean Road. (p242)

AUSTRALIA ZOO
Short on time? Check out Australia's iconic animals in Queensland's Glass House Mountains. (p151)

Bushwalking

Tramping, trekking, rambling and hiking are what you do overseas – here it's called bushwalking. Whether it's a stroll in the Blue Mountains or a hike through Tasmania's wilderness, Australia has it all. There are seriously long walks, like Western Australia's 963km Bibbulmun Track (p323), and some seriously hard tracks, like anywhere in the southwest Tasmanian wilderness...but on a short holiday, zoom in on the easy afternoon or day walks reachable by public transport from the cities, like those in Sydney's Royal National Park (p98).

Royal National Park

The Best...
National Parks

ULURU-KATA TJUTA NATIONAL PARK
Big rocks, big sky, big road trip! (p286)

KAKADU NATIONAL PARK
Top End tropical wilderness with birdlife, wetlands, crocodiles and Aboriginal rock-art galleries (p277)

SYDNEY HARBOUR NATIONAL PARK
Islands, sandstone cliffs and magical walking trails. (p64)

PORT CAMPBELL NATIONAL PARK
Victoria's Twelve Apostles are now just seven...but they sure are photogenic! (p247)

DAINTREE NATIONAL PARK
Tropical jungle, butterflies and empty white-sand beaches. (p189)

CRADLE MOUNTAIN-LAKE ST CLAIR NATIONAL PARK
Alpine wilderness with icy lakes, peaks and epic walking trails. (p340)

25

Tropical North Queensland Adventures

Adventure comes in many forms in Queensland's wild tropics. You can take in views of rainforest and reef from 9000ft on a skydive over Mission Beach, ride the foaming year-round rapids on the Tully River or swim into the technicolour underwater world of the Great Barrier Reef (p172). There's magnificent snorkelling and diving, and opportunity for downtime on pristine settings like Green Island, just off Cairns. A wide array of tour operators in North Queensland can get you above, in and under the water. White-water rafting, Tully River

Australia's
Top Itineraries

Sydney to the Blue Mountains
Big City, Big Wilderness

5 DAYS

With only five days and jet lag weighing in, focus on Sydney's must-see sights, get out onto Sydney Harbour, unwind at the beach and taste the Australian bush in the Blue Mountains, west of Sydney.

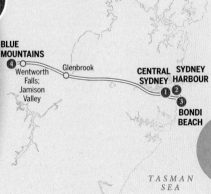

BLUE MOUNTAINS

Glenbrook

Wentworth Falls;
Jamison Valley

CENTRAL SYDNEY

SYDNEY HARBOUR

BONDI BEACH

TASMAN SEA

① Central Sydney (p64)

Arriving in **Sydney**, take a few days to get to know Australia's first city. Take a **city tour** and cross the **Sydney Harbour Bridge**. If you've booked ahead, tackle the famous **BridgeClimb** before exploring the historic **Rocks** and **Circular Quay**. Dine in a harbourside restaurant, then catch a show at the **Sydney Opera House**.

CENTRAL SYDNEY ○ SYDNEY HARBOUR
🛥 **One to three hours** Harbour cruises.
30 minutes Ferry to Manly.

② Sydney Harbour (p64)

Find your sea legs on a **harbour cruise** past sandy coves, islands, colonial history and harbourfront real estate. Catch the ferry to **Manly** for a swim, some lunch or a surfing lesson (or all three). Check out **Nielsen Park** and **Shark Bay** in Vaucluse, then wander out to the **Gap** at the entrance to Sydney Harbour, with its mesmerising cliff-top views.

SYDNEY HARBOUR ○ BONDI BEACH
🚗 **30 minutes** From central Sydney along Oxford St, then Bondi Rd. 🚆 **15 minutes** To Bondi Junction, then 🚌 **15 minutes** to Bondi.

③ Bondi Beach (p75)

Cruise out to world-famous, glamorous **Bondi Beach** for a chilled-out day of sun, sand and surf. If you're feeling chipper, propel yourself along one of New South Wales' best short walks: the **Bondi to Coogee Coastal Walk** features eye-popping coastal views and plenty of places for a swim, some lunch or a pick-me-up coffee.

BONDI BEACH ○ BLUE MOUNTAINS
🚗 **Two hours** Along Parramatta Rd, then the M4 Western Motorway. 🚆 **2.5 hours** From Bondi Junction to Katoomba.

④ Blue Mountains (p101)

The **Blue Mountains** are Sydney's overgrown backyard: hop on a tour, catch a train, or hire a car for maximum flexibility. Stop in foothills town **Glenbrook** to see some **Aboriginal hand stencils**, then go camera crazy at **Jamison Valley** and **Wentworth Falls**. Continue to the moody **Katoomba**, with its gourmet delights and atmospheric accommodation. Scan the hazy horizon from **Echo Point**, or sign up for some mountainous activities: hiking, canyoning or rock climbing.

Bondi Beach (p75)
PHOTOGRAPHER: RICHARD I'ANSON/LONELY PLANET IMAGES ©

5 DAYS

Melbourne to the Great Ocean Road
Southern Scenic

Sydney sure is pretty but Melbourne is a real city: by turns gritty, arty, complex and unfailingly authentic. Spend a few days digging the vibe, then head further south along one of the world's classic road trips: the Great Ocean Road.

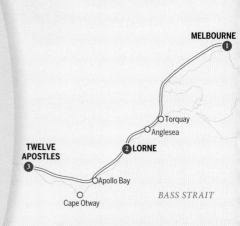

MELBOURNE ①

Torquay
Anglesea
TWELVE APOSTLES ③ ② LORNE
○ Apollo Bay
○ Cape Otway
BASS STRAIT

① Melbourne (p212)

Melbourne lives up to the hype: a burgeoning bayside city of four million-plus people, famous for the arts, Australian Rules football and exemplary coffee. It's a more introspective town than Sydney: a place to visit bookshops, go to the theatre, eat, drink and talk. Spend a couple of days exploring the cafes and bars in the downtown **laneways**, haunting the art galleries and splashing some cash in the city's shops and multicultural restaurants. Don't miss a wander along arty **Brunswick St** in Fitzroy, and a night on the tiles in tarty **St Kilda**.

MELBOURNE ⬤ LORNE

🚗 **Two hours** Along the Princes Fwy (M1) and the Great Ocean Road (B100), via Torquay (p243). 🚌 **2.5 hours** Along the same route.

② Lorne (p245)

Heading south to the scenic **Great Ocean Road**, first stop is **Torquay**, a lively surf town with surf-apparel shops, a cool surf museum and plenty of places to fuel-up on lunch. Not far away is the legendary **Bells Beach**, which starred (in name only) alongside Keanu Reeves and Patrick Swayze in *Point Break,* and hosts the annual Rip Curl Pro surf comp. Continuing west, you'll pass laid-back **Anglesea**, where you can launch into a surf lesson, and then **Lorne**, a long-time holiday hot spot for Melburnians. The beach here is perfect for a swim, after which you can take your pick of restaurants and cafes along the main drag. Lorne's accommodation is first class: renovated old guesthouses, hippie hideaways and stylish B&Bs.

LORNE ⬤ THE TWELVE APOSTLES

🚗 **Two hours** Head west along the Great Ocean Road (B100), via Apollo Bay (p246). 🚌 **Three hours** Along the same route.

③ Twelve Apostles (p247)

Heading west out of Lorne, the Great Ocean Road starts to turn on some sublime scenery: in some places the road seems to hang by a fingernail to the cliffs, twisting and turning above surf-strewn coastline. **Apollo Bay** is the next town of any size. It's a thriving, beachy place with some decent eateries, a busy pub and a good surf beach. Spend the night here, then detour to **Cape Otway** the next day to check out the old lighthouse, or take a walk through the treetops on the **Otway Fly**. Continue west to Port Campbell National Park and the highlight of the Great Ocean Road – the jaggedy rock formations of the **Twelve Apostles**. Check them out from the clifftops, or take a flight over the coastline. From here loop back to Melbourne via the agricultural inland roads.

Federation Square (p212), Melbourne
PHOTOGRAPHER: GREG ELMS/LONELY PLANET IMAGES ©

10 DAYS

Sydney to Brisbane &
the East Coast Beaches
Surf Safari

Fire-up the Kombi, strap your mini-mal to the roof and cruise into your very own Endless Summer. This stretch of Australia's east coast has some of the country's most consistent waves and a string of cheery surf communities.

NOOSA 5

BRISBANE 4
Surfers Paradise
3 GOLD COAST

Nimbin
Bangalow
2 BYRON BAY

Coffs Harbour

SOUTH
PACIFIC
OCEAN

Hunter Valley

SYDNEY 1

1 Sydney (p64)

Start with the bright lights of **Sydney**: don't miss the sparkling **harbour**, gorgeous **Sydney Opera House** and impressive **Sydney Harbour Bridge**. For bird's-eye city views, tackle the **Bridge-Climb** over the grand grey arch. Warm up your surfing muscles at the quintessentially Australian **Bondi Beach**. After two days, meander north along the coast or detour to the **Hunter Valley** for some vino-quaffing. Pit-stop in family-friendly **Coffs Harbour** before wheeling into **Byron Bay**.

SYDNEY ◗ BYRON BAY

🚗 **10 hours** Along Sydney-Newcastle Fwy, then Pacific Hwy (Route 1). 🚌 **12.5 hours** Via the same route.

2 Byron Bay (p122)

Despite big development arriving from the north and south, **Byron Bay** remains a happy hippie town with great pubs, restaurants, beaches and the famous Pass point break. Don't miss inland day-trips to pretty **Bangalow** and Australia's quasi-mythical alt-lifestyle hangout, **Nimbin**. Continue north a couple of hours to the glitzy **Gold Coast**.

BYRON BAY ◗ GOLD COAST

🚗 **1.5 hours** Via Pacific Hwy (Route 1). 🚌 **Two hours** Along the same route.

3 Gold Coast (p127)

Crossing into Queensland you'll soon hit the glam **Gold Coast**. First stop is surf-lifesaving mecca **Coolangatta**, then beautiful **Burleigh Heads** on a rocky headland (great surf and swimming). You'll soon catch sight of **Surfers Paradise**, a slightly unnerving cityscape on the horizon. Stop if you like casinos and theme parks, or continue trucking north to the easy-going river city **Brisbane**.

GOLD COAST ◗ BRISBANE

🚗 **1.25 hours** Via Pacific Motorway (M1). 🚌 **1.5 hours** Along the same route.

4 Brisbane (p131)

Once a sleepy country town, **Brisbane** (aka 'Brisvegas') is now Boom Town, growing so fast that it can be difficult to navigate. Urban charms (great dining, nightlife and the arts) meld seamlessly with the natural environment (riverside cliffs, parklands and botanic gardens). Spend a day or two, then head north to the **Sunshine Coast** and jewel-like **Noosa**.

BRISBANE ◗ NOOSA

🚗 **Two hours** Via Bruce Hwy (M1) then Eumundi–Noosa Rd (Route 12). 🚌 **2.5 hours** Along the same route

5 Noosa (p149)

Noosa really is a paradise: fabulous restaurants along Hastings St, slow-rolling surf beaches and dense national park forest. Wind up your safari with a glass of wine and a toast to 'Huey', the God of Good Surf.

Surfer, Byron Bay (p122)
PHOTOGRAPHER: PETER PTSCHELINZEW/LONELY PLANET IMAGES ©

Melbourne to Cairns
East Coast Cruiser

This classic south–north run takes in thousands of kilometres of Aussie coastline. It could take a lifetime, or, with just 10 days and a handful of airline tickets, you could taste a few east coast highlights.

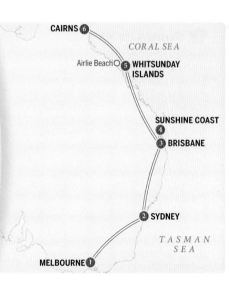

CAIRNS 6

CORAL SEA

Airlie Beach 5 WHITSUNDAY ISLANDS

SUNSHINE COAST 4

3 BRISBANE

2 SYDNEY

TASMAN SEA

MELBOURNE 1

➊ Melbourne (p212)

Kick-start this itinerary in the southern capital of **Melbourne**, a hip city famous for its live music, multicultural mix and sporting obsessions. Keep it compact: dip into the inner city's bohemian **arts** scene, linger in cafe-colonised **laneways**, catch a **live band** or watch a game of Aussie Rules **football** during winter.

MELBOURNE ➲ SYDNEY

✈ **One hour** Melbourne's Tullamarine Airport to Sydney Airport. 🚍 **25 minutes** Sydney Airport into central Sydney.

➋ Sydney (p64)

Next stop is bright 'n' breezy **Sydney**; take a couple of days to do it justice. Must-dos include a **Sydney Harbour cruise**, a stroll around **Darling Harbour** and **Chinatown**, and a plunge in the famous waves of **Bondi Beach**. On your final night, book a restaurant with spotlit views of the **Sydney Harbour Bridge** and **Sydney Opera House**.

SYDNEY ➲ BRISBANE

✈ **One hour** Sydney Airport to Brisbane Airport. 🚍 **20 minutes** Brisbane Airport into central Brisbane.

➌ Brisbane (p131)

Move north to **Brisbane**, Queensland's fast-paced capital, where you can board a river cruise to go cuddle a koala, or catch a ferry to **Moreton Island** and hand-feed wild dolphins. The **Fortitude Valley** nightlife is on the wild side, too.

BRISBANE ➲ SUNSHINE COAST

🚗 **Two hours** Via Bruce Hwy (M1), then Eumundi–Noosa Rd (Route 12). 🚍 **2.5 hours** Along the same route.

➍ Sunshine Coast (p148)

From Brisbane, explore the underrated surf towns along the **Sunshine Coast** by car, detouring into the Glass House Mountains to the famous **Australia Zoo**. Continue north to the stylish beach resort town of **Noosa** – a perfectly indulgent pit-stop.

SUNSHINE COAST ➲ WHITSUNDAY ISLANDS

🚗 **Two hours** Backtrack to Brisbane. ✈ **Two hours** Brisbane Airport to Airlie Beach or Hamilton Island.

➎ Whitsunday Islands (p173)

To access the sublime **Whitsunday Islands**, fly into party town **Airlie Beach** or direct to hedonistic **Hamilton Island**. Spend a day or two island-hopping under a billowing sail, coral-reef diving or snorkelling, or just kicking back by a resort pool.

WHITSUNDAY ISLANDS ➲ CAIRNS

✈ **1.5 hours** Hamilton Island to Cairns.

➏ Cairns (p182)

Move on to **Cairns**, Far North Queensland's tourist mecca. Day-trip into the **Daintree Rainforest** or boat-tour out to the amazing **Great Barrier Reef** to scuba dive, strap on a snorkel or just peer through a glass-bottomed boat.

Mossman Gorge, Daintree Rainforest (p189)

Sydney to Brisbane The Long Way Around

With two weeks up your sleeve, domestic flights will cover the vast distances across the desert heart of Australia. This journey runs from the big east-coast cities through the astonishing Red Centre, up to the tropical north then back to the east coast beaches.

① Sydney (p64)

Kick things off in show-stopping **Sydney** – big-city lights beckon! Take a leisurely **harbour cruise**, check out the **Art Gallery of NSW**, or hype things up with a night bar-hopping through **Kings Cross** and **Darling-hurst**. History buffs will get a kick out of the **Rocks**, while those keen for surf will head straight for the beaches: famous **Bondi**, low-key **Manly** and the chilled-out **Northern Beaches**.

SYDNEY ○ MELBOURNE

✈ **One hour** Sydney Airport to Melbourne's Tullamarine Airport. 🚌 **30 minutes** Melbourne Airport into central Melbourne.

② Melbourne (p212)

Fly south to the Victorian capital of **Melbourne**: on one side a sophisticate, with leafy **parks**, elaborate Victorian **architec-ture** and distinguished **theatres, museums and galleries**; and on the other savvy and street-wise, with hip **street art**, a vibrant independent **music scene** and a laneway **coffee culture** all its own.

MELBOURNE ○ ULURU-KATA TJUTA NATIONAL PARK

✈ **Seven hours** Melbourne to Yulara (flights via Alice Springs or Sydney).

③ Uluru-Kata Tjuta National Park (p286)

Enough urban delights: hop on a flight to **Uluru-Kata Tjuta National Park** and be moved by the commanding bulk of **Uluru**. You've seen the photos and the TV shows, but there's nothing quite like seeing an Uluru sunset firsthand. Gain a deeper under-standing from the traditional owners on an **Anangu Tour**. Nearby **Kata-Tjuta** is just as impressive; walk among the imposing red domes through the **Valley of the Winds**.

ULURU-KATA TJUTA NATIONAL PARK ○ ALICE SPRINGS

✈ **45 minutes** Yulara to Alice Springs. 🚌 **Six hours** Via Lasseter Hwy (Route 4), then Stuart Hwy (Route 87).

MacDonnell Ranges, Northern Territory
PHOTOGRAPHER: PAUL SINCLAIR/LONELY PLANET IMAGES ©

where you can peruse **Mindil Beach Sunset Market**, get wobbly on **Mitchell St** after dark, and organise an overnight tour to the World Heritage–listed **Kakadu National Park**, a wetland of international significance rich with Indigenous rock art, birdlife and crocodiles.

DARWIN & KAKADU ➲ CAIRNS
✈ **2.5 hours** Darwin to Cairns.

⑥ Cairns (p182)

Heading back east, next stop is tropical **Cairns**, a lively base for the amazing sights and activities of Far North Queensland. Swing by the hippie markets at the nearby rainforest town of **Kuranda**, and let it all hang out on the local tropical beaches. Make the most of your day-trip to the **Great Barrier Reef** with a snorkel or scuba gear.

CAIRNS ➲ BRISBANE
✈ **Two hours** Cairns to Brisbane.

⑦ Brisbane (p131)

Within reach of booming **Brisbane** (climb the bridge, cruise the river or catch a live band) is relaxing seaside **Noosa**, a perfect spot to work on your tan and catch a wave. Alternatively, head down to the brassy, bombastic **Gold Coast**, with its excellent beaches, ritzy nightlife and kid-friendly **theme parks**. Or just cool your boots at a local pub with a cold XXXX beer – you've earned it!

④ Alice Springs (p281)

Alice Springs is the only large town in this vast swathe of red-desert country. Its isolation is palpable but the wildlife at the outstanding **Alice Springs Desert Park** and grand scenery of the **MacDonnell Ranges** surprise many visitors. Alice is also the best place to see and buy Aboriginal **dot paintings** from the Central Desert.

ALICE SPRINGS ➲ DARWIN & KAKADU
✈ **Two hours** Alice Springs to Darwin.

⑤ Darwin & Kakadu (p266 & p277)

Wing your way north to the youthful, exuberant tropical capital of **Darwin**,

Australia Month by Month

January

January yawns into action as Australia recovers from its Christmas hangover, but then everyone realises: 'Hey, this is summer!' The festival scene ramps up with sun-stroked outdoor music festivals; Melbourne hosts the Australian Open tennis.

⚫ Big Day Out

(www.bigdayout.com) This touring one-day alt-rock festival visits Sydney, Melbourne, Adelaide, Perth and the Gold Coast. It features a huge line-up of big-name artists from all over the world (Metallica, Kings of Leon, Neil Young) and plenty of home-grown talent. Much head-banging, sun and beer.

⚫ Australia Day

(www.australia-day.com) Australia's 'birth-day' (when the First Fleet landed in 1788) is January 26, and Australians celebrate with barbecues, fireworks and, increas-ingly, much nationalistic flag-waving and drunkenness. In less mood to celebrate are the Aboriginal community, who refer to it as Invasion Day or Survival Day.

February

February is usually Australia's warmest month: hot and sticky up north as the wet season continues, but divine in Tasmania. Everywhere else, locals go back to work, to the beach or to the cricket.

⚫ Tropfest

(www.tropfest.com.au) The world's largest short-film festival happens on Sydney's grassy Domain on the last Sunday in February. To discourage cheating and inspire creativity, a compulsory prop appears in each entry (kiss, sneeze, key etc). Free screenings and celeb judges (Joseph Fiennes, Salma Hayek).

Sydney Gay & Lesbian Mardi Gras

March

March is harvest time in Australia's vineyards and in recent years it has been just as hot as January and February, despite its autumnal status. Melbourne's streets jam up with the Formula One Grand Prix.

❄ Sydney Gay & Lesbian Mardi Gras

(www.mardigras.org.au) A month-long arts festival culminating in a flamboyant parade along Sydney's Oxford St on the first Saturday in March (700,000 people like to watch). Gyms empty out, solariums darken, waxing emporiums tally their profits. After-party tickets are gold.

❄ WOMADelaide

(www.womadelaide.com.au) Annual festival of world music, arts, food and dance, held over four days in Adelaide's luscious Botanic Park, attracting loyal crowds from around the country. Eight stages play host to hundreds of world-music acts, it's very family friendly, and you can get a cold beer too.

April

Melbourne and the Adelaide Hills are atmospheric as European trees turn golden then maroon. Up north the rain is abating and the desert temperatures are becoming manageable. Easter = pricey accommodation everywhere.

❄ Ten Days on the Island

(www.tendaysontheisland.org) Every odd-numbered year from late March until early April, Tasmania's major cultural event takes the stage in venues around the state. Expect plenty of theatre, live music, offbeat film, dance, literature and kids' events.

May

The dry season begins in the Northern Territory, northern Western Australia and Far North Queensland: relief from humidity. A great time to visit Uluru, before the tour buses arrive in droves.

◉ Whale Watching

Along the southeastern Australian coast, migrating southern right and humpback whales come close to shore to feed, breed and calf. The whales are here between May and October; see them at Hervey Bay (New South Wales), Warrnambool (Victoria), Victor Harbor (South Australia) and Albany (Western Australia).

June

Winter begins: snow falls across the Southern Alps ski resorts and football season fills grandstands across the country. Peak season in the tropical north: waterfalls and outback tracks are accessible (accommodation prices less so).

❄ Laura Aboriginal Dance Festival

(www.laurafestival.tv) Sleepy Laura, 330kms north of Cairns on the Cape York Peninsula in Far North Queensland, hosts the largest traditional Indigenous gathering in Australia. Communities from the region come together for dance, song and ceremony. The Laura Races and Rodeo are held the following weekend.

July

Pubs with open fires, cosy coffee shops and empty beaches down south; packed markets, tours and accommodation up north. Pack warm clothes for anywhere south of Alice Springs. Don't miss 'MIFF'.

brings a stellar program of music, theatre, dance, comedy, film, Indigenous art and public exhibitions. Outdoor events held in public plazas, parks and gardens make good use of Cairns' tropical setting.

September

Spring heralds a rampant bloom of wildflowers across outback Western Australia and South Australia and flower festivals happen in places like Canberra. Football finishes and the spring horse-racing carnival begins, culminating in the Melbourne Cup in November.

Brisbane Festival

(www.brisbanefestival.com.au) One of Australia's largest and most diverse arts festivals runs through 22 days in September and features an impressive line-up of concerts, plays, dance performances and fringe events around the city. It kicks off with 'Riverfire', an elaborate fireworks show over the river.

AFL Grand Final

(www.afl.com.au) The pinnacle of the annual Australian Rules football season is this show-stopping spectacle watched (on TV) by 4 million impassioned Aussies. Tickets to the game (in Melbourne) are scarce, but at half-time everyone's neighbourhood BBQ moves to the local park for a little amateur kick-to-kick.

Melbourne International Film Festival

(MIFF; www.miff.com.au) Right up there with Toronto and Cannes, MIFF has been running since 1952 and has grown into a wildly popular event, tickets selling like piping hot chestnuts in the inner city. Myriad short films, feature-length spectaculars and documentaries flicker across city screens every winter.

August

August is when southerners, sick of winter's grey-sky drear, head to Queensland for some sun. Last chance to head to the tropical Top End and outback before things get too hot and wet.

Cairns Festival

(www.festivalcairns.com.au) Running three weeks from late August to early September, this massive art-and-culture fest

October

The weather avoids extremes everywhere: a good time to go camping. After the football and before the cricket, sports fans twiddle their thumbs, but the arts community enjoys international festivals in Melbourne and Brisbane.

Jazz in the Vines

(www.jazzinthevines.com.au) There are lots of food and wine festivals like this across Australia's wine regions (Barossa, McLaren Vale, Yarra Valley...). The Hunter Valley's proximity to the Sydney jazz scene ensures a top line-up at Tyrrell's Vineyard.

November

Northern beaches may be closed due to 'stinger season': jellyfish floating in the shallows of north Queensland, the Northern Territory and Western Australian waters. Outdoor events ramp up; the surf-lifesaving season flexes its muscles on beaches everywhere.

⭐ Melbourne Cup

(www.melbournecup.com) On the first Tuesday in November, Australia's (if not the world's) premier horse race chews up the turf in Melbourne. Country towns schedule racing events to coincide with the day, and the nation does actually stop to watch the big race.

December

Ring the bell, school's out! Holidays begin two weeks before Christmas. Cities are packed with shoppers and the weather is desirably hot. Up north, monsoon season is underway: afternoon thunderstorms bring pelting rain.

⭐ Sydney to Hobart Yacht Race

(www.rolexsydneyhobart.com) On Boxing Day, Sydney Harbour churns with competitors and onlookers for the start of the world's most arduous open-ocean yacht race (628 nautical miles!). When the yachties hit Hobart a few days later, this small city celebrates with feasting, drinking and dancing sea-legs.

Far left: Sydney to Hobart Yacht Race
Left: Laura Aboriginal Dance Festival

Get Inspired

Books

The Bodysurfers (Robert Drewe; 1983) Seductive stories from Sydney's Northern Beaches, calmly tearing shreds off the Australian suburban idyll.

Voss (Patrick White; 1957) Nobel Prize–winner White contrasts the outback with Sydney colonial life: explorer Voss plans to cross Australia coast-to-coast.

The Songlines (Bruce Chatwin; 1986) An account of Chatwin's trip to Australia; layered with outback and Indigenous insights.

Films

Lantana (director Ray Lawrence; 2001) Mystery for grown-ups: a deeply moving meditation on life, love, truth and grief.

Two Hands (director Gregor Jordan; 1999) A black-humoured look at Sydney's criminal underworld: Heath Ledger and bad-ass Bryan Brown.

Ten Canoes (director Rolf de Heer; 2006) A young man is told the story of his ancestors.

Spoken in the Ganalbingu language of Arnhem Land.

Australia (director Baz Luhrmann; 2008) Over-the-top period romance set in remote northern Australian cattle country ('Kidman in the Kimberley').

 Music

Diesel & Dust (Midnight Oil; 1987) Key track 'Beds are Burning'.

Back in Black (AC/DC; 1980) Key track 'Back in Black'.

Circus Animals (Cold Chisel; 1982) Key track 'Bow River'.

Internationalist (Powderfinger; 1998) Key track 'Passenger'.

Websites

Tourism Australia (www.australia.com) Official site with nationwide visitor info.

Lonely Planet (www.lonelyplanet.com/australia) Destination information, hotel bookings, traveller forum and more.

The Australian (www.theaustralian.com.au) National broadsheet newspaper.

Parks Australia (www.environment.gov.au/parks) National parks and reserves information.

Short on time?

This list will give you an instant insight into the country.

Read *Dirt Music* (Tim Winton; 2001) The wild west coast has its own soundtrack.

Watch *The Adventures of Priscilla, Queen of the Desert* (Director Stephan Elliot; 1994) Sydney drag queens road-tripping to Alice Springs.

Listen *Love This City* (The Whitlams; 1999) Digging into Sydney's best and worst.

Log on *First Australians* (www.sbs.com/first australians) Podcasts from the fabulous TV series on Indigenous Australia.

Left: Twin Falls (p279), Kakadu National Park;
Above: Swimming race, Bondi Beach (p75), Sydney

Need to Know

Currency
Australian dollars ($)

Language
English

ATMs
In large cities and big towns

Credit Cards
Big-brand credit cards are widely accepted

Visas
All visitors to Australia need a visa, except New Zealanders. Apply online for an ETA or eVisitor visa.

Mobile Phones
European phones work on Australia's network, but not most American or Japanese phones. Use global roaming or a local SIM card.

Wi-fi
Increasingly available in hotels, cafes and pubs

Internet Access
Internet cafes in most cities and large towns, plus many public libraries.

Driving
Drive on the left; the steering wheel is on the right.

Tipping
Not required, but tip 10% in restaurants and taxis if you're happy with the service.

When To Go

Darwin
GO Jun–Aug

Cairns
GO Sep–Nov

Perth
GO Oct–Dec

Sydney
GO Dec–Feb

Hobart
GO Jan–Mar

■ Desert, dry climate
■ Dry climate
■ Tropical climate, wet dry seasons
■ Warm to hot summers, mild winters

High Season
(Dec–Feb)

○ Summertime: local holidays and busy beaches

○ Expect to pay up to 35% more for city accommodation

○ High season is winter (June to August) in tropical north and central Australia (mild days)

Shoulder
(Sep–Nov)

○ Warm sun and clear skies

○ Local business people are not yet stressed by the summer crowds

○ Autumn (March to May) is also shoulder season – particularly nice in Melbourne

Low Season
(Jun–Aug)

○ Cool rainy days down south; sunny skies up north

○ Tourist numbers are down; restaurants and attractions keep shorter hours

○ Head for the ski resorts in Victoria and NSW

Advance Planning

○ **Three months before** Look into visa requirements and shop around for the best deal on flights.

○ **One month before** Book accommodation and regional flights, trains etc.

○ **One week before** Book a surfing lesson, reef dive or national park tour.

○ **One day before** Reserve a table at a Sydney harbourside restaurant.

Your Daily Budget

Budget less than $130

○ Dorm beds $25–35 a night

○ Big-city food markets for self-catering bargains

○ Take public transport and visit free museums

Midrange $130–$250

○ Double room in a midrange hotel/motel $100–$150

○ Midrange restaurants and a few beers at the pub

○ Hire a car and explore further

Top End more than $250

○ Double room in a top-end hotel from $200

○ Three-course meal in a classy restaurant $70

○ Go clubbing, catch a show or hit the ritzy bars

Exchange Rates

Canada	C$1	$0.96
Euro zone	€1	$1.36
Japan	¥100	$1.22
New Zealand	NZ$1	$0.79
UK	UK£1	$1.54
USA	US$1	$0.94

For current exchange rates see www.xe.com.

What To Bring

○ **Sunscreen** And don't forget sunglasses and a hat to deflect harsh UV rays

○ **Insect repellent** To fend off the merciless flies, sandflies and mosquitoes

○ **Travel insurance** Make sure it covers any planned 'risky' activities like surfing or scuba diving

○ **Visa** Confirm the latest visa situation; see p384

○ **Electricity adapter** For your digital gadgets

Arriving in Australia

○ **Sydney Airport** (p96)

Trains Every 10 minutes, from 4.30am to 12.40am

Shuttle Buses Pre-booked services to city hotels

Taxis $40–50; 30 minutes to the city

○ **Melbourne Airport** (p239)

Buses SkyBus every 10 to 30 minutes, 24-hours

Taxis $40–50; 25 minutes to the city

Hire Cars CityLink toll road is the fastest route

○ **Brisbane Airport** (p144)

Trains Every 15 to 30 minutes, 5.45am to 10pm

Shuttle Buses Pre-booked services to city hotels

Taxis $35–45; 25 minutes to the city

Getting Around

○ **Air** Save time across Australia's vast distances.

○ **Hire Car** Explore beyond the city limits, into the national parks.

○ **Train** Cross the continent on legendary trains such as the *Indian Pacific* and the *Ghan*.

○ **Bus** Private buses cover the country; cheaper than train but uncomfortable on long hauls.

○ **Boat** To islands, coral-reefs and Tasmania.

Accommodation

○ **B&Bs** Homey bed-and-breakfast choices, either hosted or nonhosted (nonhosted = more privacy).

○ **Camping** Basic national park clearings to luxury camping resorts.

○ **Hostels** Sociable, low-cost affairs packed with under-30s party people.

○ **Hotels** Three- to five-star hotels with high-standard amenities; in major cities, towns and big-ticket tourist locations.

○ **Motels** Cookie-cutter sameness tempered by value, convenience, security and cleanliness.

○ **Pubs** Aka hotels (not to be confused with three-to five-star hotels), vary from friendly country pubs to city dives. Inspect before you commit.

○ **Resorts** Luxury with pools, restaurants, spas, bars, golf courses...rooms for all budgets.

Be Forewarned

○ **Wild weather** Cyclones, floods, bushfires...it's all here, but heed local warnings and you'll be fine.

○ **At the beach** Always swim between the flags, where the lifeguards can reach you and the undertows can't.

○ **Summertime blues** Big-city prices spike and crowds are thick on the ground.

Sydney & the Blue Mountains

Sydney is the capital that every other Australian city loves to hate… But what that really means is that they all want to be just like her: sun-kissed, sophisticated and supremely self-confident.

Built around one of the most beautiful natural harbours in the world – a maze of lazy bays and sandstone headlands – Sydney plays host to three of Australia's major icons: the Sydney Harbour Bridge, Sydney Opera House and Bondi Beach. But the attractions don't stop there...

The country's oldest, largest and most diverse city is also home to magnificent museums and restaurants, a vivacious performing arts scene and yet more sublime beaches. After dark, hip bars and clubs collide as Sydneysiders wage war against sleep... So wake up! Sydney is as good as it gets.

And don't miss a trip to the Blue Mountains, the city's hazy backdrop, which delivers a slew of eye-popping lookouts, forests and quirky mountain towns.

Sydney Opera House (p65), from beneath Sydney Harbour Bridge

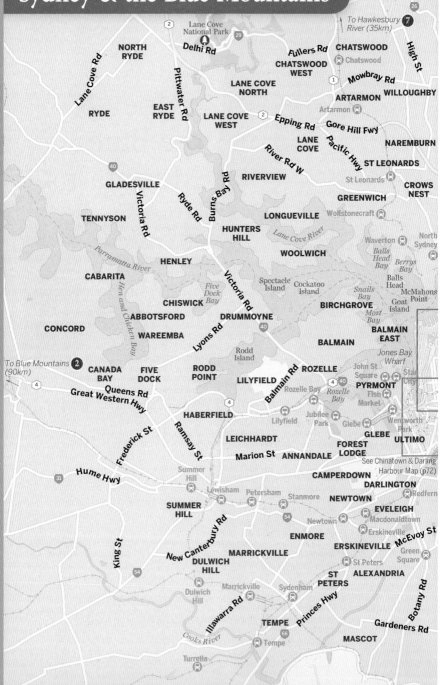

Sydney & the Blue Mountains

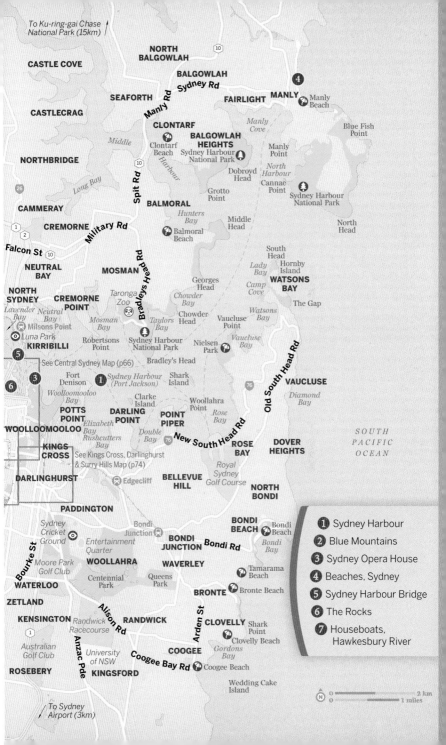

To Ku-ring-gai Chase
National Park (15km)

CASTLE COVE

NORTH
BALGOWLAH

BALGOWLAH
Sydney Rd

SEAFORTH

CASTLECRAG

FAIRLIGHT

MANLY

Manly
Beach

CLONTARF

Manly
Cove

Blue Fish
Point

Clontarf
Beach

BALGOWLAH
HEIGHTS
Sydney Harbour
National Park

Manly Point

NORTHBRIDGE

Middle

Dobroyd
Head

North
Harbour

Cannae
Point

Sydney Harbour
National Park

North
Head

Long Bay

Grotto
Point

CAMMERAY

CREMORNE

Military Rd

BALMORAL

Hunters
Bay

Balmoral
Beach

Middle
Head

Falcon St

NEUTRAL
BAY

MOSMAN

Georges
Head

South
Head

Lady
Bay

Hornby
Island

WATSONS
BAY

NORTH
SYDNEY

CREMORNE
POINT

Taronga
Zoo

Chowder
Bay

Camp
Cove

The Gap

Lavender
Bay

Neutral
Bay

Mosman
Bay

Taylors
Bay

Chowder
Head

Vaucluse
Point

Watsons
Bay

Milsons Point

Luna Park

Robertsons
Point

Sydney Harbour
National Park

Nielsen
Park

Vaucluse
Bay

KIRRIBILLI

See Central Sydney Map (p66)

Bradley's Head

Shark
Island

VAUCLUSE

Fort
Denison

Sydney Harbour
(Port Jackson)

Diamond
Bay

Woolloomooloo
Bay

Clarke
Island

Woollahra
Point

POTTS
POINT

DARLING
POINT

POINT
PIPER

Rose
Bay

WOOLLOOMOOLOO

Elizabeth
Bay

Rushcutters
Bay

Double
Bay

New South Head Rd

ROSE
BAY

DOVER
HEIGHTS

SOUTH
PACIFIC
OCEAN

KINGS
CROSS

See Kings Cross, Darlinghurst
& Surry Hills Map (p74)

DARLINGHURST

Edgecliff

BELLEVUE
HILL

Royal
Sydney
Golf Course

NORTH
BONDI

PADDINGTON

BONDI
BEACH

Bondi
Beach

Sydney
Cricket
Ground

Bondi
Junction

BONDI
JUNCTION

Bondi Rd

Bondi
Bay

Entertainment
Quarter

WOOLLAHRA

Moore Park
Golf Club

WAVERLEY

Bourke St

Centennial
Park

Queens
Park

WATERLOO

Tamarama
Beach

ZETLAND

BRONTE

Bronte Beach

KENSINGTON

Randwick
Racecourse

Alison Rd

RANDWICK

CLOVELLY

Shark
Point

Arden St

Australian
Golf Club

University
of NSW

Anzac Pde

Gordons
Bay

Clovelly Beach

ROSEBERY

KINGSFORD

COOGEE

Coogee Bay Rd

Coogee Beach

Wedding Cake
Island

To Sydney
Airport (3km)

N

0   2 km
0   1 miles

1 Sydney Harbour

2 Blue Mountains

3 Sydney Opera House

4 Beaches, Sydney

5 Sydney Harbour Bridge

6 The Rocks

7 Houseboats,
   Hawkesbury River

Sydney & the Blue Mountains Highlights

1

Sydney Harbour

Sydney Harbour is the shimmering heart of our great city. Whether you are sitting in a waterfront restaurant, walking through one of many shore-side parks, taking a ferry to Manly or being spoilt aboard a leisurely harbour cruise, there just is no better way to experience the real beauty of our city. Above: Sydney Harbour at night; Top Right: Shark Beach, Nielsen Park; Bottom Right: Sydney Harbour Bridge (p65)

Need to Know

BEST PHOTO OPPORTUNITY Catch city reflections in the still morning waters **ONLY TWO HOURS?** Board a lunch cruise (p80) for harbourside sights **For further coverage, see p64.**

Sydney Harbour Don't Miss List

BY TONY ZRILIC, HOSPITALITY MANAGER, CAPTAIN COOK CRUISES

1 FERRY TO MANLY

The Manly Ferry departs Circular Quay every half hour or so. For an unforgettable experience, take the ferry when big seas are rolling in through the entrance to Sydney Harbour, known as the Heads. When you get to **Manly** (p77), walk the Corso from the harbour beach to the ocean beach. Be sure to buy a gelato or have a cold beer while watching the mass of sun lovers enjoying this unique part of Sydney.

2 FORESHORE WALK FROM BRADLEY'S HEAD

The harbour is lined with fabulous foreshore walks. Take the ferry from Circular Quay to **Taronga Zoo** (p76), and then walk around the headland to Chowder Bay. Stop for breakfast or lunch at a foreshore brasserie.

3 WATSONS BAY & THE GAP

Catch a hop-on hop-off cruise to **Watsons Bay** (p75) and have fish and chips at world famous **Doyles on the Beach**. Walk to the **Gap** (p75), where there are great views of the Pacific and as far west as the Blue Mountains.

4 LUNCH AT FORT DENISON

One of my favourites is to take the ferry from Circular Quay to the heritage-listed island in the middle of the harbour, **Fort Denison** (p64). There's a great restaurant serving modern Australian cuisine – you can enjoy a meal while sitting in the midst of Sydney's amazing icons: the Opera House and the Harbour Bridge.

5 SWIM AT NIELSEN PARK

Nielsen Park (p75) is one of the many netted harbour beaches where you can actually swim and snorkel as yachts glide by. Part of an enormous harbourside park, it's a great place to watch the start of the Sydney to Hobart Yacht race on Boxing Day each year. When the swell is right, surfers actually get a wave here too. Catch a bus from Circular Quay.

Blue Mountains

The Blue Mountains are a magnificent natural creation, with endless stretches of sandstone cliffs, spectacular waterfalls and canyons. It's an awesome environment to experience adventure activities such as abseiling, canyoning, rock climbing, mountain biking and bushwalking. Below: Govetts Leap (p104); Top Right: Abseiling, Lithgow (p105); Bottom Right: Three Sisters (p104)

Need to Know

BEST PHOTO OPPORTUNITY Sunrise or sunset at lookouts with waterfalls **AVOID** Tour buses at Echo Point; arrive early or late in the day **For further coverage, see p101.**

Blue Mountains Don't Miss List

BY MARTY DOOLAN, ADVENTURE GUIDE,
BLUE MOUNTAINS ADVENTURE COMPANY

1 THREE SISTERS

An absolute must for all. The Three Sisters is a famous rock formation on the edge of the Jamison Valley. **Echo Point** (p102), the viewing platform for the Three Sisters, is one of the best lookouts in the Blue Mountains and is easily accessed from the town of Katoomba. If you can make it there after sundown, you will see the Three Sisters spectacularly floodlit.

2 CANYONING IN SUMMER

Canyoning is a terrific experience with plenty of thrill, excitement and adventure. Abseil down waterfalls, jump into deep pools of water, slide down natural water slides, swim and wade through geological treasures. These outdoor activities have a remarkable effect on people: after returning to their day-to-day lives refreshed and revived, most people experience a sense of renewed confidence in themselves.

3 SUNSET AT CAHILLS LOOKOUT

Cahills Lookout is a lesser known lookout near Katoomba. It has amazing views of the Megalong and Jamison Valleys, as well as Narrow Neck plateau and the remarkable Boars Head rock formation. Watch the mineralised sandstone cliffs gradually change colour as the sun dips towards the horizon.

4 KATOOMBA

Katoomba St is a great place for a leisurely lunch or an uplifting coffee after a big day out. Loads of options abound. And don't miss the **Edge Cinema** (p108), which screens a fascinating documentary about the Blue Mountains on a six-storey-high screen – a great way to learn more about the Blue Mountains, and a good wet weather option.

5 ROCK CLIMBING AT MT VICTORIA

The Blue Mountains has a long tradition of rock climbing; some of the first rock climbs in Australia were done in the Blue Mountains. Mt Victoria boasts several excellent rock climbing areas, each with a range of climbs and grades.

Sydney Opera House

Sydney's most recognisable icon is the **Sydney Opera House** (p65), its shell-like 'sails' shimmering on the blue harbour waters on a sunny Sydney day. Perfectly positioned on Bennelong Point, this curvy creation delights the eye from almost every angle and always makes a good photo. Get up close and examine the self-cleaning tiles or explore the interior on a guided tour. Better still, take in a show.

WILL SALTER/LONELY PLANET IMAGES ©

Sydney Harbour Bridge

The **Sydney Harbour Bridge** (p65) is a spookily big object – you'll catch sight of it in the corner of your eye and get a fright! Walking across it is the best way to check it out: if you start at Milsons Point you'll be walking towards the city with Opera House views. Want to get higher? Try a knee-trembling **Bridge-Climb** (p80) or scale the 200 stairs to the **Pylon Lookout** (p65).

GREG ELMS/LONELY PLANET IMAGES ©

Beaches, Beaches, Beaches...

4

From legendary **Bondi Beach** (p75) to unpretentious **Manly** (p77) and the sublime **Northern Beaches** (p77), no Sydney visit is complete without a day at the beach. And those are just the surf beaches: around the sheltered inlets of Sydney Harbour are dozens of sandy little bays – great for a swim, a picnic or just a jet-lagged snooze in the sun.

Bondi Beach

6

The Rocks

At first glance the historic Rocks area may seem a bit of a tourist trap, full of crowds and kitsch souvenir shops... But dig a little deeper and you'll uncover some fascinating stories here. Swing by the engaging **Rocks Discovery Museum** (p68), visit **Cadman's Cottage** (p67), Sydney's oldest house, or spend a while bending elbows in one of Sydney's oldest **pubs**.

7

Hawkesbury Houseboats

Stressed-out Sydneysiders love to switch off their mobile phones, pack the kids in the back of the car and flee to the slow-roaming, smoky **Hawkesbury River** (p99) for a chilled-out weekend of fishing, wine sipping and houseboat cruising. Just 30km north of Sydney, it's a brilliant (and very relaxing) way to get a feel for the national parks and landscapes that surround Australia's biggest city.

Sydney & the Blue Mountains' Best...

Fresh-air Factories

○ **Manly Ferry** (p77) Step onto the deck and suck in the sea air.

○ **Hyde Park** (p69) Sydney's lungs: a formal park with avenues of trees and swathes of lawn.

○ **Royal Botanic Gardens** (p65) A clean-breathing botany lesson.

○ **Blue Mountains** (p101) High above the big smoke (literally).

Places to Look Down & Out

○ **Sydney Harbour Bridge** (p65) The sidewalk view is good, but from the BridgeClimb (p80) it's unbelievable!

○ **Sydney Tower** (p70) Scan from Sydney Harbour to the Blue Mountains.

○ **The Gap** (p75) Impressive cliff-top lookout near the entrance to Sydney Harbour.

○ **Echo Point** (p102) Accessible Blue Mountains lookout, starring the rugged Three Sisters.

○ **Govetts Leap** (p104) Less touristed than Echo Point, but just as eye-popping.

Places to Cool Off

○ **Bondi Beach** (p75) Plunge into the waves at Sydney's famous beach.

○ **Camp Cove** (p75) Sheltered, family-friendly Sydney Harbour beach.

○ **Northern Beaches** (p77) Sandy string of unpretentious surf beaches from Manly to Palm Beach.

○ **Katoomba** (p103) Beat the city heat with a day trip to this misty mountain town.

Need to Know

Places to Wander

◦ **The Rocks & Circular Quay** (p67) Between the Opera House and the Harbour Bridge there's history and attractions aplenty.

◦ **Bondi to Coogee Clifftop Walk** (p75) Sandy beaches, cafe pit-stops and churning Pacific surf.

◦ **Darling Harbour** (p71) Walk around C-shaped Darling Harbour from King St Wharf to Pyrmont.

◦ **Royal National Park** (p98) Walk through the world's second-oldest national park.

ADVANCE PLANNING

◦ **One month before** Book a place on the hugely popular BridgeClimb (p80) over Sydney Harbour Bridge.

◦ **Two weeks before** Book tickets for a Sydney Opera House show and a Blue Mountains tour.

◦ **One week before** Book tickets for a harbour cruise and a table at one of Sydney's premier restaurants.

RESOURCES

◦ **Sydney City Council Information Kiosks** (www.cityofsydney.nsw.gov.au) At Circular Quay and the Town Hall on George St.

◦ **Sydney Visitor Centres** (www.sydneyvisitorcentre.com) At the Rocks and Darling Harbour. Information on everything; also acts as an accommodation agency.

◦ **Blue Mountains Visitor Centres** (www.visitbluemountains.com.au) At Glenbrook and Katoomba. Local information plus accommodation, tour and attraction bookings.

◦ **Tourism New South Wales** (www.visitnsw.com.au) State-wide accommodation and travel advice.

◦ **National Roads & Motorists Association** (NRMA; www.nrma.com.au) Extensive driving info and emergency roadside assistance.

GETTING AROUND

◦ **Walk** Around Circular Quay from the Rocks to the Opera House.

◦ **Ferry** To Taronga Zoo, Manly, Darling Harbour and other harbourside destinations.

◦ **Bus** All around the city, including Bondi Beach.

◦ **Train** Around the Sydney suburbs, and to the Blue Mountains.

◦ **Airport Link** Trains run to/from Sydney Airport from central Sydney.

◦ **Monorail** From Sydney CBD to Darling Harbour and back.

BE FOREWARNED

◦ **Crowds** Summer (December to February) is the busy season. Expect queues at Sydney's big-ticket sights, crowded surf, lots of tour buses at Echo Point in Katoomba and elevated accommodation prices.

Left: Ferry ride past Sydney Harbour Bridge;
Above: Hyde Park (p69)

Sydney Walking Tour

Down by Circular Quay, the Rocks was where European settlers set up shop in 1788, and it remains the first port of call for most visitors to Sydney.

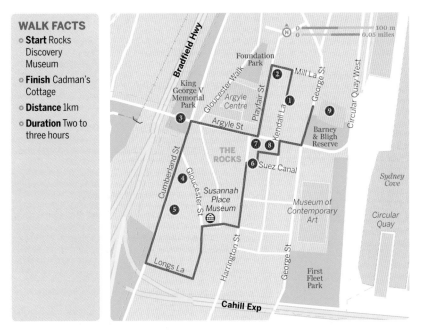

WALK FACTS

- **Start** Rocks Discovery Museum
- **Finish** Cadman's Cottage
- **Distance** 1km
- **Duration** Two to three hours

❶ Rocks Discovery Museum

The engaging **Rocks Discovery Museum** offers an overview of the Rocks' rich, disreputable history. From the museum, walk north up Kendall La to **Mill Lane**. The old flour mill here was demolished around 1920; many early Rocks' buildings suffered the same fate during the 20th century.

❷ Rocks Square

Turn left into Mill Lane and walk up to the **Rocks Square**, site of the ultimately successful 1973 'Battle for the Rocks' protests, aimed at preserving historic streets and buildings. In 1975 the state government declared that all remaining historic buildings

north of the Cahill Expressway were to be conserved and restored.

❸ Argyle Cut

Turn left into Playfair St and walk past **Argyle Terrace** (1877) and the **Argyle Stores** (1828–1913) on your right. Turn right up Argyle St to the impressive **Argyle Cut**, a road bored through the sandstone ridge between Circular Quay and Millers Point. It was excavated between the 1830s and 1860s, initially by convicts.

❹ Australian Hotel

Turn left into Cumberland St until you see the 1914 **Australian Hotel** on the Gloucester

St corner. Opposite, the 1998 **King George V Recreation Centre** is wedged between the street and the freeway; it's an interesting architectural intervention in this historic precinct.

5 Sydney Harbour YHA

Continue along Cumberland St. On the left-hand side is the recently built **Sydney Harbour YHA**, incorporating a 1994 archaeological dig which produced over 750,000 artefacts. Open to the public, the dig is preserved on the ground floor of the hostel.

6 Suez Canal

Veer left into Longs Lane, continuing through to Gloucester St and the history-focussed **Susannah Place Museum**. From here, take the Cumberland Pl stairs to Harrington St, then veer left to the infamous **Suez Canal**, a narrow laneway on the right. In the 19th century it was frequented by prostitutes and the notorious 'Rocks Push' gang.

7 Well Courtyard

Turn into Suez Canal and then left into the **Well Courtyard**, once used for dog baiting and cock fighting. Take the steps to stone-paved **Greenway Lane**, named after famous convict architect and Rocks' resident Francis Greenway.

8 Gannon House

Exit onto Argyle St. At No 45 is **Gannon House**, built in 1839 as a residence and carpentry store by former convict Michael Gannon; he was known for the quality of his coffins.

9 Cadmans Cottage

Turn right and walk down to George St. In the park opposite is Sydney's oldest house, the diminutive **Cadmans Cottage**, built in 1816 for John Cadman the Government Coxswain.

Sydney & the Blue Mountains In...

TWO DAYS

Start day one with our **Rocks** walking tour and explore **Circular Quay**, then follow the harbourside walkway to the **Art Gallery of NSW**. Catch an evening show at the **Sydney Opera House.**

Next day, board a ferry to **Manly**, where you can swim at the beach or have a long, lazy lunch. That night, head to fashionable **Surry Hills** for drinks and dinner.

FOUR DAYS

On day three, have yum cha in **Chinatown**, then catch a ferry to genteel **Balmain** or shop in pretty **Paddington**.

On day four, soak up the sun and scene at **Bondi Beach** – tackle the **Bondi to Coogee Clifftop Trail**, then boot it back to Bondi for a sunset drink at **Icebergs Dining Room & Bar**.

ONE WEEK

Spend a couple of days in the **Blue Mountains**, with a full day's bushwalking and a gourmet dinner. Back in Sydney, get out on the harbour on a yacht, then regain your land legs in infamous **Kings Cross** that night.

Sydney Opera House (p65)

Discover Sydney & the Blue Mountains

At a Glance

- **Central Sydney and Sydney Harbour** (p64) Downtown Sydney and its famous harbour

- **Kings Cross and Darlinghurst** (p73) Bohemian, red-light and gay-friendly 'hoods

- **Eastern suburbs and beaches** (p75) Golden beaches and promenading bathers

- **Manly and the Northern Beaches** (p77) Heavenly beach after heavenly beach

- **Blue Mountains** (p101) Amazing cliffs, forests and lookouts

Watsons Bay

PHOTOGRAPHER: OLIVER STREWE/LONELY PLANET IMAGES ©

SYDNEY

 Sights

Sydney will keep you busy. If you plan on seeing an exceptional number of museums, attractions and tours, check out the discount passes offered by **Australian Travel Specialists** (ATS; ✆1800 355 537; www.atstravel.com.au; ticket booths at Wharf 6, Circular Quay & Harbourside Shopping Centre, Darling Harbour).

Sydney Harbour

Stretching 20km inland from the South Pacific Ocean to the mouth of the Parramatta River, this magnificent natural harbour is the city's shimmering soul and the focus of every visitor's stay. Exploring this vast, visually arresting area by ferry (p96) is one of Sydney's great joys.

Forming the gateway to the harbour from the ocean are **North Head** and **South Head**. The former fishing village of **Watsons Bay** nestles on South Head's harbour side, and the city's favourite day-trip destination, **Manly**, occupies a promontory straddling harbour and ocean near North Head.

The focal point of the inner harbour and the city's major transport hub is **Circular Quay**, home to one of the city's flamboyant visual signatures, the Sydney Opera House.

SYDNEY HARBOUR NATIONAL PARK
Nature Reserve

This national park protects scattered pockets of harbourside bushland incorporating walking tracks, scenic lookouts,

Aboriginal engravings and historic sites. Its southern side incorporates **South Head** and **Nielsen Park** in Vaucluse; on the North Shore the park includes **North Head**, **Dobroyd Head**, **Middle Head**, **Georges Head** and **Bradleys Head**.

The park also includes five harbour islands: **Clark Island** off Darling Point, **Shark Island** off Rose Bay, **Rodd Island** in Iron Cove near Birkenhead, **Goat Island** off Balmain, and the small, fortified **Fort Denison** off Mrs Macquaries Point. All can be visited – Rodd and Goat by private vessel or water taxi ($7 landing fee per person payable at the Sydney Harbour National Park Information Centre or via its website or telephone information service; Fort Denison on a package including ferry transport, day pass and 30-minute **guided history tour** (adult/concession $27/22; ⏱12.15pm & 2.30pm, also 10.45am Wed-Sun), also booked through the Sydney Harbour National Park Information Centre; Clark on a two-hour **Aboriginal culture tour** (☎02-9206 1111; www.captaincook.com.au/tribal; adult/child $60/40; ⏱Wed-Sun) run by the Tribal Warriors Association; and Shark on a ferry operated by **Captain Cook Cruises** (www.captaincook.com.au; adult/child $20/17; ⏱five ferries daily 9.45am-3pm). There is a **cafe and restaurant** (☎bookings 02-9358 1999) on Fort Denison offering morning teas and lunches and the other islands have facilities for BYO picnickers.

SYDNEY HARBOUR BRIDGE   Landmark
Whether they're driving over it, climbing up it, rollerblading across it or sailing under it, Sydneysiders adore their 'giant coathanger' (Map p66). Opened in 1932, this majestic structure links the CBD with North Sydney, spanning the harbour at one of its narrowest points.

The best way to experience the bridge is on foot – don't expect much of a view crossing by car or train. Staircases climb up to the bridge from both shores, leading to a footpath running the length of the eastern side. Cyclists take the western side. You can climb the southeastern pylon to the **Pylon Lookout** (Map p66; www.pylonlookout.com.au; adult/child/senior $9.50/4/6.50; ⏱10am-5pm), or ascend the great arc on an adrenaline-charged bridge climb (see p80).

ROYAL BOTANIC GARDENS   Garden
(Map p66; www.rbgsyd.nsw.gov.au; Mrs Macquaries Rd; admission free; ⏱7am-sunset) One of the most accessible ways to appreciate the harbour's magnificence is by taking a walk through the city's lush, 30-hectare botanical reserve, established in 1816 as the colony's vegetable patch. The highlight is to follow the signed walkways from the Opera House around Farm Cove, past picturesque Mrs Macquaries Point and alongside Woolloomooloo Bay to the Domain and the Art Gallery of NSW. Alternatively you can take a free **guided walk** (⏱10.30am daily) or **Aboriginal Heritage Tour** (☎02-9231 8134; adult/concession $28/13; ⏱10am Fri); both depart from the Palm Grove Centre in the middle of the gardens.

SYDNEY OPERA HOUSE   Landmark
(Map p66; www.sydneyoperahouse.com; Bennelong Pt, Circular Quay E) Designed by Danish architect Jørn Utzon, this World Heritage Listed–building is Australia's most recognisable landmark. Visually referencing the billowing white sails of a seagoing yacht (but described by some local wags as more accurately resembling the sexual congress of turtles), it's a commanding presence on Circular Quay.

The complex comprises five performance spaces hosting dance, music, opera and theatre – the most spectacular is the Concert Hall. Program details and an online booking facility can be found on the website.

The best way to experience the opera house is, of course, to attend a performance, but you can also take a **guided tour** (☎02-9250 7250). The one-hour **Essential Tour** (adult/concession $35/24.50, cheaper if booked in advance online; ⏱every 30 min 9am-5pm) is an interactive audiovisual presentation that tells the story of the building's design and construction and visits one performance space. The two-hour **Backstage Tour**

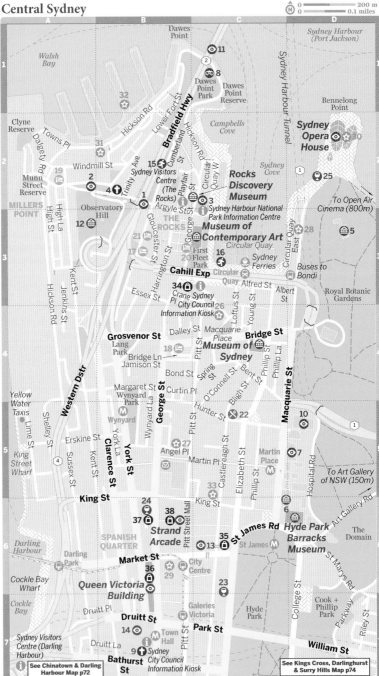

N 0 — 200 m
0 — 0.1 miles

Sydney Harbour
(Port Jackson)

Dawes
Point

11

Walsh
Bay

Dawes
Point
Park

8

Dawes
Point
Reserve

Bennelong
Point

32

Clyne
Reserve

Campbells
Cove

Sydney
Opera
House

30

Sydney
Cove

31

Windmill St

15

Sydney Visitors
Centre (The
Rocks)

Rocks
Discovery
Museum

25

Munn
Street
Reserve

19

2

4

1

Argyle St

3

Sydney Harbour National
Park Information Centre

To Open Air
Cinema (800m)

MILLERS
POINT

Observatory
Hill

12

THE
ROCKS

Museum of
Contemporary Art

28

5

21

16

Sydney
Ferries

17

First
Fleet
Park

Circular Quay

Buses to
Bondi

20

Cahill Exp

Circular
Quay

Royal Botanic
Gardens

Essex St

34

Crane Sydney
City Council
Information Kiosk

26

Alfred St

Albert
St

Grosvenor St

Dalley St

Macquarie
Place

Bridge St

Lang
Park

18

Bridge Ln
Jamison St

Museum of
Sydney

Bond St

Margaret St

Wynyard
Park

Curtin Pl

Q O'Connell St

Bligh St

Bent St

10

1

Wynyard

Hunter St

22

Yellow
Water
Taxis

King
Street
Wharf

Erskine St

Angel Pl

27

Martin Pl

7

Martin
Place

To Art Gallery
of NSW (150m)

33

King St

Art Gallery Rd

24

38

Strand
Arcade

Pitt Street Mall

35

St James Rd

6

Hyde Park
Barracks
Museum

The
Domain

37

13

St James

Darling
Harbour

Darling
Park

Market St

City
Centre

Cockle Bay
Wharf

36

29

23

Queen Victoria
Building

Cook +
Phillip
Park

Cockle
Bay

Druitt Pl

Galeries
Victoria

Hyde
Park

Druitt St

14

Town
Hall

Park St

Sydney Visitors
Centre (Darling
Harbour)

Druitt La

9

Sydney
City Council
Information Kiosk

William St

See Chinatown & Darling
Harbour Map p72

Bathurst
St

See Kings Cross, Darlinghurst
& Surry Hills Map p74

Central Sydney

($155; ⊙daily at 7am) gives access to areas normally reserved for performers and production crews and includes a breakfast in the Green Room. Note that children 12 years and under are not permitted on the Backstage Tour. There are special access tours for those with limited mobility at noon daily – bookings are essential for this and for the Backstage Tour. To purchase tickets on the spot, go to the Guided Tours desk in the Box Office Foyer.

FREE MUSEUM OF CONTEMPORARY ART Museum
(Map p66; www.mca.com.au; 140 George St; admission free except for touring exhibitions; ⊙10am-5pm) This spectacularly sited showcase for Australian and international contemporary art occupies an art deco building fronting Circular Quay West – the view from its ground floor cafe is an artwork in itself.

The Rocks & Millers Point

The site of Sydney's first European settlement, this historically rich enclave at the foot of the Harbour Bridge's southern pylon has evolved unrecognisably from the days when its residents sloshed through open sewers and squalid alleyways. Here, sailors, whalers and larrikins boozed and brawled shamelessly in countless harbourside pubs and nearly as many brothels and opium dens.

The Rocks remained a commercial and maritime hub until shipping services left Circular Quay in the late 1800s. A bubonic plague outbreak in 1900 continued the decline. Construction of the Harbour

Bridge in the 1920s brought further demolition, entire streets disappearing under the bridge's southern approach.

It wasn't until the 1970s that The Rocks' cultural and architectural heritage was recognised. The ensuing tourism-driven redevelopment saved many old buildings, but has turned the area east of the bridge highway into a tourist trap where kitsch cafes and shops hocking stuffed koalas and ersatz didgeridoos reign supreme. Nevertheless, it's a fascinating area to explore on foot – see our walking tour (p62).

Cadmans Cottage (Map p66; www. nationalparks.nsw.gov.au; 110 George St; ⏱9.30am-4.30pm Mon-Fri, 10am-4.30pm Sat & Sun), built on a buried beach, is Sydney's oldest house (1816). Water police detained criminals here in the 1840s and it was later converted into a home for retired sea captains; these days it functions as an information centre for the NSW National Parks and Wildlife Service.

The excellent **Rocks Discovery Museum** (Map p66; www.therocks.com; 2-8 Kendall Lane, The Rocks; admission free; ⏱10am-5pm) digs deep into the area's artefact-laden history and provides interactive insights into the lives of its people, including the original Indigenous inhabitants.

Beyond the **Argyle Cut** (Map p66), an impressive tunnel excavated by convicts, is **Millers Point**, a charming district of early colonial homes; stroll here to enjoy everything The Rocks is not. **Argyle Place** (Map p66) is an English-style village green overlooked by **Garrison Church** (Map p66), Australia's oldest house of worship (1848).

The Italianate **Sydney Observatory** (Map p66; www.sydneyobservatory.com; Watson Rd; free entry to building and grounds, daytime show adult/child & concession $7/5, night viewings adult/child/concession $15/10/12; ⏱10am-5pm), built from Sydney sandstone and sporting a copper-domed roof, sits atop Observatory Hill. You can visit the building and grounds, enjoy a celestial show in the 3-D theatre or see the stars and planets through the telescopes

at night (note that the hours of night viewings vary and that booking for these is essential). Sessions for the daytime shows are at 2.30pm and 3.30pm on weekdays and at 11am, noon, 2.30pm and 3.30pm on weekends.

The wharves around Dawes Point are rapidly emerging from prolonged decay. Walsh Bay's Pier 4 houses the renowned Sydney Theatre Company (p93) and several other performance troupes. The impressive Sydney Theatre (p93) is across the road.

City East

Narrow lanes lead southeast from Circular Quay up the hill towards Sydney's historic parliament precinct on Macquarie St.

MUSEUM OF SYDNEY   Museum
(Map p66; www.hht.net.au; cnr Bridge & Phillip Sts; adult/child/family $10/5/20; ⏱9.30am-5pm) Janet Laurence and Fiona Foley's evocative *Edge of the Trees* sculptural installation occupies pride of place in the forecourt of this sleek museum, marking the site of first contact between the British colonisers and Sydney's original inhabitants, the Gadigal people. Built on the site of Sydney's first Government House (1788), the foundations of which can be spotted through panels of glass in the floor, the museum also offers a modest array of permanent exhibits documenting Sydney's early colonial history – brought to life through oral histories, artefacts and state-of-the-art interactive installations – as well as a changing exhibition program in its two temporary galleries.

MACQUARIE STREET   Historic Precinct
A swathe of splendid sandstone colonial buildings graces this street, defining the central city's eastern edge. Many of these buildings were commissioned by Lachlan Macquarie, the first NSW governor with a vision of Sydney beyond its convict origins. He enlisted convict architect Francis Greenway to help realise his plans, and together they set a gold standard for architectural excellence that the city has – alas – never since managed to replicate.

FREE **Government House** (Map p66; 02-9931 5222; www.hht.net.au; ⏰10.30am-3pm Fri-Sun, grounds 10am-4pm daily), built between 1837 and 1845 in the Gothic Revival style, is just off Macquarie St in the Royal Botanic Gardens. The interior can only be visited on a tour, and bookings are essential.

Further south, the **State Library of NSW** (Map p66; www.sl.nsw.gov.au; ⏰9am-8pm Mon-Thu, 9am-5pm Fri, 10am-5pm Sat & Sun) holds over five million tomes and hosts innovative exhibitions in its galleries.

Next to the library are the deep verandahs, formal colonnades and ochre tones of the twin 1816 **Mint** (Map p66; www.hht.net.au; admission free; ⏰9am-5pm Mon-Fri) and **Parliament House** (Map p66; www.parliament.nsw.gov.au; admission free; ⏰9am-5pm Mon-Fri) buildings, originally wings of the infamous Rum Hospital, built by two Sydney merchants and the colony's principal surgeon in 1816 in return for a three-year monopoly on the rum trade.

Hyde Park Barracks Museum (Map p66; www.hht.net.au; adult/child/family $10/5/20; ⏰9.30am-5pm), is one of two nearby Greenway gems. Built in 1819, the barracks functioned as quarters for Anglo-Irish convicts (aka Oz pioneers) from 1819 to 1848, an immigrant depot (1848–86) and government courts (1887–1979) before its current incarnation as a museum offering an absolutely fascinating insight into everyday convict life through installations and exhibits.

Around Hyde Park

At the southern end of Macquarie St, this much-loved civic park (Map p66) has a grand avenue of trees and a series of delightful fountains.

AUSTRALIAN MUSEUM Museum
(Map p74; www.australianmuseum.net.au; 6 College St; adult/child/concession $12/6/8; ⏰9.30am-5pm) Occupying a prominent position opposite Hyde Park on the corner of William St, this natural history museum stuffed its first animal just 40 years after the First Fleet dropped anchor and its curatorial philosophy and exhibits don't appear to have changed much in the intervening centuries. The only exceptions are the changing exhibits in the Indigenous Australians gallery, which

Exhibit at Rocks Discovery Museum

69

often showcase contemporary Aboriginal issues and art.

FREE ART GALLERY OF NSW
Art Gallery

(off Map p66; www.artgallery.nsw.gov.au; Art Gallery Rd, The Domain; admission free, varied costs for touring exhibitions; ◷10am-5pm Thu-Tue, to 9pm Wed) Highlights at this impressive gallery include 19th- and 20th-century Australian art and Aboriginal and Torres Strait Islander art. There's also an excellent programme of touring exhibitions from interstate and overseas. The controversial, much-discussed Archibald Prize (www. thearchibaldprize.com.au) exhibits here annually, with portraits of the famous and not-so-famous bringing out the art critic in everyone.

Central Sydney

Sydney lacks a true civic centre, but **Martin Place** (Map p66) comes close. This grand pedestrian mall extends from Macquarie St to George St, and is lined with monumental financial buildings and the Victorian colonnaded General Post Office.

The 1874 **Town Hall** (Map p66) is a few blocks south of Martin Pl on the corner of George and Druitt Sts. The elaborate chamber room and concert hall inside match the fabulously ornate exterior. The neighbouring Anglican **St Andrew's Cathedral** (Map p66), built around the same time, is Australia's oldest cathedral. Next to St Andrew's, occupying an entire city block, the Queen Victoria Building is Sydney's most sumptuous shopping complex and a real highlight. Running a close second is the elegant Strand Arcade (p94) between Pitt St Mall and George St, which has a strong representation of Australian designer fashion. The newly opened Westfield Sydney (Map p66) is the city's glitziest shopping mall and has an excellent food hall on its 5th level. It's also the access point for **Sydney Tower** (Map p66; 86-100 Market St; adult/child/concession $25/15/20; ◷9am-10.30pm), where you can enjoy a stunning 360-degree view of the city.

Breathing life into the southwestern zone are Sydney's modest **Spanish Quarter** (Map p66) and thriving **Chinatown** (Map p72), an always-busy district of restaurants, shops and aroma-filled alleyways around Dixon St.

Darling Harbour

Cockle Bay on the city's western edge was once an industrial dockland full of factories, warehouses and shipyards. These days it's a sprawling and exceptionally tacky waterfront tourist development (www.darlingharbour.com), the only redeeming features of which are an excellent aquarium and maritime museum.

If you're keen to find somewhere for a coffee or meal, we suggest skipping the overpriced and underwhelming outlets on **Cockle Bay Wharf** (Map p72) and **King St Wharf** (Map p66), instead making your way to **Jones Bay Wharf**, home to the excellent Flying Fish restaurant (p88) and reliable **Café Morso**. Both have great views.

Alternatively, stroll across the restored **Pyrmont Bridge** (Map p72), which cuts over this mess with a timeless dignity. It leads to **Pyrmont**, home of the Sydney Fish Market.

Darling Harbour and Pyrmont are serviced by ferry, monorail and Metro Light Rail (MLR).

SYDNEY AQUARIUM   Aquarium
(Map p72; www.sydneyaquarium.com.au; Aquarium Pier; adult/child $35/18; ⊙9am-8pm) Celebrating the richness of Australian marine life, this phenomenally popular tourist attraction has three 'oceanariums' moored in the harbour: sharks, rays and humungous fish are in one; Sydney Harbour marine life and seals in the other two. Don't miss the kaleidoscopic colours of the Great Barrier Reef exhibit, platypuses and crocodiles at the Southern and Northern Rivers exhibits, and the cute penguins in the Southern Oceans section.

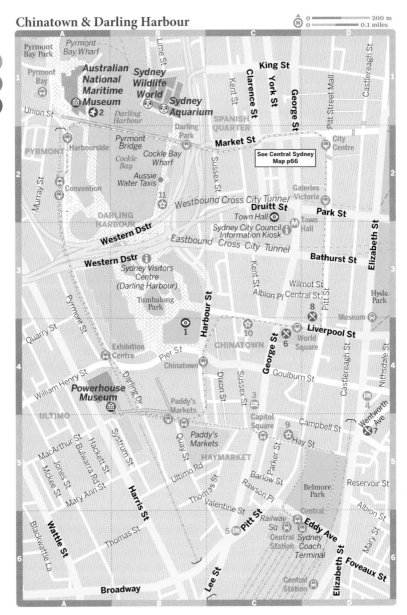

SYDNEY WILDLIFE WORLD Zoo
(Map p72; www.sydneywildlifeworld.com.au;
Aquarium Pier; adult/child $35/18; ⏰9am-
5pm) This indoor wildlife zoo next to the
aquarium offers the chance to get up
close to local critters including koalas,
red kangaroos, rock wallabies and scrub
pythons.

Chinatown & Darling Harbour

AUSTRALIAN NATIONAL MARITIME MUSEUM   Museum
(Map p72; www.anmm.gov.au; 2 Murray St; general admission free; ◷9.30am-5pm) Beneath an Utzonlike roof, this museum examines Australia's inextricable relationship with the sea through exhibits that are arranged thematically. Exhibitions range from Aboriginal canoes to surf culture and the Navy.

POWERHOUSE MUSEUM   Museum
(Map p72; www.powerhousemuseum.com; 500 Harris St, Ultimo; adult/child under 4/child 4-15 & student card holders $10/free/5, additional costs for special exhibits; ◷9.30am-5pm) Housed in the former power station for Sydney's defunct tram network, this sensational showcase for science and design is thought by many (including us) to be Australia's best museum.

CHINESE GARDEN OF FRIENDSHIP   Garden
(Map p72; www.chinesegarden.com.au; adult/Australian student & child under 12 $6/3; ◷9.30am-5.30pm) Built according to the balanced principles of Yin and Yang, this garden is an oasis of tranquillity in otherwise hectic Darling Harbour.

SYDNEY FISH MARKET   Market
(☏02-9004 1122; www.sydneyfishmarket.com.au; cnr Pyrmont Bridge Rd & Bank St, Pyrmont; ◷7am-4pm) With over 15 million kg of seafood shipped through here annually, the city's cavernous fish market is the place to introduce yourself to a bewildering array of mud crabs, Balmain bugs, lobsters, oysters, mullet, rainbow trout and more. There are plenty of fishy restaurants (including an excellent yum cha venue), a deli, a wine centre, a sushi bar and an oyster bar.

Kings Cross

Riding high above the CBD under the big **Coca-Cola sign** (Map p74) – Sydney's equivalent of LA's iconic Hollywood sign – 'the Cross' is a bizarre, densely populated dichotomy of good and evil. Once home to grand estates and stylish apartments, the neighbourhood took a left turn in the 1930s when wine-soaked intellectuals, artists, musicians, pleasure-seekers and ne'er-do-wells claimed the streets for their own.

Today the streets retain an air of seedy hedonism, but along with the strip joints and shabby drinking dens there are classy restaurants, cool bars and boutique hotels. Sometimes the razzle-dazzle has a sideshow appeal; sometimes walking up Darlinghurst Rd promotes pity. Either way, it's never boring.

Possibly the only word in the world with eight 'o's, **Woolloomooloo**, down **McElhone Stairs** from the Cross, was once a slum full of drunks and sailors (a fair few of whom were drunken sailors). Things are begrudgingly less

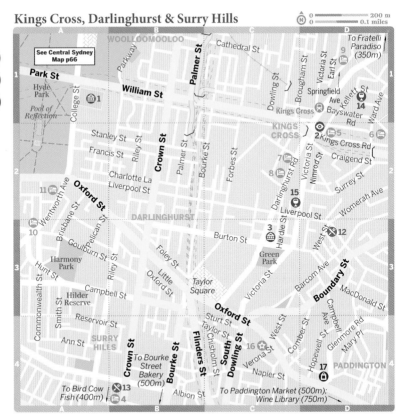

pugilistic these days – the pubs are relaxed and **Woolloomooloo Wharf** is now home to the self-consciously hip BLUE Sydney (p83) and a swathe of upmarket restaurants. Outside the wharf is the famous **Harry's Café de Wheels**, where generations of Sydneysiders have stopped to sober up over a late-night 'Tiger' (beef pie served with mushy peas, mashed potato and gravy) on the way home from a big night at the Cross.

It's a 15-minute walk to the Cross from the city, or you could hop on a train. Buses 323-7, 324-5 and 333 from the city also pass through here.

Inner East

Once the heart of Sydney's entertainment and shopping scenes, **Oxford Street** (Map p74) is now sadly tawdry. Despite

this, the area around **Taylor Square** (Map p74) is still the decadent nucleus for the city's gay community – the Sydney Gay & Lesbian Mardi Gras (p83) famously gyrates through here every February, and gay-centric pubs and clubs do a brisk trade every weekend.

Wedged between Oxford and William Sts, the boho neighbourhood of Darlinghurst is home to cafes, boutique hotels and the **Sydney Jewish Museum** (Map p74; www.sydneyjewishmuseum.com.au; 148 Darlinghurst Rd; adult/child/concession $10/6/7; ☉10am-4pm Sun-Thu, to 2pm Fri, closed Jewish holidays).

Paddington, aka 'Paddo', is an upmarket residential suburb of restored Victorian-era terrace houses, many with attractive iron 'lace' detailing. The best time to explore the Paddington's

Kings Cross, Darlinghurst & Surry Hills

jacaranda-lined streets and laneways is on Saturday, when the Paddington Market (off Map p74) is held.

FREE **Brett Whiteley Studio** (www.brettwhiteley.org; 2 Raper St, Surry Hills; ◷10am-4pm Sat & Sun) After braving the market's crowds, you can easily wander over to Surry Hills for lunch and a visit to this studio, where works by the talented and famously drug-addicted Sydney artist (1939–92) are on show.

Just southeast of Paddington, at the top end of Oxford St, is the 220-hectare **Centennial Park**, which has running, cycling, skating and horse-riding tracks, duck ponds, barbecue sites and sports pitches.

Eastern Suburbs

Handsome **Rushcutters Bay** is a five-minute walk east of Kings Cross; its harbourside park is a lovely spot for a walk or jog. The harbour-hugging New South Head Rd passes through **Double Bay** and **Rose Bay**, and then climbs east into the gorgeous enclave of **Vaucluse**, where shady **Nielsen Park** is home to one of Sydney's best harbour beaches, complete with a netted swimming enclosure, crescent-shaped stretch of sand, picnic facilities and a popular cafe-restaurant.

At the entrance to the harbour is **Watsons Bay**, where you can enjoy blissful briny breezes and a postcard-perfect view of the city skyline while eating takeaway fish and chips at **Doyle's on the Wharf** (fish & chips $11.80-17.50; ◷10am-6pm) at Fisherman's Wharf. Nearby **Camp Cove** is a lovely beach, and there's a nude beach (mostly male) near South Head at **Lady Bay**. **South Head** has great views across the harbour entrance to North Head and Middle Head. The **Gap** is an epic clifftop lookout where sunrises, sunsets, canoodling and suicide leaps transpire with similar frequency.

Buses 324 and 325 from Circular Quay service the eastern suburbs via Kings Cross (grab a seat on the left heading east to snare the best views). The Watsons Bay ferry leaves from Wharf 4 at Circular Quay, stopping at Double Bay and Rose Bay en route.

Bondi

Bondi lords it over every other beach in the city despite the crowds, the crass boardwalk, the often-treacherous rips and the less-than-consistent surf breaks. The suburb itself has a unique atmosphere due to its eclectic mix of traditional Jewish community members, dyed-in-the-wool Aussies, tourists who never went home and socially aspirational young professionals.

The simply sensational 5.5km **Bondi to Coogee Clifftop Walk** leads south from Bondi Beach along the cliff tops to Coogee via Tamarama, Bronte and Clovelly, interweaving panoramic views, patrolled beaches, sea baths, waterside parks and plaques recounting local Aboriginal myths and stories.

If You Like...
Beaches

If you like the sun, sand and sea at Bondi, we think you'll like these other beaches:

1 **BALMORAL**
Split in two by an unfeasibly picturesque rocky outcrop, Balmoral is a popular North Sydney haunt for swimming, kayaking and windsurfing. There are also some fab fish-and-chip shops here. Catch bus 246 from Wynyard, then bus 257 from Spit Junction.

2 **BRONTE**
Norfolk Island pines and sandstone headlands hug the bowl-shaped park behind Bronte, a small family-oriented beach that has a playground, rock pool and sandy cafes. Catch bus 378 from Railway Sq.

3 **CLOVELLY**
The concrete terrace skirting along skinny Clovelly bay makes it more pool than beach, but the swell still surges in. Great snorkelling. Catch bus 339 from Central Station.

4 **AVALON**
Caught in a sandy '70s time-warp, this Northern Beaches highlight is the mythical beach you always dreamed was there but could never find. Solid surf and sleepy cafes. Catch bus L88, 190 or L90 from Wynyard.

Catch bus 380 or 333 from Circular Quay to get to North Bondi (note that this service doesn't stop at Bondi Beach, which is a five-minute walk from the bus interchange at Brighton Blvd) or take a bus or train to the transport interchange at Bondi Junction, from where bus 389 or 333 will take you straight to the beach.

Inner West

West of the city centre is the higgledy-piggledy peninsula suburb of **Balmain**, once a notoriously rough neighbourhood of dockyard workers but now an arty enclave flush with beautifully restored Victorian houses, welcoming pubs, cafes and trendy shops. Catch a ferry from Wharf 5 at Circular Quay, or bus 441/2 from the QVB.

South of Sydney University is **Newtown**, a melting pot of social and sexual subcultures. King St, its relentlessly urban main drag, is full of funky clothes stores, bookshops and cafes. Take the train, or bus 422, 423, 426 or 428 from Circular Quay or Castlereagh St to King St.

North Shore

At the northern end of the Harbour Bridge are the unexpectedly tranquil waterside suburbs of **Milsons Point** and **McMahons Point**.

On the eastern shore of Lavender Bay is **Luna Park** (www.lunaparksydney.com; 1 Olympic Pl, Milsons Point; admission free, multiride passes from $20; ⊙hours vary wildly, see website for details), a classic carnival in the Coney Island mould. Operating since 1935, it boasts a Ferris Wheel, Rotor, Flying Saucer, Tumble Bug and other rides.

Just east of the bridge is the stately suburb of **Kirribilli**, home to **Admiralty House** and **Kirribilli House**, the Sydney residences of the governor-general and prime minister respectively.

You can walk across the bridge to access Milsons Point, McMahons Point, Lavender Bay and Kirribilli, or take the short ferry ride from Wharves 4 and 5 at Circular Quay.

TARONGA ZOO Zoo
(www.taronga.org.au/taronga-zoo; Bradleys Head Rd, Mosman; adult/child 4-15/concession $43/21/30; ⊙9am-5pm) Sydneysiders often joke that the animals here are housed on the best tract of real estate in the city.

Zoo ferries depart Circular Quay's Wharf 2 twice every hour – note that the entrance near the ferry stop doesn't open until 11am on weekdays. After alighting from the ferry, head to the ticket office and then to the nearby **Sky Safari cable car** (ticket included in admission), which will take you up the steep slope to the zoo's highest point. A **ZooPass** (adult/child 4-15 $49.50/24.50), sold at Circular Quay and elsewhere,

JULIET COOMBE/LONELY PLANET IMAGES ©

includes return ferry rides and zoo admission and usually represents a 10% saving.

Manly

Refreshingly relaxed Manly occupies a narrow isthmus between ocean and harbour beaches near North Head. It's the only place in Sydney where you can catch a harbour ferry to swim in the ocean.

The helpful **Manly Visitor Centre** (☎9977 1430; www.manlytourism.com; Manly Wharf; ☺9am-5pm Mon-Fri, 10am-4pm Sat & Sun) is just outside the ferry wharf.

To get to Manly, take the ferry from Circular Quay's Wharf 3 – it's one of Sydney's best-loved journeys.

Northern Beaches

The 20km-stretch of coast between Manly and well-heeled **Palm Beach** (where TV soap *Home and Away* is filmed) is often described as the most impressive urban surfing landscape in the world, and the locals who swim and catch the waves at Manly, Collaroy, Freshwater, Dee Why, Narrabeen, Mona Vale, Newport, Bilgola, Avalon, Whale and Palm Beaches would be quick to agree.

To get to Collaroy, North Narrabeen, Mona Vale, Newport, Bilgola, Avalon, Whale and Palm Beaches from the CBD, catch bus L90 from Railway Sq. From Manly Wharf, bus 136 goes to Chatswood via Curl Curl and Dee Why; bus 156 goes to McCarrs Creek via Dee Why, North Narrabeen and Mona Vale.

**KU-RING-GAI CHASE
NATIONAL PARK**   Park
(www.nationalparks.nsw.gov.au; admission per car $11) This spectacular 14,928-hectare park 24km from the city centre forms Sydney's northern boundary. It's a classic mix of sandstone, bushland and water vistas, taking in over 100km of coastline along the southern edge of Broken Bay where it heads into the Hawkesbury River.

Remnants of Aboriginal life are visible today thanks to the preservation of more than 800 sites, including rock paintings, middens and cave art. To learn about these sites and about the park's flora and fauna, enter the park through the Mt Colah entrance and visit the **Kalkari Discovery Centre** (☎02-9472 9300; Ku-ring-gai Chase Rd; admission free; ☺10am-4pm Mon-Fri, to 5pm Sat & Sun), which has displays and videos on Australian fauna and Aboriginal culture.

For information about the park, stop at the **Bobbin Head Information Centre** (☎02-9472 8949; Bobbin Inn, Bobbin Head; ⏰10am-4pm), which is operated by the NSW Parks and Wildlife Service. Also here are a marina, picnic areas, a cafe and a boardwalk leading through mangroves.

Access to the park is by car or the **Palm Beach Ferry** (www.palmbeachferry. com.au; adult/child $6.90/3.50; ⏰9am-7pm Mon-Fri, to 6pm Sat & Sun) run by Fantasea. This runs hourly from Palm Beach to Mackerel Beach, via the Basin. To get to Palm Beach from the CBD, catch bus L90 from Railway Sq or Bus 156 or 169 from Manly Wharf.

If you are arriving by car, enter Ku-ring-gai Chase Rd off Pacific Hwy, Mt Colah; Bobbin Head Rd, North Turramurra; or McCarrs Creek Rd, Terrey Hills.

 # Activities

Canoeing & Kayaking

Natural Wanders
(☎0427 225 072; www.kayaksydney.com; per person from $65) Offers exhilarating morning tours around the Harbour Bridge, Lavender Bay, Balmain and Birchgrove.

Cycling

Bicycle NSW Cycling
(www.bicyclensw.org.au) Publishes *Cycling Around Sydney*, detailing city paths; it also sells Bicycle Australia's *Where to Ride Sydney* and the NRMA's *Great Cycling Rides in NSW* from its online store.

Centennial Park Cycles Cycling
(www.cyclehire.com.au; per day/week from $50/110; ⏰9am-5pm) Branches in Randwick and Centennial Park.

Diving

Sydney's best shore dives are at Gordons Bay, north of Coogee; Shark Point, Clovelly; and Ship Rock, Cronulla. Popular boat-dive sites are Wedding Cake Island off Coogee, Sydney Heads, and off Royal National Park.

Dive Centre Bondi Diving
(☎02-9369 3855; www.divebondi.com.au; 198 Bondi Rd, Bondi; ⏰8.30am-6pm Mon-Fri, from 7.30am Sat & Sun) One-day PADI Discover Scuba course $225; shore and boat dives; rentals.

Dive Centre Manly Diving
(☎02-9977 4355; www.divesydney.com.au; 10 Belgrave St, Manly; ⏰9am-6pm Mon-Wed & Fri, 9am-8pm Thu, 8am-6pm Sat & Sun) PADI Discover Scuba course $155; shore and boat dives; rentals.

In-Line Skating

The beach promenades at Bondi and Manly and the paths of Centennial Park are the favoured spots for skating.

Rollerblading Sydney Skating
(☎0411 872 022; www.rollerbladingsydney.com. au; lessons per hr $50) Rentals, lessons and tours.

Skater HQ Skating
(www.skaterhq.com.au; 2/49 North Steyne, Manly; hire per hr adult/child $20/15; ⏰10am-7pm Mon-Thu, 10am-8pm Fri, 9am-8pm Sat, 9am-6pm Sun) Hires rollerblades, scooters and skateboards.

Sailing

Sydney has dozens of yacht clubs and sailing schools.

EastSail Sailing School Sailing
(☎02-9327 1166; www.eastsail.com.au; d'Albora Marina, New Beach Rd, Rushcutters Bay; cruises per adult/child from $119/89, 2-day 'start yachting' course $575; ⏰9am-6pm) A sociable outfit offering 'Start Yachting' courses, more advanced outings and morning/ sunset cruises.

Sydney by Sail Sailing
(Map p72; ☎02-9280 1110; www.sydneybysail. com.au; Festival Pontoon, National Maritime Museum, Darling Harbour) Daily harbour sailing tours (three hours, adult/child $150/$75), introductory weekend sailing courses ($495), whale-watching cruises (six hours, $175) and plenty of other options.

Surfing

On the South Shore, get tubed at Bondi, Tamarama, Coogee, Maroubra and Cronulla. The North Shore is home to a dozen gnarly surf beaches between Manly and Palm Beach, including Curl Curl, Dee Why, Narrabeen, Mona Vale and Newport.

Let's Go Surfing Surfing
(☎ 02-9365 1800; www.letsgosurfing.com.au; 128 Ramsgate Ave, Bondi; 2hr group lesson incl use of board & wetsuit adult/child from $89/79; ⏰ 9am-5pm, later in summer) Also offers board and wetsuit hire ($30 for two hours).

Manly Surf School Surfing
(☎ 02-9977 6977; www.manlysurfschool.com; North Steyne Surf Lifesaving Club, Manly; 2hr group lesson incl use of board & wetsuit adult/child $60/50; ⏰ 9am-6pm) Lessons cater to all levels of fitness, ability and age.

Swimming

There are 100-plus public swimming pools in Sydney, and many beaches have protected rock pools. Harbour beaches offer sheltered and shark-netted swimming, but nothing beats Pacific Ocean waves. Always swim within the flagged lifeguard-patrolled areas, and never underestimate the surf.

Some outdoor swimming pools:

Andrew 'Boy' Charlton Pool Swimming
(www.abcpool.org; 1c Mrs Macquaries Rd, The Domain; adult/child/locker $5.60/2/3; ⏰ 6am-7pm Sep-Apr, 1 hr later during daylight savings) A 50m outdoor saltwater pool and harbour-view cafe.

Bondi Icebergs Swimming Club Swimming
(http://icebergs.com.au/; adult/child & senior $5/3; ⏰ 6am-6.30pm Mon-Wed & Fri, 6.30am-6.30pm Sat

& Sun) Sydney's most famous swimming pool commands the best view in Bondi and has a cute little cafe.

North Sydney Olympic Pool Swimming
(www.northsydney.nsw.gov.au; 4 Alfred St South, Milsons Point; adult/child/senior $6.50/3.20/5.20; ⏰ 5.30am-9pm Mon-Fri, 7am-7pm Sat & Sun) Next to Luna Park, right on the harbour.

🖐 Tours

There are countless tours available in Sydney. You can book most of them at the visitor centres.

City Bus Tours

CITY SIGHTSEEING Bus Tours
(www.city-sightseeing.com) Operates two sightseeing buses around Sydney. One ticket (adult/child/senior/student 24hr ticket $35/20/25/30, 48hr ticket $56/32/40/48; ⏰ every 20 minutes from 8.30am to 7.30pm) covers both. Buses

Bronte Beach (p76)

Sydney for Children

Organised kids' activities ramp up during school holidays (December/January, April, July and September); check www.sydneyforkids.com.au, www.kidfriendly.com.au and the free *Sydney's Child* magazine for listings.

Most kids love the Sydney Aquarium (p71), Sydney Wildlife World (p72), Australian National Maritime Museum (p73) and Powerhouse Museum (p73) at Darling Harbour. Also worth investigating is the Sunday afternoon GalleryKids program at the Art Gallery of NSW (p70), which includes dance, stories, magic, cartoons, Aboriginal performances, costumed tour guides and exhibition-specific events.

Elsewhere, Taronga Zoo (p76) and Luna Park (p76) are sure-fire entertainers.

leave Central Station every 15 to 20 minutes and can be boarded at any stop. Buy your ticket on the bus. One of the two services is **Sydney Tour**, which has a 90-minute, 23-stop hop-on, hop-off loop from Central Station through Pyrmont, Darling Harbour, The Rocks, Circular Quay, the city centre, Kings Cross, the Domain, and Macquarie St.

Harbour Cruises

CAPTAIN COOK CRUISES
Harbour Cruises

(Map p66; ☏02-9206 1111; www.captaincook.com.au; Wharf 6, Circular Quay) Offers a 1¼-hour 'Harbour Highlights' cruise (adult/child 5-14 years/student $30/16/26) and a 24-hour hop-on hop-off 'Harbour Express' pass with entry to Fort Denison, Shark Island and Taronga Zoo (adult/child/student $58/32/36). Also at Aquarium Wharf, Darling Harbour.

Sydney Ferries
Harbour Cruises

(Map p66; www.sydneyferries.nsw.gov.au) Visit the website or Circular Quay ticket booth to find out everything there is to know about touring the harbour by ferry.

Walking Tours

BRIDGECLIMB
Walking Tours

(Map p66; ☏02-9240 1100; www.bridgeclimb.com; 5 Cumberland St, The Rocks; adult $188-268, child aged 10-15 $128-188; ⏲3½hr tours around the clock) Put on a headset, an umbilical cord and a naff grey jumpsuit and you'll be ready to embark on the climb of your life! Book well in advance.

SYDNEY ARCHITECTURE WALKS
Walking Tours

(☏02-8239 2211; www.sydneyarchitecture.org; adult/concession $35/25) These two-hour, architect-led tours run from September to May, departing from the Museum of Sydney. There's a tour of the city on most Wednesdays at 10.30am, one concentrating on the Opera House on Saturdays at 10.30am and an occasional tour focusing on the industrial heritage of The Rocks (various times).

 **Sleeping**

The winter months sometimes deliver bargains, but between December and February you should expect prices to jump by as much as 40%.

Circular Quay & The Rocks

SYDNEY HARBOUR YHA Hostel $

(Map p66; ☏02-8272 0900; www.yha.com.au; 110 Cumberland St, The Rocks; dm $44-59, d $148-170, d with harbour view $165-185; ✳@☏) The view from the rooftop terrace and deluxe rooms at this recently opened and exceptionally well-run YHA hostel is fabulous – right over Circular Quay to the Opera House.

RUSSELL
Boutique Hotel $$$

(Map p66; ☎02-9241 3543; www.therussell.com.
au; 143a George St, The Rocks; d $199-245, with-
out bathroom $130-199; ❄) A recent renova-
tion has seen this long-standing favourite
divest itself of frills and furbelows and
attain some contemporary style as well
as a lift and a downstairs wine bar. The
rooftop garden and location just minutes
from Circular Quay are major drawcards,
but only a few rooms have air-con.

LORD NELSON BREWERY
HOTEL
Boutique Hotel $$

(Map p66; ☎02-9251 4044; www.lordnelson.
com.au; 19 Kent St, the Rocks; d $190, without
bathroom $130; ❄ 🌐) Built in 1841, this
boutique sandstone pub has its own
brewery (try a pint of 'Nelson's Blood')
and offers elegantly understated rooms,
many with walls of the original exposed
stone. Bathrooms are regal – even those
that are shared.

B&B SYDNEY HARBOUR
B&B $$

(Map p66; ☎02-9247 1130; www.bedandbreak
fastsydney.com; 140-142 Cumberland St, The
Rocks; s $165-214, without bathroom $140-165, d
$178-260, without bathroom $155-178; ❄)

Rooms at this century-old guesthouse
in The Rocks sport a pleasant traditional
decor with an Australiana flavour; some
have harbour views. The lavish breakfast
can be enjoyed in the pretty courtyard.
Not all rooms have air-con.

City Centre

VIBE HOTEL
Hotel $$

(Map p72; ☎02-9282 0987; www.vibehotels.com.
au; 111 Goulburn St; d $165-220, ste $220-300;
❄ @ 🌐 🏊) The rooms are spacious and
extremely well priced at this excellent
choice near Central Station. All have a
seating area, flat-screen TV, work desk
and enormous closet. There's a ground-
floor cafe and a gym, sauna and good-
sized pool on the outdoor deck. Breakfast
costs an extra $22-28.

Y HOTEL
Hostel $S

(Map p74; ☎02-9264 2451; www.yhotel.com.
au; 5-11 Wentworth Ave; dm $35-65, s $70-202, d
$70-250; ❄ @ 🌐) Package tourists are in
more evidence than party animals at this
popular budget hotel. Perfectly located
in a quiet pocket of the city close to Hyde
Park, Oxford St, train stations and bus
stops, it offers simple, well-maintained

Sydney Harbour BridgeClimb

and extremely clean sleeping options that span the gamut from small dorms to spacious studios with en suites and kitchenettes.

PENSIONE HOTEL   Boutique Hotel   **$$**
(Map p72; 02-9265 8888; www.pensione.
com.au; 631-635 George St; s/d from $100/135;
❄ @ 🎅) This tastefully reworked post office features 68 smart, neutrally shaded rooms, some of which are tiny. There's also a communal lounge with kitchenette. Aim for a rear room away from traffic noise. Breakfast is an extra $10.

**ESTABLISHMENT
HOTEL**   Boutique Hotel   **$$$**
(Map p66; 02-9240 3100; www.merivale.com;
5 Bridge Lane; r $445-800; ❄ @ 🎅) Through this door pass discreet celebrities, style-conscious couples and execs hoping for a nooner with their assistant. What the hotel lacks in facilities is more than made up for in glamour, although light sleepers should beware – the hotel is in Sydney's most happening (and noisy) entertainment complexes.

WAKE UP!   Hostel   **$**
(Map p72; 02-9288 7888; www.wakeup.com.au;
509 Pitt St; dm $32-40, d & tw $112-132, without bathroom $98-118; ❄ @ 🎅) This converted 1900 department store on top of Sydney's busiest intersection is a convivial, colourful, professionally run hostel with a tour desk, 24-hour check-in, sunny cafe, bar and pronounced party atmosphere. Dorms have four to 10 beds.

TRAVELODGE SYDNEY   Hotel   **$$**
(Map p74; 02-8267 1700; www.travelodge.
com.au/travelodge-sydney-hotel/home; cnr Wentworth Ave & Goulburn St; d from $99;
❄ @ 🎅) A great location near Hyde Park (equidistant between Museum Station and Central Station) plus clean, comfortable and well-set-up rooms with basic kitchenette mean that this is a compelling choice, particularly if you can score one of the sensational internet specials (look for the five-night package).

Kings Cross, Potts Point & Wooloomooloo

DIAMANT HOTEL   Hotel   **$$$**
(Map p74; 02-9295 8888; www.evasback
packers.com.au; 14 Kings Cross Rd, Kings Cross;

Sydney Gay & Lesbian Mardi Gras

Gay & Lesbian Sydney

Gay and lesbian culture forms a vocal and vital part of Sydney's social fabric. **Taylor Square** (Map p74) on Oxford St is the centre of arguably the second-largest gay community in the world after San Francisco; Newtown is home to Sydney's lesbian scene.

Sydney's famous **Gay & Lesbian Mardi Gras** (www.mardigras.org.au) draws over 700,000 spectators; the Mardi Gras also runs the annual **Sleaze Ball** held in late September/early October at the Horden Pavilion in Moore Park (Map p66).

Free gay media includes *SX*. Online resources include www.ssonet.com.au (Sydney's main gay newspaper), www.lotl.com (Sydney's monthly lesbian magazine) and the G&L pages of the monthly *Time Out* magazine.

Most accommodation in and around Oxford St is very gay-friendly.

d $165-350, ste $305-375; ❄ @ 🛜) Standing as proudly tall as the nearby Coca-Cola sign, this supersleek member of the 8 Hotels chain offers a choice of room styles, many complete with views and courtyards. King-size beds and quality linen feature in a seriously sophisticated package, with the only disappointment being the lack of wi-fi access in rooms.

SIMPSONS OF POTTS POINT
B&B $$$

(☎ 02-9356 2199; www.simpsonspottspoint.com.au; 8 Challis Ave, Potts Point; r $235-335, ste $325-385; ❄ @ 🛜) An 1892 redbrick villa at the quiet end of a busy cafe strip, the perennially popular Simpsons looks towards Laura Ashley and her ilk for decorative flourishes. The downstairs lounge and breakfast room are lovely, and rooms are both comfortable and impeccably clean.

HOTEL 59
B&B $$

(Map p74; ☎ 02-9360 5900; www.hotel59.com.au; 59 Bayswater Rd, Kings Cross; s $88, d $110-121, f $132; ❄ 🛜) The nine rooms at this popular choice may hark back to a time when Wham! and crimped hair were in vogue, but they are spotless and oddly charming. The central location and incredibly helpful staff add to the appeal. Free wi-fi.

BLUE SYDNEY
Boutique Hotel $$$

(☎ 02-9331 9000; www.tajhotels.com/sydney; 6 Cowper Wharf Rd, Woolloomooloo; d from $200; ❄ @ 🏊) Stay here for the night and boast that you slept next to Russell Crowe (he owns one of the apartments at the end of the wharf). But even if he's not your cup of tea, you're sure to enjoy the boutique sensibilities and excellent location of this Taj-owned hotel.

MAISONETTE HOTEL
Hotel $$

(☎ 02-9357 3878; www.maisonettehotel.com; 31 Challis Ave, Potts Point; s $99-110, without bathroom $65-85, d $110-185; 🛜) You get bang for your buck at the Maisonette, a cheery hotel in the heart of Potts Point's cafe scene. Sure, the carpet's a little frayed and a lick of paint is overdue, but the rooms are welcoming and the location rocks. There are considerable discounts for stays of a week or more.

QUEST POTTS POINT
Hotel $$$

(Map p74; ☎ 02-8988 6999; www.questpottspoint.com.au; 15 Springfield Ave, Kings Cross; d from $180; ❄ @ 🛜) Occupying an art deco building in the thick of the Cross action, this branch of the franchised Quest operation offers 68 elegant and well-equipped studios and suites. Most have kitchenettes and the executive suites have stunning city-view terraces.

Inner East

ADINA APARTMENT HOTEL
SYDNEY Apartments **$$$**
(Map p74; ☎02-9212 1111; www.adinahotels.com.
au; 359 Crown St, Surry Hills; 1-bed apt $250-350,
2-bed apt $350-460; ❄️@🛜🏊) In the heart
of the Surry Hills entertainment precinct,
the recently renovated Adina offers 85
exceptionally stylish and well-equipped
apartments. Ask for an upper-floor apart-
ment, as those on the lower floors can be
noisy.

KIRKETON
Boutique Hotel **$$**
(Map p74; ☎02-9332 2011; www.8hotels.com;
229 Darlinghurst Rd, Darlinghurst; r $145-239;
❄️@) The Kirketon's 40 designer rooms
are as impeccably turned out as its hip
clientele and hot staff. The stylishly
sparse standard rooms are cramped
– upgrade to premium, executive or
superior if possible. If not, never fear –
you can always hang out in the glam Eau
de Vie bar.

HOTEL ALTAMONT
Boutique Hotel **$$**
(Map p74; ☎02-9360 6000; www.8hotels.com;
207 Darlinghurst Rd, Darlinghurst; r from $135;
❄️@🛜) The Rolling Stones have stayed
in this Georgian pile, hence the name. It's
been given a postmodern makeover since
their stay, though, with the rooms now
more Zen than rock-and-roll grunge. The
foyer bar/breakfast room is a great spot
to sit and watch the daily Darlinghurst
parade go by. Excellent value.

Bondi

BONDI BEACH HOUSE
Guesthouse **$$**
(☎0417 336 444; www.bondibeachhouse.com.
au; 28 Sir Thomas Mitchell Rd; s $95-135, without
bathroom $80-110, d $170-300, without bathroom
$120-215, ste $185-325; ❄️🛜) Tucked away in
a tranquil pocket behind Campbell Pde, this
charming place offers a real home-away-
from-home atmosphere. Though only a
five-minute walk from the beach, you may
well be tempted to stay in all day – the rear
courtyard and front terrace are great spots
for relaxing, and the rooms (particularly
the suites) are conducive to long sleep-ins.
No children under 12, and DIY breakfast.

RAVESI'S
Boutique Hotel **$$$**
(☎02-9130 3271; www.hotelbondi.com.au; 178
Campbell Pde; r weekdays $249-399, weekends
$269-42; ❄️🛜) To enjoy a sybaritic Bondi
sojourn, claim one of the 12 spacious
and stylish rooms above the fa-
mous Campbell Pde bar. Those
celebrating a big occasion
should consider booking the
Deluxe Penthouse, which
has a large private terrace
overlooking the beach.
Breakfast is not available.

Manly

101 ADDISON
ROAD B&B **$$**
(☎02-9977 6216; www.
bb-manly.com; 101 Addison
Rd; s/d $150/170) Owner
Jill Caskey offers a B&B
in the true sense of the
word – two rooms of her

Oyster tapas at Guillaume at Bennelong

charming Victorian cottage are available, but only one guest booking is accommodated. The private lounge comes complete with books, TV, DVD and grand piano. There are even beach towels and umbrellas for guests' use.

Eating

Abundant fresh produce, innovative chefs and a multicultural melange all combine to make eating out in Sydney an extremely pleasurable and popular activity – book ahead wherever possible

City Centre, the Rocks & Circular Quay

BÉCASSE   Modern Australian   **$$**
(Map p66; ☎02-9283 3440; www.becasse.com. au; Westfield Sydney, Pitt St; mains $48, 8-course tasting menu $120/130; ⏰lunch Mon-Fri, dinner Mon-Sat) Justin North's flagship restaurant has a loyal and ever-growing foodie following, particularly since he relocated to this new space and adopted a more intimate dining model – he's clearly got three chef hats in his sights. Taking inspiration from what's in season and at the markets, North constructs modern European dishes with a deft and delicious touch.

ROCKPOOL BAR & GRILL   Modern Australian   **$$**
(Map p66; ☎02-8078 1900; www.rockpool.com. au/sydney/bar-and-grill; cnr Hunter & Blight Sts, Sydney; mains $21-110; ⏰lunch Mon-Fri, dinner Mon-Sat) You'll feel like a pampered 1930s Manhattan stockbroker when you dine at this sleek operation in the art deco City Mutual Building. The bar is famous for its dry-aged, full-blood wagyu burger (make sure you also order a side of the hand-cut fat chips), but carnivores will be equally enamoured with the succulent steaks served in the grill.

GUILLAUME AT BENNELONG   French   **$$$**
(Map p66; www.guillaumeatbennelong.com. au; ☎02-9241 1999; Bennelong Pt, Circular Quay East; main $40-80; lunch Thu & Fri, dinner Mon-Sat) Indulge in master chef Guillaume

Brahimi's delectable creations under the sails of the city's most famous landmark. Snuggle into a chocolate-brown banquette or sit yourself next to the window (the views are extraordinary) to enjoy a memorable meal or nosh on tapas (four/six/eight dishes $35/40/45) at the bar. The pre-theatre dinner menu (two/three courses $66/78) offers excellent value.

Chinatown & Darling Harbour

DIN TAI FUNG   Taiwanese   **$**
(Map p72; www.dintaifungaustralia.com.au; Level 1, World Square, 644 George St, Haymarket; dumplings $9-18, noodles $5-17; ⏰lunch & dinner daily) Din Tai Fung's crabmeat, crab roe and pork dumplings deliver an explosion of fabulously flavoursome broth when you bite into their delicate casing. And the delights of this place don't stop there, with a huge choice of noodles, dumplings and buns to choose from. Come early, come hungry, come prepared to share your table.

SYDNEY MADANG   Korean   **$**
(Map p72; 371a Pitt St, Sydney; ⏰11.30am-1am) Secreted in a somewhat dingy laneway off Pitt St, Sydney Madang serves spicy steam bowls, killer kimchi dishes and lavish BBQ arrays to a loyal coterie of locals and an appreciative cast of visiting Korean nationals. No reservations, so arrive early or expect to queue.

Woolloomooloo, Potts Point & Darlinghurst

FRATELLI PARADISO   Italian   **$$**
(off Map p74; 16 Challis Ave, Potts Point; mains $20-33; ⏰7am-11pm Mon-Fri, to 6pm Sat & Sun) Challis Ave is one of the city's cafe hubs, and this bakery-bistro is in the thick of the action. The menu and atmosphere are 100% Italian, a theme that is maintained with excellent espresso and great service. Dishes change daily, and everything is delicious.

BILLS   Cafe   **$**
(Map p74; www.bills.com.au; 433 Liverpool St, Darlinghurst; breakfast $5.50-18.50, lunch $7.50-26; ⏰7.30am-3pm Mon-Sat, 8.30am-3pm Sun) Bill Granger almost single-handedly

kicked off the Sydney craze for stylish brunch. His two most famous dishes – ricotta hotcakes and sweetcorn fritters – have legions of fans, but we wish the coffee served at his three Sydney cafes was better.

Surry Hills

BIRD COW FISH Modern Australian **$$**
(off Map p74; 02-9380 4090; www.birdcowfish.com.au; 4-5/500 Crown St, Surry Hills; brunch $15.50-18.50, mains $36-37; lunch daily, dinner Mon-Sat, brunch Sat & Sun from 9am) The name sums up the ingredient list, but gives no hint of the excellence of the produce, dishes, wine list and service on offer at this terrific Surry Hills bistro. Brunch is a delight, particularly as the coffee is among the best in Sydney.

SPICE I AM Thai **$**
(Map p72; www.spiceiam.com.au; 90 Wentworth Ave; mains $14-26; lunch & dinner Tue-Sun) The signature dishes at this mega-popular BYO eatery on the city edge of Surry Hills are fragrant, flavoursome and cheap, meaning that queues are inevitable.

BOURKE STREET BAKERY Bakery **$**
(off Map p74; www.bourkestreetbakery.com.au; 633 Bourke St, Surry Hills; pastries & cakes $3-5, pies & sandwiches $4-7.50; 7am-6pm Mon-Fri, 8am-5pm Sat & Sun) Surry Hill's much-loved corner bakery makes wonderful sandwiches with its sourdough, soy-loaves and crusty white *ficelles*. Its cakes, pastries, pies and quiches are equally delicious. Grab one of the hotly contested seats and enjoy your choice with a coffee.

BILLY KWONG Chinese **$$**
(Map p74; Shop 3, 355 Crown St, Surry Hills; mains $26-48; dinner) The business strives hard to be sustainable, serving organic, seasonal and local produce wherever possible, and the results can be truly inspired (on our most recent visit, the crispy skin duck with orange was truly magnificent). However, the cramped, noisy and uncomfortable seating, sometimes lackadaisical service, lack of desserts and no-bookings

Left: Flying Fish (p88); **Below:** Chinese dumplings at Billy Kwong

policy don't seem to tally with the high prices.

Paddington & Woollahra

FOUR IN HAND French $$

(02-9362 1999; 105 Sutherland St, Paddington; mains $36-42; lunch & dinner Tue-Sun) You can't go far in Paddington and Woollahra without tripping over a beautiful old pub with amazing food. In this case, you'll be tripping over some of the best pub grub in Sydney. The restaurant here is famous for its slow-cooked meat dishes, and also offers fabulously fresh seafood dishes and a limited but delectable array of desserts. The bar menu (mains $15 to $18) is also a winner.

JONES THE GROCER Deli, Cafe $

(68 Moncur St, Woollahra; breakfast $5.50-16.50, baguettes $9-10; 8.30am-5.30pm Mon-Sat, 9am-5pm Sun) JTG offers high-end groceries, cookbooks and gourmet goodies. Enjoy a good coffee while you're here, then grab some provisions for a Centennial Park picnic.

Bondi

ICEBERGS DINING ROOM & BAR Italian $$$

(02-9365 9000; www.idrb.com; 1 Notts Ave; mains $36-97; lunch & dinner Tue-Sun) The magnificent view sweeps over Bondi Beach, making Icebergs Australia's most glamorous restaurant – bar none. The menu doesn't disappoint either, offering modern and delicious takes on classic Italian dishes and a choice of aged beef, perfectly cooked. Come for lunch so as to make the most of the view, or arrive in time to enjoy a sunset cocktail at the bar before your meal.

POMPEI'S Pizza $$

(02-9365 1233; www.pompeis.com.au; 126-130 Roscoe St, Bondi Beach; pizzas $19-23, pasta $24-26; 11am-late Fri-Sun, 3pm-late Tue-Thu) Simply sensational Roman-style pizzas, homemade pasta and the best gelato in the city are devoured by locals and

The Cult of the Celebrity Chef

Many Sydneysiders consider a sprinkling of celebrity to be an essential ingredient when it comes to dining out – whether it be courtesy of a star-studded roll-call of regulars, or a celebrity chef at the restaurant's helm.

- **Bill Granger**: Bills (p85) Lifestyle chef and author of 12 cookbooks whose food and style are thought by many to be quintessentially Sydney.
- **Kylie Kwong**: Billy Kwong (p86) Presents her own television programs (*My China* etc) and has written a number of cookbooks.
- **Neil Perry**: Rockpool Bar & Grill (p85), Rockpool and Spice Temple (www. rockpool.com.au) The city's original rock-star chef (with ponytail to match) has a long list of cookbooks and appearances on television cooking programs to his credit.
- **Adriano Zumbo**: Adriano Zumbo (p88) Everyone who watched the TV series about Sydney's hip pastry chef knows that Mr Zumbo takes his role as a celebrity chef very seriously – fortunately, his sweet concoctions live up to their hype.

visitors alike at Bondi's busiest eatery. There's indoor and outdoor seating, but no views.

Inner West

ADRIANO ZUMBO   Patisserie $
(http://adrianozumbo.com; 296 Darling St, Balmain; ☺8am-6pm Mon-Sat, to 5pm Sun) Look for the queue, and you'll find Sydney's most famous patisserie. Pastry chef Adriano Zumbo became an overnight star when he appeared on the *Masterchef* reality TV show, and he now leads a sugar-fuelled celebrity lifestyle. Try his signature macaroons (the passionfruit and basil ones are divine) and any of the cakes.

FLYING FISH   Seafood $$
(☎02-9518 6677; www.flyingfish.com.au; Lower Deck, Jones Bay Wharf, Pyrmont; mains $38-48; ☺lunch Tue-Fri & Sun, dinner Mon-Sat) Chef Peter Kuruvita is known for his aromatic Sri Lankan curries, but everything in this glamorous loft-style eatery is delicious. You can watch the action on the water as you sample sushi, freshly shucked oysters or sophisticated fish dishes. Kids' meals are $15.

North Shore & Manly

MANLY PAVILION   Italian $$
(☎02-9949 9011; West Esplanade; mains $40-45; ☺lunch & dinner) Lingering over lunch on the waterfront terrace or water-facing dining room of Manly's best restaurant is one of the quintessential Sydney dining experiences. The 1930s building (an old bathing pavilion) has been stylishly restored and the view, modern Italian cuisine, winelist and service are all impressive. It's also a great choice for a sunset aperitivo with delectable *stuzzichini* (snacks, $10 to $15) or antipasti ($26 to $30).

 **Drinking**

Pubs are a crucial part of the Sydney social scene, and you can down a glass or schooner (NSW term for a large glass) of amber nectar at elaborate 19th-century affairs, cavernous art deco joints, modern and minimalist recesses, and everything in-between. Bars are generally more stylish and urbane, sometimes with a dress code.

The Rocks & Circular Quay

OPERA BAR — Bar
(Map p66; www.operabar.com.au; Circular Quay East; ⏱11.30am-midnight Sun-Thu, to 1am Fri & Sat) The Opera Bar puts all other beer gardens to shame. Spilling into the harbour with the Opera House on one side and the Harbour Bridge on the other, this outdoor drinking den has it all. There's live music from 8.30pm Monday to Friday and from 2pm on weekends.

LORD NELSON BREWERY HOTEL — Pub
(Map p66; www.lordnelson.com.au; 19 Kent St, Millers Point; ⏱11am-11pm Mon-Sat, noon-10pm Sun) Built in 1841, the 'Nello' claims to be the oldest pub in this area (although the Fortune of War begs to differ). The on-site microbrewery produces some of Sydney's best ales.

City Centre

GRASSHOPPER — Bar
(Map p66; Temperance Lane; ⏱noon-1am Mon-Fri) The first of what is bound to be many grungy laneway bars in the inner city, Grasshopper is about as cool as the city centre gets. The food served in the upstairs restaurant is good, but the heart of the operation is the downstairs bar.

BAMBINI WINE ROOM — Wine Bar
(Map p66; www.bambinitrust.com.au; 185 Elizabeth St; ⏱from 3pm Mon-Fri, from 5.30pm Sat) This tiny darkwood-panelled room with a huge chandelier is the sort of place where you might expect to see Oscar Wilde holding court in a corner. There's an extensive wine list and a classy array of bar food ($8 to $40).

Woolloomooloo

TILBURY HOTEL — Gastropub $$
(www.tilburyhotel.com.au; 12-18 Nicholson St, Woolloomooloo; ⏱lunch & dinner Tue-Sat, brunch & lunch Sun) Once the dank domain of burly sailors and visiting ne'er-do-wells, the Tilbury now sparkles as one of the city's best gastropubs. It attracts a well-heeled crowd that hangs out in the outdoor courtyard (lunch only) or indoor restaurant, cafe and bar.

Kings Cross, Darlinghurst & Surry Hills

SHAKESPEARE HOTEL — Pub
(200 Devonshire St; ⏱11am-11pm) Surry Hills' best-loved pub is everything a neighbourhood boozer should be, with ice-cold beer, cheap bar meals and laconic locals watching the gee-gees and chewing the fat.

APERITIF — Bar
(Map p74; 7 Kellett St, Kings Cross; ⏱6pm-3am Mon & Wed-Sat, to midnight Sun) Like a gently sloping mini Bourbon St, Kellett St is a snaky, sexy laneway with as many bars as brothels. Intimate Aperitif elevates the tone with an expertly constructed all-European wine list and a late-night

Opera Bar

kitchen (last orders 2am) serving fabulous French and Spanish food.

GAZEBO WINE GARDEN   Wine Bar
(www.gazebowinegarden.com.au; 2 Elizabeth Bay Rd, Elizabeth Bay; ◔3pm-midnight Mon-Thu, from noon Fri-Sun) You've got to love a place that divides its wine list into sections including 'Unpronounceable', 'Opulent' and 'Slurpable'. Nocturnal garden parties at this bizarrely decorated Kings Cross oasis can be fantastic.

VICTORIA ROOM   Bar
(Map p74; www.thevictoriaroom.com; Level 1, 235 Victoria St, Darlinghurst; ◔6pm-midnight Tue-Thu, 6pm-2am Fri, noon-2am Sat, 1pm-midnight Sun) Plush Chesterfields, art-nouveau wallpaper, dark-wood panelling and bamboo screens – this long-standing favourite is 1920s Bombay gin palace meets Hong Kong opium den.

Woollahra

WINE LIBRARY   Wine Bar
(off Map p74; 18 Oxford St, Woollahra; ◔9am-10pm Mon-Sat, to 6pm Sun) This new wine bar is located at the top end of Oxford St, about halfway between the city and Bondi. It has an impressive range of wines by the glass and a stylish but casual feel.

Newtown

COURTHOUSE HOTEL   Pub
(202 Australia St, Newtown; ◔10am-midnight Mon-Sat, to 10pm Sun) Your drinking companions are a multifaceted lot – everyone from uni students enjoying a cheap meal in the beer garden to ferals hanging around the jukebox and nuggety locals who have propped up the front bar for half a century.

Bondi

RUM DIARIES   Cocktail Bar
(www.therumdiaries.com.au; 288 Bondi Rd, Bondi; ◔6pm-midnight Mon-Sat, to 10pm Sun) A popular addition to the Bondi drinking scene, this dark (but far from dingy) place serves fusion tapas and lots of rum-based cocktails. There's live blues music every Monday from 7pm.

Manly

Manly Wharf Hotel   Pub
(http://manlywharfhotel.com.au; East Esplanade, Manly; ◔11.30am-midnight Mon-Fri, 11am-midnight Sat & Sun) Yep, it's on the wharf. And yep again, it's got great views. The perfect place to watch the ferries roll in while indulging in beer and pub grub.

★ Entertainment

Sydney has an eclectic and innovative arts, entertainment and music scene. Outdoor cinemas and sports stadiums cater to families, the city's theatre scene is healthy and dynamic, and live music is everywhere.

Pick up the 'Metro' section in Friday's *Sydney Morning Herald* for comprehensive entertainment details. Free weekly street magazines including *The Brag* and *The Drum* specialise in gig and club information. Tickets for most shows can be purchased directly from venues or through the **Moshtix** (☎1300 438 849; www.moshtix.com.au), **Ticketmaster** (☎1300 723 038; www.ticketmaster.com.au) or **Ticketek** (☎132 849; www.ticketek.com.au) ticketing agencies.

Cinemas

First-run cinemas abound; tickets generally cost $15 to $18 for an adult, $13 to $14 for a student and $10 to $12 for a child. Sydney also has a huge following of indie and foreign films.

Dendy Opera Quays   Cinema
(Map p66; www.dendy.com.au; Shop 9, 2 Circular Quay E) A plush cinema screening first-run independent films from around the world.

Moonlight Cinema   Cinema
(www.moonlight.com.au; Belvedere Amphitheatre, cnr Loch & Broome Aves, Centennial Park; adult/child/concession $18/14/16; ◔box office 7pm, screenings 8-8.30pm Dec-Mar) Take a picnic and rug and enjoy a new-season release under the stars in magnificent Centennial Park.

ANDREW WATSON/LONELY PLANET IMAGES ©

OPEN AIR CINEMA   Cinema
(off Map p66; www.stgeorgeopenair.com.au;
Mrs Macquaries Point, Royal Botanic Gardens;
adult/concession $30/28; ⊙box office 6.30pm,
screenings 8.30pm Jan & Feb) Right on the
harbour, the outdoor three-storey screen
here comes with surround sound, sunsets, skyline and swanky food and wine.
Most tickets are purchased in advance,
but a limited number of tickets go on sale
at the door each night at 6.30 – check the
website for details.

Palace Verona   Cinema
(Map p74; www.palacecinemas.com.au/cinemas/
verona/; 17 Oxford St, Paddington) The Verona
screens international, art-house, documentary
and independent films. There's also a wine and
espresso bar, meaning that you can enjoy a
drink before, during or after the film.

Nightclubs

GOODGOD SMALL CLUB   Nightclub
(Map p72; www.goodgodgoodgod.com; 53-55
Liverpool St, Chinatown; cover charge varies, front
bar free; ⊙10pm-late Wed-Sat) In a defunct
underground taverna in the Spanish
Quarter, GoodGod's rear danceteria
hosts everything from live indie bands to

Jamaican reggae, '50s soul, rockabilly
and tropical house music. Its success lies
in the focus on great music rather than
glamorous surrounds.

HOME   Nightclub
(Map p72; www.homesydney.com; Cockle Bay
Wharf, Darling Harbour; admission varies;
⊙Thu-Sat) Welcome to the pleasuredome:
a three-level, 2000-capacity timber-
and-glass extravaganza, home to a huge
dance floor, countless bars, outdoor
balconies and an amazing DJ booth. Top-
name international DJs spin house; live
bands amp it up.

Live Music

**SYDNEY OPERA
HOUSE**   Classical Music
(Map p66; www.sydneyoperahouse.com;
Bennelong Point) Yes, it's more than a
landmark. As well as theatre and dance,
the Opera House hosts performances by
Opera Australia (✆tickets 02-9318 8200;
www.opera-australia.org.au) and the **Sydney
Symphony** (✆tickets 02-8215 4600; www.
sydneysymphony.com).

TRAVIS DREVER/LONELY PLANET IMAGES ©

CITY RECITAL HALL   Classical Music
(Map p66; ☎02-8256 2222; www.cityrecitalhall.
com; Angel Pl, Sydney; tickets free-$80; ⏰box
office 9am-5pm Mon-Fri & before performances)
Classically configured, this custom-built
1200-seat venue boasts near-perfect
acoustics. Top-billing companies here
include the Sydney Conservatorium of
Music and Sydney Symphony, plus touring international ensembles, soloists and
opera singers.

BASEMENT   Jazz
(Map p66; www.thebasement.com.au; 7 Macquarie
Pl, Circular Quay; admission varies; ⏰noon-
1.30am Mon-Thu, noon-2.30am Fri, 7.30pm-3am
Sat, 7pm-1am Sun) Sydney's premier jazz
venue presents headline touring acts and
big local talent. A broad musical mandate
also sees funk, blues and soul bands
performing. Try to book a table seated by
the stage.

ANNANDALE HOTEL   Rock
(www.annandalehotel.com; 17 Parramatta Rd,
Annandale) 'F*ck this – I'm going to the
Annandale!' is the motto at Sydney's
premier rock venue. Loads of regulars
follow its advice, enjoying live music most
Wednesdays to Sundays and cult movies

on Tuesdays; check the website for the
program.

Enmore Theatre   Rock
(☎02-9550 3666; www.enmoretheatre.com.au;
118-132 Enmore St, Newtown) Newtown is the
centre of Sydney's music scene, and the Enmore
is its mainstream heart, hosting big-name local
and international acts.

Spectator Sports

Sydneysiders are passionate about the
National Rugby League (NRL; www.nrl.
com.au; tickets through Ticketek from $25), the
season kicking off in March in suburban
stadia and the **ANZ Stadium** (www.anz
stadium.com.au; Sydney Olympic Park, Olympic
Blvd, Homebush Bay), with September finals.

Also from March right through to
September, hometown favourites the
Sydney Swans (www.sydneyswans.com.au)
play in the **Australian Football League**
(AFL; www.afl.com.au; tickets $20-40) at
the **Sydney Cricket Ground** (SCG; www.
sydneycricketground.com.au; Driver Ave, Moore
Park).

The **cricket** (http://cricket.com.au) season
runs from October to March, the SCG
hosting interstate Sheffield Shield and

sell-out international Test, Twenty20 and One Day Internationals matches.

Theatre

SYDNEY THEATRE COMPANY   Theatre
(Map p66; ☎02-9250 1777; www.sydneytheatre.com.au; level 2, Pier 4, Hickson Rd, Walsh Bay; tickets $60-65) Sydney's premier theatre company performs at its Walsh Bay base and in the Drama Theatre at the Sydney Opera House. Artistic directors Cate Blanchett and Andrew Upton program work by local and international playwrights and draw actors and directors from around the world.

Sydney Comedy Store   Theatre
(☎02-9357 1419; www.comedystore.com.au; Building 207, Entertainment Quarter, 122 Lang Rd, Moore Park; tickets $7.50-25) This purpose-built comedy hall lures big-time Australian and overseas comics, including Edinburgh Festival stand-ups.

Sydney Theatre   Theatre
(Map p66; ☎02-9250 1999; www.sydneytheatre.org.au; 22 Hickson Rd, Walsh Bay; tickets $40-79) The resplendent Sydney Theatre at the base of Observatory Hill puts 850 bums on seats for specialist drama and dance.

The following theatres host local seasons of West End and Broadway musicals, as well as concerts (tickets from $50 to $200; bookings can be made through Ticketmaster or on websites):

Capitol Theatre   Theatre
(Map p72; www.capitoltheatre.com.au; 13 Campbell St, Haymarket; ⊙box office 9am-5pm Mon-Fri)

State Theatre   Theatre
(Map p66; ☎02-9373 6655; www.statetheatre.com.au; 49 Market St)

Theatre Royal   Theatre
(Map p66; www.theatreroyal.net.au; MLC Centre, 108 King St; ⊙box office 9am-5pm Mon-Fri)

🔒 Shopping

Serious shoppers should consider downloading the suburb-by-suburb shopping guides produced by **Urban Walkabout** (www.urbanwalkabout.com); free printed versions of the maps are also available at tourist information offices and booths across the city. There are dedicated guides (with handy map) covering the CBD, Paddington, Woollahra, Surry Hills, Darlinghurst, Potts Point/Kings Cross, Balmain, Mosman, Newtown, Redfern/Waterloo, Glebe, Double Bay and Bondi.

Department Stores & Arcades

DAVID JONES   Department Store
(Map p66; www.davidjones.com.au; cnr Market & Castlereagh Sts, Sydney; ⊙9.30am-7pm Mon-Wed, 9.30am-9pm Thu & Fri, 9am-9pm Sat,

Buying Indigenous Art & Artefacts

There are plenty of shops and galleries around the state selling Indigenous-made artworks, artefacts and products, but it's sadly common to encounter Chinese-made fakes, works that breach the cultural copyright of Indigenous artists, and galleries that exploit artist poverty by buying their art unreasonably cheaply – wherever possible, look for products that are being produced and/or marketed by Indigenous-owned, not-for-profit operators.

If buying from a gallery, make sure that it's a member of the Australian Indigenous Art Trade Association or the Australian Commercial Galleries Association. Art and artefacts should be properly documented (ie by a certificate of authenticity from a reputable source, by photographs or by other evidence) and their provenance should be clearly stated (ie where, when and by whom was it made? How has it come onto the market?).

If You Like...
Markets

If you like poking around market stalls on the weekend, we think you'll like these markets:

1 BALMAIN MARKET
(www.balmainmarket.com.au; cnr Darling St & Curtis Rd, Balmain; ⏰8.30am-4pm Sat) Set in the shady grounds of St Andrews Congregational, stalls sell art, crafts, books, clothing, plants, and fruit and veg.

2 BONDI MARKETS
(www.bondimarkets.com.au; Bondi Beach Public School, cnr Campbell Pde & Warners Ave, Bondi; ⏰10am-4pm Sun) When school's out the yard fills up with stalls selling everything from vintage clothing and bric-a-brac to wooden frames and jewellery. Great for grabbing a bargain from up-and-coming fashion designers.

3 GLEBE MARKETS
(www.glebemarkets.com.au; Glebe Public School, cnr Glebe Point Rd & Derby Pl, Glebe; ⏰10am-4pm Sat) Inner-city hippies flock here for vintage duds, new designers, arts and crafts, a chai latte and restorative massage. Live bands add to the Woodstock vibe.

4 EVELEIGH MARKET
(www.eveleighmarket.com.au; 243 Wilson St, Darlington; ⏰8am-1pm Sat, closed 1st half of Jan) Over 70 regular stallholders sell home-grown produce at Sydney's best farmers market, held in a heritage-listed Eveleigh Railyards building.

5 PADDINGTON MARKETS
(www.paddingtonmarkets.com.au; St John's Church, 395 Oxford St, Paddington; ⏰10am-4pm Sat) Sydney's most popular weekend market dishes up vintage clothes and hip fashions, jewellery, books, massage and palmistry. Just as your spirits flag, you'll find something special under a little awning.

10am-7pm Sun) DJs is Sydney's premier department store. The Market St store has menswear; Castlereagh St has womenswear and childrenswear and a friendly concierge to point you in the right direction.

QUEEN VICTORIA BUILDING   Mall
(QVB; Map p66; www.qvb.com.au; 455 George St, Sydney) This high-Victorian masterpiece occupies an entire city block opposite the Town Hall, and though there are some inspiring retail offerings, they run a distant second to the magnificent wrought-iron balconies, stained-glass shopfronts and mosaic floors.

STRAND ARCADE   Mall
(Map p66; www.strandarcade.com.au; 412 George St & 193-5 Pitt St Mall, Sydney) Constructed in 1891, the Strand competes with the QVB for the title of most gorgeous shopping centre in Sydney.

Clothing & Accessories

Glenmore Rd in Paddington and Queen St in Woollahra are Sydney's premier fashion enclaves, but there are also plenty of boutiques in the CBD and in Newtown.

Akira Isagawa   Clothing
(www.akira.com.au; 12a Queen St, Woollahra) Meticulously tailored ensembles featuring gorgeous fabrics. There's another store in the Strand Arcade.

Collette Dinnigan   Clothing
(www.collettedinnigan.com.au; 104 Queen St, Woollahra) The queen of Aussie couture delivers fabulously feminine frocks with exquisite trimmings.

RM Williams   Clothing
(Map p66; www.rmwilliams.com.au; 389 George St, Sydney) Urban cowboys and country folk can't get enough of this hardwearing outback gear.

Zimmermann   Clothing
(Map p74; http://zimmermannwear.com; Shop 2, 2-16 Glenmore Rd, Paddington). Chic and cheeky street clothes and swimwear from Nicky and Simone Zimmermann. There's another store in Westfield Sydney.

Wine

Australian Wine Centre   Wine
(Map p66; Shop 3, Goldfields House, 1 Alfred St, Circular Quay) This basement shop is packed with quality Australian and New Zealand wine, as well as a healthy dose of Aussie beer and spirits.

GLENN VAN DER KNIJFF/LONELY PLANET IMAGES ©

ℹ️ Information

Medical Services

Kings Cross Travellers Clinic (☎02-9358 3066; www.travellersclinic.com.au; 13 Springfield Ave, Kings Cross; standard consultation $65; ⏰9am-1pm & 2-6pm Mon-Fri, 10am-noon Sat) General medical, travel medical and vaccinations; bookings advised.

St Vincent's Hospital (☎02-8382 1111; www.stvincents.com.au; 390 Victoria St, Darlinghurst; ⏰24hr emergency)

Sydney Hospital (☎02-9382 7111; www.sesahs.nsw.gov.au/sydhosp; 8 Macquarie St, Sydney; ⏰24hr emergency)

Money

There are plenty of ATMs throughout Sydney; foreign exchange offices are found in Kings Cross and around Chinatown, Circular Quay and Central Station.

American Express city centre (☎1300 139 060; 296 George St, Sydney; ⏰9am-5pm Mon-Fri); Haymarket (☎1300 139 060; 296 George St, Sydney; ⏰9am-5pm Mon-Fri)

ℹ️ Getting There & Away

Air

Sydney Airport (code: SYD; off Map p66; www.sydneyairport.com.au) is Australia's busiest, so don't be surprised if there are delays. The T1 (international) and T2 and T3 (domestic) terminals are a 4km bus ($5.50, 10 minutes) or train ($5, 2 minutes) ride apart (the airport is privately run so transferring terminals – a service that's free in most of the world – is seen as a profit opportunity. If you are transferring from a Qantas international flight to a Qantas domestic flight (or vice versa), free transfers are provided by the airline. Virgin Australia offers a similar service. You can fly into Sydney from all the usual international points and from within Australia. **Qantas** (☎13 13 13; www.qantas.com.au), **Jetstar** (☎13 15 38; www.jetstar.com.au), **Virgin Australia** (☎13 67 89; www.virginaustralia.com) and **Tiger Airways** (☎03-9335 3033; www.tigerairways.com/au/en) have frequent flights to other major cities.

Bus

All private interstate and regional bus travellers arrive at **Sydney Coach Terminal** (Map p72; ☎02-9281 9366; Central Station, Eddy Ave; ⏰6am-6pm Mon-Fri, 8am-6pm Sat & Sun).

The major bus companies using the depot are:

Firefly (☏ 1300 730 740; www.fireflyexpress.com.au) Wagga Wagga, Albury, Melbourne and Adelaide

Greyhound (☏ 1300 473 946; www.greyhound.com.au) Canberra, Melbourne, Byron Bay and Tamworth

Premier (☏ 13 34 10; www.premierms.com.au) Coffs Harbour, Byron Bay, Brisbane and Cairns

Train

Sydney's main rail terminus for CountryLink interstate and regional services is the huge **Central Station** (Map p72; ☏ bookings 13 22 32, 24hr transport information 13 15 00; www.countrylink.info; Eddy Ave; ☺ staffed ticket booths 6.15am-8.45pm, ticket machines 24hr).

ℹ Getting Around

For information on government buses, ferries and trains try the **Transport Infoline** (☏ 13 15 00; www.131500.com.au).

To/From the Airport

One of the easiest ways to get to and from the airport is with a shuttle company such as **Kingsford Smith Transport** (KST; ☏ 02-9666 9988; www.kst.com.au; 1 way/return from $12.60/20.70; ☺ 5am-7pm), which services central Sydney hotels.

Airport Link (☏ 13 15 00; www.airportlink.com.au; 1 way/return from Central Sydney adult $15/25, child $10/15.50, ☺ 4.30am-12.40am) is a strange service: it's a normal commuter train line (with dirty cars) but you pay through the nose to use the airport stations (punters going to Wolli Creek, the next stop *beyond* the airport pay $3.20). The trip from Central Station takes a mere 10 minutes or so.

Taxi fares from the airport are approximately $39 to the city centre ($51 between 10pm and 6am), $43 to Bondi ($55 between 10pm and 6am) and $80 to Manly ($106 between 10pm and 6am).

Boat

FERRY Harbour ferries and RiverCats (to Parramatta) operated by **Sydney Ferries** (www.sydneyferries.info) depart from Circular Quay. Most ferries operate between 6am and midnight; those servicing tourist attractions operate shorter hours. (For information about harbour cruises see p64.)

A one-way inner-harbour ride on a regular ferry costs adult/concession $5.30/2.60. A one-way ride to Manly or Parramatta costs $6.60/$3.30.

The privately owned **Captain Cook Ferries** (www.captaincook.com.au) operates ferry services to Manly from Circular Quay (return adult/child $17/8.50) and Darling Harbour (return adult/child $24/12). It also runs a Zoo Express service to Taronga Zoo from Circular Quay and Darling Harbour (return adult/child $49.50/24.50 including entrance fee).

WATER TAXI Water taxis ply dedicated shuttle routes; rides to/from other harbour venues can be booked.

Aussie Water Taxis (Map p72; ☏ 02-9211 7730; www.aussiewatertaxis.com; Cockle Bay Wharf, Darling Harbour; ☺ 9am-10pm) Darling Harbour to Circular Quay single/return adult $15/25, child $10/15; Darling Harbour to Taronga Zoo single/return adult $25/40, child $15/25; 45-minute Harbour and Nightlights Tours adult/child $35/25.

Yellow Water Taxis (Map p66; ☏ 1300 138 840; www.yellowwatertaxis.com.au; King St Wharf, Darling Harbour; ☺ 7am-midnight) Circular Quay to Darling Harbour adult/child $15/10; 45-minute Harbour 'Hop On, Hop Off' Tour stopping at Sydney Aquarium, Luna Park, Taronga Zoo and Sydney Opera House adult/child $40/20.

Bus

Sydney Buses (www.sydneybuses.info) has an extensive network; you can check route and timetable information online. Nightrider buses operate infrequently after regular services cease around midnight.

The main city bus stops are Circular Quay, Wynyard Park (York St) and Railway Sq. Many services are prepay-only during the week – buy tickets from newsagents or Bus TransitShops. On weekends you can usually purchase your ticket on the bus. There are three fare zones: $2/3.30/4.30. There's a **Bus TransitShop booth** (www.sydneybuses.info; cnr Alfred & Loftus Sts; ☺ 7am-7pm Mon-Fri, 8.30am-5pm Sat & Sun) at Circular Quay, and there are others at the Queen Victoria Building, Railway Sq and Wynyard Station.

Car & Motorcycle

Cars are good for day trips out of town, but driving one in the city is like having an anchor around your neck. Heavy traffic, elusive and very expensive parking (even at hotels, expect $30 per day) and the extra costs just aren't worth the stress.

HIRE Major car-hire agencies with offices in Sydney:

Avis (☎ 13 63 33; www.avis.com.au)

Budget (☎ 13 27 27; www.budget.com.au)

Europcar (☎ 1300 13 13 90; www.europcar.com.au)

Hertz (☎ 13 30 39; www.hertz.com.au)

Thrifty (☎ 1300 367 227; www.thrifty.com.au)

ROAD TOLLS There's a $4 southbound toll on the Sydney Harbour Bridge and Tunnel; a $5.50 northbound toll on the Eastern Distributor; a $2.10 toll on the Cross City Tunnel; and a $2.83 toll on the Lane Cove Tunnel. Sydney's main motorways (M2, M5 and M7) are also tolled ($2.50 to $7). There are a few cash booths at toll gates, but the whole system is electronic, meaning that it's up to you to organise an electronic tag or visitor's pass through any of the following websites: www.roamcom.au, www.roamexpress.com.au or www.myRTA.com.au. For info, try www.sydneymotorways.com.

Fare Deals

There are two discount options for travelling on Sydney's public transport network.

MyMulti Passes You can purchase a day pass ($20) or weekly pass (zone 1/2/3 $41/48/57) giving unlimited transport on government-operated buses, ferries and trains within Sydney, the Blue Mountains, Hunter Valley, Central Coast, Newcastle and Port Stephens.

MyBus, MyTrain and MyFerry TravelTen Tickets These offer 10 discounted rides but can only be used on one mode of transport.

You can purchase these passes and tickets at newsagencies, newsstands and bus/ferry/train ticket offices. For information, see www.myzone.nsw.gov.au.

Monorail & Metro Light Rail (MLR)

The privately operated Metro Monorail (www.metromonorail.com.au; single circuit $4.90, day pass $9.50; ☻every 5min, 7am-10pm Mon-Thu, 8am-10pm Sat & Sun) travels in a loop from Galleries Victoria on the corner of Pitt and Park Sts through Chinatown and Darling Harbour.

Run by the same outfit, the Metro Light Rail (MLR; www.metrolightrail.com.au; Zone 1 adult/concession $3.40/2.20, Zone 1 & 2 adult/concession $4.40/3.40, day pass adult $9; ☻24hr, every 10-15min 6am-midnight, every 30min midnight-6am) is a tram running between Central Station and Pyrmont via Chinatown and Darling Harbour. The Zone 2 service beyond Pyrmont to Lilyfield via the Fish Markets, Glebe and Rozelle operates from 6am to 11pm Monday to Thursday and Sunday, till midnight Friday and Saturday.

Water taxi, Sydney Harbour
PHOTOGRAPHER: DAVID WALL/LONELY PLANET IMAGES ©

Taxi

Taxis and cab ranks proliferate in Sydney. Flag fall is $3.30, then it's $1.99 per kilometre (plus 20% from 10pm to 6am). The waiting charge is $0.86 per minute. Passengers must pay bridge, tunnel and road tolls (even if you don't incur them 'outbound', the returning driver will incur them 'inbound').

The major taxi companies offering phone bookings ($2.20 fee) are:

Legion (☎13 14 51; www.legioncabs.com.au)

Premier Cabs (☎13 10 17; www.premiercabs.com.au)

Taxis Combined (☎13 33 00; www.taxiscombined.com.au)

Train

Sydney's suburban rail network is operated by CityRail (☎13 15 00; www.cityrail.info). Lines radiate from the underground City Circle (seven city-centre stations) but don't service the northern and southern beaches, Balmain or Glebe. All suburban trains stop at Central Station, and usually one or more of the other City Circle stations, too.

Trains run from around 5am to midnight. After 9am on weekdays you can buy an off-peak return ticket, valid until 4am the next day, for little more than a standard one-way fare.

Twenty-four-hour ticket machines occupy most stations, but customer service officers are usually available if you need help with the fares. If you have to change trains, buy a ticket to your ultimate destination, but don't exit the transfer station en route or your ticket will be invalid.

For train information, visit the helpful CityRail Information Booth (Circular Quay; ☺9.05am-4.50pm).

AROUND SYDNEY

Sydney's extensive urban sprawl eventually dissolves into superb national parks and historic small towns.

Royal National Park

The 15,080-hectare **Royal National Park** (www.environment.nsw.gov.au/nationalparks; pedestrians & cyclists free, cars $11; ☺gates to park areas open at sunrise & are locked at 8.30pm daily) was established in 1879, making it the oldest national park in the world after Yellowstone in the USA. Here you'll find pockets of subtropical rainforest, windblown coastal scrub, sandstone gullies dominated by gum trees, fresh- and saltwater wetlands, and isolated beaches. Traditionally the home of the Dharawal people, there are also numerous Aboriginal sites and artefacts.

Within the park there's sheltered saltwater swimming at Wattamolla, Jibbon, Little Marley and Bonnie Vale, and freshwater swimming holes at Karloo Pool (around 2km east of Heathcote Station), Deer Pool and Curracurrang. Surfers should head for Garie Beach, North Era, South Era and Burning

Surfer, Royal National Park

MICHAEL COYNE/LONELY PLANET IMAGES ©

Palms on the park's southern coastline. At the historic **Audley Boat Shed** (www.audleyboatshed.com; Farnell Ave, Audley; ☺9am-5pm Mon-Sat, to 5.30pm Sun) you can hire rowboats, canoes and kayaks ($20/40 per hour/day), aqua bikes ($15 per 30 minutes) and bicycles ($16/34 per hour/day) and paddle up Kangaroo Creek or the Hacking River.

The **park office** (☎02-9542 0648; Farnell Ave, Audley Heights; ☺8.30am-4.30pm) can assist with maps, brochures, camping permits and bushwalking details.

ℹ Getting There & Away

From Sydney, take the Princes Hwy south and turn off at Farnell Ave, south of Loftus, to the park's northern end – it's about a 45-minute drive from the city.

The most scenic route into the park is to take the CityRail train (Eastern Suburbs and Illawarra line) to Cronulla (one way adult/child $4.60/3.20), and then jump aboard a Cronulla National Park Ferry (☎02-9523 2990; www.cronullaferries.com.au; Cronulla Wharf) to Bundeena (one way adult/child $5.80/2.90, 30 minutes, hourly between 5.30am and 6.30pm, until 5.30pm Sun in winter).

Hawkesbury River

Less than an hour from Sydney, the tranquil Hawkesbury River is a favourite weekend destination for stressed-out city folk. The river – one of the longest in eastern Australia – flows past honeycomb-coloured cliffs, historic townships and riverside hamlets into bays and inlets and between a series of national parks.

The **Riverboat Postman** (☎02-9985 7566; www.hawkesburyriverferries.com.au; Riverboat Postman Wharf, Brooklyn; adult/child/family $50/30/130; ☺9.30am Mon-Fri), Australia's last operating mail boat, departs from the Brooklyn Wharf, beside the Hawkesbury River Railway Station, and chugs 40km up the Hawkesbury as far as Marlow, returning to Brooklyn at 1.15pm.

Further upstream a narrow forested waterway diverts from the Hawkesbury and peters down to the chilled-out river town of **Berowra Waters**, where a handful of businesses, boat sheds and residences cluster around the free, 24-hour ferry across Berowra Creek. If you feel like exploring, rev the river in a tinny (outboard dinghy) from the **Berowra Waters Marina** (☎02-9456 7000; www.bbqboat.info; 199 Bay Rd, Berowra Waters; per half-day $85; ☺8am-5pm).

99

Hawkesbury Houseboats

The best way to experience the Hawkesbury is on a fully equipped houseboat. Expect rates to skyrocket during summer and school holidays, but most outfits offer affordable low-season, midweek and long-term rental specials. To give a very rough guide, a two-/four-/six-berth boat for three nights costs from $650/720/1150 from September to early December, with prices doubling during the Christmas/New Year period and on weekends and holidays throughout the year.

Most companies are based in Brooklyn.

Able Hawkesbury River Houseboats (02-4566 4308, 1800 024 979; www.hawkesburyhouseboats.com.au; 3008 River Rd, Wisemans Ferry)

Brooklyn Marina (02-9985 7722; www.brooklynmarina.com.au; 45 Brooklyn Rd, Brooklyn)

Holidays Afloat (02-9985 7368; www.holidaysafloat.com.au; 65 Brooklyn Rd, Brooklyn)

Ripples Houseboats (02-9985 5555; www.ripples.com.au; 87 Brooklyn Rd, Brooklyn)

Nearby, elegant **Berowra Waters Inn** (02-9456 1027; www.berowrawatersinn.com; 4/5/6 courses $130/145/160; ☉lunch Fri-Sun, dinner Fri & Sat), housed in a waterside pavilion designed by Australia's most acclaimed contemporary architect, Glenn Murcutt, is one of the state's best restaurants, offering a degustation-style menu. The restaurant is only accessed by seaplane from Sydney or via the restaurant's own ferry, which leaves from a wharf near the village of Berowra.

CityRail trains run from Sydney's Central Station to Berowra (one way adult/child $6/3, 45 minutes, roughly hourly) and on to Brooklyn's Hawkesbury River Station (one way adult/child $6/3, one hour). Berowra Station is a solid 6km trudge from Berowra Waters. **Hawkesbury Water Taxis** (0400 600 111; www.hawkesburycruises.com.au) will take you anywhere along the river.

Hunter Valley

A filigree of narrow country lanes criss-crosses this verdant valley, but a pleasant country drive isn't the main motivator for visitors – sheer decadence is. The Hunter is one big gorge-fest: fine wine, boutique beer, chocolate, cheese, olives, you name it.

The oldest wine region in Australia, the Hunter is known for its Semillon and Shiraz. The valley's 140-plus wineries range from small-scale family-run affairs to massive commercial operations. Most offer free tastings, although a couple of the glitzier ones charge a small fee.

Here are a few picks to get you started:

Brokenwood (www.brokenwood.com.au; 401-427 McDonalds Rd, Pokolbin; ☉9.30am-5pm) One of the Hunter's most acclaimed wineries.

Hungerford Hill (www.hungerfordhill.com.au; 2450 Broke Rd, Pokolbin; ☉10am-5pm Sun-Thu, 9am-6pm Fri & Sat) Shaped like a big barrel, with its 'lid' permanently propped open, this winery stands sentinel at the entry to Broke Rd.

Margan (www.margan.com.au; 1238 Millbrodale Rd, Broke; ☉10am-5pm) Gorgeous setting, classy tasting room and the valley's best restaurant.

Pooles Rock Wines (www.poolesrock.com.au; DeBeyers Rd, Pokolbin; ☉9.30am-5pm) A big player, producing the midpriced Cockfighter's Ghost range as well as its excellent flagship wines.

Tamburlaine (www.tamburlaine.com.au; 358 McDonalds Rd, Pokolbin; ☉9am-5pm) An excellent producer focusing on sustainable viticulture.

Tours

If no-one's volunteering to stay sober enough to drive, there are plenty of winery tours available. Some operators will collect you in Sydney or Newcastle for a lengthy day trip. These are a few of the local operators:

Aussie Wine Tours (📞0402 909 090; www.aussiewinetours.com.au) You can determine your own itinerary if you take one of these private, chauffeur-driven tours.

Hunter Valley Tours (📞02-4990 8989; www.huntervalleytours.com.au) Small group local-run boutique tours; from $65 per person for a half-day tour and from $99 for a full day tour including lunch.

Wine Rover (📞02-4990 1699; www.rovercoaches.com.au) Coaches connect at Morriset in the morning with trains coming from Sydney ($55) and drop passengers back at the station after a day of visiting stopping wineries and attractions.

ℹ Information

Visitor Centre (📞02-4990 0900; www.winecountry.com.au; 455 Wine Country Dr; ⊙9am-5pm Mon-Sat, 9am-4pm Sun)

ℹ Getting There & Away

If you're driving from Sydney, consider exiting north from the M1 at the Peats Ridge Road exit and making your way along the convict-built Great North Rd to the charming colonial town of Wollombi and then heading north to Broke or east to Cessnock via Wollombi Rd.

CityRail has a line heading through the Hunter Valley from Newcastle (adult/child $6/3, 55 minutes). From Sydney (adult/child

$7.80/3.90, 3¾ hours) you'll need to catch a train to Hamilton and then change for Branxton, which is the closest station to the vineyards.

Greyhound (📞1300 473 946; www.greyhound.com.au) runs a daily bus from Sydney ($65, 4½ hours) to Branxton, departing outside Central Station at 6.30pm.

BLUE MOUNTAINS

A region with more than its fair share of gorges, gum trees and gourmet restaurants, the spectacular Blue Mountains was an obvious contender when Unesco called for Australian nominations to the World Heritage List, and its inclusion was ratified in 2000.

The foothills begin 65km inland from Sydney, rising to an 1100m-high sandstone plateau riddled with valleys eroded into the stone over thousands of years. There are eight connected conservation areas in the region, including the **Blue Mountains National Park** (www.environment.nsw.gov.au/nationalparks), which has some truly

Vineyard, Hunter Valley
PHOTOGRAPHER: OLIVER STREWE/LONELY PLANET IMAGES ©

fantastic scenery, excellent bushwalks, Aboriginal engravings and all the canyons and cliffs you could ask for.

Although it's possible to visit on a day trip from Sydney, we strongly recommend that you stay at least one night so that you can explore a few of the towns, do at least one bushwalk and enjoy a dinner at one of the excellent restaurants in Blackheath or Leura.

Purple Haze

The slate-coloured haze that gives the mountains their name comes from a fine mist of oil exuded by the huge eucalyptus gums that form a dense canopy across the landscape of deep, often-inaccessible valleys and chiselled sandstone outcrops.

 Sights

Gembrook to Blackheath

Arriving from Sydney, the first of the Blue Mountains town you will encounter is Gembrook (population 5138). From here, you can drive or walk into the **Blue Mountains National Park (per car $7, walkers free; ⊙8.30am-6pm, to 7pm during daylight savings)**; this is the only part of the park where entry fees apply. Six kilometres from the park entrance gate is the Mt Portal Lookout, which has panoramic views into the Glenbrook Gorge, over the Nepean River and back to Sydney.

Artist, author and bon vivant Norman Lindsay, infamous for his racy artworks (imagine an unfortunate conflation of Boucher and Beardsley) but much loved for his children's tale *The Magic Pudding*, lived in Faulconbridge, 14km up the mountain from Glenbrook, from 1912 until his death in 1969. His home and studio have been preserved and maintained by

Left: Hanging Rock, near Blackheath (p104); **Below:** Wentworth Falls

the National Trust as the **Norman Lindsay Gallery & Museum** (www.normanlindsay.com.au; 14 Norman Lindsay Cres, Faulconbridge; adult/child/concession $10/5/7; ⊙10am-4pm), with a significant collection of his paintings, watercolours, drawings and sculptures. There's a **cafe** (mains $19.50-24.50; ⊙9am-4.30pm) on site, but its kitchen's enthusiasm is greater than its skill – we suggest sticking to scones, jam and tea ($7.50) or a sandwich.

Further up the mountain, the town of **Wentworth Falls** (population 5650) commands views to the south across the majestic Jamison Valley. Wentworth Falls themselves launch a plume of spray over a 300m drop – check them out from Falls Reserve. This is also the starting point for a network of walking tracks into the sublime Valley of the Waters, which has waterfalls, gorges, woodlands and rainforests. Many of these walks start from the **Conservation Hut** (www.conservationhut.com.au; Fletcher St; mains $23-30; ⊙9am-4pm Mon-Fri, to 5pm Sat & Sun),

where you can enjoy a coffee or meal on a deck overlooking the valley.

Nearby **Leura** (population 4385) is a genteel town of undulating streets, heritage houses and lush gardens. At its centre is The Mall, a tree-lined main street with boutiques, galleries and cafes.

Just outside town is **Gordon Falls Reserve**, an idyllic picnic spot. From here you can trek the steep Prince Henry Cliff Walk, or take the Cliff Drive 4km west past Leura Cascades to **Katoomba** (population 7623), the region's main town, where the often-misty steep streets are lined with art-deco buildings. The population here is an odd mix of country battlers, hippies, mortgage refugees from the big smoke (Sydney) and members of a Tennessee-based messianic Christian sect called the Twelve Tribes (aka the Community of Believers), who live communally, believe in traditional lifestyle and

Katoomba

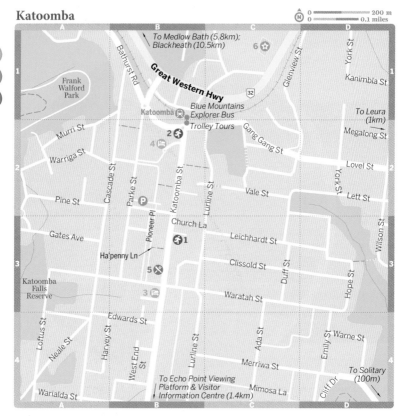

0 — 200 m
0 — 0.1 miles

To Medlow Bath (5.8km);
Blackheath (10.5km)

Great Western Hwy

Frank Walford Park

Bathurst Rd

Glenview St

York St

Kanimbla St

Katoomba

Blue Mountains
Explorer Bus
Trolley Tours

To Leura
(1km)

Megalong St

Murri St

Warriga St

Pine St

Cascade St

Parke St

Katoomba St

Lurline St

Gang Gang St

Vale St

Lovel St

York St

Lett St

Pioneer Pl

Church La

Ha'penny Ln

Leichhardt St

Clissold St

Duff St

Hope St

Wilson St

Katoomba Falls Reserve

Gates Ave

Waratah St

Edwards St

Lotus St

Neale St

Harvey St

West End St

Lurline St

Ada St

Merriwa St

Mimosa La

Emily St

Cliff Dr

Warne St

To Solitary
(100m)

To Echo Point Viewing
Platform & Visitor
Information Centre (1.4km)

Warialda St

---

operate the Common Ground Café in the main street. Extraordinarily, all of these locals seem to live together harmoniously. They also seem to cope with the huge numbers of tour buses and tourists who come here to ooh-and-aah at the spectacular view of the Jamison Valley and **Three Sisters** rock formations from the **Echo Point** viewing platforms.

There are a number of short walks from Echo Point that allow you to escape the bulk of the crowds. Parking is expensive ($3.80 for first hour, $4.40 for subsequent hours); if you're walking here from the town centre, Lurline St is the most attractive route.

Three kilometres from the centre of Katoomba you'll find **Scenic World** (www.scenicworld.com.au; cnr Cliff Dr & Violet St; cable car/railway return adult/child $21/10; 9am-5pm), with a megaplex vibe and an 1880s railway and modern cable car descending the 52-degree incline to the valley floor. Also here is the glass-floored **Scenic Skyway** (adult/child $16/8), a cable car floating out across the valley.

The next town to the west is neat and petite **Blackheath** (population 4177), which is a good base for visiting the Grose, Kanimbla and Megalong Valleys.

East of town are lookouts at **Govetts Leap** (comparable to the Three Sisters in terms of 'wow' factor), **Bridal Veil Falls** (the highest in the Blue Mountains) and **Evans Lookout**. To the northeast, via Hat Hill Rd, are **Pulpit Rock**, **Perry's Lookdown** and **Anvil Rock**.

Megalong Valley

Unless you walk in or take Katoomba's Scenic Railway, the only way you'll see a Blue Mountains gorge from the inside is in the Megalong Valley. This is straw-coloured rural Australia, a real departure from the quasi-suburbs strung along the ridgeline. The 600m **Coachwood Glen Nature Trail** features dripping fern dells, stands of mountain ash and sun-stained sandstone cliffs.

Mt Victoria, Hartley & Lithgow

With a charming alpine air, Mt Victoria sits at 1043m and is the highest town in the mountains. Historic buildings dominate and include **St Peter's Church** (1874) and the **Toll Keepers Cottage** (1849).

About 12km past Mt Victoria, on the western slopes of the range, is the tiny, sandstone 'ghost' town of Hartley, which flourished from the 1830s but declined when bypassed by the railway in 1887. It's been well preserved and a number of historic buildings remain, including several private homes and inns.

A further 14km on from Hartley in the western foothills of the Blue Mountains is Lithgow, a sombre coal-mining town popular with trainspotters for its **Zig Zag Railway** (www.zigzagrailway.com.au;

Clarence Station, Bells Line of Road; adult/child/family $28/14/70; ☺11am, 1pm & 3pm), which sits just 10km east of town. Built in the 1860s to transport the Great Western Railway tracks down from the mountains into Lithgow, today it zigzags tourists gently down the precipice (1½-hour return trip).

 **Activities**

Bushwalking

The two most popular bushwalking areas are the Jamison Valley, south of Katoomba, and the Grose Valley, northeast of Katoomba and east of Blackheath. Other great walking opportunities can be found in the area south of Glenbrook, the Kanangra Boyd National Park (accessible from Oberon or Jenolan Caves) and the Wollemi National Park, north of Bells Line of Road.

The extraordinarily helpful **NPWS Visitor Centre** (☎02-4787 8877; www.nationalparks.nsw.gov.au; Govetts Leap Rd, Blackheath; ☺9am-4.30pm) at Blackheath, about 2.5km off the Great Western Hwy and 10km north of Katoomba, can help you pick a hike, offer safety tips and will advise about camping; for information about shorter walks, ask at the Echo Point Visitor Centre (p108). Note that the bush here is dense and that it can be easy to become lost – there have been deaths as a consequence. Always leave your name and walk plan with the Katoomba Police, at the NPWS office or at one of the visitor centres; the Katoomba police station, Echo Point Visitor Centre and NPWS office also offer free use of personal locator beacons.

A range of NPWS walks pamphlets and maps ($3 to $6) are available from the NPWS office and from the visitor information centres at Glenbrook and Katoomba. All three also sell the Heama *Blue Mountains* walking map ($8.95) and Veechi Stuart's well-regarded *Blue Mountains: Best Bushwalks* ($29.95) book.

RICHARD I'ANSON/LONELY PLANET IMAGES ©

Don't Miss Jenolan Caves

The story behind the discovery of **Jenolan Caves** (www.jenolancaves.org.au; Jenolan Caves Rd; admission with tour adult/child/family from $28/18.50/68; ⊘9am-5pm) is the stuff of legends: local pastoralist James Whalan stumbled across the prehistoric caves while tracking the escaped convict and cattle rustler James McKeown, who is thought to have used the caves as a hideout.

Originally named Binoomea or 'Dark Places' by the Gundungurra people, the caves took shape more than 400 million years ago and are one of the most extensive and complex limestone cave systems in the world.

There are over 350 caves in the region, although only a handful is open to the public. You must take a **tour** to see them; there's a bewildering array of options at different levels of difficulty; staff at the ticket office are happy to explain them all. You can also don a boiler suit and squeeze yourself through narrow tunnels with only a headlamp to guide you on a **'Plughole' Adventure Tour** ($70; ⊘1.15pm daily).

The caves are 30km from the Great Western Hwy (Rte 4), a 1¼-hour drive from Katoomba. The narrow Jenolan Caves Rd becomes a one-way system between 11.45am and 1.15pm daily, running clockwise from the caves out through Oberon.

Adventure Activities & Tours

Most operators have offices in Katoomba but competition is steep, so shop around for the best deal.

Australian Eco Adventures EcoTours
(☎02-9971 2402; www.ozeco.com.au; adult/child $255/160; ⊘7am) Eco-certified deluxe day tours of the Blue Mountains departing from Sydney at 7am (maximum 16 people) and including short bushwalks. Prices drop if you choose an option without breakfast and lunch.

Australian School of Mountaineering Adventure Activities
(ASM; ☎02-4782 2014; www.asmguides.com; 166 Katoomba St, Katoomba) Rock climbing

from $175, abseiling from $145 and canyoning from $175.

Blue Mountains Adventure Company *Adventure Activities*
(02-4782 1271; www.bmac.com.au; 84a Bathurst Rd, Katoomba) Full-day adventures: abseiling from $150, canyoning from $165, rockclimbing from $180.

Blue Mountains Walkabout *Indigenous Treks*
(0408 443 822; www.bluemountainswalkabout.com) Seven-hour/half-day Aboriginal owned and guided adventurous treks with Aboriginal and spiritual themes ($95/75). Meets at Faulconbridge train station.

High 'n' Wild Mountain Adventures *Adventure Activities*
(02-4782 6224; www.highandwild.com.au; 3/5 Katoomba St) Half-/full-day abseiling (from $99/145) and climbing ($159/179), and full-day canyoning ($179).

Tread Lightly Eco Tours *EcoTours*
(02-4788 1229; www.treadlightly.com.au) Has a wide range of day and night walks ($65 to $135) that emphasise the ecology of the region.

 **Sleeping**

GLENELLA GUESTHOUSE *Guesthouse* $$
(02-4787 8352; www.glenellabluemountains\hotel.com.au; 56-60 Govetts Leap Rd, Blackheath; r $100-160, f $200-240;) Gorgeous Glenella has been functioning as a guesthouse since 1912 and is now operated with enthusiasm and expertise by a young British couple who make guests feel very welcome. There are seven comfortable bedrooms, an attractive lounge and a stunning dining room where a truly excellent breakfast is served.

BLUE MOUNTAINS YHA *Hostel* $
(02-4782 1416; www.yha.com.au; 207 Katoomba St, Katoomba; dm $29.50-31.50, d with/without bathroom $98.50/$88.50, f with/without bathroom $140/$126; @) Behind the austere art deco exterior of this popular 200-bed hostel is a selection of dorms and family rooms that are comfortable, light and spotlessly clean. Highlights include a lounge with open fire, central heating, a huge TV room, pool table, excellent communal kitchen and outdoor space with BBQs.

GREENS OF LEURA *B&B* $$
(02-4784 3241; www.thegreensleura.com.au; 24-26 Grose St, Leura; r weekdays/weekends from $145/175; @) On a quiet street parallel to The Mall, this pretty timber house set in a lovely garden offers five rooms named after English writers (Browning, Austen etc). All are individually decorated; some have four-poster beds and spas.

CARRINGTON HOTEL *Hotel* $$$
(02-4782 1111; www.thecarrington.com.au; 15-47 Katoomba St, Katoomba; r $205-315, r without bathroom $129-149, ste $340-490; @) Katoomba's social and architectural high-water mark, the Carrington has been accommodating road-weary travellers since 1880. Though much of the building has been refurbished, its historical character remains intact. Throwback amenities include a library, a billiards room and stately gardens.

 Eating

SOLITARY *Modern Australian* $$
(02-4782 1164; www.solitary.com.au; 90 Cliff Dr, Leura Falls; lunch dishes $14-33.50, dinner mains $26-33.50; lunch daily, dinner Sat, closed 2 weeks Jan) The magnificent views to Mt Solitary are the main event here, but the seasonally driven and totally delicious food lives up to this elegant restaurant's setting atop the Leura Cascades.

WHISK & PIN STORE & CAFE *Cafe* $
(www.whiskandpin.com; 1 Railway Pde, Medlow Bath; breakfast $7-17.50, sandwiches $9.50-16.50, light lunch dishes $15.50-17.50; 8.30am-4pm Mon-Fri, to 5pm Sat & Sun) This gorgeous cafe is set in a store selling gourmet pantry products and stylish gifts. Claim a seat on a couch or at the communal table and enjoy the freshly prepared and deliciously healthy food on offer.

FRESH ESPRESSO & FOOD BAR
Cafe $

(www.freshcafe.com.au; 181 Katoomba St, Katoomba; breakfast $4.50-15, lunch $13-16; ⊙8am-5pm Mon-Sat, to 4pm Sun) The organic, rainforest-alliance and fair-trade coffee served at Fresh attracts a devoted local following. Excellent all-day breakfasts are popular, too.

🍷 Entertainment

Edge Cinema
Cinema

(www.edgecinema.com.au; 225 Great Western Hwy, Katoomba; adult/child/concession $14/10/12.50; ⊙9.30am-late) A giant screen shows mainstream flicks plus a 40-minute Blue Mountains documentary (adult/child $15/10). Budget Tuesdays feature flicks for $8.50 per person.

ℹ Information

There are **Visitor Information Centres** (☎1300 653 408, 1800 641 227; www.visitbluemountains.com.au) on the Great Western Hwy at **Glenbrook** (⊙9am-4.30pm Mon-Fri, 8.30am-3.30pm Sat & Sun) and at

Lithgow (p105)

Echo Point in **Katoomba** (⊙9am-5pm). Both can provide plenty of information and will book accommodation, tours and attractions.

ℹ Getting There & Around

To reach the Blue Mountains by road, leave Sydney via Parramatta Rd. At Strathfield detour onto the toll-free M4, which becomes the Great Western Hwy west of Penrith and takes you to all of the Blue Mountains towns. It takes approximately 1½ hours to drive from central Sydney to Katoomba.

Blue Mountains Bus (☎02-4751 1077; www.bmbc.com.au) Local buses travel from Katoomba to Wentworth Falls (buses 685 and 690K), Scenic World (bus 686), Leura (bus 690K) and Blackheath (bus 698). Fares cost between $2 and $4.30.

Blue Mountains Explorer Bus (☎1300 300 915; www.explorerbus.com.au; 283 Main St, Katoomba; adult/child $36/18; ⊙9.45am-4.54pm) Offers hop-on hop-off service on a Katoomba/Leura loop. Leaves from Katoomba station every 30 minutes to one hour.

Blue Mountains ExplorerLink (☎13 15 00; www.cityrail.info; 1-day pass adult/child from $46.80/23.40, 3-day pass adult/child from $66.80/33.40 Gives return train travel from

· MTMEDIA/LONELY PLANET IMAGES ©

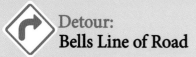

Detour:
Bells Line of Road

Bells Line of Road between Richmond and Lithgow is the most scenic route across the Blue Mountains and is highly recommended if you have your own transport. There are fine views towards the coast from Kurrajong Heights on the eastern slopes of the range, there are orchards around Bilpin and there's sandstone-cliff and bush scenery all the way to Lithgow.

Midway between Bilpin and Bell, the delightful **Blue Mountains Botanic Garden Mount Tomah** (www.mounttomahbotanicgarden.com.au; Bells Line of Road; adult/child/concession $5.50/3.30/4.40; ☺10am-4pm Apr-Sep, to 5pm Oct-Mar) is a cool-climate annexe of Sydney's Royal Botanic Gardens. As well as native plants there are displays of exotic cold-climate species, including some magnificent rhododendrons.

To access Bells Line of Road, head out on Parramatta Rd from Sydney, and from Parramatta drive northwest on Windsor Rd to Windsor. Richmond Rd from Windsor becomes the Bells Line of Road west of Richmond.

Sydney to the Blue Mountains, plus access to the Explorer Bus service.

CityRail (☎13 15 00; www.cityrail.info) Runs to the mountains from Sydney's Central Station (one way adult/child $7.80/3.90, two hours, hourly). There are stations at towns along the Great Western Hwy including Glenbrook, Faulconbridge, Wentworth Falls, Leura, Katoomba, Medlow Bath, Blackheath, Mt Victoria, Zig Zag and Lithgow.

Trolley Tours (☎02-4782 7999, 1800 801 577; www.trolleytours.com.au; 285 Main St, Katoomba; adult/family $20/60; ☺9.45am-5.42pm) Runs a 'hop-on, hop-off' bus barely disguised as a trolley. Twenty-nine stops in Katoomba and Leura.

Brisbane & the East Coast Beaches

From northern New South Wales to Queensland's Sunshine Coast, this section of Australia's east coast demands attention. Score some serious holiday points: the in-your-face seductions of the Gold Coast, hippie hinterland towns, and Brisbane, Australia's third-largest city...all caressed by surf and dappled with 300 days of sunshine a year.

Byron Bay is a gem: Australia's most easterly town is a haven for surfers, foodies and festival-goers. Further north the Gold Coast sparkles with amusement parks, surf carnivals and casino glitz. Brisbane will engage city slickers with its upbeat, cosmopolitan atmosphere, while the Sunshine Coast is criminally underrated: a relaxed span of holiday towns, white sandy beaches and wildlife-watching possibilities. Offshore, World Heritage–listed Fraser Island is studded with gorgeous forests and lakes.

Queenslander hospitality is the order of the day: down-to-earth and uncynical, the locals really know how to let it all hang out.

Burleigh Heads (p129), Gold Coast

Rubber thongs in sales display, Byron Bay (p122)
GREG ELMS/LONELY PLANET IMAGES ©

Brisbane & the East Coast Beaches

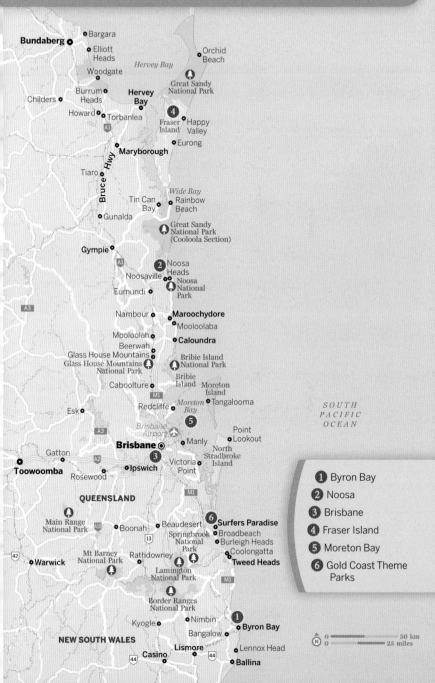

Bundaberg • Bargara
• Elliott Heads
Woodgate
Hervey Bay
• Orchid Beach

Childers • Burrum Heads **Hervey Bay** • Torbanlea
Howard • Great Sandy National Park
4 Fraser Island • Happy Valley
• Eurong
Maryborough
Tiaro
Wide Bay
Tin Can Bay • Rainbow Beach
• Gunalda
Great Sandy National Park (Cooloola Section)
Gympie •
2 Noosa Heads
Noosaville • Noosa National Park
Eumundi •
Nambour • **Maroochydore**
• Mooloolaba
Mooloolah • **Caloundra**
Beerwah
Glass House Mountains
Glass House Mountains National Park
Bribie Island National Park
Caboolture • Bribie Island
Moreton Island
Esk • Redcliffe • *Moreton Bay* • Tangalooma
Brisbane Airport
5
Brisbane ◎ • Manly
Point Lookout
Gatton
3 Victoria Point • North Stradbroke Island
Toowoomba • **Ipswich**
Rosewood
QUEENSLAND
Main Range National Park • Boonah • Beaudesert
6 **Surfers Paradise**
• Broadbeach
Springbrook National Park • Burleigh Heads
Mt Barney National Park • Rathdowney • Coolongatta
Warwick • **Tweed Heads**
Lamington National Park
Border Ranges National Park
Kyogle • Nimbin
Bangalow • **Byron Bay**
NEW SOUTH WALES
Lismore • Lennox Head
Casino • Ballina

SOUTH PACIFIC OCEAN

Bruce Hwy

1 Byron Bay
2 Noosa
3 Brisbane
4 Fraser Island
5 Moreton Bay
6 Gold Coast Theme Parks

0 —— 50 km
0 —— 25 miles

Brisbane & the East Coast Beaches Highlights

Byron Bay

Byron Bay (p122) scores points for its laid-back lifestyle, international vibe and beautiful beaches and surf breaks. It's the kind of place where people come for a week and stay six months. Twenty minutes inland, the hinterland is a maze of hills, valleys, waterfalls and hippie towns.

Need to Know

BEST SURF SEASON Winter (Good swells and fewer crowds) BEST PHOTO OPPORTUNITY Lighthouse: be the first person in Australia to see the sun rise For further coverage, see p122.

Byron Bay Don't Miss List

BY DEAN JOHNSTON, INSTRUCTOR,
BLACK DOG SURFING

1 SURF SPOTS

The Pass (p122) is my number-one spot: an awesome right-hand point break – great for beginners – with some really long rides. I also love **Tallows** (p122), a beach break for experienced surfers, with a bit more power. There's another right-hand point break called **Broken Head** (p122), and the Wreck on **Main Beach** (p122) breaks left and right, quite fast. There are so many spots, and it's so consistent – you can surf here pretty much every day.

2 CAPE BYRON LIGHTHOUSE

Nearly everyone who comes to Byron ventures up to the **lighthouse** (p122) on Cape Byron. It's about a half-hour walk from town: you can either go through the rainforest, or hug the coast and walk up along the cliffs. It's a great place to spot whales and dolphins.

3 FESTIVALS

The **East Coast International Blues & Roots Music Festival** (www.bluesfest.com.au) and **Byron Bay Writers' Festival** (www.byronbaywritersfestival.com.au) are huge here every year. Most locals are really accommodating when there are lots of visitors around: it can get crowded out in the surf, but it's such a mellow atmosphere.

4 EATING & DRINKING

You can't go past the **Beach Hotel** (p125) for a beer: a great setting with a cruisy atmosphere and live bands on Sunday arvos in summer – it pumps! **Espressohead** (p125) does the best coffee in town. Food-wise, **Earth 'n' Sea** (p125) has been around forever: great for a pizza after a three-hour surf session.

5 HINTERLAND

The Byron Bay hinterland is a really beautiful area. **Bangalow** (p126) is just 10 minutes away – a really cool little town. Backpackers love **Nimbin** (p126): local tour companies can drive you out there and back, stopping at special places like **Minyon Falls** along the way.

115

Noosa

It just keeps getting better at **Noosa** (p149), the Sunshine Coast's premier resort town, where style meets surf, or chic meets surfie chick. Noosa is developed, but the little luxuries of the well-heeled mingle effortlessly with free-of-charge natural attributes – the beach and the bush. Enjoy the culinary and shopping delights of Hastings St, take a surfing lesson, or just kick back and sip a coffee or a cocktail.

Fraser Island

They broke the mould after they made **Fraser Island** (p151): the world's largest sand island (120km long!) isn't like anywhere else on the planet. Birds, dingoes and marine life enjoy tropical forests, dunes, freshwater lakes and beaches (...the latter they also share with humans in 4WDs). It's a brilliant place to escape for a day or two in the wilds.

Brisbane

Australia's third-largest city is a booming metropolis engraved with a gracefully meandering river. Exploring **Brisbane** (p131) by river ferry and passing under the mighty **Story Bridge** (p136) will give you a wonderful appreciation of this prosperous city. On its river banks are lush subtropical gardens and magnificent vestiges of colonial architecture, as well as vibrant cafes, galleries, theatres and restaurants.

MANFRED GOTTSCHALK/LONELY PLANET IMAGES ©

DAVID WALL/LONELY PLANET IMAGES ©

Moreton Bay

Where the Brisbane River meets the sea, magnificent **Moreton Bay** (p144) is brimming with marine life, including whales, dolphins and dugongs. You can feed wild dolphins and snorkel in crystal-clear water at Tangalooma, or join Brisbane families holidaying around the pristine sandy beaches and freshwater lakes of North Stradbroke Island.

Gold Coast Theme Parks

Love it or loathe it, the **Gold Coast** (p127) never fails to elicit an opinion. It's undeniably dynamic: high-rise apartments jostle for views over the gorgeous sandy coast, while casino-fuelled nightlife goes berserk in the backstreets. But the amazing Gold Coast theme parks (p130) are what many are here for: a half-dozen adrenalin-charged excuses to stay another day. Rollercoaster, Sea World

Brisbane & the East Coast Beaches' Best...

Beaches

⊙ **Little Wategos** (p122) Byron Bay's (and mainland Australia's) most easterly stretch of sand.

⊙ **Coolangatta** (p131) Check the surf at Kirra or just snooze on the sand.

⊙ **Cylinder Beach** (p145) Lovely family-friendly beach on North Stradbroke Island.

⊙ **Surfers Paradise** (p127) The name says it all. Face the ocean and forget the high-rise backdrop.

Outdoor Activities

⊙ **Gold Coast surfing** (p128) Catch the Gold Coast surf with a board or, for an extra kick, attach a kite and power over the waves.

⊙ **Noosa bushwalking** (p149) Take a stroll through lush Noosa National Park to golden-sand beaches.

⊙ **Tangalooma dolphin feeding** (p147) Wade into the Moreton Island waters and hand-feed Flipper.

⊙ **Fraser Island 4WD beaches** (p153) It's a cliché, but it's great fun! (Consider carbon offsetting...)

Kids' Stuff

⊙ **Gold Coast theme parks** (p130) Adventure on tap for thrill seekers and restless teens.

⊙ **Australia Zoo** (p155) Take the kids for a day-trip to this fabulous wildlife park.

⊙ **Queensland Cultural Centre** (p133) Artistic, hands-on and terrific scientific education while on holiday.

⊙ **Lone Pine Koala Sanctuary** (p135) Boat along the Brisbane River to meet some koalas (just don't call them 'bears').

Need to Know

Crowd-dodging Hideaways

○ **Bangalow** (p126) Just 10 minutes from Byron Bay, Bangalow keeps things happily low-key.

○ **Rainbow Beach** (p154) A relaxed, unpretentious little town that's the departure point for Fraser Island… We hate to blow its cover!

○ **Burleigh Heads** (p129) Great surf and beachfront eateries with none of the Gold Coast hype.

○ **Springbrook National Park** (p129) Plateaus, waterfalls and rock formations in the Gold Coast hinterland.

○ **One month before** Organise internal flights, resort accommodation and a Story Bridge Adventure Climb in Brisbane.

○ **Two weeks before** Book a trip to Fraser Island or some Moreton Bay dolphin-spotting.

○ **One week before** Book a Byron Bay surfing lesson and an upmarket restaurant table in Brisbane.

RESOURCES

○ **Queensland Holidays** (www.queenslandholidays. com.au) Great resource for planning your trip.

○ **Tourism Queensland** (www.tq.com.au) Government-run body responsible for promoting Queensland.

○ **Visit Brisbane** (www. visitbrisbane.com.au) All things 'Brizzy'.

○ **Sunlover Holidays** (www.sunloverholidays.com. au) Book accommodation and tours.

○ **Royal Automobile Club of Queensland** (RACQ; www.racq.com. au) Driving info and emergency roadside assistance.

GETTING AROUND

○ **Walk** Through Noosa National Park.

○ **Drive** Around the Byron Bay hinterland.

○ **Train** From Brisbane Airport into the city.

○ **Ferry** On the Brisbane River and out to Fraser Island.

BE FOREWARNED

○ **Crowds & Festivals** Gold Coast peak season coincides with school holidays: January, early July and early October: expect theme park queues. Easter is festival time in Byron Bay – accommodation books out months in advance.

○ **Box jellyfish** Occasionally occur as far south as Fraser Island from October to April, and are potentially deadly.

○ **Fraser Island's dingoes** Keep your distance.

Left: Springbrook National Park
Above: Surfers Paradise

119

Brisbane & the East Coast Beaches Itineraries

It's not far but there's lots to see from Byron Bay to Brisbane. If you have more time, head north to explore islands, whale-filled bays and the Sunshine Coast.

3 DAYS

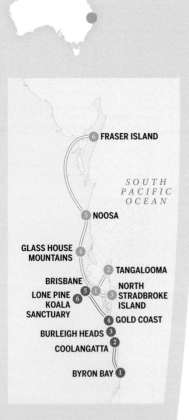

FRASER ISLAND

SOUTH PACIFIC OCEAN

NOOSA

GLASS HOUSE MOUNTAINS

TANGALOOMA

BRISBANE

LONE PINE KOALA SANCTUARY

NORTH STRADBROKE ISLAND

GOLD COAST

BURLEIGH HEADS

COOLANGATTA

BYRON BAY

BYRON BAY TO BRISBANE

Surf to City

It might be hard to leave the point breaks, cafes and chilled-out vibe of **(1) Byron Bay** behind, but point your radar north and head for Queensland. Pit-stop for a night at sandy **(2) Coolangatta** or **(3) Burleigh Heads** for some uncomplicated beach-life and a relaxed surf-side dinner. But get some sleep – the glitzy **(4) Gold Coast** awaits: parade your wares on the sand or succumb to the party atmosphere of Surfers Paradise. If the kids are in the back seat or you're craving a rollercoaster rush, swing by the Gold Coast's hugely popular theme parks.

Turn inland and check out **(5) Brisbane**, where you can take in a show and potter around the sights along the Brisbane River. Check out the West End or dissolve a few hours in New Farm's cafes, bars and live-music rooms. There are also some superb markets here, too, and a night in Fortitude Valley is usually memorable. You can also climb Brisbane's Story Bridge for some fine city views, or jump on a slow boat to the **(6) Lone Pine Koala Sanctuary**, where you can cuddle a koala and procure photographic proof of the event.

Top Left: Pool fun, Surfers Paradise (p127); **Top Right:** Surf life-saver, Noosa (p149)

5 DAYS

BRISBANE TO FRASER ISLAND

Most of the Sunshine Coast

Galleries, theatres, restaurants...Big-city **(1) Brisbane** oozes urban appeal, but there's plenty to see surrounding the big smoke and to the north along the Sunshine Coast. You could spend a day cooling off on a hinterland tour, but if you want to get wet then head to the coast and take a ferry across Moreton Bay (see any whales?) to feed the dolphins at **(2) Tangalooma**. Alternatively, spend a night on **(3) North Stradbroke Island** and wake up for an early morning surf.

Back on the mainland, navigate your way onto Glass House Mountains Rd and snake your way through the peaky **(4) Glass House Mountains**, surveying the verdant hinterland and checking out the wildlife at the world-famous Australia Zoo.

It won't be long before you feel the lure of the sea again: continue through languid Sunshine Coast towns to the elegant beachside haven of **(5) Noosa**, where you can resurrect your board-riding skills, go kayaking, explore national park rainforest and gorge on first-class multicultural cuisine.

If you've got any energy left, consider a 4WD exploration of **(6) Fraser Island**, a long sandy island littered with lakes, dunes and a rambunctious population of native wildlife.

Discover Brisbane & the East Coast Beaches

BYRON BAY

Byron Bay's reputation precedes it like no other place in Australia: it's a gorgeous town where the trademark laid-back, New Age populace lives an escapist, organic lifestyle against a backdrop of evergreen hinterland and never-ending surfable coastline.

 Sights

Cape Byron

The grandfather of the 'mad, bad and dangerous to know' poet Lord Byron was a renowned navigator in the 1760s, and Captain Cook named this spot, Australia's most easterly, after him.

The views from the summit are spectacular, particularly if you've just burnt breakfast off on the climbing track from Clarkes Beach. The surrounding ocean also jumps to the tune of dolphins and migrating humpback whales in June and July. Towering over all is the 1901 **lighthouse** (☏02-6685 6585; Lighthouse Rd; ⊙8am-sunset), Australia's most easterly and powerful.

Beaches

Main Beach, immediately in front of town, is terrific for people watching and swimming. At the western edge of town, **Belongil Beach** is clothing optional. **Clarkes Beach**, at the eastern end of Main Beach, is good for surfing, but the best surf is at the next few beaches: the **Pass**, **Wategos** and **Little Wategos**.

Tallow Beach is an amazing stretch that extends 7km south of Cape Byron to a rockier patch around **Broken Head**,

Cape Byron
PHOTOGRAPHER: HOLGER LEUE/LONELY PLANET IMAGES ©

where a succession of small beaches dots the coast before opening onto **Seven Mile Beach**, which goes all the way to Lennox Head.

 **Activities**

ALTERNATIVE THERAPIES

The *Body & Soul* guide, available from the visitor centre, is a handy guide to therapies on offer.

Bikram Hot Yoga (☑02-6685 6334; www.bikramyogabyronbay.com.au; 35 Childe St; casual 90min class $20)

Buddha Gardens (☑02-6680 7844; www.buddhagardensdayspa.com.au; Arts Factory Village, 21 Gordon St; treatments from $85; ⏱10am-6pm) Balinese-style day spa.

KAYAKING

Exhibitionist dolphins enhance scenic, half-day kayaking tours in and around Cape Byron Marine Park. Tours go for $60 to $65 per adult, less for children.

Cape Byron Kayaks (☑02-6680 9555; www.capebyronkayaks.com; ⏱8.30am & 1pm)

Dolphin Kayaking (☑02-6685 8044; www.dolphinkayaking.com.au; tours ⏱8.30am)

SURFING

Black Dog Surfing (☑02-6680 9828; www.blackdogsurfing.com; Shop 8, The Plaza, Jonson St) Intimate group lessons and women's courses.

Surfing Byron Bay (☑02-6685 7099; www.gosurfingbyronbay.com; 84 Jonson St) Has courses for kids.

 Tours

Byron Bay Eco Tours (☑02-6685 4030; www.byron-bay.com/ecotours; tours $85; ⏱9am) Excellent commentary.

Jim's Alternative Tours (☑0401 592 247; www.jimsalternativetours.com; tours $40; ⏱10am) Entertaining tours (with soundtrack!) to Nimbin.

Mountain Bike Tours (☑1800 122 504, 0429 122 504; www.mountainbiketours.com.au; tours $99; ⏱9.30am) Environmentally friendly bike tours.

 Sleeping

ATLANTIC Guesthouse **$**
(☑02-6685 5118; www.atlanticbyronbay.com.au; 13 Marvell St; dm/d from $25/150; ❄☎🛜) This little residential compound has been transformed into a shiny white seaside haven with varying room combos to suit everyone. Rooms are bright and cheery; the cheapest share bathrooms and kitchens, and dorm rooms are bunk-free. Ask about sleeping in the retro polished aluminium caravan ($175).

ARTS FACTORY LODGE Hostel/Campground **$**
(☑02-6685 7709; www.artsfactory.com.au; Skinners Shoot Rd; dm/d from $34/80, camp-sites $17; @☎) For an archetypal Byron experience, pull up stumps here. The complex has didgeridoo lessons and yoga and meditation workshops delivered in a serene hippie-esque setting on a pictur-esque swamp. Choose from colourful six- to 10-bed dorms, a cottage, teepees or wagons. Couples can opt for aptly titled 'cube' rooms, island retreat canvas huts (both $90) or the pricier love shack with bathroom ($100).

BEACH HOTEL RESORT Resort **$$$**
([☑02-6685 6402; www.beachhotelresort.com.au; Bay St; r incl breakfast from $260; ❄☎) In Byron's hub, this beachfront icon attracts a classy crowd slightly more reserved than that of the massive hotel beer garden next door. Ground-floor rooms open onto lush gardens and a heated pool where a family of lizards sunbake; rooms in the upper storeys have ocean views.

BAY BEACH MOTEL Motel **$$**
(☑02-6685 6090; www.baybeachmotel.com.au; 32 Lawson St; r $155-180, 2-bed apt from $235; ❄☎) Unpretentious but smart, this white-brick hotel with IKEA-esque furnishings is close to town and the beach, but not so close that party-goers keep guests awake.

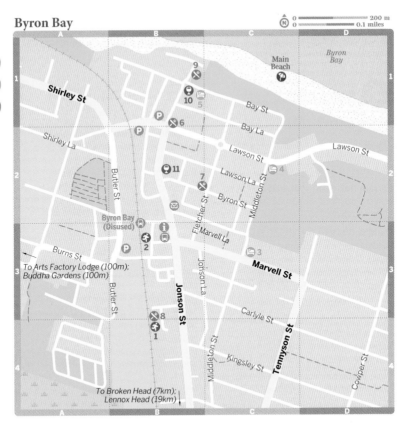

Byron Bay

Byron Bay

 Eating

BALCONY Restaurant, Bar **$$**

(☏ 02-6680 9666; www.balcony.com.au; cnr Lawson & Jonson Sts; dinner $9-39; ☺ breakfast, lunch & dinner; 🛜) The eponymous architectural feature here wraps around the building and gives you tremendous views of the passing Byron parade and the always-clogged traffic circle. The food is Mediterranean fusion, with global influences. The drink list is long.

FISHHEADS Seafood **$**

(www.fishheadsbyronbay.com.au; 1 Jonson St; mains $6-27; ☺ breakfast, lunch & dinner; 🛜) Right on the beach this fabulous takeaway shop sells traditional battered fish and chips ($12.50) or take it up a notch with grilled prawns and salad ($18). The restaurant is fine too, but why wouldn't you dine on the beach?

ESPRESSOHEAD Espresso Bar **$**
(Shop 13, 108 Jonson St) Tucked away behind Woolworths, locals flock to this place for its excellent coffees. See if you can count the number of dodgy vans for sale on the bulletin board.

EARTH 'N' SEA Italian **$$**
(www.earthnsea.com.au; cnr Fletcher & Byron sts; mains $14-34; ☉lunch & dinner) The pizza list at this old favourite is long and full of flavoursome options. Pasta is on the menu too. Beers include several excellent microbrews from the Northern Rivers Brewing Co.

Drinking

GREAT NORTHERN Pub
(www.thenorthern.com.au; Byron St; ☉noon-late) You won't need your fancy duds at this boisterous pub. It's loud and beery with live music most nights and even louder when hosting headline acts. There's live music almost nightly. Soak up the booze with a wood-fired pizza.

BEACH HOTEL Pub
(www.beachhotel.com.au; cnr Jonson & Bay Sts; ☉11am-late) The mothership of all pubs is close to the main beach and is shot through with a fabulously infectious atmosphere that makes everyone your best mate. There's live music and DJs some nights.

ℹ Information

Visitor Centre (☎02-6680 9279; www.visitbyronbay.com; Stationmaster's Cottage, Jonson St) Ground zero for tourist information (and when it's busy this cramped office feels like it).

ℹ Getting There & Away

Air
The closest airport is at Ballina and with its rapidly expanding service it is the best airport for Byron.

♥ If You Like...
Surfing

If you like carving up the swell (or just trying your darndest to stand up) at Byron Bay, check out these other hot-spots with curling point breaks, gentle shore breaks or gnarly sandbars:

1 BURLEIGH HEADS
In the right conditions there's an awesome point break off the headland at Burleigh Heads National Park. Bring buckets of experience.

2 COOLANGATTA
Coolangatta heralds the start of the Gold Coast if you're arriving from the south: a great stretch of beach with consistent shore breaks. The very B-grade 1984 surf flick *Coolangatta Gold* is mandatory local viewing.

3 NOOSA
Before the yuppies, Noosa was full of hippies, all with bushy-bushy blonde hair dos, surfboards and Kombi vans. Surf for all levels of experience.

4 SURFERS PARADISE
It's a crowded, urban beach-scene with high-rise apartments as a backdrop, but they didn't call it Surfers Paradise for nothing! A great place to learn to surf.

It also has shuttle services and rental cars for Byron travellers.

Bus
Long-distance buses for Greyhound (☎1300 473 946; www.greyhound.com.au) and Premier (☎13 34 10; www.premierms.com.au) stop on Jonson St.

Train
CountryLink (☎13 22 32; www.countrylink.info) has buses connecting to trains at the Casino train station (70 minutes).

ℹ Getting Around

Byron Bay Bicycles (☎6685 6067; The Plaza, 85 Jonson St) Hires mountain bikes for $28 per day.

If You Like...
That Small Town Vibe

If you like changing down a gear and checking out small towns like Bangalow, we think you might like these other great little places:

1 NIMBIN
At face value Nimbin can seem a little gimmicky and debased, but it's actually a really interesting place. The free-love ideology that started the town was pure: look through the hemp haze and it's still there.

2 RAINBOW BEACH
Most people swing through Rainbow Beach on their way to Fraser Island and don't stop to look around. Good thing too – there'd be too many people here! It's a relaxed place, with beaut beaches, dunes and cliffs, plus national park access and Fraser Island if you *must*.

3 EUMUNDI
Eumundi's famous market happens on Wednesday and Saturday mornings, but visit any other day of the week and discover lovely cafes and artisan shops washed over by a simple highland lifestyle.

4 BURLEIGH HEADS
It's technically part of the glittering Gold Coast, but the Burleigh vibe is understated and laconic. There's a beautiful little national park here too, and with the right swell there's a kick-ass point break off the headland.

Byron Bay RentaCar (☏6685 5517; 84 Jonson St) Rents a wide range of vehicles.

Byron Bay Taxis (☏6685 5008; www.byronbaytaxis.com.au) On call 24 hours.

FAR NORTH COAST HINTERLAND

Beach bums and surfers might not credit it, but there are people who not so secretly regard the hinterland – as opposed to Byron Bay – as the jewel in the Far North Coast crown.

Bangalow

Boutiques, fine eateries, bookshops and an excellent pub – a mere 14km from Byron Bay. Beautiful Bangalow, with its character-laden main street, is the kind of place that turns Sydneysiders into tree-changers.

There's a good weekly **farmers market** (Byron St; ☉8-11am Sat) and a praised **cooking school** (☏02-6687 2799; www.bangalowcookingschool.com).

RIVERVIEW GUESTHOUSE
(☏02-6687 1317; www.riverviewguesthouse.com.au; 99 Byron St; d/tw from $195/150) Stately old Riverview sits on the river's edge ensuring guests see platypuses and oversized lizards as they take on breakfast. It's the stuff of B&B dreams.

BANGALOW DINING ROOMS
(www.bangalowdining.com; Byron St; mains $15-32; ☉lunch & dinner) Located at Bangalow Hotel, this is a classy place with just the right amount of cool. Reserve a table in the dining room or sit on the deck and order from the cheaper menu; gourmet burgers and the like.

Blanch's Bus Service (☏02-6686 2144; www.blanchs.com.au) operates a service to Ballina ($8) and Byron Bay ($7).

Nimbin

A trip in Nimbin, or rather, a trip *to* Nimbin – is, erm, *high*-ly recommended for anyone visiting the Far North Coast. Wordplays aside, this strange little place, a hangover from an experimental 'Aquarius Festival' in the '70s, still feels like a social experiment where anything goes. A day or two here will reveal there's a growing artist community, a New Age culture and welcoming locals. The **visitor centre** (☏02-6689 1388; Cullen St) has great local info.

NIMBIN MUSEUM & CAFÉ   Museum
(www.nimbinmuseum.com; 62 Cullen St) An interpretive and expressionistic museum,

that packs an eclectic collection of local art into a modest space. It's far more a work of art than of history.

HEMP EMBASSY

(www.hempembassy.net; 51 Cullen St) Across the street, this place raises consciousness about marijuana legalisation, as well as providing all the tools and fashion items you'll need to get high (or at least attract more police raids). Smokers are welcome at the tiny Hemp Bar next door, which is like Haight-Ashbury in a bottle.

GOLD COAST

Behind the long, unbroken ribbon of sand of some of the world's best surfing beaches is a shimmering strip of high-rises, eateries, bars and theme parks that attracts a perpetual stream of sun-loving holidaymakers. The undisputed capital is Surfers Paradise, where the dizzying fun sucks you into a relentless spin and spits you back out exhausted. The hype diminishes drastically outside the epicentre; Broadbeach's beach chic and Burleigh Heads' seaside charm mellowing into Coolangatta's laid-back surfer ethos.

❶ Getting There & Around

The Gold Coast international airport at Coolangatta is 25km south of Surfers Paradise.

The Gold Coast Tourist Shuttle (☎ 1300 655 655, 07-5574 5111; www.gcshuttle.com.au; 1 way per adult/child/family $18/9/45) will meet your flight and drop you at most Gold Coast accommodation.

Coachtrans (☎ 1300 664 700, 07-3358 9700; www.coachtrans.com.au) runs transfers between Brisbane airport and most Gold Coast accommodation (one way adult/child $44/20).

Surfers Paradise & Broadbeach

Some say the surfers prefer other beaches and the paradise is tragically lost, but there's no denying this wild and trashy party zone attracts phenomenal visitor numbers all year round.

Directly south is Broadbeach (population 3800), where the decibel level is considerably lower, but it offers some chic restaurants and a gorgeous stretch of golden beach.

Surfers Paradise

RICHARD I'ANSON/LONELY PLANET IMAGES ©

Surfers Paradise

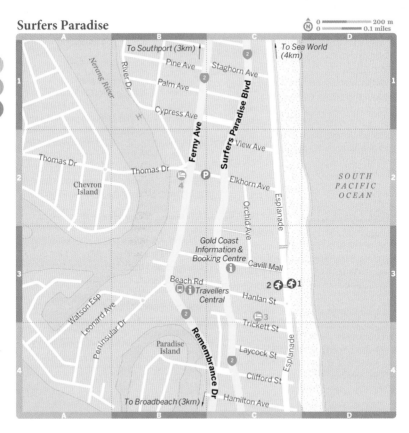

Surfers Paradise

🟢 Activities, Courses & Tours

🔵 Sleeping

🏃 Activities

Cheyne Horan School of Surf   Surfing
(📞 1800 227 873, 0403 080 484; www.cheyne
horan.com.au; 2hr lessons $45) World Champion
surfer Cheyne Horan offers excellent tuition.

Go Ride a Wave   Surfing
(📞 1300 132 441, 07-5526 7077; www.goride
awave.com.au; Cavill Ave Mall; 2hr surfing or
kayaking lessons from $55; ⏰ 9am-5pm) Also
rents out surfboards, kayaks, beach chairs and
umbrellas.

Splash Safaris Sea Kayaking   Kayaking
(📞 0407 741 748; half-day tours $85) Tour
includes kayaking, snorkelling, fish feeding,
bushwalking and morning or afternoon tea.

🛏 Sleeping

VIBE HOTEL   Boutique Hotel **$$**
(📞 07-5539 0444; www.vibehotels.com.au; d
from $140; ❄ @ 🏊) You won't miss this
chocolate and lime-green high-rise on
the Nerang River, a vibrant gem among
Surfers' bland plethora of hotels and
apartments. The rooms are subtle-
chic and the poolside is the spot for

Detour:
Springbrook National Park

The breathtaking landscape of Springbrook is a remnant of the huge shield volcano that centred on nearby Mt Warning in NSW more than 20 million years ago. The national park is directly west of Coolangatta, just 29km from Mudgeeraba or 42km from Nerang.

The park is divided into four reserves. The **Springbrook Plateau** is a 900m-high section with numerous waterfalls and spectacular lookouts.

The beautiful **Natural Bridge** section, off the Nerang–Murwillumbah road, has a 1km walking circuit leading to a rock arch spanning a water-formed cave, which is home to a huge colony of glow-worms.

The **Mt Cougal** section, accessed via Currumbin Creek Rd, has several waterfalls and swimming holes. The **Numinbah** forest reserve was recently added as the fourth section of the national park.

There's a **ranger's office** (87 Carrick Rd; ☺8am-3.30pm Mon-Fri) at Springbrook where you can pick up a copy of the national park's walking tracks. There's also an unstaffed **information centre** at the end of Old School Rd.

sundowners. The aqua-view rooms have superb views over the river.

SURFERS INTERNATIONAL APARTMENTS Apartments **$$**
(☏1800 891 299, 07-5579 1299; www.surfers -international.com.au; 7-9 Trickett St; 1-/2-bed-room apt 3-night minimum stay from $450/630; @ ☲) This high-rise just off the beach has large, comfortable apartments with full ocean views. The complex comes with a small gym and a rooftop pool. This is a good option, close to everything.

Getting There & Away

Long-distance buses stop at the Surfers Paradise Transit Centre (Beach Rd). Greyhound Australia (☏1300 473 946, 07-5531 6677) and Premier Motor Service (☏13 34 10; www.premierms.com.au) have frequent services to/from Brisbane ($20 to $30, 75 minutes). The bus stops for Burleigh Heads and Southport are on Ferny Ave.

Burleigh Heads
A little further south and the true essence of the Gold Coast – far removed from the frenzied party atmosphere of Surfers – permeates the chilled-out surfie town of Burleigh Heads. With its cheery cafes and beachfront restaurants overlooking a gorgeous stretch of white sand, and its small but beautiful national park on the rocky headland, Burleigh Heads charms everyone.

◉ Sights & Activities

A walk around the headland through **Burleigh Heads National Park** is a must for any visitor – it's a 27-hectare eucalypt forest reserve with plenty of bird life and several walking trails. The natural rock slides and water cascades at the **Currumbin Rock Pools** are wonderful in the summer months.

The **Currumbin Wildlife Sanctuary** (☏07-5534 1266; www.cws.org.au; Gold Coast Hwy, Currumbin; adult/child $49/31; ☺8am-5pm) has Australia's biggest rainforest aviary, where you can hand feed rainbow lorikeets. There's also kangaroo feeding, photo opportunities with koalas, Aboriginal dance displays and a Snakes Alive show.

Don't Miss Gold Coast Theme Parks

The roller-coasters and water slides at these American-style theme parks offer so much dizzying action that keeping your lunch down can be a constant battle. Discount tickets are sold in most of the tourist offices on the Gold Coast; the 3 Park Super Pass (adult/child $177/115) covers entry to Sea World, Movie World and Wet'n'Wild.

Australian Outback Spectacular (07-5519 6200; www.myfun.com.au; Entertainment Rd, Oxenford; adult/child incl dinner $99/69) Between Movie World and Wet'n'Wild, this is not actually a theme park but rather a 1½-hour dinner and show in a 1000-seat arena. The venue captures the spirit of the Australian outback with displays of brilliant horsemanship, stampeding cattle and even a little boot scootin' to music written by Australian country singer Lee Kernaghan.

Dreamworld (07-5588 1111; www.dreamworld.com.au; Pacific Hwy, Coomera; adult/child $72/47; 10am-5pm) Home to the Big 6 Thrill Rides, including the Giant Drop and Tower of Terror. Get your photo taken with a Bengal tiger at Tiger Island.

Sea World (07-5588 2222, show times 07-5588 2205; www.seaworld.com.au; Sea World Dr, The Spit, Main Beach; adult/child $75/50; 10am-5pm) See polar bears, sharks and performing dolphins at this aquatic park (pictured above), or ride one of the original Gold Coast roller-coasters, the Corkscrew.

Warner Bros Movie World (07-5573 8485; www.myfun.com.au; Pacific Hwy, Oxenford; adult/child $75/50; 10am-5pm) Movie-themed shows, rides and attractions including the Batwing Spaceshot and Lethal Weapon roller-coaster.

Wet'n'Wild (07-5573 2255; www.wetnwild.com.au; Pacific Hwy, Oxenford; adult/child $55/35; 10am-5pm Feb-Apr & Sep-Dec, to 4pm May-Aug, to 9pm 27 Dec-25 Jan) The ultimate water slide here is the Kamikaze, where you plunge down an 11m drop in a two-person tube at 50km/h.

WhiteWater World (07-5588 1111; www.whitewaterworld.com.au; Dreamworld Parkway, Coomera; adult/child $45/30; 10.30am-4.30pm) Connected to Dreamworld; features the Cave of Waves, Pipeline Plunge and more than 140 water activities and slides.

Sleeping

**HILLHAVEN HOLIDAY
APARTMENTS**　　　Apartments　$$
(☑07-5535 1055; www.hillhaven.com.au; 2 Goodwin Tce, Burleigh Heads; d $170, minimum 3-night stay; @) The pick of these upmarket apartments is the gold deluxe room at $300 per night. Situated on the headland adjacent to the national park these apartments have a grand view of Burleigh Heads.

**BURLEIGH PALMS HOLIDAY
APARTMENTS**　　　Apartments　$$
(☑07-5576 3955; www.burleighpalms.com; 1849 Gold Coast Hwy; 1-bedroom apt per night/week from $130/550, 2-bedroom apt from $160/660; ⊠) Even though they're on the highway, these large and comfortable self-contained units, so close to the beach, are solid value. The owner is a mine of information and is happy to organise tours and recommend places to visit.

Eating

**Elephant Rock
Café**　　　Modern Australian　$$
(☑07-5598 2133; 776 Pacific Pde, Currumbin; mains $16-34; ⊙breakfast & lunch daily, dinner Tue-Sat; ☑) A cool cafe specialising in Mod Oz and 'gourmet vegetarian' cuisine, this trendy cafe morphs from beach-chic by day to ultrachic at night. Great ocean views from the top deck.

Coolangatta

A laid-back seaside resort on Queensland's southern border, Coolangatta is proud of its good surf beaches and tight community. With a sleek makeover transforming the esplanade, this once sleepy town is now the pick of the Gold Coast.

Cooly Surf (cnr Marine Pde & Dutton St; ⊙9am-5pm) hires out high-performance surfboards as well as Malibu surfboards (half/full day $30/45) and stand-up paddleboards ($40/55). Learn to surf with **Walkin' on Water** (☑07-5534 1886, 0418 780 311; www.walkinonwater.com; 2hr group lesson per person $40) or **Gold Coast Surf Coaching** (☑0417 191 629).

Sleeping

KOMUNE　　　Boutique Hotel　$$
(☑07-5536 6764; www.komuneresorts.com; 146 Marine Pde; dm from $45, 2-bedroom apt $220, penthouses $695, penthouses incl Sky-House party room $1500; @ ⊠ ⊠)With beach-funk decor, tropical poolside and an ultra laid-back vibe, this is the ultimate surf retreat. The new concept in accommodation – from budget dorms (including a girls-only dorm), self-contained apartments, and a hip penthouse begging for a party – attracts a broad range of travellers, and fosters eclectic friendships.

BRISBANE

One of Australia's most underrated destinations, Brisbane is an easy-going city with a vibrant arts scene, burgeoning nightlife and first-rate dining, with lush gardens, iconic sights and historic buildings all woven into the urban landscape.

Brisbanites are an active bunch and make good use of the temperate climate and lovely riverside setting. You can go jogging, cycling, kayaking and rock climbing, wander through outdoor markets or relax on palm-fringed artificial beaches just a short jaunt from the highrises looming over the winding Brisbane River.

 Sights & Activities

City Centre

**CITY BOTANIC GARDENS
& AROUND**　　　Park
(Albert St; ⊙24hr) On the river, Brisbane's favourite green space is a mass of lawns, towering Moreton Bay figs, bunya pines, macadamia trees and other tropical flora, descending gently from the Queensland University of Technology (QUT) campus. Its lawns are popular with lunching office workers, joggers and picnickers.

Central Brisbane

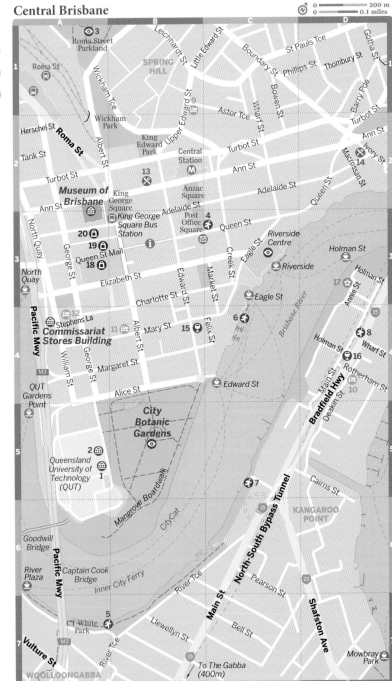

Central Brisbane

In the grounds of QUT is the **QUT Art Museum** (2 George St; admission free; ⏱10am-5pm Tue-Fri, noon-4pm Sat & Sun), which has regularly changing exhibits of contemporary Australian art and works by Brisbane art students. Next door is the former **Old Government House**, a beautiful colonnaded building dating from 1860 and now the home of the National Trust.

FREE **MUSEUM OF BRISBANE** Museum (www.museumofbrisbane.com.au; 157 Ann St; admission free; ⏱10am-5pm) Around the corner from City Hall, this museum illuminates the city from a wide variety of viewpoints, with interactive exhibits that explore both social history and the current cultural landscape.

COMMISSARIAT STORES BUILDING Museum
(115 William St; adult/child $5/2.50; ⏱10am-4pm Tue-Fri) Built by convicts in 1829, the former government storehouse is one of Brisbane's oldest buildings and houses a museum devoted to Brisbane's convict and colonial history.

South Bank

QUEENSLAND CULTURAL CENTRE Museums, Concert Hall
On South Bank, just over Victoria Bridge from the CBD, the Queensland Cultural Centre is the epicentre of Brisbane's cultural confluence. It's a huge compound that includes a concert and theatre venue, four museums and the Queensland State Library.

Queensland Museum (www.southbank.qm.qld.gov.au; cnr Grey & Melbourne Sts; admission free; ⏱9.30am-5pm) occupies imaginations with all manner of curiosities. Queensland's history is given a once-over with an interesting collection of exhibits, including a skeleton of the state's own dinosaur, *Muttaburrasaurus,* and the *Avian Cirrus,* the tiny plane in which Queensland's Bert Hinkler made the first England-to-Australia solo flight in 1928.

The museum also houses the **Sciencentre** (adult/child/family $12/9/40), with over 100 hands-on, interactive exhibits that delve into life science and technology in fun, thought-provoking ways.

The **Queensland Art Gallery** (www.qag.qld.gov.au; Melbourne St, South Brisbane; admission free; ⏱10am-5pm Mon-Fri, 9am-5pm Sat & Sun) houses a fine permanent

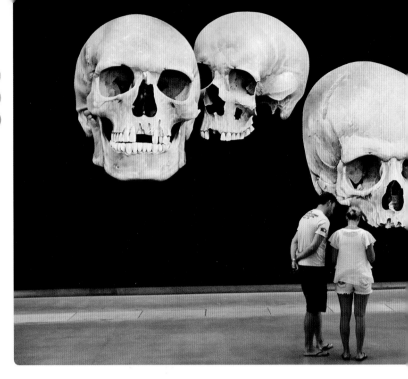

collection, mostly of domestic and European artists.

The massive **Queensland Gallery of Modern Art** (GoMA; Stanley Pl; admission free; ☺10am-5pm Mon-Fri, 9am-5pm Sat & Sun) displays Australian art from the 1970s to today in a variety of changing exhibitions and media: painting, sculpture and photography sit alongside video, installation and film.

SOUTH BANK PARKLANDS   Park
(☺dawn-dusk) This beautiful smear of green park, skirting the western side of the Brisbane River, is home to cultural attractions, fine eateries, small rainforests, hidden lawns and gorgeous flora. The standout attractions here are **Streets Beach**, a funky artificial beach resembling a tropical lagoon, and, behind the beach, **Stanley Street Plaza**, a renovated section of historic Stanley St, with shops, cafes and a tourist information centre.

The London Eye–style **Wheel of Brisbane** (www.thewheelofbrisbane.com.au; Russell St, South Brisbane; adult/child $15/10;

☺11am-9pm) offers 360-degree views from its 60m heights; rides last around 15 minutes and include audio commentary of Brisbane sights.

The South Bank Parklands are within easy walking distance of the city centre, but CityCat and Inner City Ferries also stop there; you can also get there by bus or train from Roma St or Central Station.

Fortitude Valley & New Farm

For over a decade the alternative neighbourhoods of Fortitude Valley and nearby New Farm have been the hub of all things contemporary and cool, thanks to a confluence of artists, restaurateurs and various fringe types flooding the area.

Brisbane's very own **Chinatown** occupies only one street (Duncan St) but exhibits the same flamboyance and flavour of its counterparts in Sydney and Melbourne.

The **Institute of Modern Art** (www.ima.org.au; ☺11am-5pm Tue-Sat, to 8pm Thu), a noncommercial gallery with an industrial

Left: Schaedel-03-Painting-2008, Shirana Shahbazi, Queensland Gallery of Modern Art; **Below:** Streets Beach, South Bank Parklands

PHOTOGRAPHERS: (LEFT) ANDREW WATSON/LONELY PLANET IMAGES ©; (BELOW) LINDSAY BROWN/LONELY PLANET IMAGES ©

exhibition space, has regular showings by local names.

On the eastern fringes of New Farm Park stands the **Brisbane Powerhouse** (119 Lamington St, New Farm; ◷farmers market 6am-noon 2nd & 4th Sat), a former power station that has been superbly transformed into a contemporary arts centre.

Greater Brisbane
LONE PINE KOALA SANCTUARY
Nature Reserve

(☎07-3378 1366; Jesmond Rd, Fig Tree Pocket; adult/child/family $30/21/80; ◷8.30am-5pm) A 35-minute bus ride south of the city centre, Lone Pine Koala Sanctuary is set in attractive parklands beside the river. It is home to 130 or so koalas, as well as kangaroos, possums and wombats. The koalas are undeniably cute and most visitors readily cough up the $16 to have their picture taken hugging one.

To get here catch bus 430 ($4.70, 43 minutes, hourly), which leaves from the Queen St bus station. Alternatively, **Mirimar II** (☎1300 729 742; www.mirimar.com; incl park entry per adult/child/family $60/35/180) cruises to the sanctuary along the Brisbane River from North Quay, next to Victoria Bridge. It departs daily at 10am, returning from Lone Pine at 1.45pm.

 **Activities**

The riverside paths are popular among runners, cyclists and walkers. There's also great rock climbing as well as kayaking on the river.

A good one-stop shop for a wide range of activities is **Riverlife Adventure Centre** (☎07-3891 5766; www.riverlife.com.au; Naval Stores, Kangaroo Point), located near the Kangaroo Point cliffs. It offers rock climbing ($45 per session), abseiling (rappelling, $39) and kayaking instruction ($39), and hires out bicycles ($15/30 per 90 minutes/four hours), kayaks ($25 per 90 minutes) and in-line skates ($20/40 per 90 minutes/four hours).

STORY BRIDGE ADVENTURE
CLIMB Bridge Climbing
(☎1300 254 627; www.storybridgeadventure climb.com.au; 170 Main St, Kangaroo Point; adult/child from $89/76) Fast becoming a Brisbane must-do, the bridge climb offers breathtaking views of the city. The 2½-hour climb takes place on the southern half of the bridge and reaches heights of 80m above the Brisbane River.

CITYCAT Ferry Rides
Ditching the tourist bus and catching one of the sleek CityCat ferries down the Brisbane River has become the sightseeing journey of choice for visitors to the city. Ferries run every 15 to 30 minutes, between 5.40am and 11.45pm, from the University of Queensland in the southwest to Apollo Rd, Bulimba, stopping at 15 terminals including New Farm Park, North Quay (for the Queen St Mall), Riverside (for the CBD) and West End.

 Tours

CASTLEMAINE-PERKINS XXXX
BREWERY Brewery
(☎07-3361 7597; www.xxxxalehouse.com.au; cnr Black & Paten Sts; adult/child $22/15; ⏱hourly 11am-4pm Mon-Fri & 6pm Wed, 12.30pm, 1pm & 1.30pm Sat) If you're a fan of the golden nectar, you'll enjoy touring the XXXX brewery. Adult entry includes four ales to quench your thirst at the end of the tour, so leave the car at home. Call or go online for details. The brewery is a 20-minute walk west from the transit centre, or you can take the Citytrain to Milton Station.

CITY SIGHTS City
(day tickets per adult/child $25/20) This hop-on-hop-off shuttle bus takes in 19 of Brisbane's major landmarks. Tours depart every 45 minutes between 9am and 3.45pm from Post Office Sq on Queen St.

The same ticket covers you for unlimited use of CityCat ferry services.

BRISBANE LIGHTS TOURS City
(☎07-3822 6028; www.brisbanelightstours. com; adult/child from $65/30) Tour departs at 6.30pm nightly (pick-up from your hotel included in price) and covers a dozen city landmarks, dinner or refreshments at Mt Coot-tha Lookout, and a CityCat cruise.

KOOKABURRA RIVER
QUEENS River Cruises
(☎07-3221 1300; www.kookaburrariverqueens. com; lunch/dinner cruises per person from $39/75) Chug up and down the river in a restored wooden paddle steamer. Meals are a three-course seafood and carvery buffet, and there's live entertainment (bands, DJs, dancing) on evening cruises. Steamers depart from the Eagle Street Pier.

River City Cruises River Cruises
(☎0428 278 473; www.rivercitycruises.com.au; South Bank Parklands Jetty A; adult/child/family $25/15/60) River City has 1½-hour cruises with commentary departing South Bank at 10.30am and 12.30pm (plus 2.30pm during summer).

🛏 Sleeping

City Centre
TREASURY Hotel $$$
(☎07-3306 8888; www.treasurybrisbane.com. au; 130 William St; r $200-349; ❄@) Brisbane's classiest hotel is in the beautifully preserved former Land Administration Building. Every room is unique and awash with heritage features, with high ceilings, framed artwork on the walls and polished wood furniture and elegant furnishings. Even the standard rooms are quite spacious. The best rooms have river views.

M ON MARY Apartments $$
(☎07-3503 8000; www.monmary.com.au; 70 Mary St; apt from $170; ❄) Handily located a few blocks from the botanic gardens, this 43-storey building has modern, comfortably furnished one- and two-bedroom apartments. Some have poor layouts and are gloomy, but the best apartments have balconies.

ACACIA INNER-CITY INN　　B&B **$**
(☎07-3832 1663; www.acaciainn.com; 413 Upper Edward St; s/d incl breakfast $70/80/, with bathroom $95) This well-maintained B&B has small, motel-style rooms in a functional environment. The singles are fairly snug, but the doubles have more space and it's clean throughout. All rooms come with TV and bar fridge. It's a great setup for the price and location.

Spring Hill

SPRING HILL TERRACES　　Guesthouse **$$**
(☎07-3854 1048; www.springhillterraces. com; 260 Water St; r $85-110, studio/terrace units $130/160; ❄@ 🛜🏊) Offering good old-fashioned service, Spring Hill has motel-style rooms and roomier terrace units with balconies and leafy courtyards. It's set amid greenery within 10 minutes' walk of Fortitude Valley.

Fortitude Valley

LIMES　　Boutique Hotel **$$$**
(☎07-3852 9000; www.limeshotel.com.au; 142 Constance St; d from $229; ❄@ 🛜🏊) A stylish newcomer to the Valley, Limes

has handsomely outfitted rooms that make good use of tight space – each has plush furniture, kitchenettes and thoughtful extras (iPod docks, free wi-fi, a free gym pass). The rooftop bar is smashing.

CENTRAL BRUNSWICK APARTMENTS　　Apartments **$$**
(☎07-3852 1411; www.centralbrunswickhotel. com.au; 455 Brunswick St; r $135-155; ❄) These modern serviced apartments, favourites with business travellers, have fully equipped kitchens and there's an on-site gym, sauna and spa.

New Farm

BOWEN TERRACE　　Guesthouse **$**
(☎07-3254 0458; www.bowentceaccom modation.com; 365 Bowen Tce; dm/s/d $35/60/85, deluxe r $99-145; Ⓟ@🏊) A beautifully restored Queenslander, this guesthouse is tucked away in a quiet area of New Farm. The friendly owners have installed a TV and bar fridge in every room and there's a lovely back deck overlooking the pool.

Story Bridge Adventure Climb

South Bank

EDMONDSTONE MOTEL   Motel **$$**
(07-3255 0777; www.edmondstonemotel.
com.au; 24 Edmondstone St, South Bank; s/d
$109/119; ❄ @ 🔊 ☲) A 10-minute walk
from both the South Bank Parklands
and West End, the Edmondstone Motel
has small, comfortable rooms with new
mattresses, kitchenettes and LCD TVs –
and yellow brick walls. Most have small
balconies, and there's a small pool and
BBQ.

Kangaroo Point

IL MONDO   Boutique Hotel **$$**
(07-3392 0111; www.ilmondo.com.au; 25
Rotherham St; r/apt $160/250; ❄ @ ☲) In a
fine location near the Story Bridge, this
boutique hotel has handsome three- and
four-star rooms with contemporary,
minimalist design, high-end fixtures and
plenty of space. The cheaper options are
standard hotel rooms while the more
expensive are self-contained apartments.

✕ Eating

City Centre

E'CCO   Modern Australian **$$$**
(07-3831 8344; 100 Boundary St; mains $43;
🕑 lunch Tue-Fri, dinner Tue-Sat) One of the
finest restaurants in the state, award-
winning E'cco is a must for any culinary
aficionado. Masterpieces on the menu
include Milly Hill lamb rump with baby
beetroot, roast pumpkin, blue cheese and
pine nuts. The interior is suitably swish
and you'll need to book well in advance.

**🍃 BLEEDING HEART
GALLERY**   Cafe **$**
(www.bleedingheart.com.au; 166 Ann St; mains
$6-8; 🕑 8am-5pm Mon-Fri; 🔊) Set back from
busy Ann St in a charming, two-storey
Queenslander with verandah, this spa-
cious cafe and gallery has a bohemian
vibe and hosts art openings, occasional
concerts and other events.

Chinatown & Fortitude Valley

**VIETNAMESE
RESTAURANT**   Vietnamese **$$**
(194 Wickham St; mains $8-15; 🕑 lunch & din-
ner) Aptly if unimaginatively named, this
is indeed *the* place in town to eat Vietnamese, with exquisitely prepared
dishes served to an always crowded house. The real delights are
to be found on the 'Authentic
Menu'. The shredded beef in
spinach rolls are tops, as
is any dish containing the
word 'sizzling'. BYO and
licensed.

**CAFÉ
CIRQUE**   Cafe **$$**
(618 Brunswick St;
breakfast mains $14-17;
🕑 8am-4pm) One of the
best breakfast spots
(served all day) in town,
the buzzing Café Cirque

Lone Pine Koala Sanctuary (p135)

Brisbane for Children

From toddlers to teenagers, there's no shortage of places to keep youngsters busy (and parents happy) in Brisbane.

South Bank Parklands (p134) have a smattering of playgrounds and the **Wheel of Brisbane** (p134) would be the highlight of any kids' day out. **Streets Beach** (p134) is also located here with a shallow paddling pool for really small tots. The **Roma Street Parkland** and **New Farm Park** are other good spots to roam free.

One of the best attractions for children is the **Queensland Cultural Centre** (p133). Here the Queensland Museum runs some fantastic, hands-on programmes for little tackers during school holidays. The incorporated Sciencentre is made for inquisitive young minds and will keep them inventing, creating and discovering for hours. The Queensland Art Gallery has a Children's Art Centre in which it runs regular programmes throughout the year.

The river is a big plus. Many children will enjoy a river-boat trip, especially if it's to **Lone Pine Koala Sanctuary** (p135) where they can cuddle up to one of the lovable creatures.

serves rich coffees and daily specials, along with open-face sandwiches and gourmet salads for lunch.

New Farm

ORTIGA　　　　　Spanish　**$$$**
(☏07-3852 1155; 446 Brunswick St; sharing plates $18-36; ⏲dinner Tue-Sun) One of Brisbane's best new restaurants, Ortiga opened in 2010 to much fanfare. You can dine in the stylish upstairs tapas bar with rustic wood tables or head to the elegant subterranean dining room where chefs work their magic in an open kitchen.

South Bank

AHMET'S　　　　　Turkish　**$$**
(☏07-3846 6699; 164 Grey St; mains $20-28; ⏲lunch & dinner) On restaurant-lined Grey St, Ahmet's serves delectable Turkish fare amid a riot of colours. The *pide* (oven-baked Turkish pizza) here is sublime. There's belly dancing on Friday and Saturday nights, plus live 'gypsy-jazz' on Thursday night.

West End

MONDO ORGANICS　　Modern Australian　**$$**
(☏07-3844 1132; 166 Hardgrave Rd; mains $26-38; ⏲lunch Fri-Sun, dinner Wed-Sat, breakfast Sat & Sun) Using the highest-quality organic and sustainable produce, Mondo Organics earns top marks for its delicious seasonal menu. Recent hits include pumpkin, leek and ricotta tortellini; lamb rack with wild mushroom risotto; and ocean trout with shaved fennel and saffron-infused mashed potatoes.

🍷 Drinking

City Centre

BELGIAN BEER CAFE　　　　　Bar
(cnr Mary & Edward Sts; ⏲noon-late) Tin ceilings, wood-panelled walls and globe lights lend an old-fashioned charm to the front room of this buzzing space, while out the back, the beer garden provides a laid-back setting for sampling brews (including 30-plus Belgian beers) and high-end bistro fare.

Fortitude Valley & New Farm

PRESS CLUB   Cocktail Bar

(www.thepressclub.net.au; 339 Brunswick St; ⏰5pm-late Thu-Sat) The Press Club is an elegant spot of amber hues, leather sofas and ottomans, glowing chandeliers and fabric-covered lanterns, giving it a touch of Near Eastern glamour. Live music happens on Thursday – jazz, funk, rockabilly – while DJs spin on weekends.

ALLONEWORD   Bar

(www.alloneword.com.au; 188 Brunswick St) On a seedy stretch of Brunswick, this underground spot is the antidote to sleek cocktail bars taking over the Valley. The front room is pure whimsy: vintage wallpaper, velvety banquettes and a mirrored ceiling, while the back patio has graffiti murals and DJs.

West End

LYCHEE LOUNGE   Cocktail Bar

(94 Boundary St) Sink into the lush furniture and stare up at the macabre doll-head chandeliers at this exotic oriental lounge bar, with mellow beats, mood lighting and an open frontage to Boundary St.

Breakfast Creek

BREAKFAST CREEK HOTEL   Bar, Restaurant

(2 Kingsford Smith Dr; ⏰lunch & dinner) In a great rambling building dating from 1889, this historic pub is a Brisbane institution. Built in French Renaissance style, the pub encompasses various bars (including a beer garden and an art deco 'private bar' where you can still drink draft beer tapped from a wooden keg). The stylish, modern Substation No 41 bar serves boutique beers and cocktails.

Kangaroo Point & South Bank

STORY BRIDGE HOTEL   Bar

(200 Main St, Kangaroo Point) Beneath the bridge at Kangaroo Point, this beautiful old pub with beer garden is the perfect place for a pint after a long day exploring. Live jazz on Sunday (from 3pm).

Entertainment

Most touring international bands have Brisbane on their radar and the city's nightclubs regularly attract top-class DJs. Theatres, cinemas and other performing-arts venues are among Australia's biggest and best.

Pick up one of the free entertainment papers: **Time Off** (www.timeoff.com.au), **Rave** (www.ravemagazine.com.au) and **Scene** (www.scenemagazine.com.au).

Nightclubs

CLOUDLAND   Nightclub

(641 Ann St, Fortitude Valley; ⏰11.30am-late Wed-Sun) Like stepping into a cloud forest (or at least the Ann St version of it), this sprawling, multilevel nightclub has a huge, open, plant-filled lobby with a retractable roof, a wall of water and wrought-iron birdcage-like nooks sprinkled about; you'll also find a rooftop garden and a cellar bar.

MONASTERY   Nightclub

(☎07-3257 7081; 621 Ann St, Fortitude Valley) Monastery really does look like a monastery inside (apart from the heaving, sweaty hordes churning up the dance floor), with its iconic, plush design and gothic lighting.

Live Music

ZOO   Eclectic

(www.thezoo.com.au; 711 Ann St, Fortitude Valley; ⏰Wed-Sat) The long queues at Zoo start early for a good reason: whether you're into hard rock, hip hop, acoustic, reggae or electronic soundscapes, Zoo has a gig for you. It's one of your best chances to hear some raw local talent.

BRISBANE JAZZ CLUB   Jazz

(☎07-3391 2006; www.brisbanejazzclub.com.au; 1 Annie St, Kangaroo Point) Beautifully sited overlooking the river, this tiny club has been a beacon for jazz purists since 1972. The space is small and intimate, and anyone who's anyone in the jazz scene plays here when they're in town.

Cinemas

From March to April, you can see films in the open air at the South Bank Parklands (www.brisbaneopenair.com.au). New Farm Park also hosts alfresco cinema between December and February at the **Moonlight Cinema** (www.moonlight.com.au; adult/child $15/11; ☾7pm Wed-Sun).

Near Roma St Station, **Palace Barracks** (www.palacecinemas.com.au; Petrie Tce) shows a mix of Hollywood and alternative fare.

South Bank Cinema (www.cineplex.com.au; cnr Grey & Ernest Sts, South Bank) is the cheapest cinema for mainstream flicks.

Performing Arts

Brisbane is well stocked with theatre and dance venues, most of them located at South Bank. For bookings at the Queensland Performing Arts Centre and all South Bank theatres, contact **Qtix** (☏13 62 46; www.qtix.com.au).

Queensland Performing Arts Centre Theatre, Live Music (QPAC; ☏07-3840 7444; www.qpac.com.au; Queensland Cultural Centre, Stanley St, South Bank) This centre consists of three venues and features concerts, plays, dance and performances of all genres. Catch anything from flamenco to *West Side Story* revivals.

BRISBANE POWERHOUSE Theatre, Live Music (☏07-3358 8600; www.brisbanepowerhouse.org; 119 Lamington St, New Farm) The former 1940 power station continues to bring electricity to the city – albeit in the form of nationally acclaimed theatre, music and dance productions.

Sport

Like most other Australians, Brisbanites are sports-mad. You can see interstate cricket matches and international test cricket at the **Gabba** (Brisbane Cricket Ground; www.thegabba.org.au; 411 Vulture St) in Woolloongabba, south of Kangaroo Point. If you're new to the game, try to get along to a Twenty20 match, which is cricket in its most explosive form. The cricket season runs from October to March.

The Gabba is also a home ground for the Brisbane Lions, an Australian Football League (AFL) team. Watch them in action,

Lychee Lounge

Market-Lovers Guide to Brisbane

○ **James Street Market** (James St, New Farm; ◔8.30am-6pm) Paradise for gourmands, this small but beautifully stocked market has gourmet cheeses, a bakery-patisserie, fruit, vegetables, and lots of gourmet goodies. The fresh seafood counter serves excellent sushi and sashimi.

○ **Jan Power's Farmers Market** (Brisbane Powerhouse, 119 Lamington St, New Farm; ◔7am-noon 2nd & 4th Sat of month) Don't miss this excellent and deservedly popular farmers market if it's on when you're in town: over 120 stalls selling fresh produce, local wines, jams, juices, snacks (waffles, sausages, desserts, coffees) and much more. The CityCat takes you there.

○ **West End Markets** (Davies Park, cnr Montague Rd & Jane St; ◔6am-2pm Sat) This sprawling flea market has loads of fresh produce, herbs, flowers, organic foodstuffs, clothing and bric-a-brac. It's an apt representation of the diverse West End and a good place for noshing, with stalls selling a wide range of cuisines; there's also live music in the park.

○ **South Bank Lifestyle Markets** (Stanley St Plaza, South Bank; ◔5-10pm Fri, 10am-5pm Sat, 9am-5pm Sun) These popular markets have a great range of clothing, craft, art, handmade goods and interesting souvenirs.

often at night under lights, between March and September.

During the other half of the year, rugby league is the big spectator sport. The Brisbane Broncos play home games at **Suncorp Stadium** (www.suncorpstadium.com.au; 40 Castlemaine St, Milton).

🅐 Shopping

The Queen St Mall and Myer Centre in the CBD have large chain stores, upmarket outlets and the obligatory tourist tat. Smaller independent and specialist shops are in Fortitude Valley.

Paddington Antique Centre Antiques
(167 Latrobe Tce, Paddington) The city's biggest antique emporium houses over 50 dealers selling all manner of treasure/trash from the past. Clothes, jewellery, dolls, books, artwork, lamps, musical instruments, toys and more.

Blonde Venus Clothing
(707 Ann St, Fortitude Valley) One of the top boutiques in Brisbane, Blonde Venus has been around for 20-plus years, stocking a well-curated selection of both indie- and couture labels. Other great boutiques line this street.

Record Exchange Music
(Level 1, 65 Adelaide St) Record Exchange is home to an astounding collection of vinyl, plus CDs, DVDs, posters and other memorabilia.

ⓘ Information

Medical Services

Royal Brisbane & Women's Hospital (☎07-3636 8111; cnr Butterfield St & Bowen Bridge Rd, Herston) Has 24-hour casualty ward.

Travel Clinic (☎1300 369 359, 07-3211 3611; 1st fl, 245 Albert St)

Money

There are foreign-exchange bureaus at Brisbane Airport's domestic and international terminals, as well as ATMs. ATMs are prolific throughout Brisbane.

American Express (☎ 1300 139 060; Shop 3, 156 Adelaide St)

Travelex (☎ 07-3210 6325; Shop 149F, Myer Centre, Queen St Mall)

Tourist Information

Brisbane Visitor Information Centre (☎ 07-3006 6290; Queen St Mall; ⏰ 9am-5.30pm Mon-Thu, to 7pm Fri, to 4.30pm Sat, 9.30am-4pm Sun) Great one-stop info counter for all things Brisbane.

🛈 Getting There & Away

Air

Brisbane's main airport is about 16km northeast of the city centre at Eagle Farm and has separate international and domestic terminals about 2km apart, linked by the **Airtrain** (per person $5; ⏰ every 15-30min).

Bus

Brisbane's main terminus and booking office for all long-distance buses and trains is the **Brisbane Transit Centre** (Roma St, Brisbane), about 500m west of the city centre.

Car & Motorcycle

There are five major routes, numbered from M1 to M5, into and out of the Brisbane metropolitan area. If you're just passing through, take the Gateway Motorway (M1) at Eight Mile Plains, which bypasses the city centre to the east and crosses the Brisbane River at the Gateway Bridge ($3 toll).

Train

Brisbane's main station for long-distance trains is the Brisbane Transit Centre. For reservations and information visit the **Queensland Rail Travel Centre** (☎ 13 16 17; www.queenslandrail.com.au) Central Station (Ground fl, Central Station, 305 Edward St); Brisbane Transit Centre (Brisbane Transit Centre, Roma St).

🛈 Getting Around

Obtain bus, train and ferry info at the **Transit Information Centre** (www.translink.com.au; cnr Ann & Albert Sts) or call ☎ 13 12 30.

West End Markets

Fares on buses, trains and ferries operate on a zone system. There are 23 zones in total, but the city centre and most of the inner-city suburbs fall within zone 1, which translates into a single fare of $3.90/2 per adult/child. To save money (around 30% off individual fares), purchase a **Go Card** ($5), which is sold (and recharged) at transit stations and newsagents.

To/From the Airport

The easiest way to get to and from the airport is via the **Airtrain** (📞07-3215 5000; www.airtrain. com.au; adult/child $15/7.50; ⏱6am-7.30pm), which runs every 15 to 30 minutes from the airport to Fortitude Valley, Central Station, Roma St Station (Brisbane Transit Centre) and other key destinations. There are also half-hourly services to the airport from Gold Coast Citytrain stops.

If you prefer door-to-door service, **Coachtrans** (📞07-3358 9700; www. coachtrans.com.au) runs regular shuttle buses between the airport and any hotel in the CBD (adult/child $15/8); it also connects Brisbane Airport to Gold Coast accommodation (adult/ child $44/20).

A taxi into the centre from the airport will cost around $40.

Boat

In addition to the CityCats (p136), Inner City Ferries zigzag back and forth across the river between North Quay, near the Victoria Bridge, and Mowbray Park. Services start at 6am and run till about 11pm. There are also several cross-river ferries; most useful is the Eagle Street Pier to Thornton St (Kangaroo Point) service.

As with all Brisbane public transport, fares are based on zones (zone 1 adult/child $3.90/2).

Bus

The Loop, a free bus service that circles the city area, stops at QUT, Queen Street Mall, City Botanic Gardens, Central Station and Riverside. It runs every 10 minutes on weekdays between 7am and 6pm.

The main stop for local buses is in the underground Queen Street Mall bus station, where there's an information centre, and King George Sq bus station.

Buses generally run every 10 to 30 minutes Monday to Friday, from 5am till about 11pm, and with the same frequency on Saturday morning (starting at 6am).

Taxi

The major taxi companies are **Black & White** (📞13 10 08) and **Yellow Cab Co** (📞13 19 24).

Train

The fast Citytrain network has seven lines, which run as far as Gympie North in the north (for the Sunshine Coast) and Robina in the south (for the Gold Coast). All trains go through Roma St, Central and Brunswick St Stations; there's also a handy South Bank Station.

MORETON BAY

The patch of water lapping at Brisbane's urban edges is packed full of marine life including whales, dolphins and

CityCat ferry (p136) heading towards Story Bridge

SALLY DILLON/LONELY PLANET IMAGES ©

dugongs. Moreton Bay also has some startlingly beautiful islands that are very accessible from the mainland.

 Tours

Humpback whales are a regular sight in the bay between June and November when they migrate to and from their southern feeding grounds.

Dolphin Wild Boat
(✆ 07-3880 4444; www.dolphinwild.com.au; per adult/child/family incl lunch $110/60/290) Departing from Redcliffe, these full-day ecotours include a cruise to Moreton Island with commentary from a marine naturalist and guided snorkel tours ($20/10 per adult/child) around the Tangalooma wrecks.

Manly Eco Cruises Boat
(✆ 07-3396 9400; www.manlyecocruises.net; per adult/child $99/44) Ride on the catamaran boom nets, enjoy free canoe rides or sit back on the MV *Getaway* and spot marine life. The two-hour Sunday BBQ breakfast tour ($29/14 per adult/child) is especially popular.

North Stradbroke Island

Brisbanites are lucky to have such a brilliant holiday island on their doorstep. A mere 30-minute ferry ride from Cleveland, this sand island has a string of glorious powdery white-sand beaches. Between June and November, hundreds of humpback whales can also be seen here.

 **Sights & Activities**

At Point Lookout, the breathtaking **North Gorge Headlands Walk** is an absolute must for any visitor to Straddie. Turtles, dolphins and manta rays can be spotted any time of year from the wooden boardwalk that skirts the rocky outcrops, and the view from the headland down Main Beach is sublime.

There are several gorgeous **beaches** huddled around Point Lookout. A patrolled swimming area, Cylinder Beach is popular with families and is flanked by Home Beach and Deadman's Beach.

 Tours

North Stradbroke Island 4WD Tours & Camping Holidays (☎ 07-3409 8051; straddie@ecn.net.au) Generally, half-day tours cost $35/20 per adult/child.

Straddie Kingfisher Tours (☎ 07-3409 9502; www.straddiekingfishertours.com.au; adult/child $79/59) Operates six-hour 4WD and fishing tours; also has whale-watching tours in season.

Sleeping

PANDANUS PALMS RESORT   Apartments   **$$$**
(☎ 07-3409 8106; www.pandanus.stradbroke resorts.com.au; 21 Cumming Pde; apt $245-315; ☎) Perched high above the beach, with a thick tumble of vegetation beneath, the large two-bed townhouses here are a good size and boast modern furnishings; the best face the ocean, with private yards and BBQs. There is an excellent restaurant on site.

STRADBROKE ISLAND BEACH HOTEL   Hotel   **$$$**
(☎ 07-3409 8188; www.stradbrokeislandbeach hotel.com.au; East Coast Rd; d $230-310; ❄ ☎) Straddie's only hotel has an intriguing modern design, with 12 cool, inviting rooms in muted colour schemes, each with high-end fixtures and a balcony. The open bar downstairs with outdoor beer garden is a delight, and there's also a restaurant and spa.

Getting There & Away

The gateway to North Stradbroke Island is the seaside suburb of Cleveland. Regular Citytrain (www.translink.com.au) services run from Central Station or Roma St to Cleveland station ($6.70, one hour) and buses to the ferry terminals meet the trains at Cleveland station (10 minutes).

Stradbroke Ferries (☎ 07-3488 5300; www. stradbrokeferries.com.au) goes to Dunwich almost every hour from about 6am to 6pm ($19 return, 25 minutes). It also has a slightly

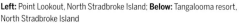

Left: Point Lookout, North Stradbroke Island; **Below:** Tangalooma resort, North Stradbroke Island

PHOTOGRAPHERS: (LEFT) SALLY DILLON/LONELY PLANET IMAGES ©: (BELOW) PHILIP GAME/LONELY PLANET IMAGES ©

less frequent vehicle ferry ($135 return per vehicle including passengers, 40 minutes).

Moreton Island

City life rapidly fades from memory when you're cruising on the ferry from Brisbane out to this sand island north of Stradbroke. Day trippers, campers and folks staying at the island's resort love to explore its extremes, diving deep into crystal-clear waters to view marine life or rising to the summits of enormous sand dunes for tobogganing.

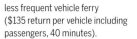 **Sights & Activities**

Tangalooma, halfway down the western side of the island, is a popular tourist resort sited at an old whaling station. The main attraction is the **dolphin feeding**, which takes place each evening around sunset. Between five and nine dolphins swim in from the ocean and take fish from the hands of volunteer feeders. Although you have to be a guest of the resort to participate, onlookers are welcome. The resort also organises **whale-watching** cruises (June to October), plus loads of other activities.

 **Tours**

Moreton Bay Escapes Activities, Camping
(☎ 1300 559 355; www.moretonbayescapes.com. au; 1-day tours adult/child from $165/125, 2-day camping tours $249/149) A certified ecotour, the one-day Moreton Island 4WD tour includes sand-boarding, tobogganing, marine wildlife watching and a picnic lunch.

Sunrover Expeditions Camping
(☎ 1800 353 717, 07-3203 4241; www.sunrover. com.au; adult/child $120/100) A friendly and reliable 4WD-tour operator with good day tours and camping tours.

147

🛏 Sleeping

**TANGALOOMA WILD DOLPHIN
RESORT** Hotel, Apartments **$$$**
(☎ 1300 652 250, 07-3637 2000; www.
tangalooma.com; 1-night packages from $310;
❄ @ ☲) This beautifully sited but ageing
resort is the only formal setup on the
island. There is a plethora of options,
starting with pretty bland hotel-style
rooms. A step up are the units and suites,
where you'll get beachside access and
rooms kitted out in cool, contemporary
decor with good facilities. Look for online
deals through www.wotif.com. The resort
has several eating options.

ⓘ Getting There & Around

The Tangalooma Flyer (☎ 07-3268 6333; www.
tangalooma.com; adult/child return day trips
from $45/25) is a fast catamaran operated by
Tangalooma Resort. It makes the 1¼-hour trip to
the resort on Moreton Island daily from a dock
at Eagle Farm, at Holt St off Kingsford Smith Dr.
A bus (adult/child one way $19/9) goes to the
Flyer from the CBD. Return service also available.
Bookings essential (☎ 07-3637 2000).

NOOSA & THE SUNSHINE COAST

If your idea of the perfect summer
holiday involves lazy days in the sun,
sand between your toes, and fish and
chips on the beach then pack a smile,
ditch the bling and immerse yourself
in the laid-back beach-chic culture of
the refreshingly natural and unaffected
Sunshine Coast.

ⓘ Getting There & Away

Air

The Sunshine Coast Airport is at Mudjimba,
10km north of Maroochydore and 26km south of
Noosa. Jetstar (☎ 13 15 38; www.jetstar.com.
au) and Virgin Australia (☎ 13 67 89; www.
virginaustralia.com) have daily flights from
Sydney and Melbourne. Tiger Airways (☎ 03-
9999 2888; www.tigerairways.com) has flights
from Melbourne.

Bus

Greyhound Australia (☎ 1300 473 946;
www.greyhound.com.au) has daily services
from Brisbane to Caloundra ($30, two hours),

Noosa National Park

RICHARD I'ANSON/LONELY PLANET IMAGES ©

Detour:
Eumundi

Sweet little Eumundi is a quaint highland village with a quirky new-age vibe greatly amplified during its famous market days. The historic streetscape blends well with modern cafes, unique boutiques, silversmiths, crafts people and body-artists doing their thing.

The **Eumundi markets** (⊘6.30am-2pm Sat, 8am-1pm Wed) attract thousands of visitors to their 300-plus stalls and have everything from hand-crafted furniture and jewellery to homemade clothes and alternative-healing booths, plus food and live music.

Sunbus runs hourly from Noosa Heads ($3.20, 40 minutes) and Nambour ($4.10, 30 minutes). A number of Noosa tour operators visit the Eumundi markets on Wednesdays and Saturdays.

Maroochydore ($30, two hours) and Noosa ($32, 2½ hours). Premier Motor Service (☑13 34 10; www.premierms.com.au) also services Maroochydore and Noosa from Brisbane.

Veolia (☑1300 826 608; www.vtb.com.au) has an express service from Brisbane to Noosa (one way/return $25/46) twice daily.

ⓘ Getting Around

Several companies offer transfers from Sunshine Coast Airport and Brisbane to points along the coast. The following are recommended:

Henry's (☑07-5474 0199; www.henrys.com.au)

Noosa Transfers & Charters (☑07-5450 5933; www.noosatransfers.com.au)

Sun-Air Bus Service (☑1800 804 340, 07-5477 0888; www.sunair.com.au)

Train

Citytrain has services from Nambour to Brisbane ($22, two hours). Trains also go to Beerwah ($12, 1½ hours), near Australia Zoo.

Noosa

Once a little-known surfer hang-out, gorgeous Noosa is now a stylish resort town and one of Queensland's star attractions. Noosa's stunning natural landscape of crystalline beaches and tropical rainforests blends seamlessly with its fashionable boulevard, Hastings St, and the sophisticated beach elite who flock here.

Sights

One of Noosa's best features, the lovely **Noosa National Park**, covering the headland, has fine walks, great coastal scenery and a string of bays with waves that draw surfers from all over the country.

The most scenic way to access the national park is to follow the boardwalk along the coast from town. Pick up a walking-track map from the **QPWS centre** (⊘9am-3pm), at the entrance to the park.

 Activities

Noosa River is excellent for canoeing and kayaking. **Noosa Ocean Kayak Tours** (☑0418 787 577; www.learntosurf.com; 2hr tours $66, kayak hire per day $55) hires kayaks and offers sea-kayaking tours around Noosa National Park and Noosa River.

Numerous companies offer surf lessons and board hire, including **Merrick's Learn to Surf** (☑0418 787 577; www.learntosurf.com.au; 2hr lessons $60), **Go Ride A Wave** (☑1300 132 441; www.gorideawave.com.au; 2hr lessons $60, 2hr surfboard hire $25, 1hr stand-up paddleboard hire $25) and **Noosa Kite Surfing** (☑0458 909 012; www.noosakitesurfing.com.au; 2hr lessons $160).

Noosa

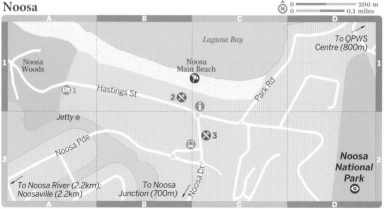

Laguna Bay

To QPWS
Centre (800m)

Noosa
Woods

Noosa
Main Beach

Hastings St

Jetty

Noosa Pde

Noosa Dr

Park Rd

Noosa
National
Park

To Noosa River (2.2km);
Noosaville (2.2km)

To Noosa
Junction (700m)

0   200 m
0   0.1 miles

ISLANDER NOOSA RESORT   Resort **$$**
(☎07-5440 9200; www.islandernoosa.com.au;
187 Gympie Tce, Noosaville; 2-/3-bedroom villas
$178/205; ❄@🛜🏊) Set on more than
1.5 hectares of lush tropical gardens,
with a central tropical pool and wooden
boardwalks meandering through the trees
to your comfortable bungalow, this resort
is excellent value. It's bright and cheerful
and packs a cocktail-swilling, island-
resort ambience.

#2 HASTINGS ST   Apartments **$$$**
(☎07-5448 0777; www.2hastingsst.com.
au; 2 Hastings St, Noosa Heads; units from
$225; ❄🛜) These two-bedroom, two-
bathroom units at the Noosa Woods
end of Hastings St are great value as a
four-share. Units overlook the river or the
woods, and you're within a short walk of
everything. Minimum two-night stay.

ANCHOR MOTEL NOOSA   Motel **$$**
(☎07-5449 8055; www.anchormotelnoosa.
com.au; cnr Anchor St & Weyba Rd, Noosaville;
r from $115; ❄🛜🏊) There's no escap-
ing the nautical theme in this colourful
motel. Blue-striped bedspreads, porthole
windows and marine motifs will have you
wearing stripes and cut-offs while grilling
prawns on the barbie.

 Eating

**BERARDO'S ON
THE BEACH**   Modern Australian **$$**
(☎07-5448 0888; On the Beach Resort, Hastings
St; mains $20-36; ⏰breakfast, lunch & dinner)
Reminiscent of the French Riviera, this
stylish bistro is only metres from the
waves. Classy without being pretentious,
this is Noosa in a seashell. The Mod Oz
menu uses local produce with a focus on
seafood.

GASTON   Modern Australian **$$**
(5/50 Hastings St; mains $17-25; ⏰breakfast,
lunch & dinner) This casual alfresco bar
and bistro is highly recommended by the
locals. It's also a great place to watch the
passing parade of beautiful people.

ℹ **Getting There & Around**

Long-distance buses stop at the bus stop near
the corner of Noosa Dr and Noosa Pde; see p148
for fares. At the time of research a new transit
centre was under construction in Noosa Dr, Noosa
Junction. Once completed, long-distance buses
will arrive here.

Sunbus (☎13 12 30) has frequent services to
Maroochydore ($5, one hour) and the Nambour
train station ($5, one hour).

Glass House Mountains

Rising high above the green subtropical hinterland are the 16 volcanic crags known as the Glass House Mountains. Mt Beerwah (556m), the highest of these ethereal cornices, is the mother according to Dreamtime mythology. These stunning natural formations lend an eerie otherworldliness to a region brimming with life.

Hikers are spoilt for choice here. If you're in a hurry, the **Glass House Mountains lookout** provides a fine view of the peaks and the distant beaches. The **lookout circuit** (800m) is a short and steep walking track that leads through open scribbly-gum forest and down a wet gully before circling back.

FRASER ISLAND & THE FRASER COAST

Fraser Island

Sculpted from wind, sand and surf, the striking blue freshwater lakes, crystalline creeks, giant dunes and lush rainforests of this gigantic sandbar form an enigmatic island paradise unlike any other in the world. Created over hundreds of thousands of years from sand drifting off the east coast of mainland Australia, Fraser Island is the largest sand island in the world (measuring 120km by 15km) and the only place where rainforest grows on sand.

◎ Sights & Activities

From Fraser's southern tip, use the high-tide access track between Hook Point and **Dilli Village**, rather than the beach. From here on, the eastern beach is the main thoroughfare. Stock up at nearby **Eurong**, the start of the inland track, across to Central Station and Wanggoolba Creek (for the ferry to River Heads).

About 4km north of Eurong along the beach is a signposted walking trail to **Lake Wabby**. Wabby is edged on three sides by eucalypt forest, while the fourth side is a massive sandblow, which is encroaching on the lake at a rate of about 3m a year.

Driving north along the beach you'll pass **Happy Valley**, with many places to stay, and **Eli Creek**. About 2km from Eli Creek is the wreck of the *Maheno,* a

Glass House Mountains

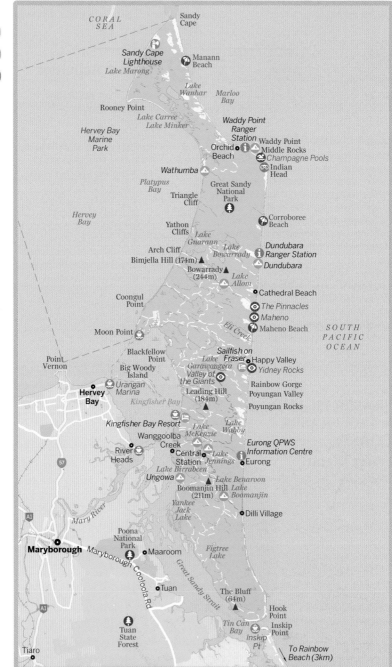

passenger liner that was blown ashore by a cyclone in 1935 while being towed to a Japanese scrap yard.

Roughly 5km north of the *Maheno* you'll find the **Pinnacles** (a section of coloured sand cliffs) and, about 10km beyond, **Dundubara**. Then there's a 20km stretch of beach before you come to the rocky outcrop of **Indian Head**, the best vantage point on the island. Sharks, manta rays, dolphins and (during the migration season) whales can often be spotted from the top of the headland.

From Indian Head the trail branches inland, passing the **Champagne Pools**, the only safe spot on the island for saltwater swimming. This inland road leads back to **Waddy Point** and **Orchid Beach**, the last settlement on the island.

Sleeping & Eating

SAILFISH ON FRASER Apartments $$$
(07-4127 9494; www.sailfishonfraser.com.au; Happy Valley; d from $230-250, extra person $10;) Any notions of rugged wilderness and roughing it will be forgotten quick smart at this plush, indulgent retreat. These two-bedroom apartments are cavernous and classy, with wall-to-wall glass doors, spas and mod cons; and there's an alluring pool.

**KINGFISHER BAY RESORT** Resort $$
(1800 072 555, 07-4194 9300; www.kingfisherbay.com; Kingfisher Bay; d $160, 2-bedroom villas $198;) This elegant eco-resort has

---

Sand Safaris: Exploring Fraser Island

The only way to explore Fraser Island is with a 4WD vehicle. For most travellers there are three transport options: tag-a-long tours, organised tours or 4WD hire.

TAG-ALONG TOURS

Popular with backpackers, these tag-along tours feature a group of travellers that pile into a 4WD convoy and follow a lead vehicle with an experienced guide and driver.

Rates hover around $300 to $320 for three-day/two-night packages and exclude food, fuel and alcohol. See p155 for operators.

ORGANISED TOURS

Package tours leave from Hervey Bay, Rainbow Beach and Noosa and typically cover rainforests, Eli Creek, Lakes McKenzie and Wabby, the coloured Pinnacles and the *Maheno* shipwreck.
Footprints on Fraser (1300 765 636; www.footprintsonfraser.com.au; 4-/5-day walks $1375/1825) Highly recommended guided walking tours of the island's natural wonders.
Fraser Explorer Tours (1800 249 122, 07-4194 9222; www.fraserexplorertours.com.au; day tours $175, 2-day tours $312) Highly recommended.

4WD HIRE

Hire companies lease out 4WD vehicles in Hervey Bay, Rainbow Beach and on the island itself. Most companies will help arrange ferries and permits and hire camping gear.

On the island, **Kingfisher Bay 4WD Hire** (07-4120 3366) hires out 4WDs from $175/280 per half-/full day. Also see Getting Around in the Hervey Bay (p157) section for rental companies.

hotel rooms with private balconies, and sophisticated timber villas, some with spas on their private decks. There's a three-night minimum stay in high season. The resort has restaurants, bars and shops and operates daily tours of the island (adult/child $169/99).

ℹ️ Information

The main ranger station, Eurong QPWS Information Centre (☎07-4127 9128), is at Eurong. Others can be found at Dundubara (☎07-4127 9138) and Waddy Point (☎07-4127 9190).

If your vehicle breaks down, call Fraser Island Breakdown (☎07-4127 9173) or the tow-truck service (☎07-4127 9449, 0428 353 164), both based in Eurong.

Permits

You will need permits for vehicles (per month/year $39.40/197.20) and camping (per person/family $5.15/20.60), and these must be bought before you arrive. It's best to buy the permits online at www.derm.qld.gov.au or contact QPWS (☎13 74 68). Permits aren't required for private camping grounds or resorts. Permit-issuing offices:

Great Sandy Information Centre (☎07-5449 7792; 240 Moorinidil St, Tewantin; ◷8am-4pm) Near Noosa.

Rainbow Beach QPWS (☎07-5486 3160; Rainbow Beach Rd)

River Heads Information kiosk (☎07-4125 8485; ◷6.15-11.15am & 2-3.30pm) Ferry departure point at River Heads, south of Hervey Bay.

ℹ️ Getting There & Away

Vehicle ferries connect Fraser Island with River Heads, about 10km south of Hervey Bay, or further south at Inskip Point, near Rainbow Beach.

Fraser Island Barges (☎1800 227 437; www.fraserislandferry.com.au) makes the crossing (vehicle and four passengers $150 return, 30 minutes) from River Heads to Wanggoolba Creek on the western coast of Fraser Island. It departs daily from River Heads at 8.30am, 10.15am and 4pm, and returns from the island at 9am, 3pm and 5pm.

Coming from Rainbow Beach, the operators Rainbow Venture & Fraser Explorer (☎07-4194 9300; pedestrian/vehicle return $10/80) and

Manta Ray (☎07-5486 8888; vehicle return $90) both make the 15-minute crossing from Inskip Point to Hook Point on Fraser Island continuously from about 7am to 5.30pm daily.

Air Fraser Island (☎07-4125 3600; www.airfraserisland.com.au) charges from $125 for a return flight (20 minutes each way) to the island's eastern beach, departing Hervey Bay airport.

Rainbow Beach

Gorgeous Rainbow Beach is a tiny town at the base of the Inskip Peninsula with spectacular multicoloured sand cliffs overlooking its rolling surf and white sandy beach. Still relatively untouched, the town has friendly locals and a relaxed vibe. Convenient access to Fraser Island (only 15 minutes by barge) and the Cooloola section of the Great Sandy National Park has made it a rising star of Queensland's coastal beauty spots.

The town is named for the **coloured sand cliffs**, a 2km walk along the beach. A 600m track along the cliffs at the southern end of Cooloola Dr leads to the **Carlo Sandblow**, a spectacular 120m-high dune.

🏃 Activities

For those not wishing to hire a 4WD, **Surf & Sand Safaris** (☎07-5486 3131; www.surfandsandsafaris.com.au; per adult/child $70/35) runs 4WD tours through the national park, and along the beach to the coloured sands and lighthouse at Double Island Point.

Rainbow Beach Dolphin View Sea Kayaking (☎0408 738 192; 4hr tours per person $85) operates kayaking safaris and rents kayaks ($65 per half-day). It also runs the **Rainbow Beach Surf School** ($55 per two-hour session).

🛏️ Sleeping

DEBBIE'S PLACE   B&B $
(☎07-5486 3506; www.rainbowbeachaccommodation.com.au; 30 Kurana St; d/ste from $79/89, 3-bedroom apt from $99; ❄) Inside

BAMSE009 ISTOCKPHOTO ©

Don't Miss **Creature Feature: Australia Zoo**

Just north of Beerwah is one of Queensland's, if not Australia's, most famous tourist attractions. **Australia Zoo** (☎07-5494 1134; www.australiazoo.com.au; Steve Irwin Way, Beerwah; adult/child/family $49/29/146; ⊙9am-4.30pm) is a fitting homage to its founder, zany celebrity wildlife enthusiast Steve Irwin. As well as all things slimy and scaly the zoo has an amazing wildlife menagerie complete with a Cambodian-style Tiger Temple, the Asian-themed Elephantasia, as well as the famous Crocoseum. There are macaws, birds of prey, giant tortoises, snakes, otters, camels, and more crocs and critters than you can poke a stick at. Plan to spend a full day at this amazing wildlife park.

Various companies offer tours from Brisbane and the Sunshine Coast. The zoo operates a free courtesy bus from towns along the coast, as well as from the Beerwah train station (bookings essential).

this beautiful timber Queenslander the charming rooms are fully self-contained and have private entrances and veran-dahs. The effervescent Debbie is a mine of information and makes this a cosy home away from home.

ⓘ Getting There & Around

Greyhound Australia (☎1300 473 946; www.greyhound.com.au) and Premier Motor Service (☎13 34 10; www.premierms.com.au) have daily services from Brisbane ($65, five hours), Noosa ($33, 2½ hours) and Hervey Bay ($30, 1½ hours).

Hervey Bay

Once the caravanning capital of Queensland, Hervey Bay has matured from a welfare-by-the-sea escape into a top tourist-dollar destination thanks to its lovely sandy bay (and soothing sea breezes), energetic resort development and huge pods of humpback whales.

Fraser Island

Hervey Bay is great for arranging a 4WD adventure on Fraser Island. Some hos-tels in Hervey Bay put groups together

BOB CHARLTON/LONELY PLANET IMAGES ©

Don't Miss Giants of the Sea: Whale Watching in Hervey Bay

Every year, from August to early November, thousands of humpback whales (*Megaptera novaeangliae*) cruise into Hervey Bay's sheltered waters for a few days before continuing their arduous migration south to the Antarctic.

Boat cruises go from the Urangan Marina out to Platypus Bay and then zip around from pod to pod to find the most active whales. In a very competitive market, vessels offer half-day (four-hour) tours that include breakfast or lunch and cost around $115 for adults and $60 for children. The larger boats run six-hour day trips and the amenities are better, but they take around two hours to reach Platypus Bay. Some recommended operators:

○ **Spirit of Hervey Bay** (☏1800 642 544; www.spiritofherveybay.com; ⏱8.30am & 1.30pm) The largest vessel with the greatest number of passengers. Has an underwater hydrophone and underwater viewing window.

○ **That's Awesome** (☏1800 653 775; www.awesomeadventure.com.au; ⏱7am, 10.30am & 2.30pm) This rigid inflatable boat speeds out to the whales faster than any other vessel. The low deck level means you're nearly eyeball-to-eyeball with the big fish.

○ **MV Tasman Venture** (☏1800 620 322; www.tasmanventure.com.au; ⏱8.30am & 1.30pm) Maximum of 80 passengers; underwater microphones and viewing windows.

○ **Blue Dolphin Marine Tours** (☏07-4124 9600; www.bluedolphintours.com.au; ⏱7.30am) Maximum 20 passengers on a 10m catamaran.

in tag-along tours. A maximum of five vehicles follow a lead vehicle with an experienced guide and driver.

Recommended operators:

Colonial Village YHA (✆ 1800 818 280; www.cvyha.com)

Fraser Roving (✆ 1800 989 811, 07-4125 6386; www.fraserroving.com.au)

Next Backpackers (✆ 07-4125 6600; www. nextbackpackers.com.au)

 **Sleeping**

QUARTERDECKS HARBOUR RETREAT   Apartments $$
(✆ 07-4197 0888; www.quarterdecksretreat. com.au; 80 Moolyyir St, Urangan; 1-/2-/3-bedroom villas $150/195/225; ❄ 🛜 ☁) Backing onto a nature reserve, these excellent villas are stylishly furnished with a private courtyard, all the mod cons you could wish for, and little luxuries like fluffy bathrobes. It's a short stroll to the beach.

BAY B&B   B&B $$
(✆ 07-4125 6919; www.baybedandbreakfast. com.au; 180 Cypress St, Urangan; s $75, d $135-150; ❄ @ ☁) This great-value B&B is run by a friendly, well-travelled Frenchman. Guest rooms are in a comfy annexe out the back, and breakfast is served on an outdoor patio in a tropical garden surrounded by birds and masses of greenery.

ℹ Information

Hervey Bay visitor centre (✆ 1800 649 926; 401 The Esplanade, Torquay; internet per hr $4)

Friendly, privately run booking office with internet access.

Hervey Bay Visitor Information Centre (✆ 1800 811 728; www.herveybaytourism.com.au; cnr Urraween & Maryborough Rds) Helpful tourist office on outskirts of town.

ℹ Getting There & Away

Boat

Boats to Fraser Island leave from River Heads, about 10km south of town, and Urangan Marina; see p154). Most tours leave from Urangan Harbour.

Bus & Train

Long-distance buses depart **Hervey Bay Coach Terminal** (✆ 07-4124 4000; Central Ave, Pialba).

Queensland Rail (✆ 13 12 30; www. queenslandrail.com.au) connects Brisbane with Maryborough West ($74, five hours), where a Trainlink bus ($8) transfers you to Hervey Bay.

ℹ Getting Around

Seega Rent a Car (✆ 07-4125 6008; 463 The Esplanade) has small cars from $40 to $55 a day.

Plenty of rental companies makes Hervey Bay the best place to hire a 4WD for Fraser Island:

Fraser Magic 4WD Hire (✆ 07-4125 6612; www.fraser-magic-4wdhire.com.au; 5 Kruger Crt, Urangan)

Hervey Bay Rent A Car (✆ 07-4194 6626) Also rents out scooters ($30 per day).

Safari 4WD Hire (✆ 1800 689 819; www. safari4wdhire.com.au; 102 Boat Harbour Dr, Pialba)

Tropical North Queensland

Awash with picture-perfect landscapes and vibrant towns, Queensland's tropical north is intriguing. Three unmissable highlights provide a backdrop of natural splendour: the Whitsunday Islands archipelago, the luminous green Daintree Rainforest, and the Great Barrier Reef, with its hyper-coloured coral and clear blue waters.

Also here are some of the country's lesser-known treasures, delivering wow-factor with gusto. You only have to peel back the postcard to find corners seemingly untouched by other visitors – spectacular national parks with tumbling waterfalls, hippie villages and foodie towns, white sandy beaches fringed by kaleidoscopic coral, vibrant and unique Indigenous festivals and jaw-dropping sunsets.

Cairns is a travellers' mecca, a far-flung town on the way up that's surprisingly worldly and cosmopolitan. From here you can launch yourself into the jungle or out onto the reef with ease.

Hardy Reef, Whitsunday Islands (p173)

159

Tropical North Queensland

PAPUA NEW GUINEA

CORAL SEA

Great Barrier Reef

1. Great Barrier Reef
2. Whitsunday Islands
3. Daintree Rainforest
4. Cairns
5. Port Douglas
6. Northern Reef Islands
7. Southern Reef Islands

Cape York
Bamaga

Jardine River National Park

Shelburne Bay

Weipa

Iron Range National Park
Lockhart River

Mungkan Kandju National Park

Coen

Princess Charlotte Bay

Cape Melville National Park
Barrow Point

Lizard Island

Hope Vale
Cooktown

Lakefield National Park

Laura

Pormpuraaw

Cape York Peninsula

Kowanyama

Mitchell River

Staaten River National Park

Aurukun

Wujal Wujal
Cape Tribulation

Daintree National Park

Mossman

Port Douglas

Kuranda
Mareeba
Atherton Tableland
Atherton

Cairns

Fitzroy Island

Frankland Islands

Tropical North Queensland's Highlights

1

Great Barrier Reef

Queensland's Great Barrier Reef (or just GBR or the Reef) is an amazing place: battered by natural and now chronic human impacts, which are causing a continuing decline, the Reef is remarkably resilient and always seems to offer something new.

Need to Know

MAINLAND GATEWAYS Operators in Airlie Beach and Cairns arrange reef visits **BEST TRUE REEF ISLAND RESORTS** Heron Island, Lady Elliot Island, Lizard Island and Green Island

Great Barrier Reef Don't Miss List

BY LEN ZELL, GREAT BARRIER
REEF GUIDE & AUTHOR – WWW.LENZELL.COM

1 THE REEF BY NIGHT

If possible, take an extended dive charter or stay overnight on a sand cay resort or camping ground. An overnight stay allows you to 'feel' some of the many moods of this gigantic system, especially during an atmospheric night dive. During the summer breeding seasons of sea turtles and birds, the fish, worms and corals turn the waters into a thriving 'gamete soup'.

2 GETTING WET

Staff at all snorkelling and diving destinations will help you get wet in the best way for your ability or, best of all, take you way beyond your imagined ability – safely. Seeing an 80-year-old Scottish woman who had never gone beyond knee-deep be led into the water and stay there for more than an hour shows anyone can do it. Once in you won't want to come out!

3 WATERY WILDLIFE ENCOUNTERS

Don't miss the magnificent manta rays at **Lady Elliot Island** (p172), the most southerly of the reef's islands. Tranquil **Heron Island** (p173) is a nesting ground for birds, and green and loggerhead turtles, and features the 'bommie', a fish-filled mini-reef or coral head. Snorkel with minke whales midyear between Cairns and Lizard Island, eyeball massive cod at the Cod Hole on No 10 Ribbon Reef, and dive with sea snakes in the Swain Reefs.

4 THE CHANCE TO EXPLORE

Take a deeper look into this magnificent ecosystem by exploring beyond the well-known cays. Seek out the remote and the less-visited reefs to witness the unexpected, which may include reefs recently smashed by cyclones, devoured by crown-of-thorns sea stars, or reefs in recovery mode. Check out the fascinating wreck of the *Yongala*, between Bowen and Townsville, the outer reefs far off **Cairns** (p182), and the rarely visited islands and reefs north of **Lizard Island** (p196), towards Torres Strait.

Whitsunday Islands

There is no better way to experience the breathtaking Whitsunday Islands than to set sail on an overnight sailing adventure. Get out there and explore the best of the 74 Whitsunday Islands and make the most of your time. Be one with the crystal clear waters and amazing marine life. Below: Daydream Island (p179); Top Right: Yacht race, Hamilton Island (p179); Bottom Right: Whitsunday Island (p179)

Need to Know

BEST PHOTO OPPORTUNITY Take to the air for a fabulous angle on Whitehaven Beach **Best snorkelling** Hook and Whitsunday Islands **For further coverage,** see p173.

Whitsunday Islands Don't Miss List

BY MICHAEL O'CONNOR, WHITSUNDAY BOOKINGS MANAGER & SKYDIVING & SCUBA DIVING INSTRUCTOR

1 THE WHITSUNDAY NGARO SEA TRAIL

Follow in the footsteps of the Ngaro people, the traditional owners of the Whitsunday area, and undertake a journey through a region of unsurpassed natural beauty and rich cultural history. Blending seaways with kayaking and a range of walks, the Whitsunday Ngaro Sea Trail highlights many iconic features that have made the area famous. Walk pure white sands, sail turquoise waters, see ancient rock art, rugged headlands, dry rainforest and rolling grasslands, and experience breathtaking views.

2 BAIT REEF

Having been a dive instructor for over 15 years and diving my way around the world, Bait Reef is still one of my favourite dive sites. It is one of the most pristine and spectacular diving sites on the Great Barrier Reef and is classed as a Special Management Area. Limited numbers of boats are allowed to visit Bait Reef and no fishing is allowed. The best dive sites are Manta Ray Drop Off, The Stepping Stones and Paradise Lagoon.

3 CRAYFISH BEACH, HOOK ISLAND

Crayfish is my favourite camping getaway in the Whitsundays. It is at the top of **Hook Island** (p179) and offers fantastic snorkelling, a beautiful beach and a secluded camp site that takes a maximum of 13 people. If you want a few days away from the rat race this is the place.

4 THE ESPLANADE, AIRLIE BEACH

The Esplanade at **Airlie Beach** (p174) is a great spot to just relax and watch people pass by while enjoying great food and drinks at one of the many restaurants. The Airlie Beach markets are at the end of the Esplanade every Saturday morning, and Sunday sessions are a great way to end the week: from around 2pm there's live music on the beachfront opposite the Esplanade restaurants.

Daintree Rainforest

Everyone in Australia knows its name, but the Daintree (p189) still suffers from an identity crisis: is it a village? Is it a national park? A river? A World Heritage area? It's actually all four, but mostly it's a rainforest – an amazing, remote tropical wilderness with incredible biodiversity and more precious jungle-meets-sea beaches than you have lazy afternoons to spare.

Port Douglas

Keep going 70km north from Cairns and you'll hit Port Douglas (p191), a well-heeled tourist hub that comes as an unexpected delight. Hospitality industry standards are sky-high here, with first-rate resorts accompanying some awesome restaurants and hip bars and pubs. It's also a great place from which to launch your Daintree Rainforest and Great Barrier Reef excursions.

Cairns

Cairns (p182) is the kind of regional outpost where, 30 years ago, you might have feared to tread if you were anyone other than a fisherman or a sugarcane farmer. But these days it's a lively tourist hotspot with multicultural eateries, some great places to stay and easy access to Tropical North Queensland's iconic sights: the Daintree Rainforest and the Great Barrier Reef.

Northern Reef Islands

The Great Barrier Reef is visible from space! It's no wonder that down here on earth it just seems to keep stretching northwards, studded by some gorgeous islands off Cairns (p188): Green Island, Fitzroy Island and the Frankland Islands offer brilliant snorkelling, diving and beach-bumming. Further north, Lizard Island (p196) sees less visitors – perfect for castaway fantasies-come-true. Green Island

Southern Reef Islands

The photogenic Whitsunday Islands get all the good press, but along the Great Barrier Reef's southern reaches off the Capricorn Coast there are some other fabulous isles (p172) that have all the hallmarks without the hype. Check out Lady Elliot Island and Lady Musgrave Island for some magical dive sites, and secluded Heron Island for a pristine coral encounter. Lady Elliot Island

Tropical North Queensland's Best...

Island Escapes

o **Whitsunday Island** (p179) Lovely enough to lend its name to the surrounding archipelago.

o **Green Island** (p188) Day trippers from Cairns come for the beaches and snorkelling, or you can opt for a luxury overnight stay.

o **Hamilton Island** (p179) Not for Robinson Crusoes, this luxury resort has abundant activities and entertainment options.

o **Lizard Island** (p196) Bask like a lizard atop a rock on this remote and un-touristed isle.

Diving & Snorkelling

o **Green Island** (p188) Quick and easy access from Cairns with super offshore snorkelling.

o **Hook Island** (p179) Superb access to coral coupled with fabulous camping or simple budget digs.

o **Frankland Islands National Park** (p189) Fabulous coral reef surrounds these uninhabited national park islands off Cairns.

Tropical Wilds

o **Daintree Rainforest** (p189) Crocodiles, rivers, swamps, palm-fringed beaches...it's all here.

o **Great Barrier Reef** (p172) OK, so it's underwater, but what a wild place!

o **Cape Tribulation** (p197) Jungle-meets-sea photogenics north of Port Douglas.

Need to Know

Urban Delights

○ **Port Douglas** (p191) Cool in the tropical heat, 'Port' is a classy town with superior restaurants, cafes and bars.

○ **Cairns** (p182) The Big Smoke in Tropical North Queensland, Cairns delivers plenty of city-size comforts.

○ **Mission Beach** (p180) Low-key in the best possible way, Mission Beach is the perfect little tropical town.

○ **Airlie Beach** (p174) Party hard in Airlie, then recover on the Whitsunday Islands.

○ **ADVANCE PLANNING**

○ **One month before** Organise internal flights and resort accommodation.

○ **Two weeks before** Book a seat (and a snorkel) on a Great Barrier Reef tour from Cairns or Port Douglas.

○ **One week before** Book a table at a top Port Douglas eatery.

RESOURCES

○ **Queensland Holidays** (www.queenslandholidays. com.au) Great resource for planning your trip.

○ **Tourism Queensland** (www.tq.com.au) Government-run body responsible for promoting Queensland.

○ **Tourism Tropical North Queensland** (www.ttnq.org. au) Helpful office for TNQ.

○ **Sunlover Holidays** (www.sunloverholidays.com. au) Book accommodation and tours.

○ **Royal Automobile Club of Queensland** (RACQ; www.racq.com. au) Driving info and emergency roadside assistance.

GETTING AROUND

○ **Walk** The esplanades of Cairns and Airlie Beach.

○ **Train** Ride the *Tilt Train* to Cairns, and from there the scenic railway to Kuranda.

○ **Fast Cat** To the reef and islands on superfast catamarans.

○ **Drive** Through the Atherton Tableland.

BE FOREWARNED

○ **Box jellyfish** Appear in coastal waters north of Agnes Water from October to April and are potentially deadly.

○ **Saltwater crocodiles** A real danger in Tropical North Queensland and can be found in estuaries, creeks and rivers. Observe signs.

Left: Mossman Gorge, Daintree Rainforest
Above: Boulder coral, Great Barrier Reef

Tropical North Queensland Itineraries

Queensland's far north is a remarkable place with a tropical pace. Change down a gear or two, slip into beach (or reef) mode and enjoy the good life under the sun.

3 DAYS

PORT DOUGLAS TO CAIRNS
Leisure Stations

An hour or so north of Cairns is a gem worth discovering: **(1) Port Douglas** is the kind of town where you plan to spend the night but end up staying a week. The lure here is quality accommodation, great restaurants, relaxed but still-stylish bars and pubs (a rarity in these latitudes), and access to both the Daintree Rainforest and Great Barrier Reef. Spend a day unwinding then sign up for a reef snorkelling trip or a Daintree excursion (look for cassowaries).

The next day, point yourself south and travel along the scenic inland road (Hwy 1), through the **(2) Atherton Tablelands**, to **(3) Mission Beach**. Mission Beach itself has instant appeal: a quiet little seaside town with just enough cafes and restaurants to keep your pulse ticking over.

After a night in Mission Beach, track north again to **(4) Cairns**, a city where you could easily blow your budget on fine food, shopping or daiquiris by the pool. There are some great galleries here too, plus the educational Indigenous-owned Tjapukai Cultural Park, and day-trips and activities aplenty.

Top Left: Mission Beach (p180); **Top Right:** Kuranda Scenic Railway (p190)

5 DAYS

CAIRNS TO HAMILTON ISLAND

Reef Madness

Kick off this coral-coloured escapade in the hub of all things Great Barrier Reef, the tropical town of **(1) Cairns**. Spend a day splashing around in the lagoon and hitting the bars and restaurants. And no visit to Cairns is complete without a boat ride to the nearby coral-fringed islands – **(2) Green Island** is our pick – or a snorkelling day-trip to the pristine outer reef. If you didn't pack your sea legs, take the scenic railway out to explore the hippie markets and Australian Butterfly Sanctuary at **(3) Kuranda** in the hinterland.

From Cairns head down to **(4) Airlie Beach**, which offers plenty of accommodation, water-based activities and excuses to drink beer. It's the logical base for exploring the sandy **(5) Whitsunday Islands** archipelago. From here you can ferry or fly directly to **(6) Hamilton Island**, where the resort lifestyle grips you as soon as you step off the plane. Spend a day fooling around with watercraft or lazing by the pool, then explore other islands in the group: shoot for Whitsunday Island, with dazzling Whitehaven Beach, or the laid-back and naturally beautiful Hook or South Molle Islands.

Discover Tropical North Queensland

Newly hatched green turtle, Lady Elliot Island
PHOTOGRAPHER: BOB CHARLTON/LONELY PLANET IMAGES ©

GREAT BARRIER REEF
Southern Reef Islands

More and more savvy travellers are doing their Great Barrier Reef thing here – and for good reason. These sparkling coral cays are as good as it gets in Australia, without nearly the same crowds, storms or miles to travel.

Tours to the islands (from $175) stop at a number of beaches and snorkelling spots and include lunch.

Lady Elliot Island

On the southern frontier of the Great Barrier Reef, Lady Elliot is a 40-hectare vegetated coral cay popular with divers, snorkellers and nesting sea turtles. Divers can walk straight off the beach to explore an ocean bed of ship-wrecks, coral gardens, bommies (coral pinnacles or outcroppings) and blowholes, and abundant marine life including barracuda, giant manta rays and harmless leopard sharks.

Lady Elliot Island is not a national park, and camping is not allowed. Your only option is the low-key **Lady Elliot Island Resort** (☎1800 072 200; www.ladyelliot.com.au; per person $160-326).

Most resort guests travel to the island on light aircraft.Seair flies guests in from Bundaberg and Hervey Bay for $254/136 per adult/child return; book through the resort. Day trippers can visit the island on cruises from Bundaberg and Hervey Bay for $300/170 including tours and activities, lunch and snorkelling gear.

Lady Musgrave Island

Wannabe castaways look no further – this is the perfect desert island! This tiny 15-hectare cay 100km north-east of Bundaberg sits on the western rim of a stunning, turquoise-blue reef lagoon renowned for its safe swimming, snorkelling and diving. Birds nest from October to April, green turtles from November to February.

Day trips to Lady Musgrave depart from the Town of 1770 marina (see p192).

Heron Island

With the underwater reef world accessible directly from the beach, Heron Island is famed for scuba diving and snorkelling, although you'll need a fair amount of cash to visit.

Heron Island Resort (☏ 07-4972 9055, 1800 737 678; www.heronisland.com; s/d incl buffet breakfast from $399/479) has comfortable accommodation suited to families and couples; the Point Suites have the best views. Meal packages are extra, and guests will pay $200/100 per adult/child for launch transfer, or $440/270 for helicopter transfer. Both are from Gladstone.

Agnes Water & Town of 1770

Surrounded by national parks, sandy beaches and the blue Pacific, the twin coastal towns of Agnes Water and Town of 1770 are among Queensland's most appealing seaside destinations. The tiny settlement of Agnes Water has a lovely white-sand beach, the east coast's most northerly surf beach, while the even tinier Town of 1770 (little more than a marina!) marks Captain Cook's first landing in Queensland.

Activities

The action around here happens on and in the water. Agnes Water is Queensland's northernmost **surf beach**. Learn to surf on the gentle breaks of the main beach with the highly acclaimed **Reef 2 Beach Surf School** (☏ 07-4974 9072; www.reef2beachsurf.com; 1/10 Round Hill Rd, Agnes Water).

1770 Liquid Adventures (☏ 0428 956 630; www.1770liquidadventures.com.au; tours $40) runs a spectacular twilight kayak

tour. **Dive 1770** (☏ 07-4974 9359; www.dive1770.com) offers PADI courses (from $250) and Great Barrier Reef dives (from $30). **1770 Underwater Sea Adventures** (☏ 1300 553 889; www.1770underseaadventures.com.au) also offers dive courses, and Great Barrier Reef and wreck dives.

Tours

LADY MUSGRAVE CRUISES   Cruises
(☏ 07-4974 9077; www.1770reefcruises.com; Captain Cook Dr, Town of 1770; adult/child $175/85) Has excellent day trips to Lady Musgrave Island aboard the *Spirit of 1770*. Trips include snorkelling, fishing gear, coral viewing in a semisubmersible, lunch and snacks.

🛏 Sleeping

SANDCASTLES 1770 MOTEL & RESORT   Motel, Resort $$
(☏ 07-4974 9428; www.sandcastles1770.com.au; 1 Grahame Colyer Dr, Agnes Water; motel r from $120, villas/beach-home apt from $160-650; ❄ @ ➿) Set on 4 hectares of landscaped gardens and subtropical vegetation, Sandcastles has a mix of motel-style rooms (from $90) luxury beach-home apartments and airy Balinese-themed villas.

Beach Shacks   Apartments $$
(☏ 07-4974 9463; www.1770beachshacks.com; 578 Captain Cook Dr, Town of 1770; d from $178) These delightful self-contained tropical 'shacks' are decorated in timber, cane and bamboo. They offer grand ocean views just a minute's walk from the water.

ℹ Getting There & Away

Only one of several daily **Greyhound** (☏ 13 20 30; www.greyhound.com.au) buses detours off the Bruce Hwy to Agnes Water; the direct bus from Bundaberg ($24, 1½ hours) arrives opposite Cool Bananas at 6.10pm. Others, including **Premier Motor Service** (☏ 13 34 10; www.premierms.com.au), drop passengers at Fingerboard Rd.

Whitsunday Islands

The Whitsunday group of islands off the north-eastern Queensland coast is, as the cliché goes, a tropical paradise. Sheltered

If You Like…
Watching Wildlife

If you like peering at technicoloured fish on the Great Barrier Reef (p172), you might want to hunt down some of these other Tropical North Queensland critters:

1 CROCODILES IN THE DAINTREE RIVER
Queensland is the happy home of the world's largest crocodile species, the estuarine (or saltwater) crocodile. Photograph them safely on a cruise along the Daintree River.

2 CASSOWARIES AROUND MISSION BEACH
The captivating cassowary (a tropical ostrich!) lives in Queensland's northern rainforests. Look for them around Mission Beach.

3 SEA TURTLES ON LADY ELLIOT ISLAND
Sea turtles drag themselves onto the sandy shores of Lady Elliot Island in the southern reaches of the Great Barrier Reef.

4 KOALAS ON MAGNETIC ISLAND
Koalas live along Australia's entire eastern seaboard: in Queensland you can often spot them on Magnetic Island off Townsville.

by the Great Barrier Reef, the waters are perfect for sailing.

Only seven of the islands have tourist resorts – catering to every budget and whim from the basic accommodation at Hook Island to the exclusive luxury of Hayman Island.

ⓘ Getting There & Around

The two main airports for the Whitsundays are at Hamilton Island and Proserpine, 36km southwest of Airlie Beach. Virgin Australia (☎13 67 89; www.virginaustralia.com) and Jetstar (☎13 15 38; www.jetstar.com.au) connect Hamilton Island with Brisbane, Sydney and Melbourne. QantasLink (☎13 13 13; www.qantas.com.au) flies there from Cairns.

Transfers between Abel Point Marina and Daydream, Long and South Molle Islands are provided by Cruise Whitsundays (☎07-4946 4662; www.cruisewhitsundays.com; adult/child 1 way $30/20). It also runs airport transfers from Abel Point Marina to Hamilton Island. Transfers between Shute Harbour and Hamilton Island are provided by Fantasea (☎07-946 5111; www.fantasea.com.au; adult/child 1 way $49/27).

Airlie Beach

Tacky and tremendous, exploited and exploitative, Airlie Beach is not so much a stepping-off point for the Whitsunday Islands as a high-voltage launching pad! Airlie is the kind of town where humanity celebrates its close proximity to natural beauty by partying very hard, fast and frequently.

 Activities

Sailing is the leisure activity of choice here, in all its nautical variations. For **sailing tours** see p176 but if you've got salt water in your veins, a **bareboat charter** might be more your style. Expect to pay between $500 to $800 a day in the high season (September to January) for a yacht that will comfortably sleep four to six people.

There are a number of bareboat charter companies around Airlie Beach:

Charter Yachts Australia Sailing Charters
(☎1800 639 520; www.cya.com.au; Abel Point Marina)

Whitsunday Escape Sailing Charters
(☎1800 075 145; www.whitsundayescape.com; Abel Point Marina)

Whitsunday Rent A Yacht Sailing Charters
(☎1800 075 000; www.rentayacht.com.au; Trinity Jetty, Shute Harbour)

These are also a great place to learn to sail:

Whitsunday Marine Academy Sailing Lessons
(☎1800 810 116; www.explorewhitsundays.com; 4 The Esplanade) Run by Explore Whitsundays.

Whitsunday Sailing Club Sailing Lessons
(☎07-4946 6138; Airlie Point)

Whitsunday Coast

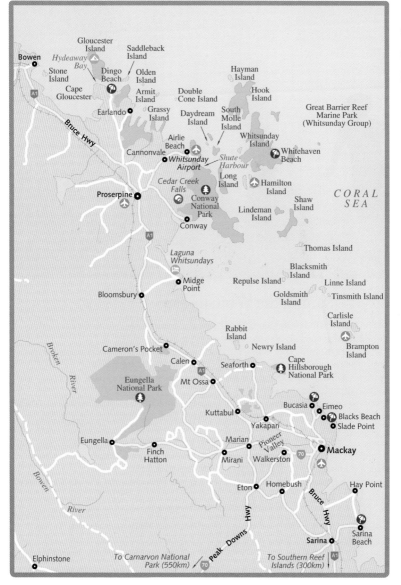

Whitsunday Dive Adventures Diving, Snorkelling
(☎07-4948 1239; www.adventuredivers.com.au; 303 Shute Harbour Rd) Offers a range of instruction, including open-water PADI-certified dive courses ($565). Half-day dive trips cost $175. Many boat cruises.

Salty Dog Sea Kayaking Kayaking
(☎07-4946 1388; www.saltydog.com.au; half-/full-day trips $70/125) Offers guided full-day

175

TIM BARKER/LONELY PLANET IMAGES ©

Don't Miss **Sailing the Whitsundays**

Dream of an island holiday and alongside the swaying palms, sand-fringed bays, and calm blue seas there's usually a white sailboat skimming lightly across the water. In the Whitsundays it isn't hard to put yourself in the picture but with the plethora of charters, tours, and specials on offer, deciding how to go about it can be confusing.

Aside from day trips, most overnight sailing packages are for three days/two nights or two days/two nights.

Most vessels offer snorkelling on the fringing reefs (the reefs around the islands). Check if snorkel equipment, stinger suits and reef taxes are included in the package. Diving usually costs extra.

Once you've decided what suits, book at one of the many booking agencies in town such as **Whitsundays Central Reservation Centre** (☏1800 677 119; www.airliebeach.com; 259 Shute Harbour Rd) or a management company such as **Whitsunday Sailing Adventures** (☏07-4940 2000; www.whitsundaysailing.com; Shute Harbour Rd) or **Explore Whitsundays** (☏07-4946 4999; www. explorewhitsundays.com; 4 The Esplanade).

Some of the recommended sailing trips are listed below:

○ **Camira** (day trip $165) This good value day-trip includes Whitehaven Beach, snorkelling, morning and afternoon tea, a barbecue lunch, and all refreshments (including wine and beer).

○ **Maxi Action Ragamuffin** (day trip $156) Choose between a cruise to Whitehaven Beach (Thu & Sun) or snorkelling at Blue Pearl Bay (Mon, Wed, Fri & Sat).

○ **Derwent Hunter** (3-day/2-night trip from $590) A very popular sailing safari on a timber gaffe-rigged schooner. Good for couples and those wanting to experience nature and the elements.

Detour:
Carnarvon National Park

One of the highlights of all Queensland, **Carnarvon Gorge** is a dramatic rendition of Australian natural beauty. The 30km-long, 200m-high gorge was carved out over millions of years by Carnarvon Creek and its tributaries twisting through soft sedimentary rock. What was left behind is a lush, other-worldly oasis, where life flourished, shielded from the stark terrain.

You'll find giant cycads, king ferns, river oaks, flooded gums, cabbage palms, deep pools and platypuses in the creek. The area was made a national park in 1932 after defeated farmers forfeited their pastoral lease.

The entrance road leads to an **information centre** (📞 07-4984 4505; 🕒 8-10am & 3-5pm) and scenic picnic ground. The main walking track also starts here, following Carnarvon Creek through the gorge, with detours to various points of interest. These include the **Moss Garden** (3.6km from the picnic area), **Ward's Canyon** (4.8km), the **Art Gallery** (5.6km) and **Cathedral Cave** (9.3km).

tours and kayak rental ($50/60 per half-/full day), plus longer kayak/camping missions (the six-day challenge costs $1500). It's a charming and healthy way to see the islands.

Skydive Airlie Beach Skydiving
(📞 07-4946 9115; www.skydiveairliebeach.com. au) Tandem skydives from $249.

Air Whitsunday Seaplanes Scenic Flights
(📞 07-4946 9111; www.airwhitsunday.com. au) Offers three-hour Reef Adventures (adult/ child $315/280), a Whitehaven experience ($240/210) and the signature four-hour Panorama Tour ($425/390) where you fly to Hardy Lagoon to snorkel or ride a semi-submersible then fly to Whitehaven Beach for a picnic lunch. It also offers day trips to exclusive Hayman Island ($195).

Other operators:

HeliReef Scenic Flights
(📞 07-4946 9102; www.avta.com.au) Helicopter flights to the reef (from $129), day trips to Hayman Island ($399) and a picnic lunch on Whitehaven Beach ($399).

Aviation Adventures Scenic Flights
(📞 07-4946 9988; www.av8.com.au) Helicopter flights ranging from scenic island trips ($99) to picnic rendezvous ($199) and reef adventures ($649).

Tours

Voyager 3 Island Cruise Boat
(📞 07-4946 5255; www.wiac.com.au; adult/child $140/80) A good-value day cruise that includes snorkelling at Hook Island, beachcombing and swimming at Whitehaven Beach, and checking out Daydream Island.

Ocean Rafting Speed Boat
(📞 07-4946 6848; www.oceanrafting.com; adult/ child/family $120/78/360) Swim at Whitehaven Beach, view Aboriginal cave paintings at Nara Inlet and snorkel the reef at Mantaray Bay or Border Island.

🛏 Sleeping

WATER'S EDGE RESORT Apartments $$$
(📞 07-4948 4300; www.watersedgewhitsun days.com.au; 4 Golden Orchid Dr; 1-bedroom apt $210-260, 2-bedroom apt $275-345; ❄ 🏊) The reception area immediately tells you that you're on holiday. Its open-air plan and gently revolving ceiling fans stir the languid, tropical heat. In the rooms, soft colours, cane headboards and shutters sealing off the bedroom from the living space immediately put your mind at ease.

WATERVIEW Apartments $$
(📞 07-4948 1748; www.waterviewairliebeach. com.au; 42 Airlie Cres; studios/1-bedroom units

177

Detour:
Conway National Park

The mountains of this national park and the Whitsunday Islands are part of the same coastal mountain range. Rising sea levels following the last ice age flooded the lower valleys, leaving only the highest peaks as islands, now cut off from the mainland.

The road from Airlie Beach to Shute Harbour passes through the northern section of the park. Several **walking trails** start from near the picnic and day-use area. About 1km past the day-use area, there's a 2.4km walk up to the **Mt Rooper lookout**, which provides good views of the Whitsunday Passage and islands. Further along the main road, towards Coral Point (before Shute Harbour), there's a 1km track leading down to **Coral Beach** and **The Beak lookout**.

To reach the beautiful **Cedar Creek Falls**, turn off the Proserpine–Airlie Beach road onto Conway Rd, 18km south-west of Airlie Beach. It's then about 15km to the falls; the roads are well signposted.

from $135/149; ❄ 📶) An excellent choice for location and comfort, this boutique accommodation overlooks the main street and has gorgeous views of the bay. The rooms are modern, airy and spacious and have kitchenettes for self-caterers.

WHITSUNDAY ORGANIC B&B
B&B $$
(☎07-4946 7151; www.whitsundaybb.com. au; 8 Lamond St; s/d $155/210) Rooms are comfortable, but it's the organic garden walk and the orgasmic three-course organic breakfasts (nonguests $22.50) that everyone comes here for. You can book a healing massage, meditate in the garden teepee, or just indulge in all things organic.

Eating

FISH D'VINE
Seafood $$
(☎07-4948 0088; 303 Shute Harbour Rd; mains $10-25; ☉lunch & dinner) Of course, rum and fish – what a perfect combination! But somehow this quirky concept has taken off like a storm. Seafood dishes will keep you happy, and the selection of over 100 different rums is bound to unleash your inner pirate.

ALAIN'S RESTAURANT
French $$$
(☎07-4946 5464; 44 Coral Esplanade, Cannonvale; mains $25-35; ☉dinner Thu-Sat) For fine dining this intimate French restaurant opposite Cannonvale beach is first-rate. White linen, silverware and soft candle-light add up to romance. Indulge in the six-course table d'hote menu and you'll have time to ask about that Citroën parked in the corner.

WATERLINE
Modern Australian $$
(☎07-4948 1023; 1 Shingley Dr; mains $20-30; ☉lunch & dinner Wed-Sun, breakfast Sun) With stunning views over the marina, this restaurant at Shingley Beach Resort has one of the best locations for waterfront dining. The decor is tropical beach-chic. Recommended by the locals for its good service, great food and consistent quality.

❶ Getting There & Around

The closest major airports are at Proserpine and on Hamilton Island. The small Whitsunday Airport (☎07-4946 9933) is about 6km southeast of town; see p174 for flight details.

Greyhound (☎13 20 30; www.greyhound. com.au) and Premier Motor Service (☎13 34 10; www.premierms.com.au) have bus connections to Brisbane ($230, 19 hours), Mackay ($38, two hours), Townsville ($58, 4½ hours) and Cairns ($140, 11 hours).

South Molle Island

Lovers of birds and long, sandy beaches will enjoy the largest of the Molle archipelago. Nearly 15km of splendid walking tracks traverse this mountainous 4-sq-km island; the highest point is Mt Jeffreys (198m), but the climb up Spion Kop is also worthwhile.

The **Adventure Island Resort** (☏1800 464 444; www.koalaadventures.com.au; dm from $49-100, d $180-240; ✱ @ ⚊) is far from luxurious, with basic motel-style rooms and beachfront bungalows. There's a three-night minimum stay.

Daydream Island

Daydream Island is more manufactured than dreamy, but at just 1km long and a 15-minute ferry ride from Shute Harbour, it's a good compromise for busy families.

Daydream Island Resort & Spa (☏1800 075 040; www.daydreamisland.com; 3-night packages $900-2500; ✱ 🛜 ⚊) is the tackier side of the Whitsundays, with five grades of accommodation. Still, it's efficiently operated and set in beautifully landscaped tropical gardens.

Hook Island

The second largest of the Whitsundays, the 53-sq-km Hook Island is predominantly national park and rises to 450m at Hook Peak. There are a number of good beaches dotted around the island, and Hook boasts some of the best diving and snorkelling locations in the Whitsundays.

Those who don't mind roughing it book in at the **Hook Island Wilderness Resort** (☏07-4946 9380; www.hookislandresort.com; campsites per person $20, d with/without bathroom $120/100; ✱ ⚊), a battered place with basic quarters and a licensed **restaurant** (mains $16 to $27) that serves seafood, steak and pasta.

Whitsunday Island

Whitehaven Beach, on Whitsunday Island, is a pristine 7km-long stretch of dazzling white sand bounded by lush tropical vegetation and a brilliant blue sea. There's excellent snorkelling from its southern end. Whitehaven is one of Australia's most beautiful beaches.

Hamilton Island

Hamilton Island can come as quite a shock for the first-time visitor. Swarms of people and heavy development make

The Cassowary

The flightless cassowary is as tall as a grown man, has three toes, a blue-and-purple head, red wattles (fleshy lobes hanging from its neck), a helmet-like horn and unusual black feathers, which look more like ratty hair. The Australian cassowary is also known as the southern cassowary, though it's only found in the north of Queensland.

The cassowary is an endangered species; there are less than 1000 left. Its biggest threat is loss of habitat, and eggs and chicks are vulnerable to dogs and wild pigs. A number of birds are also hit by cars: heed road signs warning drivers to be cassowary-aware. You're most likely to see cassowaries around Mission Beach and the Cape Tribulation section of the Daintree National Park.

Next to the Mission Beach visitor centre, there are cassowary-conservation displays at the **Wet Tropics Environment Centre** (☏07-4068 7197; www.wettropics.gov.au; Porter Promenade, Mission Beach; ◷10am-4pm), which is staffed by volunteers from the **Community for Cassowary & Coastal Conservation** (C4; www.cassowaryconservation.asn.au).

Hamilton seem like a busy town rather than a resort island. Although this is not everyone's idea of a perfect getaway, it's hard not to be impressed by the sheer range of accommodation options, bars restaurants and activities.

Hamilton Island Resort (☎ 07-4946 9999; www.hamiltonisland.com.au; d from $314; ❄ @ 🛜 🏊) has extensive options, including bungalows, luxury villas, plush hotel rooms and self-contained apartments.

Hamilton is a ready-made day trip from Shute Harbour, and you can use some of the resort's facilities; see p174 for transport details.

Mission Beach

Less than 30km east of the Bruce Hwy's rolling sugar-cane and banana plantations, the hamlets that make up greater Mission Beach are hidden among World Heritage rainforest.

Fanning out around Mission are picturesque walking tracks, which are fine places to see wildlife, including cassowaries – in fact Australia's highest density of cassowaries (around 40) roam the surrounding rainforests.

Mangroves, Mission Beach

◉ Sights & Activities

Adrenaline junkies flock to Mission Beach for extreme and water-based sports, including white-water rafting on the nearby Tully River (see the boxed text, p181). And, if you've got your own board, Bingil Bay is one of the rare spots inside the reef where it's possible to **surf**, with small but consistent swells of around 1m.

The **walking** in the area is superb. The visitor centre stocks walking guides detailing trails in the area.

Jump the Beach Skydiving
(☎ 1800 444 568; www.jumpthebeach.com. au; 9000/11,000/14,000ft tandem dives $249/310/334)

Skydive Mission Beach Skydiving
(☎ 1800 800 840; www.skydivemissionbeach. com; 9000/11,000/14,000ft tandem dives $249/310/334)

Spirit of the Rainforest Rainforest Trips
(☎ 07-4088 9161; www.echoadventure.com.au; 4-hr tours adult/child $80/60; ⏱ Tue, Thu & Sat) Local Aboriginal guides offer a unique insight into the ancient rainforest around Mission Beach.

LAWRIE WILLIAMS/LONELY PLANET IMAGES ©

Tully River Rafting

The Tully River provides thrilling white water year-round thanks to all that rain and the river's hydroelectric floodgates. Rafting trips are timed to coincide with the daily release of the floodgates, resulting in grade four rapids, with stunning rainforest scenery as a backdrop.

Day trips with **Raging Thunder Adventures** (07-4030 7990; www.ragingthunder. com.au/rafting.asp; standard trips $185, 'xtreme' trips $215) or **R'n'R White Water Rafting** (07-4041 9444; www.raft.com.au; trips $185) include a BBQ lunch and transport from Tully or nearby Mission Beach. It only costs an extra $10 for transfers from Cairns and as far north as Palm Cove, but you'll save yourself several tedious hours' return bus ride if you pick up a trip here.

Coral Sea Kayaking   Kayaking
(07-4068 9154; www.coralseakayaking.com; half/full day $77/128) To Dunk Island.

Fishin' Mission   Fishing
(07-4088 6121; www.fishinmission.com.au; half/full day $130/190) Island or reef fishing trips.

Sejala on the Beach   Cabins $$$
(07-4088 6699; http://missionbeachholidays. com.au/sejala; 26 Pacific Pde; d $239; ❄ 🐾) Three huts (go for one of the two facing the beach) with rainforest showers, decks with private BBQs and loads of character.

 **Sleeping**

MISSION BEACH

ECOVILLAGE   Cabins $$
(07-4068 7534; www.ecovillage.com.au; Clump Point Rd; d $145-190; ❄ 🛜 🐾) It's not eco-certified, but with its own banana and lime trees scattered around its gardens and a direct path through the rainforest to the beach, this 'ecovillage' makes the most of its environment. Higher-priced bungalows have spas, and there's a free-form pool and **restaurant** (mains $19; ⏱dinner Tue-Sat).

CASTAWAYS RESORT & SPA   Resort $$$
(1800 079 002; www.castaways.com.au; Pacific Pde; d $145-185, 1-/2-bedroom units $205/295; ❄ @ 🛜 🐾) Castaways' cheapest rooms don't have balconies, so it's worth splashing out a bit more for one of the 'Coral Sea' rooms, with extended deck and day bed. Even the units are small, but perks include two elongated pools, a luxurious **spa** (www.driftspa.com.au) and live entertainment at the **bar-restaurant** (mains $12-32; ⏱breakfast, lunch & dinner).

 Eating

NEW DELI   Cafe, Deli $
(shop 1, 47 Porter Promenade; mains $7.50-15.50; ⏱9.30am-6pm Sun-Fri; 🥗) Tuck into blue-berry pancakes or smoked salmon and brie bagels for breakfast, or zucchini and feta tart for lunch. Or stock up on goodies for a gourmet picnic.

SHRUBBERY TAVERNA   Seafood $$
(David St; mains $19-36; ⏱5pm-late Wed, noon-late Thu-Sun) Shaded by bamboo gardens, this local hang-out is great for seafood tapas, salt and pepper prawns and creamy seafood chowder. Live music on Friday night and Sunday afternoon.

❶ Getting There & Around

Greyhound Australia (1300 473 946; www. greyhound.com.au) and Premier (13 34 10; www.premierms.com.au) buses stop in Wongaling Beach next to the giant 'big cassowary'; fares with Greyhound/Premier are $21/19 to Cairns, $40/46 to Townsville. Sun Palm (07-4087 2900; www. sunpalmtransport.com) has daily services to Cairns and Cairns Airport ($49) as well as Innisfail and Tully.

Cairns

Cairns has come a long way from struggling cane town to international resort city.

For many visitors this is the end of the line on the east-coast jaunt (or the start for those flying into Cairns' international airport), and the city is awash with bars and nightclubs, as well as accommodation and eateries in all price ranges.

⊙ Sights

CAIRNS FORESHORE & LAGOON
Swimming, Walking

In the absence of a beach, sunbathers flock around Cairns' shallow but spectacular saltwater swimming **lagoon** (admission free; ⊙6am-10pm Thu-Tue, noon-10pm Wed) on the city's reclaimed foreshore.

FLECKER BOTANIC GARDENS
Botanic Gardens

(www.cairns.qld.gov.au; Collins Ave, Edge Hill; ⊙7.30am-5.30pm Mon-Fri, 8.30am-5.30pm Sat & Sun) These beautiful tropical gardens are an explosion of greenery and rainforest plants. Free guided walks depart Tuesday and Thursday at 10am and 1pm from the **information centre** (⊙8.30am-5pm Mon-Fri). There's an excellent **cafe (mains $14-19;** ⊙7am-4.30pm) here.

CAIRNS REGIONAL GALLERY
Gallery

(www.cairnsregionalgallery.com.au; cnr Abbott & Shields Sts; adult/child under 16 $5/free; ⊙10am-5pm Mon-Sat, 1-5pm Sun) In a colonnaded 1936-built heritage building, Cairns' acclaimed regional gallery hosts exhibitions reflecting the consciousness of the tropical north region, with an emphasis on local and Indigenous works.

TJAPUKAI CULTURAL PARK
Cultural Centre

(⊿07-4042 9900; www.tjapukai.com.au; Kamerunga Rd, Smithfield; adult/child $35/17.50; ⊙9am-5pm) Allow at least three hours at this Indigenous-owned cultural extravaganza, incorporating the Creation Theatre, which tells the story of creation using

Left: Cairns foreshore promenade; **Below:** Flecker Botanic Gardens
PHOTOGRAPHERS: (LEFT) LINDSAY BROWN/LONELY PLANET IMAGES ©; (BELOW) RICHARD I'ANSON/LONELY PLANET IMAGES ©

giant holograms and actors, a dance theatre and a gallery, as well as boomerang- and spear-throwing demonstrations and turtle-spotting during a canoe ride on the lake.

REEF TEACH Interpretive Centre
(☎07-4031 7794; http://reefteach.wordpress.com; 2nd fl, Main Street Arcade, 85 Lake St; adult/child $15/8; ⏰lectures 6.30-8.30pm Tue-Sat) Before heading out to the reef, take your knowledge to greater depths at this excellent and informative centre, where marine experts explain how to identify specific types of coral and fish and how to treat the reef with respect.

Sleeping

FLORIANA GUESTHOUSE Guesthouse $$
(☎07-4051 7886; www.florianaguesthouse.com; 183 The Esplanade; s $69, d $79-120; ❄@📶🏊) Run by charismatic jazz musician Maggie, Cairns-of-old still exists at this old-fashioned guesthouse, which retains its original polished floorboards and art deco fittings. The swirling staircase leads to 10 individually decorated rooms, some with bay windows and window seats, others with balconies.

SHANGRI-LA Hotel $$$
(☎07-4031 1411; www.shangri-la.com; Pierpoint Rd; r from $270; ❄@📶🏊) In an unbeatable waterfront setting, towering over the marina, Shangri-La is Cairns' top hotel, a super-swish five-star that ticks all the boxes for location, views, facilities (including a gym and pool bar) and attentive service. The Horizon Club rooms are top notch.

REEF PALMS Apartments $$
(☎1800 815 421; www.reefpalms.com.au; 41-7 Digger St; apt $125-145; ❄@📶🏊) The crisp white interiors of Reef Palms' apartments will have you wearing your

Cairns

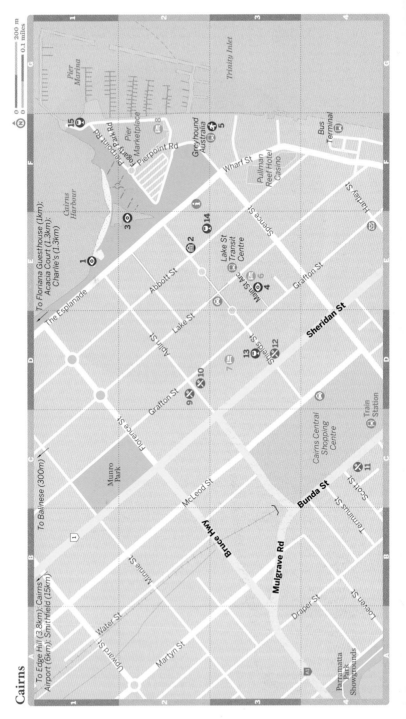

Cairns

sunglasses inside. All rooms in this traditional Queenslander-style place have kitchen facilities; larger ones include a lounge area and a spa. Good for couples and families.

NORTHERN GREENHOUSE Hostel **$$**
(☎1800 000 541; www.friendlygroup.com.au; 117 Grafton St; dm/tw/apt $28/95/120; ❄@🛜🏊) It fits into the budget category with dorm accommodation and a relaxed attitude, but this friendly place is a cut above, with neat studio-style apartments with kitchens and balconies. The central deck, pool and games room are great for socialising. Freebies include breakfast and a Sunday barbie.

INN CAIRNS Apartments **$$**
(☎07-4041 2350; www.inncairns.com.au; 71 Lake St; apt $125-188; ❄@🛜🏊) Behind the unassuming facade, this is true inner-city apartment living. Take the lift up to the 1st-floor pool or to the rooftop garden for a sundowner. The elegant self-contained apartments come with wrought-iron and glass furnishings.

ACACIA COURT Hotel **$$**
(☎1300 850 472; www.acaciacourt.com; 223-227 The Esplanade; d $120-145; ❄🛜🏊) A stroll along the foreshore from town, this waterfront high-rise has beachy touches like bright aqua bedspreads and a choice of ocean or mountain views, making it great value for money. Most rooms have private balconies. The famed buffet restaurant Charlie's is downstairs.

BALINESE Motel **$$**
(☎1800 023 331; www.balinese.com.au; 215 Lake St; d from $138; ❄@🛜🏊) Bali comes to Cairns at this low-rise complex: waking up among the authentic wood furnishings and ceramic pieces, you may be taken with the sudden urge to have your hair beaded.

Eating

OCHRE Modern Australian **$$$**
(☎07-4051 0100; www.ochrerestaurant.com.au; 43 Shields St; mains $30-36; ⏰lunch Mon-Fri, dinner nightly; 🅿) In an ochre- and plum-toned dining room, the changing menu at this innovative restaurant utilises native Aussie fauna (such as croc with native pepper, or roo with quandong-chilli glaze) and flora (wattle-seed damper loaf with peanut oil and native dukka; lemon-myrtle panacotta). If you can't decide, try a tasting plate, or go all-out with a six-course tasting menu.

GREEN ANT CANTINA Mexican **$$**
(☎07-4041 5061; www.greenantcantina.com; 183 Bunda St; mains $17-40; ⏰dinner) This funky little slice of Mexico behind the railway station is worth seeking out for its homemade quesadillas, enchiladas and Corona-battered tiger prawns. Great cocktail list, cool tunes (including an open-mic night on Sunday).

CHARLIE'S Seafood **$$**
(223-227 The Esplanade; buffets $28.50; ⏰dinner) It's not the fanciest place in town, but Charlie's, at the Acacia Court hotel, is legendary for its nightly all-you-can-eat seafood buffet. Fill your plate with prawns, oysters, clams or hot food and eat out on the poolside terrace. Great cocktails, too.

FUSION ORGANICS Cafe $

(cnr Aplin & Grafton Sts; dishes $4-19.50; ☉7am-4pm Mon-Fri, to 1pm Sat; ✈) In the wicker-chair-strewn corner courtyard of an historic 1921 redbrick former ambulance station, Indian chefs spice up Fusion's organic, allergy-free fare like quiches, frittatas, corn fritters and filled breads. Healthy brekkie options include buckwheat waffles and pick-me-up 'detox' juices.

ADELFIA GREEK TAVERNA Greek $$

(☎07-4041 1500; www.adelfiagreektaverna. com; cnr Aplin & Grafton Sts; mains $21-30; ☉lunch Fri, dinner Tue-Sun) Plate-smashing, Mediterranean music, belly dancing and heaping portions of authentic Greek cuisine make this taverna a fun family night out. Call for entertainment times.

🍷 Drinking

SALT HOUSE Bar

(www.salthouse.com.au; 6/2 Pierpoint Rd; ☉9am-2am) Next to Cairns' new yacht club, Salt House has a sleek nautical design that has seen it become the city's most sought-after bar since it opened a couple of years ago. It's actually two bars: the luxury yacht–styled Sailing Bar, with live music, and the Balinese-influenced Deck Bar, with killer cocktails and DJs hitting the decks.

COURT HOUSE HOTEL Pub

(38 Abbott St; ☉9am-late) In Cairns' gleaming white former courthouse building, dating from 1921, the Court House pub is replete with a polished timber island bar and Scales of Justice statue – and canetoad races on Wednesday night.

12 BAR BLUES Jazz

(62 Shields St; ☉7pm-late Tue-Sun) The best place in Cairns for loungy live music, this intimate bar grooves to the beat of jazz, blues and swing. Songwriter open-mic night takes place on Thursday, general open-mic night on Sunday.

ℹ Information

Medical Services

Cairns Base Hospital (☎07-4050 6333; The Esplanade) Has a 24-hour emergency service.

Cairns City 24 Hour Medical Centre (☎07-4052 1119; cnr Florence & Grafton Sts) General practice and dive medicals.

Money

American Express (63 Lake St) In Westpac Bank.

Travelex (75 Abbott St)

Tourist information

Cairns & Tropical North Visitor Information Centre (www.tropicalaustralia.com.au; 51 The Esplanade; ☉8.30am-6.30pm) Government-run centre that doles out impartial advice and can book accommodation and tours.

ℹ Getting There & Away

Air

Qantas (☎13 13 13; www.qantas.com.au; cnr Lake & Shields Sts), **Virgin Australia** (☎13 67 89; www.virginaustralia.com) and **Jetstar** (☎13 15 38; www.jetstar.com.au) all service Cairns, with flights to/from Brisbane, Sydney, Melbourne, Darwin (including via Alice Springs) and Townsville.

Bus

Greyhound Australia (☎1300 473 946; www. greyhound.com.au) Has four daily services down the coast to Brisbane ($310, 29 hours) via Townsville ($81, six hours), Airlie Beach ($139, 11 hours) and Rockhampton ($215, 18 hours).

Premier (☎13 34 10; www.premierms.com. au) Runs one daily service to Brisbane ($205, 29 hours) via Innisfail ($19, 1½ hours), Mission Beach ($19, two hours), Tully ($26, 2½ hours), Cardwell ($30, three hours), Townsville ($55, 5½ hours) and Airlie Beach ($90, 10 hours).

John's Kuranda Bus (☎0418-772 953) Runs a service between Cairns and Kuranda two to five times daily ($4, 30 minutes). Departs Lake Street Transit Centre.

CATHY FINCH/LONELY PLANET IMAGES ©

Don't Miss **Tours from Cairns**

GREAT BARRIER REEF

Reef operators generally include transport, lunch and snorkelling gear in their tour prices. Many have diving options including introductory dives requiring no prior experience.

Boats depart from the Pier Marina and Reef Fleet Terminal around 8am, returning 6pm.

Great Adventures — Diving

(☏07-4044 9944; www.greatadventures.com.au; adult/child from $190/95) Fast catamaran with day trips to a floating pontoon, with an optional stopover on Green Island (from $210/105), as well as semisubmersibles and a glass-bottomed boat.

Silverswift — Diving

(☏4044 9944; www.silverseries.com.au; adult/child from $167.50/125.50) Popular catamaran snorkelling/diving three outer reefs.

Sunlover — Diving

(☏4050 1333; www.sunlover.com.au; adult/child from $180/65) Fast catamaran to a pontoon on the outer Moore Reef. Options include semisubmersible trips and helmet diving. Good for families.

CAPE TRIBULATION & THE DAINTREE

After the Great Barrier Reef, Cape Trib is the next most popular day trip – usually including a cruise on the Daintree River.

Billy Tea Bush Safaris — EcoTour

(☏07-4032 0077; www.billytea.com.au; day trips adult/child $170/120) Exciting eco day tours to Cape Trib and along the 4WD Bloomfield Track to Emmagen Creek.

Cape Trib Connections — Sightseeing

(☏07-4041 7447; www.capetribconnections.com; day trips $124) Includes Mossman Gorge, Cape Tribulation Beach and Port Douglas. Also overnight tours.

Tropical Horizons Tours — Sightseeing

(☏07-4035 6445; www.tropicalhorizonstours.com.au; day tours from $161) Day trips to Cape Trib and the Daintree; overnight tours available.

If You Like...
Coral Reefs

If you like diving the coral reefs off Cairns, we think you might like these other amazing diving locations in Tropical North Queensland:

1 HERON ISLAND
This exclusive and tranquil coral cay sits amid a huge spread of reef. You can step straight off the beach into a party of colourful fish.

2 LADY ELLIOT ISLAND
The most southerly of the Great Barrier Reef islands, and also a coral cay, Lady Elliot is home to 19 highly regarded dive sites, so it's hard to know where to begin.

3 LIZARD ISLAND
Remote and rugged, Lizard Island boasts what are arguably Australia's best-known dive sites – Cod Hole, famous for its resident giant and docile potato cod, and Pixie Bommie.

4 SS YONGALA
Rated as one of Australia's best wreck dives and bristling with abundant marine life, this rusty relic is accessible from Townsville.

Sun Palm (☎07-4087 2900; www.sunpalmtransport.com) Runs two northern services from Cairns to Cape Tribulation ($78, three hours) via Port Douglas ($35, 1½ hours) and Mossman ($40, 1¾ hours) with additional services direct to Port Douglas and south to Mission Beach ($49, two hours).

Car & Motorcycle
All the major car-rental companies have branches in Cairns and at the airport, with discount car- and campervan-rental companies proliferating throughout town.

Train
The *Sunlander* departs Cairns' train station (Bunda St) on Tuesday, Thursday and Saturday for Brisbane (one way from $219, 31½ hours); the Scenic Railway (p190) runs daily to/from Kuranda. Contact Queensland Rail (☎1800 872 467; www.traveltrain.com.au).

❶ Getting Around

To/From the Airport
The airport is about 7km north of central Cairns; many accommodation places offer courtesy pick-ups. Sun Palm (☎07-4087 2900; www.sunpalmtransport.com) meets all incoming flights and runs a shuttle bus (adult/child $10/5) to the CBD. You can also book airport transfers to/from Cairns' northern beaches ($18), Palm Cove ($18), Port Douglas ($35), Mossman ($45) and Cape Tribulation ($78, two services daily). Black & White Taxis (☎13 10 08) charges around $26.

Bus
Sunbus (☎07-4057 7411; www.sunbus.com.au) runs regular services in and around Cairns from the Lake Street Transit Centre, where schedules are posted.

Taxi
Black & White Taxis (☎13 10 08) has a rank near the corner of Lake and Shields Sts, and one on McLeod St, outside Cairns Central Shopping Centre.

Islands Off Cairns

Cairns day trippers can easily head out to Green Island, as well as Fitzroy Island and Frankland Islands National Parks for a bit of sunning, snorkelling and indulging.

Green Island
Green Island's long, doglegged jetty heaves under the weight of boatloads of day trippers. This beautiful coral cay is only 45 minutes from Cairns and has a rainforest interior with interpretive walks, a fringing white-sand beach and snorkelling just offshore. You can walk around the island in about 30 minutes.

Great Adventures (☎07-4044 9944; www.greatadventures.com.au; 1 Spence St, Cairns; adult/child $75/37.50) and Big Cat (☎07-4051 0444; www.greenisland.com.au; adult/child from $75/37.50) run day trips, with optional glass-bottomed boat and semisubmersible tours.

Alternatively, sail to the island aboard **Ocean Free** (07-4052 1111; www.oceanfree.com.au; adult/child from $135/90), spending most of the day offshore at Pinnacle Reef, with a short stop on the island.

Fitzroy Island

A steep mountaintop rising from the sea, Fitzroy Island has coral-strewn beaches, woodlands and walking tracks, and Australia's last staffed lighthouse. The most popular snorkelling spot is around the rocks at **Nudey Beach** (1.2km from the resort), which, despite its name, is not clothing-optional, so bring your togs.

Raging Thunder (07-4030 7900; www.ragingthunder.com.au; adult/child $42/21; Reef Fleet Terminal, Cairns; adult/child $58/31.50) runs one trip a day from Cairns (departing 8.30am).

Frankland Islands

If the idea of hanging out on one of five uninhabited coral-fringed islands with excellent snorkelling and stunning white sandy beaches appeals – and if not, why not? – cruise out to the Frankland Group National Park.

Frankland Islands Cruise & Dive (07-4031 6300; www.franklandislands.com.au; adult/child from $136/84) runs excellent day trips, which include a cruise down the Mulgrave River, snorkelling gear and lunch.

DAINTREE RAINFOREST
Atherton Tableland

Waterfalls, lush green pastures complete with well-fed dairy cows and patches of remnant rainforest make up the tablelands, though the bordering areas are dramatically different; expect dry, harsh outback and much thinner cattle. Plenty of people self-drive around the area, though since most towns are close together, bike tours are popular. Either way, allow plenty of time to visit the plethora of waterfalls and local-produce outlets.

Daintree National Park: Then & Now

The greater Daintree rainforest is protected as part of Daintree National Park. The area has a controversial history: despite conservationist blockades, in 1983 the Bloomfield Track was bulldozed through lowland rainforest from Cape Tribulation to the Bloomfield River, and the ensuing international publicity indirectly led the federal government to nominate Queensland's wet tropical rainforests for World Heritage listing. The move drew objections from the Queensland timber industry and the state government, but in 1988 the area was inscribed on the World Heritage list, resulting in a total ban on commercial logging within its boundaries.

World Heritage listing doesn't affect land ownership rights or control, and since the 1990s efforts have been made by the Queensland government and conservation agencies to buy back and rehabilitate freehold properties, add them to the Daintree National Park and install visitor-interpretation facilities. Check out **Rainforest Rescue** (www.rainforestrescue.org.au) for more information.

BIODIVERSITY

Far North Queensland's wet tropics area has amazing pockets of biodiversity. The Wet Tropics World Heritage Area stretches from Townsville to Cooktown and covers 894,420 hectares of coastal zones and hinterland, diverse swamp and mangrove-forest habitats, eucalypt woodlands and tropical rainforest. It covers only 0.01% of Australia's surface area, but has 36% of all the mammal species, 50% of the bird species, around 60% of the butterfly species and 65% of the fern species.

ⓘ Getting There & Around

Trans North (☎07-4095 8644; www.transnorthbus.com) has regular bus services connecting Cairns with the tableland, departing from 46 Spence St and running to Kuranda ($8, 45 minutes), Mareeba ($16.80, one hour), Atherton ($22, 1¾ hours), Herberton ($28, two hours, three per week). **John's Kuranda Bus** (☎0418 772 953; www.kuranda.org) runs a service between Cairns and Kuranda two to five times daily ($4, 20 minutes).

Kuranda

Kuranda is a hop, skip and jump – or make that a historic train journey, sky-rail adventure or winding bus trip – from Cairns. The village itself is basically sprawling sets of markets nestled in a spectacular tropical-rainforest setting and selling everything from made-in-China Aboriginal art to emu oil. There's little reason to stay overnight, as this is really a day trippers' domain.

Behind the train station, hop aboard the **Kuranda Riverboat** (☎07-4093 7476; adult/child $14/7; ☺hourly 10.30am-2.30pm) for a 45-minute calm-water cruise along the Barron River.

The **Australian Butterfly Sanctuary** (☎07-4093 7575; www.australianbutterflies.com; 8 Rob Veivers Dr; adult/child $16/8; ☺10am-4pm) offers half-hour tours through its butterfly aviary or head next door to **Birdworld** (☎07-4093 9188; www.birdworldkuranda.com; Heritage Markets; adult/child $16/8; ☺9am-4pm), which displays 75 species of bird.

ⓘ Getting There & Away

TransNorth (☎07-4095 8644; www.transnorthbus.com; 46 Spence St) has five daily bus services from Cairns to Kuranda ($8, 45 minutes).

Kuranda Scenic Railway (☎07-4036 9333; www.ksr.com.au; Cairns train station, Bunda St; adult/child $45/23; return $68/34) winds 34km from Cairns to Kuranda through picturesque mountains and 15 tunnels. The trip takes 1¾ hours and trains depart Cairns at 8.30am and 9.30am daily, returning from pretty Kuranda station on Arara St at 2pm and 3.30pm.

Skyrail Rainforest Cableway (☎07-4038 1555; www.skyrail.com.au; adult/child one way $42/21, return $61/30.50; ☺9am-5.15pm), at 7.5km, is one of the world's longest gondola cableways. The Skyrail runs from the corner of Kemerunga Rd and the Cook Hwy in the northern Cairns suburb of Smithfield (15 minutes' drive north of Cairns) to Kuranda (Arara St), taking 90 minutes. The last departure from Cairns and Kuranda is at 3.30pm; transfers to/from the terminal. Combination Scenic Railway and Skyrail deals are available.

Mareeba

At the centre of industrious cattle, coffee and sugar enterprises, Mareeba is essentially an administrative and supply town for the northern tableland and parts of Cape York Peninsula.

Kuranda's Markets

With revamped boardwalks terraced in the rainforest and wafting incense, the **Kuranda Original Rainforest Markets** (www.kurandaoriginalrainforestmarket.com.au; Therwine St; ☺9am-3pm) first opened in 1978 and are still the best place to see artists such as glassblowers at work, pick up hemp products, and sample local produce such as honey and fruit wines.

Across the road, the **Heritage Markets** (www.kurandamarkets.com.au; Rob Veivers Dr; ☺9am-3pm) overflow with souvenirs and crafts such as ceramics, emu oil, jewellery, clothing (lots of tie-dye) and pistachio-nut figurines.

The **New Kuranda Markets** (www.kuranda.org; 21-23 Coondoo St; ☺9am-4pm), the first you come to if you're walking up from the train station, are essentially just an ordinary group of shops.

RICHARD I'ANSON/LONELY PLANET IMAGES ©

First stop is the **Mareeba Heritage Museum & Tourist Information Centre** (07-4092 5674; www.mareebaheritagecentre.com.au; Centenary Park, 345 Byrnes St; admission free; 8am-4pm), which has a huge room filled with displays on the area's past and present commercial industries, as well as its natural surrounds.

Mareeba Wetlands (1800 788 755; www.jabirusafarilodge.com.au; adult/child $12/6; 9am-4.30pm Apr-Jan) is a 20-sq-km reserve of woodlands, grasslands, swamps and the expansive Clancy's Lagoon, a birdwatchers' nirvana. A huge range of bird species flock here, and you might see other animals such as kangaroos and freshwater crocs. Over 12km of walking trails crisscross the wetlands. Various safari tours (from $38) depart during the week, or you can take a 30-minute eco-cruise (adult/child $15/7.50) or paddle in a canoe ($15 per hour).

Port Douglas

Port Douglas (or just 'Port') is the flashy playground of tropical northern Queensland. For those looking to escape Cairns' bustling traveller scene, Port Douglas is more sophisticated and more intimate. It also has a beautiful white-sand beach right on its doorstep, and the Great Barrier Reef is less than an hour offshore.

 **Sights & Activities**

On a sunny, calm day, Four Mile Beach will take your breath away; it is sand and palm trees for as far as you can see (head up to **Flagstaff Hill Lookout** for a great view).

At the Cooktown Hwy turn-off, **Wildlife Habitat Port Douglas** (07-4099 3235; www.wildlifehabitat.com.au; Port Douglas Rd; adult/child $30/15; 8am-5pm) endeavours to keep and showcase native animals in enclosures that closely mimic their natural environment. It's home to koalas, cassowaries, black-necked storks, crocs, tree kangaroos and other species.

On Sunday the grassy foreshore of Anzac Park spills over with the **Port Douglas Markets** (end of Macrossan St; 8am-1.30pm Sun). You'll find stalls selling arts, crafts and jewellery, locally produced tropical fruits, ice creams and coconut milk, and hot food stalls.

191

Home-grown Cuppa

All the ingredients for a cuppa – coffee, tea, milk and sugar – are produced on and around the Atherton Tableland.

Coffee is one of the area's biggest crops; producers open to the public include the following:

Jacques Coffee Plantation (☎07-4093 3284; www.jaquescoffee.com; 232 Leotta Rd; tours adult/child $15/8; ☺9am-5pm) Ride around Jaques' plantation in its 'bean machine' and sip its coffee liqueur. Signposted off the Kennedy Hwy, 8km east of Mareeba.

North Queensland Gold Coffee Plantation (☎07-4093 2269; www.nqgoldcoffee. com.au; Dimbulah Hwy; tours $5; ☺8am-5pm) Local icon Bruno Maloberti leads entertaining personal tours of his family's plantation. Be sure to try his dark chocolate-coated coffee beans. Located 10.2km southwest of Mareeba.

Skybury Coffee Plantation (☎07-4093 2190; www.skybury.com.au; Dimbulah Hwy; adult/child $23.75/11.90; ☺tours 10.30am, 11.45am & 2.15pm) Snazzy plantation and visitor centre; tours include a film and laboratory tasting. Licensed onsite restaurant. Situated 9km west of Mareeba.

 Tours

Low Isles Trips

There are several cruises to Low Isles, a small coral cay surrounded by a lagoon and topped by a lighthouse. The cay offers good snorkelling and the chance to see turtle-nesting grounds.

Reef Sprinter (☎07-4099 3175; www. reefsprinter.com.au; adult/child $100/80) Superfast 15-minute trip to the Low Isles for speed snorkelling (and no seasickness!).

Sailaway (☎07-4099 4772; www.sailaway portdouglas.com; adult/child $191/121) Popular sailing and snorkelling trip (maximum 27 passengers) to the Low Isles that's great for families. Also offers 90-minute twilight sails ($50 Monday to Friday) off the Port Douglas coast.

Reef Trips

Tours typically make two to three stops on the outer and ribbon reefs, including St Crispins, Agincourt, Chinaman and Tongue Reefs. Reef trips generally include reef tax, snorkelling and transfers from your accommodation, plus lunch and refreshments.

Calypso (☎07-4099 6999; www.calypso charters.com.au; adult/child $195.50/140.50) Large catamaran visiting three outer reefs.

Haba (☎07-4098 5000; www.habadive.com. au; Marina Mirage; adult/child $180.50/104.50) Long-standing, well-regarded local dive company; 25-minute glass bottom boat tours ($16/8) available.

Poseidon (☎07-4099 4772; www.poseidon -cruises.com.au; adult/child $195.50/135.50) Friendly family-owned and -operated luxury catamaran with trips to Agincourt reefs.

Silversonic (☎07-4087 2100; www. silverseries.com.au; adult/child $180.50/129.50) Smooth trips out to Agincourt Reef.

Wavelength (☎07-4099 5031; www.wave length.com.au; adult/child $200/150) Outer reef snorkelling (only) at three sites with a marine biologist. Maximum 30 passengers.

Other Tours

BTS Tours (☎07-4099 5665; www.btstours. com.au; adult/child $154/110) Tours to the Daintree Rainforest and Cape Trib, including canoeing.

Reef & Rainforest Connections

(☎ 07-4099 5333; www.reefandrainforest. com.au; adult/child from $163/105) A range of day-long ecotours including Cape Trib and Bloomfield Falls, Kuranda and Mossman Gorge.

🛏 Sleeping

PINK FLAMINGO   Boutique Resort $$
(☎ 07-4099 6622; www.pinkflamingo. au; 115 Davidson St; r $125-195; ❄ @ 🤶 ☲) Flamboyant fuchsia-, purple- and orange-painted rooms opening to private walled courtyards (with hammocks, outdoor baths and outdoor showers) and a groovy mirror-balled alfresco bar make the Pink Flamingo Port Douglas' hippest digs. Outdoor movie nights screen under the palms; tone your abs in the gym or rent a bike for a spin around town. Gay-owned, gay-friendly and all-welcoming (except for kids).

HIBISCUS GARDENS   Resort $$$
(☎ 1800 995 995; www.hibiscusportdouglas. com.au; 22 Owen St; d from $205; ❄ @ ☲) Balinese influences of teak furnishings and fixtures, bi-fold doors and plantation shutters – as well as the occasional Buddha – give this stylish resort an exotic ambience. The in-house day spa, specialising in Indigenous healing techniques and products, has a local reputation as the best of the many places to be pampered in town.

**BY THE SEA
PORT DOUGLAS**
Apartments $$
(☎ 07-4099 5387; www. bytheseaportdouglas.com. au; 72 Macrossan St; d from $175; ❄ @ 🤶 ☲) Close to the beach and town centre, the 12 self-contained rooms here are spread over

three levels – the upper rooms have 'filtered' views through the palm trees to the beach. Refitted rooms have neutral tones livened up with bright splashes of colour.

Port Douglas Motel   Motel $
(☎ 07-4099 5248; www.portdouglasmotel.com; 9 Davidson St; d $96; ❄ ☲) No views but bright rooms and a great location.

🍃 Port o' Call Lodge   Hostel $
(☎ 07-4099 5422; www.portocall.com.au; cnr Port St & Craven Cl; dm $35, d $99-119; ❄ @ 🤶 ☲) Low-key solar- and wind-powered, YHA-associated hostel with a good-value bistro.

Port Douglas Retreat   Apartments $$
(☎ 07-4099 5053; www.portdouglasretreat. com.au; 31-33 Mowbray St; d $149-179; ❄ 🤶 ☲) Recline on a sun lounge on the wide wooden decking that surrounds the palm-lined swimming pool at this traditional Queenslander-style complex of 36 apartments.

Low Isles

PHOTOGRAPHER: RICHARD I'ANSON/LONELY PLANET IMAGES ©

 Eating

BEACH SHACK
Modern Australian **$$**

(☎07-4099 1100; www.the-beach-shack.com.au; 29 Barrier St, Four Mile Beach; mains $21-29.50; ☺dinner; ☝) There'd be an outcry if this locals' favourite took its lovely macadamia-crumbed eggplant (with grilled and roast vegies, goat's cheese and wild rocket) off the menu. But it's the setting that makes it really worth heading to the southern end of Four Mile Beach: a lantern-lit garden with sand underfoot. Good reef fish, sirloins and blackboard specials, too.

ZINC
Modern Australian **$$**

(☎07-4099 6260; www.zincportdouglas.com; 53-61 Macrossan St; mains $25-34; ☺7am-midnight) Over 70 wines (40 by the glass) and 110 spirits and liqueurs set Zinc apart from its neighbours – as do dishes like pan-seared bugs with apple- and vanilla-scented sweet-potato puree and candied cashews. Don't leave without checking out the floor-to-ceiling, fish-filled aquarium in the bathrooms!

ON THE INLET
Seafood **$$**

(☎07-4099 5255; www.portdouglasseafood.com; 3 Inlet St; mains $22-39.50; ☺lunch & dinner) At this restaurant jutting out over Dickson Inlet, tables spread out along a huge deck where you can await the 5pm arrival of George the grouper, who comes to feed most days. Take up the bucket of prawns and a drink deal for $18 from 3.30pm to 5.30pm, or choose your own crayfish and mud crabs from the live tank. Great service, cool atmosphere.

RE:HAB
Cafe, Gallery **$**

(www.beijaflordesign.com.au; 7/42 Macrossan St; ☺8am-6pm; @☎) Coffee is literally an art form at this chilled cafe—local art gallery, with astoundingly intricate designs etched in the froth of its fresh-roasted brews. Home-baked cakes, muffins and slices, and a Zen little courtyard out back.

Left: Iron Bar; **Below:** Zinc

🍷 Drinking

TIN SHED   Licensed Club
(www.thetinshed-portdouglas.com.au; 7 Ashford
Ave) Port Douglas' Combined Services
Club is a locals' secret. This is a rare find:
bargain dining on the waterfront, and
even the drinks are cheap. Sign in, line up
and grab a table on the river- or shore-
fronting deck.

IRON BAR   Pub
(5 Macrossan St) A bit of whacky outback-
shearing-shed decor never goes astray
in Queensland. It's well done – all rustic
iron and ageing timber; even the outdoor
furniture is old wood and hessian. After
polishing off your Don Bradman eye fillet
(the steaks are named after famous Aussies), head upstairs for a flutter on the
cane-toad races ($5).

ℹ️ Information

The **Port Douglas Tourist Information Centre**
(☎ 07-4099 5599; www.tourismportdouglas.com.
au; 23 Macrossan St; ⊙8am-6.30pm) has maps
and makes tour bookings.

ℹ️ Getting There & Away

For further information about getting to Cairns,
see p186.

    Coral Reef Coaches (☎ 07-4098 2800; www.
coralreefcoaches.com.au) connects Port Douglas
with Cairns ($36, 1¼ hours) via Cairns Airport and
Palm Cove.

    Sun Palm (☎ 07-4087 2900; www.
sunpalmtransport.com) has frequent daily
services between Port Douglas and Cairns ($35,
1½ hours) via the northern beaches and the
airport, and up the coast to Mossman ($10, 20
minutes), Daintree Village and the ferry ($20, one
hour), and Cape Tribulation ($48, three hours).

    Airport Connections (☎ 07-4099 5950;
www.tnqshuttle.com; ⊙3.20am-5.20pm) runs

195

Detour:
Lizard Island

The spectacular islands of the Lizard group are clustered just 27km off the coast about 100km from Cooktown. Jigurru (Lizard Island), a sacred place for the Dingaal Aboriginal people, has dry, rocky and mountainous terrain offering bushwalking; glistening white swimming beaches; and a relatively untouched fringing reef for snorkelling and diving.

There are good dives right off the island, and the outer Barrier Reef is less than 20km away, including two of Australia's best-known dive sites – Cod Hole and Pixie Bommie. Lizard Island Resort offers a full range of diving facilities to its guests.

There are great walks through country that switches from mangrove to rainforest to dry and rocky in mere minutes, including a superb hike up to **Cook's Look** (368m); allow three hours return.

Lizard Island Resort (☏ 1300 863 248; www.lizardisland.com.au; Anchor Bay; d from $1700; ❄ @ 🛜 ⛱) has luxurious villas, spa treatments and a top restaurant. Kids aren't allowed.

Book through the resort for all air transfers to/from Cairns (return $530).

Daintree Air Services (☏ 1800 246 206; www.daintreeair.com.au) has full-day tours from Cairns at 8am ($690). The trip includes lunch, snorkelling gear, transfers and a local guide.

---

a shuttle-bus service ($36; hourly) between Port Douglas, Cairns' northern beaches and Cairns Airport, continuing on to Cairns CBD.

ℹ Getting Around

Bus

Sun Palm (☏ 07-4087 2900; www. sunpalmtransport.com; ⏱ 7am-midnight) runs in a continuous loop every half-hour from Wildlife Habitat Port Douglas to the Marina Mirage, stopping regularly en route. Flag down the driver at marked bus stops.

Car & Motorcycle

Port Douglas has plenty of small, local car-hire companies as well as major international chains. Expect to pay around $65 a day for a small car and $130 a day for a 4WD, plus insurance.

Latitude 16 (☏ 07-4099 4999; www.latitude16. com.au; 54 Macrossan St) Also rents open-sided Mokes (per day from $49).

Thrifty (☏ 07-4099 5555; www.thrifty.com.au; 50 Macrossan St)

Daintree Village

Surprisingly, given its rainforest surrounds, **Daintree Village** is not tree-covered; cattle farms operate in large clearings next to the Daintree River. Most folk come here to see crocodiles, and there are several small operators who will take you on croc-spotting boat tours.

Bruce Belcher's Daintree River Cruises   River Cruises
(☏ 07-4098 7717; www.daintreerivercruises.com; 1hr cruises adult/child $25/10) One-hour cruises on a covered boat.

Crocodile Express   River Cruises
(☏ 07-4098 6120; www.daintreeconnection. com.au; Daintree Village; 1hr cruises adult/child $25/13; ⏱ from 8.30am daily) The original Daintree River cruise operator.

Daintree River Experience   Birdwatching Cruises
(☏ 07-4098 7480; www.daintreecruises.com.au; 2hr cruises adult/child $50/35) Serene sunrise and sunset cruises specialising in birdwatching.

Sleeping & Eating

DAINTREE ECO
LODGE & SPA   Boutique Resort **$$$**
(☎07-4098 6100; www.daintree-ecolodge.
com.au; 20 Daintree Rd; s/d from $550/598;
❄@ 🛜 ☎) The 15 boutique 'banyans'
(pole cabins; 10 with private spas) sit high
in the rainforest canopy a few kilometres
south of Daintree Village. Even the day
spa is eco-minded, with its own range of
organic, Indigenous-inspired products and
treatments. Nonguests are welcome at its
superb **Julaymba Restaurant** (mains $29-32;
☺breakfast, lunch & dinner), utilising local pro-
duce, including Indigenous berries, nuts,
leaves and flowers. Don't miss a Flaming
Green Ant cocktail!

RED MILL HOUSE   B&B **$$$**
(☎07-4098 6233; www.redmillhouse.com.
au; 11 Stewart St; s/d $160/200; ❄@☎)
Birdwatchers will love the Red Mill. The
large verandah overlooking the rainforest garden is a prime spot to observe the
resident wildlife. There are four well-ap-
pointed rooms, a large communal lounge
and library, and a two-bedroom family
unit (from $260). Guided birding walks
are available on request.

Daintree Escape   Cabins **$$**
(☎07-4098 6021; www.daintreeescape.com.au;
17 Stewart St; d $175; ❄@☎) Cute cabins amid
grassy gardens strolling distance from the village.

Cape Tribulation

This little piece of paradise retains a
frontier quality, with low-key develop-
ment, road signs alerting drivers to cas-
sowary crossings and crocodile warnings
that make beach strolls that little bit less
relaxing.

The rainforest tumbles right down to
two magnificent, white-sand beaches
– Myall and Cape Trib – separated by a
knobby cape.

  Ocean Safari (☎07-4098 0006; www.
oceansafari.com.au; adult/child $108/69; ☺9am
& 1pm) leads small groups (25 people
maximum) on snorkelling cruises to
the Great Barrier Reef, just half an hour
offshore.

  Jungle Surfing (☎07-4098 0043;
www.junglesurfing.com.au; $90) is an
exhilarating zipline (flying fox) through
the rainforest canopy, stopping at five
tree platforms. Tours depart from Cape
Tribulation Pharmacy (next to the IGA
supermarket).

Tours

Cape Trib Horse Rides   Horse Riding
(☎1800 111 124; per person $95; ☺8am &
1.30pm) Leisurely rides along the beach.

Cape Tribulation Kayak   Kayaking
(☎07-4098 0077; www.capetribcamping.com.au;
2hr tours $60) Guided kayaking trips and kayak
hire (single/double kayaks $20/30 per hour).

Mason's Tours   Walking, 4WD
(☎07-4098 0070; www.masonstours.com.au,
Mason's Store, Cape Tribulation Rd) Interpretive
walks lasting two hours (adult/child $49/40) or
a half-day ($70/55), and a croc-spotting night
walk ($49). Also 4WD tours up the Bloomfield
Track (from $135/114).

ℹ️ Getting There & Away

Sun Palm (☎07-4087 2900; www.
sunpalmtransport.com) runs daily buses from
Cairns to Cape Tribulation (adult/child $78/39).
Services depart from Cairns at 7am and 1pm and
take 3½ hours.

Melbourne & the Great Ocean Road

Melbourne, Australia's second-largest city and Victoria's urban epicentre, is the nation's artistic heartland. A truly global melting pot, it's a place where culture junkies and culinary perfectionists can feast on art, music, theatre, cinema and cuisine. Australia's best baristas compete for your morning trade, and you're never far from a live-music gig, a gallery opening or a quirky street-art installation. It's a big town, but Melbourne retains a vibrant neighbourhood spirit, embodied in the fierce rivalries between local Australian Rules football teams (Carlton vs Collingwood at the MCG is a quasi-religious experience).

Further south, scalloping its way around coves, beaches and cliffs, the Great Ocean Road is one of the world's great road trips. Wild surf pounds the shoreline and enigmatic coastal towns mingle with lush national parks. Also down south is the Australian mainland's southernmost tip – the spiritually reviving Wilsons Promontory National Park.

Street art, Hosier Lane (p203), Melbourne

199

Historic W class tram, Melbourne
CHRISTOPHER GROENHOUT/LONELY PLANET IMAGES ©

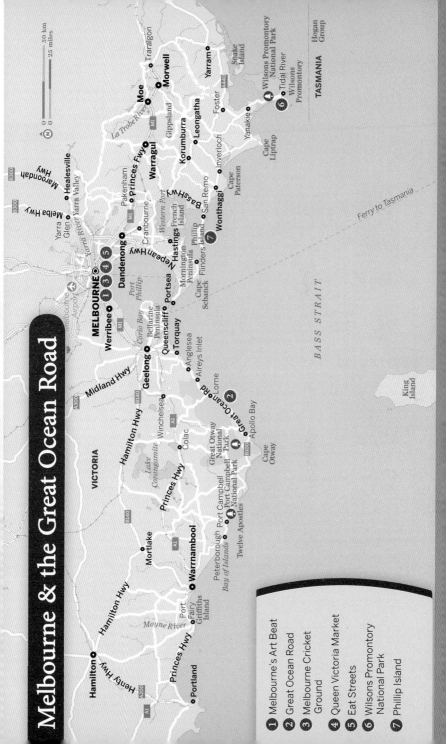

Melbourne & the Great Ocean Road

1 Melbourne's Art Beat
2 Great Ocean Road
3 Melbourne Cricket Ground
4 Queen Victoria Market
5 Eat Streets
6 Wilsons Promontory National Park
7 Phillip Island

Melbourne &
the Great Ocean Road Highlights

1 Melbourne's Art Beat

What makes the Melbourne art scene tick? Locals say it's the many dedicated public spaces made available for art: quirky spaces down side alleys or in anonymous buildings where artists can interpret, exploit and explain the city on their own terms.

Need to Know

FORMS OF STREET ART Stencil, freehand spray **BEST PHOTO OPPORTUNITY** Look out around town and Fitzroy for some great work by Miso and Ghostpatrol, two extremely talented artists

Melbourne's Art Beat Don't Miss List

BY BERNADETTE ALIBRANDO, ART
CONSULTANT & GUIDE (WWW.WALKTOART.COM.AU)

1 COMMISSIONED LANEWAY ART

The Melbourne City Council started the Laneways Commissions project in 2001. Pick up a Laneways Commissions map and explore – for locals it's a bit like being a tourist in your own city. It's always changing: it's about just taking a moment to look up and about and see what's happening around town. In 2011 commissions celebrated the work of Victoria-based Indigenous artists.

2 PLATFORM

Beneath Flinders St, in a pink-tiled pedestrian subway called Campbell Arcade, is a great space run by a group called Platform Artists Group. Platform has ever-changing exhibits behind glass windows – the last window is always used for video media and can be quite idiosyncratic.

3 CENTRE PLACE & HOSIER LANE

Melbourne is rated in the top five street-art cities of the world, with New York, London, Berlin and Barcelona. In some lanes, such as Hosier and Union, the city has sanctioned colourful and political stencil art and graffiti. A lot of credit for the vibrancy and legitimacy of Melbourne's street-art scene goes to Andy Mac – check out the street art, light boxes and Mac's **Until Never Gallery** (www.untilnever.net) in Hosier Lane. Platform also has three windows on the beautiful Majorca Building in Centre Place, which are used for emerging artists to show their work.

4 GALLERIES

The **Australian Centre for Contemporary Art** (p216) is a great contemporary art space. Around Gertrude St and Smith St in Fitzroy and Collingwood, pop into **Gertrude Contemporary Art Space** (www.gertrude.org.au) and **Lamington Drive** (www.lamingtondrive.com) for great illustration. **Stephen McLaughlan Gallery** (www.stephenmclaughlangallery.com.au) on Swanston St in the city provides great art and views. Also there's **Sarah Scout** (www.sarahscoutpresents.com) on Crossley St, and **Utopian Slumps** (www.utopianslumps.com) and **Screen Space** (www.screenspace.com) in Guildford Lane.

Great Ocean Road

The wild ocean beaches and bushland along the Great Ocean Road have long been holiday hot-spots for Melburnians. Torquay is Victoria's 'surf city' and the gateway to this spectacular coast: an inspirational combination of beach and bush awaits as you travel west towards the famous Twelve Apostles. Below: Erskine Falls (p245); Top Right: Great Ocean Road; Bottom Right: Twelve Apostles

Need to Know

ONLY A FEW HOURS? Take a **helicopter tour** over the Twelve Apostles **AVOID** Standing beneath and on top of the crumbly cliffs behind the beaches **For further coverage, see p242.**

Great Ocean Road Don't Miss List

BY CRAIG BAIRD, CURATOR, SURF WORLD MUSEUM

1 TORQUAY
Torquay (p243) offers a chance to immerse yourself in surf culture. The **Surf World Museum** (p243) is recognised as the world's largest, and is dedicated to telling the story of Australian surfing. Torquay's surf shops can provide you with all the latest gear and fashion, local surfing schools offer the chance to learn how to get on board, and there are funky galleries encapsulating surfing cool.

2 BELLS BEACH
The Great Ocean Road heads slightly inland between Torquay and Anglesea, with a turn-off about 7km from Torquay to the famous **Bells Beach** (p244). Bells is a spectacular surf beach with a rich history and is home to the world's longest running surfing competition, the Rip Curl Pro. It's worth a detour as cliff-top platforms provide great views of the waves and surfers.

3 LORNE
It's not all about the beaches – exquisite natural beauty extends inland as well, and there are a number of waterfalls and bushwalks around **Lorne** (p245) that can give you a chance to unwind and plug back into nature. If you can tug yourself away from Lorne's pretty bay, head to the **Qdos Gallery** (p245), among the trees just out of Lorne, which features some great contemporary art.

4 THE RIDE
There is a beautiful rhythm to the Great Ocean Road. At a number of spots you are only metres from the water and there are some great sandy beaches and secluded little coves that can be accessed by simply parking and walking to them.

5 PORT CAMPBELL NATIONAL PARK
The rugged and beautiful coastline beyond **Cape Otway** (p247) is known as the Shipwreck Coast. At **Port Campbell National Park** (p247), sheer 70m cliffs confront relentless seas, which have carved out spectacular arches, blowholes and stacks, such as the **Twelve Apostles** (p247), from the soft limestone.

Melbourne Cricket Ground

Melbourne hosts several big-ticket international events (the Australian Open tennis and the Australian Formula 1 Grand Prix spring to mind), but it's home-grown Australian Rules football that dominates many local hearts and minds. Between March and September arenas reverberate with the roar of thousands of passionate supporters, and the number one stadium is the 100,000-capacity **Melbourne Cricket Ground** (p217), aka the MCG or just 'the G'.

Eat Streets

Inner Melbourne's neighbourhoods each have a multicultural main street. **Brunswick St** in Fitzroy is home to cafes, bars, live-music pubs and urban bohemians; **Smith St** in Collingwood is grittier, with everything from Greek patisseries to Balinese. **Victoria St** in Richmond is the city's Vietnamese strip; **Little Bourke St** is the hub of Chinatown. Head to **Lygon St** in Carlton for Italian, and to Brunswick's **Sydney Rd** for Middle Eastern. Lygon St

DAVID WALL/LONELY PLANET IMAGES ©

Queen Victoria Market

The largest open-air market in the southern hemisphere, the **Queen Victoria Market** (p213) hosts more than 600 traders and has a history dating back over 130 years. Saturdays are hectic, with thousands of Melburnians stocking up on fresh fruit, veg, meat and fish. On Sundays clothing stalls proliferate: you mightn't be looking for a VB beer singlet or an Eminem T-shirt, but the prices might tempt you.

4

6

Wilsons Promontory National Park

Close enough to Melbourne to make a decent day tip, the untamed **Wilsons Promontory National Park** (p249), usually just called 'the Prom', features squeaky white-sand surf beaches, curious native wildlife, ferny gullies and lichen-covered granite outcrops. The southern tip of mainland Australia also boasts over 80km of trails for avid bushwalkers.

7

Phillip Island

The curious, rather English **Phillip Island** (p239) sits at the entrance to Western Port Bay, 140km southeast of Melbourne. Dappled with farmland and beachy holiday towns, it's most famous for staging the Penguin Parade, one of Victoria's biggest tourist drawcards. Hundreds day-trip down from Melbourne to watch the tiny wet birds waddle back to their burrows after a hard day's fishing.

Melbourne & the Great Ocean Road's Best…

Arts & Culture

○ **Arts Precinct** (p216) Under the spire in Southbank are concert halls, theatres and Victoria's premier art gallery.

○ **Ian Potter Centre: National Gallery of Victoria Australia** (p212) Amazing Australian art: colonial, contemporary and Indigenous.

○ **Federation Square** (p212) Striking 'Fed Square' is Melbourne's favourite meeting point and host to galleries and cultural events.

○ **Melbourne Museum** (p221) Contemporary building with a broad natural and cultural-heritage collection.

Places with a View

○ **Twelve Apostles** (p247) There may only be six left, but these rocky stacks battling the ocean make for a magnificent cliff-top spectacle.

○ **Eureka Tower & Skydeck 88** (p216) Big Melbourne building, big Melbourne views.

○ **Seal Rocks** (p240) Ogle magical views of the ocean and the Nobbies rock formation or turn your attention to Phillip Island's fur seals below.

Nature Escapes

○ **Wilsons Promontory** (p249) Take a hike! Silvery beaches, verdant gullies of tree ferns and inquisitive wombats.

○ **The Otways** (p246) Cycle or hike through the national park, spotting kookaburras and koalas in the treetops.

○ **Phillip Island** (p239) Check out cavorting fur seals then rug-up for the famous Penguin Parade.

Places for Lunch

- **Chinatown** (p213) Garish scarlet-and-gold restaurants entice you to yum cha.

- **Melbourne's pubs** (p232) It's not just about beer: Melbourne's pubs do hefty meals (...and beer).

- **Queen Victoria Market** (p213) Fill a hamper with cheese, smallgoods and fresh bread.

- **Melbourne Cricket Ground** (p217) Bite into a pie and sauce while barracking for your team.

Need to Know

ADVANCE PLANNING
- **One month before** Reserve Melbourne theatre seats and check live-music listings.

- **Two weeks before** Plan your Great Ocean Road journey, including booking accommodation and a hire car.

- **One week before** Book a table at a top-notch restaurant or a reserve seat at the Melbourne Cricket Ground.

RESOURCES
- **Tourism Victoria** (www.visitvictoria.com) For information, ideas and contacts.

- **Melbourne Visitor Centre** (www.visitmelbourne.com) At Federation Square in the central city.

- **Parks Victoria** (www.parkweb.vic.gov.au) Managers of Victoria's national parks.

- **Information Victoria** (www.information.vic.gov.au) Government body producing a variety of publications about Melbourne and Victoria. Bookshop at 505 Little Collins St in central Melbourne.

- **Royal Automobile Club of Victoria** (RACV; www.racv.com.au) Produces the excellent *Experience Victoria* guide, full of accommodation and touring info. Also offers emergency roadside assistance for drivers.

GETTING AROUND
- **Walk** Through the caffeine-infused laneways of inner Melbourne.

- **Tram** Between Melbourne's inner neighbourhoods.

- **Drive** Along the curves and bends of the Great Ocean Road.

- **Train** To Melbourne's outer suburbs.

- **Bus** To the Phillip Island Penguin Parade and to/from Melbourne Airport on Skybus.

BE FOREWARNED
- **Driving in Melbourne** Watch out for passengers alighting from trams, and for the 'hook turn' at many city intersections – to turn right, pull into the *left* lane, wait until the *other* light turns green, then complete the turn.

- **Phillip Island's Penguin Parade** It kicks off *after* sunset.

Left: Arts Centre spire; **Above:** The Otways
PHOTOGRAPHERS: (LEFT): WIBOWO RUSLI/LONELY PLANET IMAGES © (ABOVE) RICHARD I'ANSON/LONELY PLANET IMAGES ©

Melbourne & the Great Ocean Road Itineraries

From Australia's hippest city to sleepy surf towns along the Great Ocean Road, Victoria is (as the local licence plates suggest) 'the place to be'.

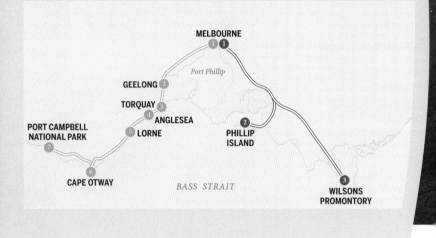

3 DAYS — MELBOURNE TO WILSONS PROMONTORY RETURN
Nightlife & Wildlife

Start your trip in Victoria's cool capital **(1) Melbourne**, where you can indulge in global cuisines, see raucous live bands and check out eclectic theatre. Once you've had your fill of nightlife, overdosed on lattes and long blacks, seen a show or yelled yourself hoarse at the football, it's time to leave the city lights behind and experience Victoria's wild side.

It's easy to organise a tour or hire a car to visit **(2) Phillip Island**. Phillip Island is home to the famous Penguin Parade, where cute little penguins march up the beach in a quirky floodlit spectacle. There's more to see here, too, including a colony

of Australian fur seals and some excellent beaches (bring your airport novel).

From Phillip Island head to **(3) Wilsons Promontory**, or 'the Prom' as it is affectionately known. The Prom offers abundant wildlife, pristine beaches and excellent bushwalking tracks. Go barefoot on the white sand at Squeaky Beach to find out where the name comes from, then loop back to Melbourne.

5 DAYS

MELBOURNE TO PORT CAMPBELL NATIONAL PARK

Along the Great Ocean Road

Pick up a set of wheels in **(1) Melbourne** and head west. The regional hub of **(2) Geelong** has come a long way in recent years: check out the waterfront and grab a bite before continuing to the fabulous Great Ocean Road.

The Great Ocean Road officially starts at **(3) Torquay**, the energetic hub of Victoria's surfing scene. Visit the surf museum, shop for some hypercoloured surf clothes or hire a board and hurl yourself into the waves. There are gentle breaks and surf schools here, and nearby is the famous Bells Beach (not for beginners).

Next up is **(4) Anglesea**, home to a more relaxed surf culture, while **(5) Lorne** offers wonderful bushwalks, waterfalls and beaches, plus some quality places to eat and stay. There are more quiet towns, secluded beaches, spectacular views and the ever-winding road all the way to **(6) Cape Otway**, on a rugged part of the coast that earned the moniker 'the Shipwreck Coast'. Beyond the cape is the eye-popping **(7) Port Campbell National Park**, where crumbling limestone cliffs retreat from the pounding surf, leaving natural arches, blowholes and the eerie Twelve Apostles rock stacks.

Bells Beach (p244)

PHOTOGRAPHER: DAVID WALL/LONELY PLANET IMAGES ©

Discover Melbourne & the Great Ocean Road

MELBOURNE

There's a lot of fun packed into this city of some four million people. Coffee, food, art and fashion are taken mighty seriously, but that doesn't mean they're only for those in the know; all you need to eat well, go bar-hopping or shopping is a bit of cash and a deft ability to find hidden stairways down graffiti-covered laneways.

 Sights

Central Melbourne

FEDERATION SQUARE   Public Space
(Map p218; www.federationsquare.com.au; cnr Flinders & Swanston Sts) Striking Federation Square has become the place to celebrate, protest or party. Its undulating forecourt of Kimberley stone echoes the town squares of Europe. Here you'll find the subterranean Melbourne **Visitor Centre** (☎03-9928 0096; ◷9am-6pm; tours per adult $12).

IAN POTTER CENTRE: NATIONAL GALLERY OF VICTORIA AUSTRALIA   Art Gallery
(NGVA; Map p218; www.ngv.vic.gov.au; ◷10am-5pm Tue-Sun) This houses the NGV's extensive collection of Australian paintings, decorative arts, photography, prints, drawings, sculpture, fashion, textiles and jewellery.
    The gallery's indigenous collection dominates the ground floor and seeks to challenge ideas of the 'authentic'. Upstairs there are permanent displays of colonial paintings and drawings by 19th-century Aboriginal artists.

Birrarung Marr, Giant Sky Wheel and Federation Bells (designed by Neil McLachlan and Anton Hasell in collaboration with Swaney Draper Architects)

AUSTRALIAN CENTRE FOR THE MOVING IMAGE
Museum

(ACMI; Map p218; www.acmi.net.au; ⏰10am-6pm) ACMI manages to educate, enthral and entertain in equal parts, and has enough games and movies on call for days, or even months of screen time. 'Screenworld' is an exhibition that celebrates the work of mostly Australian cinema and TV and, upstairs, the Australian Mediatheque is a venue set aside for the viewing of programs from the National Film and Sound Archive, and ACMI.

BIRRARUNG MARR
Park

(Map p218; btwn Federation Sq & the Yarra River) Featuring grassy knolls, river promenades and a thoughtful planting of Indigenous flora, Birrarung Marr is a welcome addition to Melbourne's patchwork of parks and gardens. It houses the sculptural and musical **Federation Bells**, which ring according to a varying schedule.

CHINATOWN
Neighbourhood

(Map p218; Little Bourke St, btwn Spring & Swanston Sts) Chinese miners arrived in search of the 'new gold mountain' in the 1850s and settled in this strip of Little Bourke St, now flanked by red archways. Here you'll find an interesting mix of bars and restaurants, including one of Melbourne's best, Flower Drum (p228). Come here for yum cha, or explore its attendant laneways for late-night dumplings or cocktails. Chinatown hosts the city's vibrant Chinese New Year celebrations and the interesting **Chinese Museum** (Map p218; www.chinesemuseum. com.au; 22 Cohen Pl; adult/child $7.50/5.50; ⏰10am-5pm), which showcases the history of Chinese in Victoria.

OLD MELBOURNE GAOL
Historic Building

(Map p218; ☎03-8663 7228; www.oldmelbourne gaol.com.au; Russell St; adult/child/family $21/11/49; ⏰9.30am-5pm) This forbidding monument to 19th-century justice is now a museum. It was built of bluestone in 1841, and was a prison until 1929. The last sound that legendary bushranger Ned Kelly heard was the clang of the trap here in 1880. His death mask, armour and history are on display.

QUEEN VICTORIA MARKET
Market

(Map p218; www.qvm.com.au; 513 Elizabeth St; ⏰6am-2pm Tue & Thu, 6am-5pm Fri, 6am-3pm Sat, 9am-4pm Sun) This site has been the market for more than 130 years, prior to which it was a burial ground. This is where Melburnians shop for fresh produce including organics and Asian specialities. There's a deli, meat and fish hall as well as a fast food and restaurant zone. On Wednesday evenings from mid-November to the end of February, a night market with hawker-style food stalls, bars and music takes over.

🖋 KOORIE HERITAGE TRUST
Cultural Centre

(Map p218; www.koorieheritagetrust.com; 295 King St; entry by gold-coin donation, tours $15; ⏰10am-4pm) This cultural centre is devoted to southeastern Aboriginal culture, and cares for artefacts and oral history. Its gallery spaces show a variety of contemporary and traditional work, a model scar tree at the centre's heart, as well as a permanent chronological display of Victorian Koorie history.

IMMIGRATION MUSEUM
Museum

(Map p218; www.museumvictoria.com.au/ immigrationmuseum; 400 Flinders St; adult/ child $8/free; ⏰10am-5pm) The Immigration Museum uses personal and community voices, images and memorabilia to tell the many stories of immigration. It's symbolically housed in the old Customs House (1858–70).

MELBOURNE AQUARIUM
Aquarium

(Map p218; ☎03-9923 5999; www.melbourne aquarium.com.au; cnr Queenswharf Rd & King St; adult/child/family $33/19/88; ⏰9.30am-6pm) This aquarium is home to rays, gropers and sharks, all of which cruise around a 2.2-million-litre tank, watched closely by visitors through a see-through tunnel. Three times a day divers are thrown to the sharks; for between $150 and $345 you can join them.

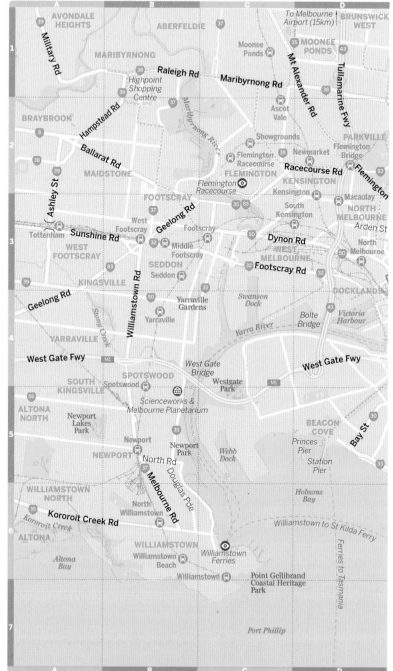

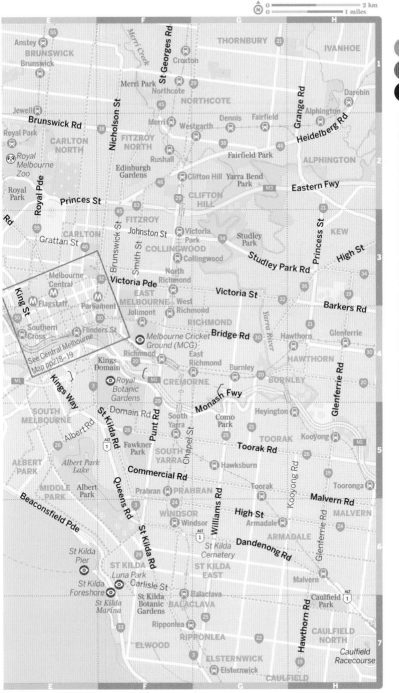

YOUNG & JACKSON'S
Historic Building

(Map p218; www.youngandjacksons.com.au; cnr Flinders & Swanston Sts) Across the street from Flinders Street Station is a pub known for more than beer (which its been serving up since 1861); it's known for its painting of pre-pubescent *Chloe*. Painted by Jules Joseph Lefebvre, her yearning gaze, cast over her shoulder and out of the frame, was a hit at the Paris Salon of 1875.

Southbank & Docklands

FREE NATIONAL GALLERY OF VICTORIA INTERNATIONAL
Art Gallery

(NGVI; off Map p218; www.ngv.vic.gov.au; 180 St Kilda Rd; ◎10am-5pm Wed-Mon) Beyond the water wall you'll find international art that runs from the ancient to the contemporary. Completed in 1967, the original NGV building – Roy Grounds' 'cranky icon' – was one of Australia's most controversial but ultimately re-spected Modernist masterpieces. Interior remodelling was undertaken from 1996 to 2003, overseen by Mario Bellini. Don't miss a gaze up at the Great Hall's stained-glass ceiling.

EUREKA TOWER & SKYDECK 88
Notable Building

(Map p218; www.eurekaskydeck.com.au; 7 Riverside Quay, Southbank; adult/child/family $18/9/40, The Edge extra $12/8/29; ◎10am-10pm, last entry 9.30pm) Eureka Tower, built in 2006, has 92 storeys. Take a wild elevator ride to almost the top (don't miss a glance at the photo on the floor) and you'll do 88 floors in less than 40 seconds. 'The Edge' – not a member of U2, but a slightly sadistic glass cube – propels you out of the building.

FREE AUSTRALIAN CENTRE FOR CONTEMPORARY ART
Gallery

(ACCA; www.accaonline.org.au; 111 Sturt St; ◎10am-5pm Tue-Fri, 11am-6pm Sat & Sun; 🚊1) The ACCA is one of Australia's most exciting and challenging contemporary galleries. The building is fittingly sculptural, with a deeply rusted exterior

Left: Etihad Stadium (p224) and Bolte Bridge, Docklands; **Below:** Waterwall, National Gallery of Victoria International

PHOTOGRAPHERS: (LEFT) CHRISTOPHER GROENHOUT/LONELY PLANET IMAGES ©; (BELOW) KRZYSZTOF DYDYNSKI/ LONELY PLANET IMAGES ©

evoking the factories that once stood on the site, and a slick, soaring, ever-adapting interior designed to house often massive installations.

VICTORIAN ARTS CENTRE
Notable Building

(Map p218; www.theartscentre.com.au; 100 St Kilda Rd) The Arts Centre is made up of two separate buildings: the concert hall (**Hamer Hall**, which at the time of writing was undergoing a major redevelopment) and the **theatres building** (under the spire). Both are linked by a series of landscaped walkways.

DOCKLANDS
Precinct

(Map p214; www.docklands.vic.gov.au; 🚋 70, 86) This waterfront area was the city's main industrial and docking area until the mid-1960s. In the mid-1990s a purpose-built studio complex and residential, retail and entertainment area was built. Of most interest to travellers is the first-born, **New Quay**, with public art, promenades and a wide variety of cafes and restaurants.

East Melbourne & Richmond

MELBOURNE CRICKET GROUND
Sport Stadium

(MCG; Map p214; ☎ 03-9657 8888; www.mcg.org. au; Brunton Ave; 🚃 Jolimont, 🚋 48, 75) It's one of the world's great sporting venues, and for many Australians the 'G' is considered hallowed ground. The **AFL Grand Final** is held here every year in September, and in 1858 the first game of Aussie Rules football was played where the MCG and its car parks now stand. The first Test cricket match between Australia and England was held here in 1877. The MCG was also the central stadium for the 1956 Melbourne Olympics and the 2006 Commonwealth Games.

If you want to make a pilgrimage, **tours** (☎ 03-9657 8879; adult/child/family $20/10/50) take you through the stands,

217

Central Melbourne

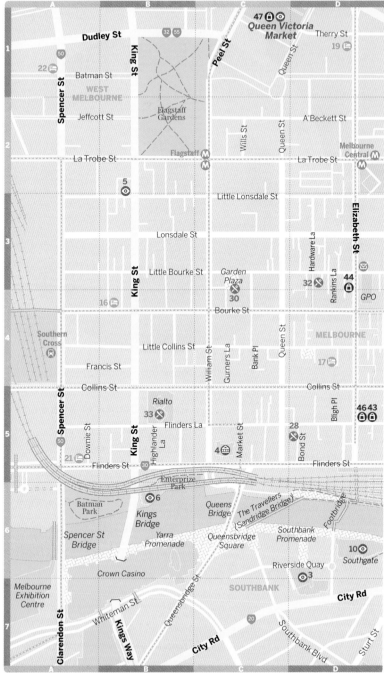

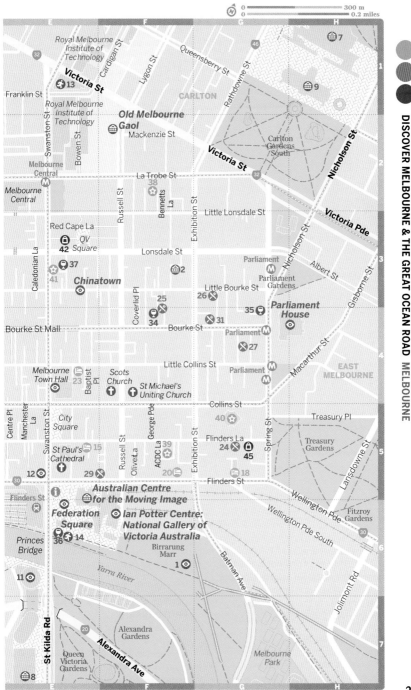

0   300 m
0   0.2 miles

Royal Melbourne Institute of Technology

Victoria St

13

Franklin St

Royal Melbourne Institute of Technology

CARLTON

Old Melbourne Gaol

Mackenzie St

Victoria St

Carlton Gardens South

Nicholson St

Melbourne Central

Melbourne Central

La Trobe St

38

Bennetts La

Exhibition St

Little Lonsdale St

Victoria Pde

Red Cape La

42 QV Square

37

41

Chinatown

Lonsdale St

2

Little Bourke St

Parliament

Parliament Gardens

Albert St

Gisborne St

Coverlid Pl

25

34

31

26

35

Parliament House

Bourke St Mall

Bourke St

Parliament

27

Little Collins St

Parliament

EAST MELBOURNE

Melbourne Town Hall

23

Baptist Pl

Scots Church

St Michael's Uniting Church

Parliament

Macarthur St

Collins St

City Square

St Paul's Cathedral

15

29

12

George Pde

Russell St

Oliver La

ACDC La

39

40

24

20

Flinders La

45

18

Treasury Pl

Treasury Gardens

Spring St

Lansdowne St

Flinders St

Flinders St

Australian Centre for the Moving Image

Federation Square

36   14

Ian Potter Centre: National Gallery of Victoria Australia

Birrarung Marr

1

Yarra River

Batman Ave

Wellington Pde

Wellington Pde South

Fitzroy Gardens

30

Jolimont Rd

Princes Bridge

11

St Kilda Rd

20

Alexandra Gardens

Alexandra Ave

Queen Victoria Gardens

8

Melbourne Park

Central Melbourne

corporate and coaches' areas, the Long Room and (subject to availability) the players change rooms and out onto the ground. They run (on non-match days) between 10am and 3pm. Bookings are not essential but recommended. The MCG houses the **National Sports Museum**; you can incorporate both the MCG tour and entrance to the museum (adult/child/family incl tour $30/15/60).

FITZROY GARDENS Gardens
(Map p214; btwn Wellington Pde, Clarendon, Lansdowne & Albert Sts; Parliament, City Circle, 48, 75) The city drops away suddenly just east of Spring St, giving way to Melbourne's beautiful backyard, the Fitzroy Gardens. The stately avenues lined with English elms, flowerbeds, expansive lawns, strange fountains and a creek are a short stroll from town.

Fitzroy & Around

CENTRE FOR CONTEMPORARY PHOTOGRAPHY Art Gallery
(CCP; www.ccp.org.au; 404 George St, Fitzroy; admission by donation; 11am-6pm Wed-Fri, noon-5pm Sat & Sun; 86) This not-for-profit centre has a changing schedule of exhibitions across a couple of galleries. Shows

traverse traditional techniques and the highly conceptual.

FREE ABBOTSFORD
CONVENT Historic Site
(📞03-9415 3600; www.abbotsfordconvent
.com.au; 1 St Heliers St, Abbotsford;
⏰7.30am-10pm; 🚉Victoria Park, 🚌203)
The convent, which dates back to
1861, is spread over nearly 7 hectares
of riverside land just 4km from the
CBD. The nuns are long gone – no
one is going to ask you if you've been
to Mass lately – and there's now a
rambling collection of creative studios
and community offices. There's a
Slow Food Market (www.mfm.com.
au; admission $2; ⏰8am-1pm) every
fourth Saturday and **Shirt and Skirt
Market** every third Sunday. On the
other side of the bicycle track is the
Collingwood Children's Farm (www.
farm.org.au; adult/child/family $8/4/16;
⏰9am-5pm; 🚉Victoria Park, 🚌203), a
rustic riverside retreat with a range of
frolicking farm animals and a terrific
on-site cafe.

Carlton & Around

MELBOURNE MUSEUM Museum
(off Map p214 (📞13 11 02; www.museum
victoria.com.au; 11 Nicholson St, Carlton;
adult/child $8/free, exhibitions $24/16;
⏰10am-5pm; 🚉Parliament, 🚌City Circle,
86, 96, 🚌250, 251, 402) This confident
postmodern exhibition space mixes
old-style object displays with themed
interactive display areas. The museum's
reach is almost too broad to be cohe-
sive, but it provides a grand sweep of
Victoria's natural and cultural histo-
ries. Walk through the reconstructed
laneway lives of the 1800s or become
immersed in the legend of champion
racehorse Phar Lap. Bunjilaka, on the
ground floor, presents Indigenous
stories and history told through objects
and Aboriginal voices. There's also an
open-air forest atrium featuring Victorian plants and animals and an **Imax
cinema** next door.

♥ **If You Like…
Museums &
Galleries**

If you like the interesting exhibits at the
Melbourne Museum, you might like to
spend a few hours at these other awesome
museums around town:

1 **NATIONAL SPORTS MUSEUM**
Melbourne is a sports-mad town, and what better
place to celebrate all things Aussie and sporty than
the National Sports Museum at the Melbourne Cricket
Ground.

2 **AUSTRALIAN CENTRE FOR THE MOVING
IMAGE**
Yeah, we know, you're not on holiday to watch TV, but a
visit to this archive of Australian film and TV takes TV
to a whole new level.

3 **OLD MELBOURNE GAOL**
It's an undeniably spooky place (a lot of very
unhappy people spent time here), but a visit to the
Old Melbourne Gaol provides an amazing insight into
the city's history (and will right your rudder if you're
contemplating a life of crime).

4 **IMMIGRATION MUSEUM**
Australia is a country of immigrants, and no
melting pot is as multicultural as Melbourne! This
engaging museum in the old Customs House tells
the stories of the city's immigrant origins.

**ROYAL EXHIBITION
BUILDING** Historic Building
(off Map p214; www.museumvicoria.com.au/
reb; Nicholson St, Carlton; 🚉Parliament, 🚌City
Circle, 86, 96, 🚌250, 251, 402) Built for the
International Exhibition in 1880, and
winning Unesco World Heritage status
in 2004, this beautiful Victorian edifice
symbolises the glory days of the Industrial Revolution, Empire and 19th-
century Melbourne's economic supremacy. **Tours**
(📞bookings 13 11 02; adult/child $5/3.50) leave
from the Melbourne Museum most days
at 2pm.

ROYAL MELBOURNE ZOO   Zoo

(Map p214; ☎03-9285 9300; www.zoo.org.
au; Elliott Ave, Parkville; adult/child/family
$25/13/57; ☺9am-5pm; ☒Royal Park, ☒55)
Melbourne's zoo is one of the city's most
popular attractions. Walkways pass
through some enclosures; you can stroll
through the bird aviary, cross a bridge
over the lions' park or enter a tropical
hothouse full of colourful butterflies.
There's also a large collection of native
animals in natural bush settings, a platypus aquarium, fur seals, lions and tigers,
plenty of reptiles, and an 'am I in Asia?'
elephant enclosure. In summer, the zoo
hosts **Twilight Concerts**. **Roar 'n' Snore**
(adult/child $195/145; ☺Sep-May) allows you
to camp at the zoo and join the keepers
on their morning feeding rounds.

South Yarra, Prahran & Windsor

ROYAL BOTANIC GARDENS   Garden

(Map p214; www.rbg.vic.gov.au; admission free;
☺7.30am-8.30pm Nov-Mar, to 5.30pm Apr-Oct;
☒8) The RBG is one of Melbourne's most
glorious attractions. Sprawling beside
the Yarra River, the beautifully designed
gardens feature a global selection of

plantings as well as specific Australian gardens. There's also the excellent,
nature-based **Ian Potter Children's
Garden**.

During the summer months, the
gardens play host to the **Moonlight
Cinema** (p234) and theatre
performances.

PRAHRAN MARKET   Market

(www.prahranmarket.com.au; 163 Commercial
Rd, South Yarra; ☺7am-5pm Tue, Thu & Sat,
to 6pm Fri, 10am-3pm Sun; ☒Prahran, ☒72,
78, 79) The Prahran Market has been a
Melbourne institution for over a century
and is one of the finest produce markets
in the city.

St Kilda & Around

LUNA PARK   Amusement Park

(Map p214; www.lunapark.com.au; Lower
Esplanade, St Kilda; adult/child single-ride
ticket $9.40/7.50, unlimited-ride ticket $42/32;
☺check website for seasonal opening hours;
☒16, 96) It opened in 1912 and still
retains the feel of an old-style amusement park with creepy Mr Moon's gaping
mouth swallowing you up whole on
entering. There's a heritage-listed scenic

Entrance to Luna Park

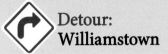

Detour:
Williamstown

Williamstown is a yacht-filled gem just a short boat ride (or drive) from Melbourne's CBD. It has stunning views of Melbourne, and a bunch of touristy shops along its esplanade.

Gem Pier is where passenger ferries dock to drop off and collect those who visit Williamstown by boat. It's a fitting way to arrive, given the area's maritime ambience. **Williamstown Ferries** (03-9517 9444; www. williamstownferries.com.au) plies Hobsons Bay daily, stopping at **Southgate** (Map p218) and visiting a number of sites along the way, including Docklands. **Melbourne River Cruises** (03-9629 7233; www.melbcruises.com.au) also docks at Gem Pier, travelling up the Yarra River to Southgate. Ticket prices vary according to your destination. Pick up a timetable from the very useful visitors centre in Williamstown or at Federation Square, or contact the companies directly; bookings are advised.

railway and the full complement of gut-churning modern rides.

ST KILDA FORESHORE · Beach
(Map p214; Jacka Blvd, St Kilda; 16, 96)
There are palm-fringed promenades, a parkland strand and a long stretch of sand. Still, don't expect Bondi or Noosa. St Kilda's seaside appeal is more Brighton, England than *Baywatch*, despite 20-odd years of glitzy develop-ment. And that's the way Melburnians like it; a certain depth of character and an all-weather charm, with wild days on the bay providing for spectacular cloudscapes and terse little waves, as well as the more predictable sparkling blue of summer.

JEWISH MUSEUM OF
AUSTRALIA · Museum
(03-9534 0083; www.jewishmuseum.com. au; 26 Alma Rd, St Kilda; adult/child/family $10/5/20; 10am-4pm Tue-Thu, 11am-5pm Sun; Balaclava) Interactive displays tell the history of Australia's Jewish community from the earliest days of European set-tlement, while permanent exhibitions celebrate Judaism's rich cycle of festivals and holy days.

South Melbourne, Port Melbourne & Albert Park

SOUTH MELBOURNE MARKET · Market
(cnr Coventry & Cecil Sts, South Melbourne; 8am-4pm Wed, to 6pm Fri, to 4pm Sat & Sun; 96) The market's labyrinthine interior is packed to overflowing with an eccentric collection of stalls selling everything from carpets to *bok choy* (Chinese greens). Its hangover-relieving dim sims are famous and sold at various cafes around Mel-bourne (as 'South Melbourne Market Dim Sims' no less!).

ALBERT PARK LAKE · Lake
(Map p214; btwn Queens Rd, Fitzroy St, Aughtie Dr & Albert Rd, Albert Park; 96, 112) El-egant black swans give their inimitable bottoms-up salute as you circumnavigate the 5km perimeter of this man-made lake. Jogging, cycling, walking or clamouring over play equipment is the appropriate human equivalent.

 **Activities**

Canoeing & Kayaking

KAYAK MELBOURNE · Kayak Tours
(0418 106 427; www.kayakmelbourne.com.au; tours $89) Two-hour long tours by Kayak

If You Like...
Spectator Sports

If you like hollering along with the fans at big stadiums like the Melbourne Cricket Ground, get yourself to some of these other sporting hotspots:

1 ETIHAD STADIUM
(✆ 03-8625 7700; www.etihadstadium.com. au; Docklands) This 52,000-seat stadium is the city's alternative footy arena, with a state-of-the-art sliding roof. Other sporting events (A-league soccer) and live concerts also happen here on a regular basis. **Stadium tours** (✆ 03-8625 7277; adult/child/ family $14/7/37; ⏱11am, 1pm & 3pm) are conducted on weekdays.

2 FLEMINGTON RACECOURSE
(Map p214) The horse race that stops the nation, the **Melbourne Cup** (www.vrc.net.au), is always run here and always on the first Tuesday in November. See the website for other racing dates throughout the year.

3 OLYMPIC PARK
(✆ 03-9286 1600; www.mopt.com.au; Batman Ave, Jolimont) Olympic Park is the home ground for the **Melbourne Storm** (www.melbournestorm. com.au), the only Melbourne side in winter's **National Rugby League** (NRL; www.nrl.com.au) competition.

4 ROD LAVER ARENA
(✆ 03-9286 1600; www.mopt.com.au; Batman Ave, Jolimont) This arena hosts the **Australian Open** (www.ausopen.org) – the top tennis players from around the world come to compete in the first of each year's four Grand Slam tournaments. It features a retractable roof which keeps the summer sun at bay.

Melbourne take you past Melbourne city's newest developments and explain the history of the older ones. Moonlight tours are most evocative and include a 'fish 'n' chips' dinner.

STUDLEY PARK BOATHOUSE   Canoe Hire
(✆ 03-9853 1828; www.studleyparkboathouse. com.au) Pack a picnic then hire a two-person canoe or kayak from the boathouse for $30 for the first hour.

Cycling

Cycling maps are available from the Visitor Information Centre at Federation Sq (Map p218) and **Bicycle Victoria** (✆ 03-8636 8888; www.bv.com. au). Wearing a helmet while cycling is compulsory in Australia. Borrow a bike from the public scheme (p239), a private scheme or go vintage.

HUMBLE VINTAGE   Bike Hire
(✆ 0432 032 450; www.thehumblevintage. com) Get yourself a set of special wheels from this collection of retro racers, city bikes and ladies' bikes. Rates start at $30 per day, or $80 per week, and include lock, helmet and a terrific map. Bikes can be picked up from St Kilda, the CBD and Fitzroy. Give them a ring as the exact locations change.

Swimming

FITZROY SWIMMING POOL   Swimming
(✆ 03-9205 5180; Alexandra Pde, Fitzroy; adult/child $4.60/2.10; 🚊112) Between laps, locals love catching a few rays up in the bleachers or on the lawn. The pool's Italian 'Aqua Profonda' sign was painted in 1953 – an initiative of the pool's manager who frequently had to rescue migrant children who couldn't read the English signs.

MELBOURNE CITY BATHS   Swimming
(Map p218; ✆ 03-9663 5888; www.melbourne citybaths.com.au; 420 Swanston St, Melbourne; casual swim adult/child/family $5.50/2.60/12, gym $20; ⏱6am-10pm Mon-Thu, 6am-8pm Fri, 8am-6pm Sat & Sun) Enjoy a swim in the 1903 heritage-listed building.

Tours

 ### ABORIGINAL HERITAGE
WALK Indigenous
(🕿03-9252 2429; www.rbg.vic.gov.au; Royal
Botanic Gardens; adult/child $25/10; ⏰11am
Tue, Thu & 1st Sun of the month) The Royal
Botanic Gardens are on a traditional
camping and meeting place of the original
owners, and this tour takes you through
their story – from song lines to plant lore,
all in 90 fascinating minutes.

`FREE` City Circle Trams Tram Tour
(www.metlinkmelbourne.com.au) Free W-class
trams that trundle around the city perimeter
(and into the depths of Docklands) from 10am
to 6pm daily.

`FREE` MELBOURNE CITY
TOURIST SHUTTLE Bus Tour
(www.thatsmelbourne.com.au; ⏰9am-4.30pm)
This tourist bus takes about 1½ hours to
make its stops around Melbourne and its
inner suburbs. Stops include Lygon St,
Carlton, Queen Victoria Market, Melbourne Museum and, on non-sporting
days, the MCG.

`FREE` GREETER
SERVICE Walking Tour
(🕿03-9658 9658; Melbourne Visitor
Centre, Federation Sq) This free two-
hour 'orientation tour' departs
Fed Sq daily at 9.30am
(bookings required) and is
run by volunteer 'greeters'
who are keen to share
their knowledge. It's
aimed at giving visitors
to Melbourne a good
understanding of the
layout and sights of
Melbourne.

Hidden Secrets Tours Laneways
(🕿03-9663 3358; www.hiddensecretstours.
com; tours $70-145) Offers a variety of walking
tours covering everything, including lanes and
arcades, wine, architecture, coffee and cafes and
vintage Melbourne.

REAL MELBOURNE
BIKE TOURS Cycling
(Map p218; 🕿0417 339 203; www.rentabike.net.
au; Federation Sq; tours incl lunch adult/child
$110/79) Offers four-hour cycling tours
covering the CBD, parts of the Yarra and
Fitzroy. Also has bike hire (including child
seats and 'tagalongs') with hourly ($15)
daily ($30) and weekly ($100) rates.

Sleeping

CENTRAL MELBOURNE
MELBOURNE CENTRAL YHA Hostel $
(Map p218; 🕿03-9621 2523; www.yha.com.
au; 562 Flinders St; dm/d 32/100; @ 🛜)
This heritage building has been totally

Studley Park Boathouse on Yarra River
PHOTOGRAPHER: GLENN BEANLAND/LONELY PLANET IMAGES ©

transformed by the YHA gang; expect a lively reception, handsome rooms, and kitchens and common areas on each of the four levels. Entertainment's high on the agenda, there's a fab restaurant (Bertha Brown) on the ground floor and a grand rooftop area.

MEDINA EXECUTIVE FLINDERS STREET
Serviced Apartments $$

(Map p218; ☎03-8663 0000; www.medina.com. au; 88 Flinders St; apt from $165; ✳) These cool monochromatic apartments are extra large and luxurious. Ask for one at the front for amazing parkland views or get glimpses into Melbourne's lanes from the giant timber-floored studios, all boasting full kitchens.

ADELPHI HOTEL
Hotel $$

(Map p218; ☎03-8080 8888; www.adelphi.com. au; 187 Flinders Lane; r from $185; ✳@🖥️🏊) This discreet Flinders Lane property, designed by Denton Korker Marshall in the early 1990s, was one of Australia's first boutique hotels. The cosy rooms with original fittings have stood the test of time, and its pool, which juts out over Flinders Lane, has sparked imitators.

ROBINSONS IN THE CITY
Boutique Hotel $$

(Map p218; ☎03-9329 2552; www.ritc.com. au; 405 Spencer St; r incl breakfast from $185; ✳🖥️) Robinsons is a gem with six large rooms and warm service. The building is a former bakery, dating from 1850, but it's been given a modern, eclectic look. Bathrooms are not en suite; each room has its own in the hall.

ALTO HOTEL ON BOURKE
Hotel $$

(Map p218; ☎03-9606 0585; www.altohotel. com.au; 636 Bourke St; r from 160, apt from $190; ✳@🖥️) This environment-minded hotel has water-saving showers, energy-efficient light globes, and double-glazed windows that open, and in-room recycling is promoted. Rooms are also well equipped, light and neutrally decorated.

CAUSEWAY 353
Hotel $$

(Map p218; ☎03-9660 8888; www.causeway. com.au; 353 Little Collins St; r incl breakfast from $150; ✳@🖥️) Who needs a view when you've got laneway location? Causeway 353's breakfast is in a cafe on a bustling laneway, and you'll be more than relaxed after a night in its simple, stylish rooms which feature long and dark timber bedheads, king-sized beds and smart leather furniture.

HOTEL LINDRUM
Hotel $$$

(Map p218; ☎03-9668 1111; www.hotellindrum. com.au; 26 Flinders St; r from $245; ✳@🖥️) This attractive hotel was once the pool hall of the legendary and literally unbeatable Walter Lindrum. Expect rich tones, subtle lighting and tactile fabrics. Spring for a deluxe room and you'll snare either arch or bay windows and marvellous

Melbourne for Children

○ **ACMI** (p213) Free access to computer games and movies may encourage square eyes, but it's a great spot for a rainy day.

○ **Melbourne Zoo** (p222) Roar 'n' Snore packages (sleeping at the zoo) take you behind the scenes.

○ **National Sports Museum** (p217) Just walking in will get your junior champion's heart rate up.

○ **Melbourne Museum** (p221) The Children's Museum has hands-on exhibits that make kids squeal.

Snow leopard, Royal Melbourne Zoo (p222)

ALEX DISSANAYAKE/LONELY PLANET IMAGES ©

Melbourne views. And yes, there's a pool table.

JASPER HOTEL
Hotel **$$**

(Map p218; ☎03-8327 2777; www.jasperhotel.
com.au; 489 Elizabeth St; r from $180; ❄@🛜)
The old Hotel Y has had a makeover by
Jackson Clements Burrows and now
sports moody down lighting, a veritable
Pantone swatch-book of colours, louvred
bathrooms and some lovely graphic soft
furnishings. It's a tad soulless, though.
Guests have complimentary use of the
sporting facilities at the nearby
Melbourne City Baths.

VICTORIA HOTEL
Hotel **$$**

(Map p218; ☎03-9669 0000; www.victoria
hotel.com.au; 215 Little Collins St; s/d $99/110;
❄@🛜🏊) The original Vic opened its
doors in 1880, but don't worry, they've
updated the plumbing since then. This
city institution has around 400 rooms,
and all differ slightly. The Bellerive
and Heritage rooms are more upmarket,
but all have down lights and are
comfortable.

FITZROY & AROUND

BROOKLYN ARTS
HOTEL
Boutique Hotel **$$**

(☎03-9419 9328; www.brooklynartshotel.
com; 48-50 George St, Fitzroy; s/d incl breakfast
$95/135; 🛜; 🚃86) There are seven very
different rooms in this character-filled
hotel. Owner Maggie has put the call out
for artistic people and they've responded
by staying, so expect lively conversation
around the continental breakfast. Rooms
are clean, colourful and beautifully
decorated; one even houses a piano.

Carlton & Around

DOWNTOWNER ON LYGON
Hotel **$$**

(☎03-9663 5555; www.downtowner.com.au;
66 Lygon St, Carlton; r from $169; ❄@🛜;
🚃1, 8) The Downtowner is a surprising complex of different-sized rooms,
including joining rooms perfect for
families and couples travelling together.
Ask for a light-bathed room if you can.
It's perfectly placed between the CBD
and Lygon St restaurants.

DISCOVER MELBOURNE & THE GREAT OCEAN ROAD MELBOURNE

SOUTH YARRA, PRAHRAN & WINDSOR

PUNTHILL APARTMENTS
SOUTH YARRA
Apartments $$
(✆1300 731 299; www.punthill.com.au; 7 Yarra St, South Yarra; r from $180; ❄🛜; 🚇South Yarra) It's the little things, like a blackboard and chalk in the kitchen for messages, and individually wrapped liquorice all-sorts by the bed, that make this a great choice. The bright rooms have laundry facilities and those with balconies come complete with their own (tin) dog on fake grass.

ART SERIES
(CULLEN)
Boutique Hotel $$
(✆03-9098 1555; www.artserieshotels.com.au/cullen; 164 Commercial Road, Prahran; r from $169; ❄@🛜; 🚇78,79) Expect visions of Ned Kelly shooting you from the glam opaque room/bathroom dividers in this new and lively hotel resplendent in the works of Sydney artist Adam Cullen. Borrow the 'Cullen Car' ($60 per day) or Kronan bike ($5 per hour) and let the whole of Melbourne know where you're staying.

ST KILDA & AROUND

PRINCE
Hotel $$$
(✆03-9536 1111; www.theprince.com.au; 2 Acland St, St Kilda; r incl breakfast from $260; ❄@🛜; 🚇16, 79, 96, 112) The Prince has a suitably dramatic lobby and the rooms are an interesting mix of the original pub's proportions, natural materials and a pared-back aesthetic. On-site 'facilities' take in some of the city's most men-tioned: bars, band rooms and even a wine shop downstairs.

BASE
Hostel $$
(✆03-8598 6200; www.basebackpackers.com; 17 Carlisle St, St Kilda; dm from $30, r from $110; ❄@🛜; 🚇16, 79, 96) Accor spin-off Base has streamlined dorms, each with en suite, or slick doubles. There's a 'sanctu-ary' floor for female travellers, and a bar and live music nights to keep that good-time vibe happening.

HOTEL TOLARNO
Hotel $$
(✆03-9537 0200; www.hoteltolarno.com.au; 42 Fitzroy St, St Kilda; r from $155; ❄@🛜; 🚇16, 79, 96, 112) Tolarno was once the site of Georges Mora's seminal gallery Tolar-no. Rooms upstairs are brightly coloured and eclectically furnished, with good beds and crisp white linen. Those at the front of the building might get a bit noisy for some, but have balconies, floorboards and enormous windows.

Around St Kilda

MIDDLE PARK HOTEL
Pub $$
(✆03-9690 1958; www.middleparkhotel.com.au; 102 Canterbury Rd, Middle Park; r incl breakfast from $180; 🚇112; ❄🛜) With a locked bedside drawer labeled 'x', and an 'x' keyring to match (hello $70 'intimacy' pack), you might be wondering what kind of hotel you've booked yourself into, but relax. A Six Degrees renovation has ensured the rooms feel luxurious and modern – expect ipod docks and rain showerheads when you reach the top of the wooden staircase. There's a modern pub and restaurant downstairs, and the cooked gourmet breakfast in the dining room is a treat.

 Eating

CENTRAL MELBOURNE

VUE DE
MONDE
French, Modern Australian $$$
(Map p218; ✆03-9691 3888; www.vuedemonde.com.au; Rialto, 525 Collins St; lunch/dinner menu gourmand from $100/150; ⏱lunch & dinner Tue-Fri, dinner Sat). Melbourne's favoured spot for occasion dining has relocated to the old 'observation deck' of the Rialto, so its view will finally match its name. Expect the usual fantastic French cuisine thanks to visionary Shannon Bennett. Book ahead.

FLOWER DRUM
Chinese $$$
(Map p218; ✆03-9662 3655; www.flower-drum.com; 17 Market Lane; mains $35-55; ⏱lunch Mon-Sat, dinner daily) The Flower Drum con-tinues to be Melbourne's most celebrated Chinese restaurant. The finest, freshest

produce prepared with absolute attention to detail keeps this Chinatown institution booked out for weeks in advance.

GINGERBOY   Modern Hawker **$$**
(Map p218; ☎03-9662 4200; www.gingerboy.com.au; 27-29 Crossley St; small dishes $13-16, large dishes $30-36; ☺lunch & dinner Mon-Fri, dinner Sat) Brave the aggressively trendy surrounds and weekend party scene, as talented Teague Ezard does a fine turn in flash hawker cooking. Flavours pop in dishes such as scallops with green chilli jam or coconut kingfish with peanut and tamarind dressing. There are two dinner sittings, and bookings are required.

CUMULUS INC   Modern Australian **$$**
(Map p218; www.cumulusinc.com.au; 45 Flinders Lane; mains $21-38; ☺breakfast, lunch & dinner Mon-Sat) One of Melbourne's best for breakfasts, lunches and dinners; it gives you that wonderful Andrew McConnell style along with really reasonable prices. The focus is on beautiful produce and simple but artful cooking: from breakfasts of sardines and smoked tomato on toast to suppers of freshly shucked clair de lune oysters, as you sit tucked away on the leather banquettes.

MOVIDA   Spanish **$$**
(Map p218; ☎03-9663 3038; www.movida.com.au; 1 Hosier Lane; tapas $4-6, raciones $10-17; ☺lunch & dinner) Movida is nestled in a cobbled laneway emblazoned with one of the world's densest collections of street art; it doesn't get much more Melbourne than this. Line up along the bar, cluster around little window tables or, if you've booked, take a table in the dining area. **Movida Next Door** (next door!) is the perfect place for a pre-show beer and tapas, while way over in the lawyer-end of town is larger **Movida Aqui**, with its lovely terrace.

ITALIAN WAITERS CLUB   Italian **$$**
(Map p218; 1st fl, 20 Meyers Pl; mains $15-18; ☺lunch & dinner) Once only for Italian and Spanish waiters to unwind after work over a game of *scopa* (a card game) and a glass of wine, now everyone from suits to students is allowed in for hearty plates of red-sauce pasta and the roster of regularly changing specials.

Movida Next Door

GERARD WALKER/LONELY PLANET IMAGES ©

PORTELLO ROSSO Tapas $$
(Map p218; www.portellorosso.com.au; 15 Warburton Lane; tapas $15; ⏲lunch Tue-Fri, dinner Tue-Sat) Chef Aaron Whitney has travelled to Melbourne via Byron Bay and Majorca so expect excellent (read: real) tapas. There's an olde-worlde cocktail bar upstairs (Murmur), and the whole space harks back to its industrial past.

MAHA Middle Eastern $$
(Map p218; ☎03-9629 5900; www.mahabg.com.au; 21 Bond St; small dishes $8-10, large dishes $20-26; ⏲lunch & dinner Mon-Fri, dinner Sat) Get your reservation in for a meal at this sexy subterranean space. It pays homage to the richness and complexity of Middle Eastern and Eastern Mediterranean cooking, but is done with a light, modern touch. Chef Shane Delia's Maltese heritage gets a look in too – rabbit is only off the menu when it's not in season.

**PELLEGRINI'S
ESPRESSO BAR** Italian, Cafe $
(Map p218; ☎03-9662 1885; 66 Bourke St; mains $12-16; ⏲breakfast, lunch & dinner) The iconic Italian equivalent of a classic 1950s diner, Pellegrini's has remained genuinely

unchanged for decades. Pick and mix from the variety of pastas and sauces; from the table out the back you can watch it all thrown together from enormous ever-simmering pots. In summer, finish with a ladle of watermelon granita.

NORTH MELBOURNE

COURTHOUSE HOTEL Pub Fare $$
(www.thecourthouse.net.au; 86 Errol St, North Melbourne; mains $18-41; ⏲lunch & dinner Mon-Sat; 🚊57) This corner pub has managed to retain the comfort and familiarity of a local while taking food, both in its public bar and its more formal dining spaces, very seriously. Lunch deals, including a glass of wine, are good value at $37, or head to the front bar for (cheaper) finds.

RICHMOND

DEMITRI'S FEAST Greek $
(www.dimitrisfeast.com.au; 141 Swan St Richmond; mains $14-16; ⏲breakfast & lunch Tue-Sun; 🚊70) Warning: don't even attempt to get a seat here on the weekend; aim for a quiet weekday when you'll have time and space to fully immerse yourself in lunches like a calamari salad with ouzo aioli.

RICHMOND HILL CAFE & LARDER
Cafe $$

(www.rhcl.com.au; 48-50 Bridge Rd, Richmond; brunch $12-30; ⊙breakfast & lunch; ⌖West Richmond, ⊟48, 75) Once the domain of well-known cook Stephanie Alexander, it still boasts its lovely cheese room and simple, comforting food like cheesy toast. There are breakfast cocktails for the brave. Wellington St in the CBD becomes Bridge Rd.

FITZROY & AROUND

CUTLER & CO   Modern Australian $$$

(☎03-9419 4888; www.cutlerandco.com.au; 55 Gertrude St, Fitzroy; ⊙dinner Tue-Sun, lunch Fri & Sun; ⊟86) Hyped for all the right reasons, this is Andrew McConnell's latest restaurant and though its decor might be a little over the top, its attentive, informed staff and joy-inducing meals (suckling pig is a favourite) have quickly made this one of Melbourne's best.

ST JUDE'S CELLARS   Modern Australian $$

(www.stjudescellars.com.au; 389-391 Brunswick St, Fitzroy; mains around $22-26; ⊙lunch & dinner Tue-Sun, breakfast Sat & Sun; ⊟112) A cavernous warehouse space has been given a clever, cool and humanising fit-out while not losing its airy industrial feel. The restaurant stretches out from behind the shopfront cellar, affording respite from the Brunswick St hustle. Mains include mussels and leek in Coldstream cider and goat ragout, but try their innovative desserts, too.

MOROCCAN SOUP BAR   North African, Vegetarian $$

(☎03-9482 4240; 183 St Georges Rd, North Fitzroy; banquet $18; ⊙6pm-10pm Tue-Sun; ⊟112) Prepare to queue before being seated by stern Hana, who will then go through the menu verbally. Best bet is the banquet, which, for three courses, is tremendous value. It's an alcohol-free zone, but (shhh) there's a cute bar next door.

BABKA BAKERY CAFE   Bakery, Cafe $

(358 Brunswick St, Fitzroy; mains $8-16; ⊙breakfast & lunch Tue-Sun; ⊟112) Russian flavours infuse the lovingly prepared breakfast and lunch dishes, and the heady aroma of cinnamon and freshly baked bread makes even just a coffee worth queuing for. Cakes are notable and can be taken away whole.

MARIOS   Cafe $

(303 Brunswick St, Fitzroy; mains around $14-25; ⊙breakfast, lunch & dinner; ⊟112) Mooching at Marios is part of the Melbourne 101 curriculum. Breakfasts are big and served all day, the service is swift and the coffee is old-school strong.

CARLTON & AROUND

ABLA'S   Lebanese $$

(☎03-9347 0006; www.ablas.com.au; 109 Elgin St, Carlton; mains $25; ⊙lunch Thu & Fri, dinner Mon-Sat; ⊟1, 8, 96, ⊟205) The kitchen here is steered by Abla Amad, whose authentic, flavour-packed food has inspired a whole generation of local Lebanese chefs. Bring a bottle of your favourite plonk and settle in for the compulsory banquet on Friday and Saturday night.

EMBRASSE RESTAURANT   French $$

(☎03-9347 3312; www.embrasserestaurant.com.au; 312 Drummond St, Carlton; mains $27-37; ⊙dinner Wed-Sun, lunch Thu-Sun) Pressure cooking chickpeas and daintily serving up emulsions, purees and flowers is Nicolas Poelaert's game, and the crowd is responding enthusiastically. Just off the main Lygon St drag, the space is intimate and formal. Sunday lunch is a four-course ode to France.

TIAMO   Italian $$

(303 Lygon St Carlton; mains $13-10) When you've had enough of pressed, siphoned, slayered, pour over filtered and plunged coffee, head here to one of Lygon Street's original Italian cafe-restaurants. There's laughter and the relaxed joie de vivre only a time-worn restaurant can have.

ST KILDA & AROUND

ATTICA   Contemporary $$$

(☎03-9530 0111; www.attica.com.au; 74 Glen Eira Rd, Ripponlea; 8-course tasting menu $144; ⊙dinner Tue-Sat; ⌖Ripponlea) Staking its claim to fame by being the only Melbourne restaurant to make it onto San Pellegrino's Best Restaurant list in 2010, Attica is a suburban restaurant that serves Ben Shewry's creative dishes degustation-style. Expect small portions of texture-oriented delight, like potatoes cooked in earth.

CICCIOLINA   Mediterranean $$
(www.cicciolinastkilda.com.au; 130 Acland St, St Kilda; mains $19-40; ☺lunch & dinner; ☒16, 96) This warm room of dark wood, subdued lighting and pencil sketches is a St Kilda institution. The inspired Mod-Med menu is smart and generous, and the service warm. They don't take bookings; eat early or while away your wait in the moody little back bar.

I CARUSI II   Pizza $$
(231 Barkly St, St Kilda; pizza $14-18; ☺dinner; ☒16, 96) I Carusi pizzas have a particularly tasty dough and follow the less-is-more tenet, with top-quality mozza, pecorino and a small range of other toppings. Bookings are advised.

SOUTH YARRA, PRAHRAN & WINDSOR

JACQUES REYMOND   Modern Australian $$$
(☎03-9525 2178; www.jacquesreymond.com.au; 78 Williams Rd, Prahran; 3 courses from $98; ☺lunch Thu-Fri, dinner Tue-Sat; ☒6) Reymond was a local pioneer of degustation dining. Degustation plates are now entrée-size, and there's an innovative vegetarian version. Expect a French-influenced, Asian-accented menu with lovely details including house-churned butter.

WINDSOR CASTLE   Pub $$
(89 Albert St, Windsor; mains $15-25; ☒Windsor) Cosy nooks, sunken pits, fire places (or, in summer, a beer garden) and yummo pub meals make the Windsor Castle an extremely attractive option.

🍷 Drinking

CENTRAL MELBOURNE

RIVERLAND   Bar
(Map p218; www.riverlandbar.com; Vaults 1-9, Federation Wharf (below Princes Bridge); ☺7am-midnight) This bluestone beauty sits by the water and keeps things simple with good wine, beer on tap and bar snacks.

SECTION 8   Bar
(Map p218; www.section8.com.au; 27-29 Tattersalls Lane; ☺8am-late Mon-Fri, noon-late Sat & Sun) The latest in shipping-container habitats, come and sink a Mountain Goat with the after-work crowd, who make do with packing cases for decor.

MELBOURNE SUPPER CLUB   Bar
(Map p218; 1st fl, 161 Spring St; ☺5pm-3am Mon-Sat) Melbourne's own Betty Ford's (the place you go when there's nowhere left to go), the Supper Club is open very late and is a favoured after-work spot for performers and hospitality types. Browse the encyclopaedic wine menu and relax; the sommeliers will cater to any liquid desire.

CROFT INSTITUTE   Bar
(Map p218; www.thecroftinstitute.net; 21-25 Croft Alley; ☺5pm-late Mon-Fri, 8pm-late Sat) Located in a laneway off a laneway, the lab-themed Croft is a test of drinkers' determination. Prescribe yourself a beaker of house-distilled vodka in the downstairs laboratory (some come complete with fat plastic syringes).

EAST MELBOURNE & RICHMOND

DER RAUM   Bar
(www.derraum.com.au; 438 Church St, Richmond; ☺5pm-late; ☒East Richmond, ☒70) The name conjures up images of a dark Fritz Lang flick and there's definitely something noir-ish about the space and their extreme devotion to hard liquor. It's hard to miss the bottles hanging from the ceiling as evidence of past boozing.

MOUNTAIN GOAT BREWERY
Microbrewery

(www.goatbeer.com.au; cnr North & Clark Sts, Richmond; ⏰from 5pm Wed & Fri only) This local microbrewery is set in a massive beer-producing warehouse; enjoy its range of beers while nibbling on pizza, or join a free brewery tour on Wednesday night.

FITZROY & AROUND

NAPIER HOTEL
Pub

(www.thenapierhotel.com; 210 Napier St, Fitzroy; ⏰3-11pm Mon-Thu, 1pm-1am Fri & Sat, 1-11pm Sun; 🚋112, 86) The Napier has stood on this corner for over a century and many pots have been pulled as the face of the neighbourhood changed. It's still a great spot for pub grub.

LITTLE CREATURES DINING HALL
Beer Hall

(www.littlecreatures.com.au; 222 Brunswick St Fitzroy; 📶; 🚋112) With free wi-fi, community bikes and a daytime kid-friendly groove, this vast drinking hall is the perfect place to spend up big on pizzas and enjoy local wine and beer.

NAKED FOR SATAN
Bar

(www.nakedforsatan.com.au; 285 Brunswick St; ⏰daily from noon until late; 🚋112) Vibrant, loud and reviving an apparent Brunswick St legend (a man nicknamed Satan who would get down and dirty, naked because of the heat, in an illegal vodka distillery under the shop), this place packs a punch both with its popular *pintxos* (bite-sized sandwiches; $2) and cleverly named beverages.

CARLTON & AROUND

GERALD'S BAR
Wine Bar

(386 Rathdowne St, Carlton North; ⏰5-11pm Mon-Sat; 🚋1, 8, 🚌253) Wine by the glass is democratically selected at Gerald's

and they spin some fine vintage vinyl from behind the curved wooden bar. If you get hungry, there are delightful morsels (of the likes of terrine and pork belly) to sink your teeth into.

ST KILDA & AROUND

CARLISLE WINE BAR
Wine Bar

(137 Carlisle St, Balaclava; ⏰brunch Sat & Sun, dinner daily; 🚉Balaclava, 🚋3, 16) Locals love this often rowdy, wine-worshiping former butcher's shop. The staff will treat you like a regular and find you a glass of something special, or effortlessly throw together a cocktail amid the weekend rush. Carlisle St runs east off St Kilda Rd.

GEORGE PUBLIC BAR
Bar

(www.georgepublicbar.com.au; Basement, 127 Fitzroy St, St Kilda; 🚋96, 16) Behind the crumbling paint and Edwardian arched windows of the George Hotel, there's the Melbourne Wine Room and a large front bar that keeps the after-work crowd happy. In the bowels of the building is

the George Public Bar, often referred to as the Snakepit.

⭐ Entertainment

Nightclubs

ALUMBRA Club
(www.alumbra.com.au; Shed 9, Central Pier, 161 Harbour Esplanade, Docklands; ⏱4pm-late Fri-Sun) Great music and a stunning location will impress – even if the Bali-meets-Morocco follies of the decorator don't.

REVOLVER UPSTAIRS Club
(www.revolverupstairs.com.au; 229 Chapel St, Prahran; ⏱noon-4am Mon-Thu, 24hr Fri-Sun; 🚃Prahran, 🚌6) Rowdy Revolver can feel like an enormous version of your own lounge room, but with 54 hours of nonstop music come the weekend, you're probably glad it's not.

Cinemas

Cinema multiplexes are spread throughout Melbourne city, and there are quite a few treasured independent cinemas in both the CBD and surrounding suburbs.

ASTOR Cinema
(www.astor-theatre.com; cnr Chapel St & Dandenong Rd, St Kilda; 🚃Windsor, 🚌64)

CINEMA NOVA Cinema
(www.cinemanova.com.au; 380 Lygon St, Carlton; 🚌1, 8).

KINO CINEMAS Cinema
(Map p218; www.palacecinemas.com.au; Collins Pl, 45 Collins St)
Outdoor cinemas are very popular in the summer; check the websites for seasonal opening dates and program details.

MOONLIGHT CINEMA Outdoor Cinema
(www.moonlight.com.au; Gate D, Royal Botanic Gardens, Birdwood Ave, South Yarra; 🚌8) Bring along a rug, pillow and moonlight supper, or buy food and drinks there, and set up

Left: Corner Hotel; **Below:** Esplanade Hotel (p236)

an outdoor living room in the middle of the gardens.

ROOFTOP CINEMA Outdoor Cinema
(Map p218; www.rooftopcinema.com.au; Level 6, Curtin House, 252 Swanston St, Melbourne) Here we have amazing views, a burger stall to keep you fed and a bar.

Theatre

MALTHOUSE THEATRE Theatre
(☎ 03-9685 5111; www.malthousetheatre. com.au; 113 Sturt St, South Melbourne; ☒ 1) The Malthouse Theatre Company often produces the most exciting theatre in Melbourne.

MELBOURNE THEATRE COMPANY Theatre
(MTC; ☎ 03-8688 0800; www.mtc.com.au; 140 Southbank Blvd, Southbank) Melbourne's major theatrical company stages around 15 productions annually, ranging from contemporary and modern (including many new Australian works) to Shakespearean and other classics.

Live Music

NORTHCOTE SOCIAL CLUB Live Music
(☎ 03-9489 3917; www.northcotesocialclub. com; 301 High St, Northcote; ☒ 86) This is one of Melbourne's best live-music venues, with a stage that's seen plenty of international folk just one album out from star status. If you're just after a drink, the front bar buzzes every night of the week, or there's a large deck out the back for lazy afternoons.

CORNER HOTEL Live Music
(☎ 03-9427 9198; www.cornerhotel.com; 57 Swan St, Richmond; ⊙ closed Mon; ☒ Richmond, ☒ 70) The band room here is one of Melbourne's most popular midsized venues and has seen plenty of loud and live action over the years. The rooftop has stunning city views, but gets superpacked, and often with a different crowd from the music fans below.

BENNETTS LANE — Live Music

(Map p218; www.bennettslane.com; 25 Bennetts Lane, Melbourne; tickets from $15; ⏰8.30pm-late) Bennetts Lane has long been the boiler room of Melbourne jazz. It attracts the cream of local and international talent and an audience that knows when it's time to applaud a solo.

ESPLANADE HOTEL — Live Music

(http://espy.com.au; 11 The Esplanade, St Kilda; ⏰noon-late Mon-Fri, 8am-late weekends; 🚋96, 16) Rock-pigs rejoice. The Espy remains gloriously shabby and welcoming to all. Bands play most nights and there's a spruced-up kitchen out the back. And for the price of a pot you get front row seats for the pink-stained St Kilda sunset.

TOTE — Live Music

(www.thetotehotel.com; cnr Johnston & Wellington Sts, Fitzroy; ⏰Thu-Sun 4pm-late; 🚋86) The Tote's closure in 2010 brought Melbourne to a stop. People protested on the CBD streets against the liquor-licensing laws that were blamed for the closure, and there were howls of displeasure on the radio waves. The punters won; there were changes to Melbourne's liquor-licensing laws, and, armed with new 'white knight' owners, the Tote reopened to continue its tradition of live bands playing dirty rock.

CHERRY — Live Music

(Map p218; ACDC Lane, Melbourne; ⏰5pm-late Tue-Fri, 9pm-late Sat) This rock 'n' roll refuge is still going strong. There's often a queue, but once inside a relaxed, slightly anarchic spirit prevails. Music is rarely live, but never electronic.

🔒 Shopping

CENTRAL MELBOURNE

CAPTAINS OF INDUSTRY — Clothing

(Map p218; www.captainsofindustry.com.au; Level 1, 2 Somerset Pl) Where can you get a haircut, a bespoke suit and pair of shoes made in the one place? Here. The hard-working folk at Captains also offer homey breakfasts and thoughtful lunches. To work!

COUNTER — Craft, Design

(Map p218; www.craftvic.au.au; 31 Flinders Lane) The retail arm of Craft Victoria, Counter showcases the handmade. Its range of jewellery, textiles, accessories, glass and ceramics bridges the art/craft divide and makes for some wonderful mementos of Melbourne.

AESOP — Beauty

City Centre (Map p218; QV, 35 Albert Coates Lane & 268 Flinders Lane); Fitzroy (242 Gertrude St, Fitzroy); Prahran (143 Greville St, Prahran) This home-grown skincare company specialises in products made from simple ingredients in simple packaging. The range is wide and based on botanical extracts.

FITZROY & AROUND

CRUMPLER — Accessories

(www.crumpler.com.au; cnr Gertrude & Smith Sts, Fitzroy; 🚋86) Crumpler's bike-courier bags started it all. Its durable, practical designs can now be found around the world, and it makes bags for cameras, laptops and iPods as well as its original messenger style.

THIRD DRAWER DOWN — Design

(www.thirddrawerdown.com; 93 George St, Fitzroy; 🚋86)
This seller-of-great-things makes life beautifully unusual by stocking everything from sesame-seed grinders to beer o'clock beach towels and 'come in, we're closed' signs.

POLYESTER RECORDS — Music

(387 Brunswick St, Fitzroy; 🚋112) This great record store has been selling Melburnians independent music from around the world for decades, and also sells tickets for gigs. There's a CBD **branch** (Map p218; 288 Flinders Lane, Melbourne).

CARLTON & AROUND

READINGS — Books

(309 Lygon St, Carlton; www.readings.com.au; 🚋16) A potter around this defiantly prospering indie bookshop can occupy an entire afternoon if you're so inclined. There's a dangerously loaded (and good-value) specials table, switched-on staff and everyone from Lacan to *Charlie & Lola* on the shelves.

WILL SALTER/LONELY PLANET IMAGES ©

Don't Miss **Melbourne Markets**

○ **Rose Street Artists' Market** (www.rosestmarket.com.au; 60 Rose St, Fitzroy; ◷11am-5pm Sat &Sun; ⬚112) One of Melbourne's best and most popular art-and-craft markets, just a short stroll from Brunswick St.

○ **Camberwell Sunday Market** (www.sundaymarket.com.au; Station St, behind the cnr of Burke & Riversdale Rds, Camberwell; gold coin donation; ◷7am-12.30pm Sundays; ⬚Camberwell, ⬚70,72,75) This is where Melburnians come to offload their unwanted items and antique hunters come to find them.

○ **Esplanade Market** (www.esplanademarket.com; Upper Esplanade, btwn Cavell & Fitzroy Sts, St Kilda; ◷10am-5pm Sun; ⬚96) Fancy shopping with a seaside backdrop? A kilometre of trestle tables joined end to end carry individually crafted products from toys to organic soaps to large metal sculptures of fishy creatures.

○ **Queen Victoria Market** (Queen Vic Market; Map p218; www.qvm.com.au; 513 Elizabeth St, Melbourne; ◷6am-2pm Tue & Thu, 6am-5pm Fri, 6am-3pm Sat, 9am-4pm Sun) Don't miss this 130-year old market (pictured above) with its meat hall, deli and expansive fruit and vegie sections. On Wednesdays during summer it also plays host to a lively and musical night market.

SOUTH YARRA, PRAHRAN & WINDSOR

CHAPEL STREET BAZAAR Collectables (217-223 Chapel St, Prahran; ⬚Prahran, ⬚78, 79) Calling this a 'permanent undercover collection of market stalls' won't give you any clue to what's tucked away here. This old arcade is a retro-obsessive riot. It doesn't matter if Italian art glass or Noddy egg cups are your thing, you'll find it here.

ⓘ Information

Medical Services

The Travel Doctor (TVMC; www.traveldoctor. com.au) City Centre (☎03-9935 8100; Level 2,

JOHN BANAGAN/LONELY PLANET IMAGES ©

393 Little Bourke St); Southgate (☎03-9690 1433; 3 Southgate Ave, Southgate) specialises in vaccinations.

The Royal Melbourne Hospital (☎03-9342 7666; www.rmh.mh.org.au; 300 Grattan St, Parkville) is a public hospital with an emergency department.

Money

There are ATMs throughout Melbourne. Bigger hotels offer a currency exchange service, as do most banks during business hours. There's a bunch of exchange offices on Swanston St.

Tourist Information

Melbourne Visitor Centre (MVC; ☎03-9658 9658; Federation Sq; ☺9am-6pm daily)

❶ Getting There & Away

Air

Two airports serve Melbourne: Avalon and Tullamarine, though at present only domestic airlines Tiger (☎03-9335 3033; www.tigerairways.com) and Jetstar (☎13 15 38; www.jetstar.com) operate from Avalon. These two airlines also fly from and to Tullamarine Airport, in addition to the domestic and international flights offered by Qantas (☎13 13 13; www.qantas.com) and Virgin Australia (☎13 67 89; www.virginaustralia.com).

Boat

Spirit of Tasmania (☎1800 634 906; www.spiritoftasmania.com.au) crosses Bass Strait from Melbourne to Devonport, Tasmania, at least nightly; there are also day sailings during peak season.

Bus, Car & Motorcycle

Southern Cross Station (Map p218; www.southerncrossstation.net.au) is the main terminal for interstate bus services.

V/Line (www.vline.com.au; around Victoria)

Firefly (www.fireflyexpress.com.au) From/to Adelaide & Sydney.

Greyhound (www.greyhound.com.au) Bus services Australia-wide.

Train

Interstate trains arrive and depart from Southern Cross Station.

ⓘ Getting Around

To/from the Airport

TULLAMARINE AIRPORT

There are no trains or trams to Tullamarine airport. Taxis charge from $40 for the trip to Melbourne's CBD, or you can catch SkyBus (☏03-9335 3066; www.skybus.com.au; adult/child one-way $16/6), a 20-minute express bus service to/from Southern Cross Station.

AVALON AIRPORT

Avalon Airport Transfers (www.sitacoaches.com.au; one-way $20; 50 min) meets all flights flying into and out of Avalon. It departs from Southern Cross Station; check website for times. There is no pre-booking required.

Bike

Melbourne Bike Share (www.melbourne bikeshare.com.au; ☏1300 711 590) began in 2010 and has had a slow start, mainly blamed on Victoria's compulsory helmet laws. Subsidised safety helmets are now available at 7Eleven stores around the CBD ($5 with a $3 refund on return). Each first half-hour of hire is free. Daily ($2.50) and weekly ($8) subscriptions require a credit card and $300 security deposit.

Car & Motorcycle

CAR HIRE

Avis (☏13 63 33; www.avis.com.au)

Budget (☏1300 362 848; www.budget.com.au)

Hertz (☏13 30 39; www.hertz.com.au)

Europcar (☏1300 131 390; www.europcar .com.au)

Thrifty (☏1300 367 227; www.thrifty.com.au)

Rent a Bomb (☏03-9696 7555; www.renta bomb.com.au)

TOLL ROADS

Motorcycles travel free on CityLink; car drivers will need to purchase a pass if they are planning on using one of the two toll roads (CityLink or EastLink, which runs from Ringwood to Frankston).

Public Transport

Flinders Street Station is the main metro train station connecting the city and suburbs. The City Loop runs under the city, linking the four corners of town.

An extensive network of tram lines covers every corner of the city, running north–south and east–west along most major roads. Trams run roughly every 10 minutes Monday to Friday, every 10 to 15 minutes on Saturday, and every 20 minutes on Sunday. Check Metlink (www. metlinkmelbourne.com.au) for more information. Also worth considering is the free City Circle tram, which loops around town.

TICKETING

The myki (www.myki.com.au) transport system covers Melbourne's buses, trams and trains and uses a 'touch on, touch off' system. Myki cards ($10 full fare) are available online; from Flinders Street Station; the MetShop (☏13 16 38; Melbourne Town Hall, cnr Swanston & Little Collins Sts); and the myki discovery centre at Southern Cross Station.

You need to top up your myki card with cash at machines located at most stations (or online, though it can take 24 hours to process). If you're only in town for a few days, short-term tickets can be bought from machines on buses, trains and trams, though fares are slightly more expensive than using a myki.

Costs:

○ Zone 1: myki money 2hr $2.94, short term 2hr $3.70

○ Zone 1: myki money daily $5.88, short term daily $6.80

Taxi

Melbourne's taxis are metered and require an estimated prepaid fare when hailed between 10pm and 5am. You may need to pay more or get a refund depending on the final fare. Toll charges are added to fares.

PHILLIP ISLAND

Famous for the Penguin Parade and Grand Prix racing circuit, Phillip Island is a spectacular natural environment, attracting a curious mix of surfers, petrolheads and international tourists making a beeline for those little penguins.

At its heart, 100-sq-km Phillip Island is still a farming community, but along with the penguins, there's a large seal colony, abundant bird life around the Rhyll wetlands, and a koala colony.

Sights & Activities

Phillip Island Nature Parks

The nature parks comprises three of the islands biggest attractions: the **Penguin Parade** (☏03-5951 2800; www.penguins. org.au; Summerland Beach; adult/child/family $20/10/50; ☺10am-dusk); the **Koala Conservation Centre** (☏03-5952 1307; adult/child/family $10/5/25; ☺10am-5pm, extended hr in summer), off Phillip Island Rd, with elevated boardwalks; and trips to **Churchill Island** (☏03-5956 7214; adult/child/family $10/5/25; ☺10am-4.30pm, extended hr in summer), a working farm also off Phillip Island Rd, where Victoria's first crops were planted and today features historic displays, including butter churning and blacksmithing.

Most people come for the **Little Penguins**, the world's smallest and probably cutest of their kind. The penguin complex includes concrete amphitheatres that hold up to 3800 spectators who visit to see the little fellas just after sunset as they waddle from the sea to their land-based nests. There are a variety of specialised **tours (adult $35-70)** so you can be accompanied by rangers or see them from the vantage of a Skybox (an elevated platform).

Seal Rocks & the Nobbies

The extreme southwestern tip of Phillip Island leads to the Nobbies and beyond them is **Seal Rocks**, inhabited by Australia's largest colony of fur seals. The **Nobbies Centre** (☏03-5951 2816; admission free, tours adult/child $10/5; ☺10am-8pm summer, 11am-5pm autumn, 11am-4pm winter; 11am-6pm spring) houses an interesting interpretive centre with interactive panels and games, and the huge windows afford great views of the 6000 Australian fur seals who loll here during the October to December breeding season.

Motor Racing Circuit

Even when the motorbikes aren't racing, petrolheads love the **Grand Prix Motor**

Hot-air ballooning over Domain Chandon vineyard, Yarra Valley

JULIET COOMBE/LONELY PLANET IMAGES ©

Detour:
Yarra Valley Wineries

The **Yarra Valley** (www.wineyarravalley.com), about an hour northeast of Melbourne, has more than 80 wineries and 50 cellar doors scattered around its rolling hills – the first vines were planted at Yering Station in 1838. The region produces cool-climate, food-friendly drops such as Chardonnay, Pinot Noir and Pinot Gris.

Boat O'Craigo (☎03-8357 0188; 458 Maroondah Hwy, Healesville) Boutique winery with two vineyards producing fruity reds and whites like Shiraz and Pinot Gris.

Domain Chandon (☎9738 9200; www.chandon.com.au; 727 Maroodah Hwy, Coldstream) Established by the makers of Moet, this slick operation is worth a visit for the free guided tours at 1pm and 3pm where you can sample the bubbly.

Rochford (☎03-5962 2119; www.rochfordwines.com; cnr Maroondah Hwy & Hill Rd, Coldstream) Rochford is a huge complex with restaurant, cafe and regular concerts.

TarraWarra Estate (☎03-5957 3510; www.tarrawarra.com.au; 311 Healesville–Yarra Glen Rd, Yarra Glen) Convivial bistro and a superb art gallery ($5) come together in a striking building.

Yering Farm Wines (☎03-9739 0461; www.yeringfarmwines.com; St Huberts Rd, Yering) A rustic and friendly little cellar door in an old hay shed with lovely views.

Yering Station (☎03-9730 0100; www.yering.com; 38 Melba Hwy, Yering) A modern complex with a fine restaurant, gourmet provedore and bar, it's home to the heady Shiraz-Viognier blend.

Racing Circuit (☎03-5952 9400; www.phillipislandcircuit.com.au; Back Beach Rd; ⊗8.30am-5.30pm Mon-Fri), which was souped up for the Australian Motorcycle Grand Prix in 1989, although the island hosted its first Grand Prix way back in 1928. The **visitor centre** (☎03-5952 9400; ⊗9am-6pm) runs 45-minute **guided circuit tours** (adult/child/family $19/10/44; ⊗tours 11am & 2pm), which include a visit to the History of Motorsport Museum, as well as the chance to cut laps of the track in hotted-up V8s (one/two/three people $210/315/365, booking essential).

Beaches & Surfing

Ocean beaches on the south side of the island include **Woolamai**, a popular surf beach with dangerous rips and currents. The surf at **Smiths Beach** is more family-friendly, though it gets busy on summer weekends. There are calm, sheltered beaches at Cowes.

Island Surfboards (www.islandsurfboards.com.au; surfing lessons $55, surfboard hire per hr/day $13/40) Smiths Beach (☎03-5952 3443; 65 Smiths Beach Rd); Cowes (☎03-5952 2578; 147 Thompson Ave) can start your waxhead career with wetsuit hire and lessons for all standards.

Birds & Wildlife

A good range of wildlife can be spotted at **Phillip Island Wildlife Park** (☎03-5952 2038; Thompson Ave; adult/child/family $15/8/40; ⊗10am-5.30pm, later in summer), about 1km south of Cowes, including Tasmanian devils, cassowaries and quolls.

Tours

Go West Day Tour
(☎1300 736 551; www.gowest.com.au; 1-day tour $125) One-day tour from Melbourne that includes lunch and iPod commentary in several languages.

Wildlife Coast Cruises Wildlife, Cruises
(☎1300 763 739; 5952 3501; www.wildlifecoastcruises.com.au; Rotunda Bldg, Cowes Jetty; tours $35-70; ⊗Nov-May) Runs a variety of cruises from Cowes including seal-watching,

twilight and cape cruises; also a half-day cruise to French Island (adult/child $55/75) and full day to Wilsons Promontory ($140/190).

Sleeping

SURF & CIRCUIT ACCOMMODATION
Apartments **$$**

(☎03-5952 1300; www.surfandcircuit.com; 113 Justice Rd, Cowes; apt $135-380; ❄❂) Ideal for families or groups, these eight spacious, modern and comfortable two- and three-bedroom units accommodate up to six and 10 people, and have kitchens and lounges with plasma TVs and patios, and some have spas.

Waves Apartments
Apartments **$$**

(☎03-5952 1351; www.thewaves.com.au; Esplanade; d/tr/q from $180/195/210; ❄) These slick apartments overlook Cowes main beach so you can't beat your balcony views if you go for a beachfront unit. The modern self-contained apartments come with spa and balcony or patio.

Eating

INFUSED
Modern Australian **$$**

(☎03-5952 2655; www.infused.com.au; 115 Thompson Ave, Cowes; mains $25-38; ⊙lunch & dinner Wed-Mon) Infused's groovy mix of timber, stone and lime-green decor makes a relaxed place to enjoy a beautifully presented lunch or dinner, or just a late-night cocktail. The eclectic Mod Oz menu is strong on seafood and moves from freshly shucked oysters to Asian curries and Black Angus rib eye.

MADCOWES
Cafe, Deli **$**

(☎03-5952 2560; 17 The Esplanade, Cowes; mains $7-17; ⊙breakfast & lunch) This stylish cafe-foodstore looks out to the beach. Try the ricotta hotcakes or the grazing platter, and browse the selection of wine and produce.

ⓘ Information

Phillip Island Visitors Centres (☎1300 366 422, 03-5956 7447; www.visitphillipisland.com; ⊙9am-5pm, to 6pm during school holidays; @)

Newhaven (**895 Phillip Island Tourist Rd**); Cowes (**cnr Thompson & Church Sts**)

ⓘ Getting There & Away

By car, Phillip Island can only be accessed across the bridge at San Remo to Newhaven. From Melbourne take the Monash Fwy (M1) and exit at Packenham, joining the South Gippsland Hwy at Koo Wee Rup.

Bus

V/Line (☎13 61 96; www.vline.com.au) has train/bus services from Melbourne's Southern Cross Station via Dandenong Station or Koo Wee Rup ($10.40, 2½ hours). There are no direct services.

Ferry

Inter Island Ferries (☎03-9585 5730; www.interislandferries.com.au; return adult/child/bike $21/10/8) runs between Stony Point on the Mornington Peninsula and Cowes via French Island (45 minutes). There are two sailings on Monday and Wednesday, and three on Tuesday, Thursday, Friday, Saturday and Sunday.

ⓘ Getting Around

Hire bicycles from **Ride On Bikes** (☎03-5952 2533; www.rideonbikes.com.au; 43 Thompson Ave, Cowes; half-/full-day $25/35).

GREAT OCEAN ROAD

The Great Ocean Road (B100) is one of Australia's most famous road-touring routes. It takes travellers past world-class surfing breaks, through pockets of rainforest and calm seaside towns, and under koala-filled tree canopies. Walk it, drive it, enjoy it.

ⓘ Getting There & Away

The following tours depart from Melbourne and often cover the Great Ocean Road in a day:

Go West Tours (☎1300 736 551; www.gowest.com.au)

Ride Tours (☎1800 605 120; www.ridetours.com.au)

Autopia Tours (☎03-9391 0261; www.autopiatours.com.au)

Goin South (☎ 1800 009 858; www.goinsouth.com.au)

Otway Discovery (☎ 03-9654 5432; www.otwaydiscovery.com.au)

Adventure Tours (☎ 1800 068 886; www.adventuretours.com.au)

Bus

Three buses a week (Monday, Wednesday and Friday) travel from Geelong along the Great Ocean Road to Warrnambool ($27, six hours). There are around 10 V/Line (☎ 13 61 96; www.vline.com.au) buses a day to Port Fairy ($3.40, 30 minutes) and three continue on to Portland ($9.20, 1½ hours). There's a bus on Monday, Wednesday and Friday to Apollo Bay ($15.80, 3½ hours). **Christians Bus Co** (☎ 03-5562 9432) runs services on Tuesday, Friday and Saturday to Port Fairy ($3.30, departing 8am).

Train

V/Line (☎ 13 61 96; www.vline.com.au; Merri St) trains run to Melbourne ($26, 3¼ hours, three or four daily).

Torquay

In the 1960s and '70s, Torquay was just another sleepy seaside town. Back then surfing in Australia was a decidedly counter-cultural pursuit, and its devotees were crusty hippy drop-outs living in clapped-out Kombis, smoking pot and making off with your daughters. Since then surfing has become unabashedly mainstream and a huge transglobal business. The town's proximity to world-famous Bells Beach and status as home of two iconic surf brands – Ripcurl and Quicksilver, both initially wetsuit makers – ensures Torquay is the undisputed capital of Australian surfing.

Sights & Activities

SURFWORLD MUSEUM Museum
(www.surfworld.org.au; Surf City Plaza, Beach Rd; adult/child/family $10/6/20; ☺9am-5pm) Imbedded at the rear of the Surf City Plaza is this homage to Australian surfing, with shifting exhibits, a theatre and displays of old photos and monster balsa mals. Two-hour surfing lessons start at $50, try:

Go Ride A Wave Surfing Lessons
(☎ 1300 132 441; www.gorideawave.com.au; 1/15 Bell St, Torquay; 143b Great Ocean Rd, Anglesea; ☺9am-5pm)

Torquay Surfing Academy Surfing Lessons
(☎ 03-5261 2022; www.torquaysurf.com.au; 34a Bell St, Torquay; ☺9am-5pm)

Sleeping

BELLBRAE HARVEST Apartments $$$
(☎ 03-5266 2100; www.bellbraeharvest.com.au; 45 Portreath Rd; d $200; ❄) Far from the

Torquay front beach

madding crowd, here are three separate (and stunning) split-level apartments looking onto a dam. Expect rainwater shower heads, kitchenettes, huge flat-screen TVs and lots and lots of peace.

Eating

SCORCHED   Modern Australian   **$$**
(☎03-5261 6142; www.scorched.com.au; 17 The Esplanade; mains $26-36; ◷lunch Fri-Sun, dinner Wed-Sun) This might be the swankiest restaurant in Torquay, overlooking the waterfront, with classy understated decor and windows that open right up to let the sea breeze in. Try the seasonal grazing plate.

❶ Information

Torquay Visitors Centre (www.greatoceanroad. org; Surf City Plaza, Beach Rd; @)

Torquay to Anglesea

About 7km from Torquay is **Bells Beach**. The powerful point break at Bells is part of international surfing folklore (it's here, in name only, that Keanu Reeves and Patrick Swayze had their ultimate showdown in the film *Point Break*). Since 1973, Bells has hosted the **Rip Curl Pro** (www.asp worldtour.com) every Easter – *the* glamour event on the world-championship ASP World Tour.

Nine kilometres southwest of Torquay is the turn-off to spectacular **Point Addis**, 3km down this road. It's a vast sweep of pristine 'clothing optional' beach that attracts surfers, hang-gliders and swimmers. At Point Addis there's a signposted **Koorie Cultural Walk**, a 1km circuit trail to the beach through the **Ironbark Basin** nature reserve.

Anglesea

Anglesea's **Main Beach** is the ideal spot to learn to surf, while sheltered **Point Road-knight Beach** is good for kiddies. Check out the resident **kangaroo** population at the town's golf course, or hire a paddle boat and cruise up the Anglesea River.

🏃 Activities

Go Ride A Wave   Surfing
(☎1300 132 441; www.gorideawave. com.au; 143b Great Ocean Rd; ◷9am-5pm) Rents out kayaks and surfboards and runs two-hour surfing lessons (from $75).

❶ Information

Visitor Centre (16/87 Great Ocean Rd; ◷9am-5pm Sep-May, 10am-4pm Jun-Aug)

Kangaroos, Anglesea Golf Club
PHOTOGRAPHER: BERNARD NAPTHINE/LONELY PLANET IMAGES ©

Great Ocean Road Distances & Times

Melbourne to Geelong	75km	1hr
Geelong to Torquay	21km	15 mins
Torquay to Anglesea	21km	15 mins
Anglesea to Aireys Inlet	10km	10 mins
Aireys Inlet to Lorne	22km	15 mins
Lorne to Apollo Bay	45km	1hr
Apollo Bay to Port Campbell	88km	1hr 10mins
Port Campbell to Warrnambool	66km	1hr
Warrnambool to Port Fairy	28km	20 mins
Port Fairy to Portland	72km	1hr
Portland to Melbourne	440km	6½hrs

Lorne

Lorne has an incredible natural beauty; tall gum trees line its hilly streets and Loutit Bay gleams irresistibly. Lorne gets busy; in summer you'll be competing with day trippers for restaurant seats and boutique bargains, but, thronged with tourists or not, Lorne is a lovely place to hang out.

Sights & Activities

QDOS ART GALLERY   Gallery
(03-5289 1989; www.qdosarts.com; 35 Allenvale Rd; 8.30am-6pm Thu-Mon, daily school holidays) Qdos, tucked in the hills behind Lorne, always has something arty in its galleries, and sculptures dot its lush landscape. Its cafe fare is nothing but delicious, and you can stay the night in one of its luxury Zen treehouses ($200 per night, two-night minimum, no kids).

ERSKINE FALLS   Waterfall
Head out of town to see this lovely waterfall. It's an easy walk to the viewing platform or 250 (often slippery) steps down to its base, from which you can explore further or head back on up.

Sleeping

CHAPEL   Cottage $$$
(03-5289 2622; thechapellorne@bigpond.com; 45 Richardson Blvd; d $200;) This contemporary two-level bungalow has been lifted from the pages of a glossy magazine, with tasteful Asian furnishings, splashes of colour and bay windows that open into the forest. It's secluded and romantic, with double shower and complimentary robes.

ALLENVALE COTTAGES   Cottages $$
(03-5289 1450; www.allenvale.com.au; 150 Allenvale Rd; d from $175) These four self-contained early-1900s timber cottages, that each sleep four (or more), have been luxuriously restored. They're 2km north-west of Lorne, arrayed among shady trees and green lawns, complete with bridge and babbling brook. It's ideal for families.

GREAT OCEAN ROAD COTTAGES & BACKPACKERS YHA   Hostel $
(03-5289 1070; www.yha.com.au; 10 Erskine Ave; tents $25, dm $20-30, d $55-75, cottages $170) Tucked away in the bush among the cockatoos and koalas, this two-storey timber lodge has spacious dorms, bargain tents with beds already set up, and top-value doubles. The more expensive

245

A-frame cottages sleep up to six with kitchens and en suites.

Eating

BA BA LU BAR Spanish $$$
(www.babalubar.com.au; 6a Mountjoy Pde; mains $32-42; ⏰breakfast, lunch & dinner) It's all a bit Spanish at Ba Ba Lu Bar, what, with its wintery paella nights and Chilean singers popping in for a gig in summer. The menu has inspired tapas and plenty of meat-based mains, and the bar kicks on into the wee hours.

Kafe Kaos Cafe $
(www.kafekaos.com.au; 52 Mountjoy Pde; lunch $8-15; ⏰breakfast & lunch) Bright and perky, Kafe Kaos typifies Lorne's relaxed foodie philosophy – barefoot patrons in boardies or bikinis tucking into first-class paninis, bruschettas, burgers and chips.

ℹ️ Information

Lorne Visitors Centre (☏1300 891 152; www.visitsurfcoast.com.au; 15 Mountjoy Pde; ⏰9am-5pm)

Apollo Bay

Apollo Bay is synonymous with music festivals, the Otways and lovely beaches, and it's one of the least claustrophobic hamlets along the Great Ocean Road.

👁️ Sights & Activities

COMMUNITY MARKET Market
(www.apollobay.com/market_place; ⏰8.30am-4.30pm Sat) This market is held along the main strip and is the perfect spot for picking up local apples, locally made souvenirs and just-what-you've-always-wanted table lamps made from tree stumps.

MARK'S WALKING TOURS Walking Tours
(☏0417 983 985; www.greatoceanwalk.asn.au/markstours; 2-3hr tours adult/child $50/15) Take a walk around the area with local Mark Brack, son of the Cape Otway Lighthouse

keeper. He knows this stretch of coast, its history and ghosts better than anyone around.

Apollo Bay Sea Kayaking Kayaking Tours
(☏0405 495 909; www.apollobaysurfkayak.com.au; 2hr tours $65) Head out to an Australian fur-seal colony on a two-seated kayak. Tours depart from Marengo beach and are suitable for children over 12.

Otway Expeditions Outdoor Adventure
(☏03-5237 6341; http://otwayexpeditions.tripod.com; argo rides from $45) Take a dual suspension bike through the Otways (minimum six people), or go nuts in an amphibious all-terrain 8x8 argo buggy.

🛏️ Sleeping

YHA ECO BEACH Hostel $
(☏03-5237 7899; 5 Pascoe St; dm $32-38, d $88-95, f $109-145; ❄️ @) Even if you're not on a budget this three-million-dollar, architect-designed hostel is an outstanding place to stay. Its eco-credentials are too many to list here, but it's a wonderful piece of architecture with great lounge areas, kitchens, TV rooms, internet lounge and rooftop terraces.

Nelson's Perch B&B B&B $$
(☏03-5237 7176; www.nelsonsperch.com; 54 Nelson St; d $160; ❄️ @ 📶) Nelson's looks fresher than some of the town's weary B&Bs. There are three rooms, each with a courtyard, and free wireless internet.

Eating

Vista Seafood $$
(www.thevistaseafoodrestaurant.com; 155 Great Ocean Rd; mains $25-35; ⏰dinner) This is fab, upmarket dining on the main drag. Spend hours cracking a locally caught crab, supported in your endeavours by local wine.

La Bimba Modern Australian $$$
(125 Great Ocean Rd; mains $25-45; ⏰breakfast, lunch & dinner Wed-Mon) This upstairs Mod Oz restaurant is outstanding – definitely worth the splurge. It's a warm,

relaxed smart-casual place with views, friendly service and a good wine list.

● Information

Great Ocean Road Visitor Centre (⌀ 03-5237 6529; 100 Great Ocean Rd; ⊙ 9am-5pm)

Cape Otway

Cape Otway is the second-most southerly point of mainland Australia (after Wilsons Promontory) and one of the wettest parts of the state. This coastline is particularly beautiful, rugged and dangerous. More than 200 ships came to grief between Cape Otway and Port Fairy between the 1830s and 1930s, which led to the 'Shipwreck Coast' moniker.

The turn-off for Lighthouse Rd, which leads 12km down to the lighthouse, is 21km from Apollo Bay. The **Cape Otway Lighthouse** (⌀ 03-5237 9240; www.lightstation.com; adult/child/family $17/8/42; ⊙ 9am-5pm) is the oldest surviving lighthouse on mainland Australia and was built in 1848 by more than 40 stonemasons without mortar or cement.

Port Campbell National Park

The road levels out after leaving the Otways and enters narrow, relatively flat scrubby escarpment lands that fall away to sheer, 70m cliffs along the coast between Princetown to Peterborough – a distinct change of scene. This is Port Campbell National Park – home to the Twelve Apostles – the most famous and most photographed stretch of the Great Ocean Road.

The **Gibson Steps**, hacked by hand into the cliffs in the 19th century by local landowner Hugh Gibson (and more recently replaced by concrete steps), lead down to feral Gibson Beach, an essential stop. The lonely **Twelve Apostles** are rocky stacks that have been abandoned to the ocean by retreating headland. Today, only seven Apostles can be seen from the viewing platforms (see the boxed text, below). The understated roadside **lookout** (Great Ocean Rd; ⊙ 9am-5pm), 6km past Princetown, has public toilets and a cafe. Helicopters zoom around the Twelve Apostles, giving passengers an amazing view of the rocks. **12 Apostles Helicopters** (⌀ 03-5598 6161; www.12apostleshelicopters.com.au) is just behind the car park at the lookout and offer a 10-minute tour covering the Twelve Apostles, Loch Ard Gorge, Sential Rock and Port Campbell from $95 per person.

Nearby **Loch Ard Gorge** is where the Shipwreck Coast's most famous and haunting tale unfolded when two young

How Many Apostles?

The Twelve Apostles are not 12 in number, and, from all records, never have been. From the viewing platform you can clearly count seven Apostles, but maybe some obscure others? We consulted widely with Parks Victoria officers, tourist office staff and even the cleaner at the lookout, but it's still not clear. Locals tend to say 'It depends where you look from', which, really, is true.

The Apostles are called 'stacks' in geologic lingo, and the rock formations were originally called the 'Sow and Piglets'. The soft limestone cliffs are dynamic and changeable, constantly eroded by the unceasing waves – one 70m-high stack collapsed into the sea in July 2005 and the Island Archway lost its archway in June 2009. If you look carefully at how the waves lick around the pointy part of the cliff base, you can see a new Apostle being born.

survivors of the wrecked iron clipper *Loch Ard* made it to shore (see the boxed text, below).

Port Campbell

This small, windswept town is poised on a dramatic, natural bay, eroded from the surrounding limestone cliffs, and almost perfectly rectangular in shape. It's a friendly place with some great bargain accommodation options, and makes an ideal spot for debriefing after the Twelve Apostles.

Tours

Port Campbell Touring Company   Tours
(📞 03-5598 6424; www.portcampbelltouring.com.au; half-day tours $65) Runs Apostle Coast tours, a Loch Ard evening walk and fishing trips to Crofts Bay.

Sleeping & Eating

PORT CAMPBELL GUESTHOUSE   Guesthouse $
(📞 0407 696 559; www.portcampbellguesthouse.com.au; 54 Lord St; guesthouse/flashpackers per person $35/38) It's great to find a home away from home, and this property close to town has a cosy house with four

bedrooms out back and a separate motel-style 'flashpackers' section up front. Great for families.

ROOM SIX   Restaurant $$
(28 Lord St; mains $15-30; ⊙ breakfast, lunch & dinner Fri-Wed) Come here for delightful dinners (featuring all the good seafood of the area) or a simple snack during the day. Although only new, its ambience suggests a lovely maturity.

ℹ️ Information

Port Campbell Visitor Centre (📞 1300 137 255; www.visit12apostles.com.au; 26 Morris St; ⊙ 9am-5pm)

Port Campbell to Warrnambool

The Great Ocean Road continues west of Port Campbell passing more rock stacks. The next one is the **Arch**, offshore from Point Hesse.

Nearby is **London Bridge**...fallen down! Now sometimes called London Arch, it was once a double-arched rock platform linked to the mainland. Visitors could walk out across a narrow natural bridge to the huge rock formation. In January 1990, the bridge collapsed leaving two terrified tourists marooned on the world's newest

---

The Wreck of the Loch Ard

The Victorian coastline between Cape Otway and Port Fairy was a notoriously treacherous stretch of water in the days of sailing ships, due to hidden reefs and frequent heavy fog. More than 80 vessels came to grief on this 120km stretch in just 40 years.

The most famous wreck was that of the iron-hulled clipper *Loch Ard,* which foundered off Mutton Bird Island at 4am on the final night of its long voyage from England in 1878. Of 37 crew and 19 passengers on board, only two survived. Eva Carmichael, a nonswimmer, clung to wreckage and was washed into a gorge, where apprentice officer Tom Pearce rescued her. Eva and Tom were both 19 years old, leading to speculation in the press about a romance, but nothing actually happened – they never saw each other again and Eva soon returned back to Ireland (this time, perhaps not surprisingly) via steamship.

Detour:
Port Fairy

This seaside township at the mouth of the Moyne River was settled in 1835, and the first arrivals were whalers and sealers. Port Fairy still has a large fishing fleet and a relaxed, salty feel, with its old bluestone and sandstone buildings, whitewashed cottages, colourful fishing boats and tree-lined streets. The town is very much a luxury tourist destination and is home to art galleries, antique shops and boutiques.

The visitors' centre has brochures and maps that show the popular **Shipwreck Walk** and **History Walk**. On **Battery Hill** there's a lookout point, and cannons and fortifications positioned here in the 1860s. Down below there's a lovely one-hour walk around **Griffiths Island** where the Moyne River empties into the sea.

island – they were eventually rescued by helicopter.

The **Bay of Islands** is 8km west of tiny **Peterborough**, where a short walk from the car park takes you to magnificent lookout points.

The Great Ocean Road ends near here where it meets the Princess Hwy, which continues through the traditional lands of the Gunditjmara people into South Australia.

GIPPSLAND

It might not be as well known as the Great Ocean Road to the west, but Victoria's southeast coast easily boasts the state's best beaches, impossibly pretty lakeside villages and Victoria's finest coastal national parks, typified by the glorious Wilsons Promontory.

Wilsons Promontory National Park

If you like wilderness bushwalking, stunning coastal scenery and secluded white-sand beaches, you'll absolutely love this place. 'The Prom', as it's affectionately known, is one of the most popular national parks in Australia and our favourite coastal park.

The southern-most part of mainland Australia, the Prom once formed a land bridge that allowed people to walk to Tasmania.

Tidal River, 30km from the park entry, is the hub, and home to the Parks Victoria office, a general store, cafe and accommodation. The wildlife around Tidal River is remarkably tame: kookaburras and rosellas lurk expectantly (resist the urge to feed them), and wombats nonchalantly waddle out of the undergrowth.

Although there's a staffed **entry station** (⊙9am-sunset) where you receive a ticket, entry is free.

 **Activities**

There are more than 80km of marked **walking trails** here, taking you through forests, marshes, valleys of tree ferns, low granite mountains and along beaches backed by sand dunes. Even nonwalkers can enjoy much of the park's beauty, with car park access off the Tidal River road leading to gorgeous beaches and lookouts.

Swimming is safe from the beautiful beaches at **Norman Bay** (Tidal River) and around the headland at **Squeaky**

Beach – the ultra-fine quartz sand here really does squeak beneath your feet!

Tours

Bunyip Tours   Nature
(☏1300 286 947, 03-9650 9680; www.bunyiptours.com; day tour $120) One-day guided tour to the Prom from Melbourne, with the option of staying on another two days to explore by yourself.

Hiking Plus   Nature
(☏0418-341 537; www.hikingplus.com; 3-/5-day tours $1100/1800) This tour company organises fully catered and guided hikes to the Prom from nearby Foster. Packages include meals, a massage and spa, and you need only carry a light pack.

 Sleeping

Tidal River
Situated on Norman Bay and a short walk to a stunning beach, Tidal River is justifiably popular. Book well in advance through **Parks Victoria** (☏1800 350 552, 13 19 63; www.parkweb.vic.gov.au), especially for weekends and holidays. For the Christmas school-holiday period there's a ballot for sites (apply online by 31 July).

Accommodation includes **camp sites** (unpowered sites per car & 3 people $20-24, powered sites per vehicle & up to 8 people $44-52); **huts** (4-/6-bed $65/100); **cabins** (d $110-172, extra adult $23); luxury **safari tents** (d $250, extra person $20); and the isolated **Lighthouse Keepers' Cottage** (8-bed cottages per person $51-83) at the southern tip of the Prom.

Yanakie & Foster
BLACK COCKATOO
COTTAGES   Cottages $$
(☏03-5687 1306; www.blackcockatoo.com; 60 Foley Rd, Yanakie; d $160) You can take in glorious views of the national park without leaving your very comfortable bed – or without breaking the bank – in these private, stylish, black-timber cottages. There are three modern cottages and a three-bedroom house.

Prom Coast Backpackers   Hostel $
(☏03-5682 2171; www.yha.com.au; 40 Station Rd, Foster; dm/d/f from $30/70/90; @) This

Whale Rock, Tidal River, Wilsons Promontory National Park

Top Prom Short Walks

○ **Lilly Pilly Gully Nature Walk** An easy 5km (two hour) walk through heathland and eucalypt forests, with lots of wildlife.

○ **Mt Oberon Summit** Starting from the Mt Oberon car park, this moderate-to-hard 7km (2½ hour) walk is an ideal introduction to the Prom with panoramic views from the summit. The free Mt Oberon shuttle bus can take you to the Telegraph Saddle car park and back.

○ **Squeaky Beach Nature Walk** Another easy 5km return stroll through coastal tea trees and banksias to a sensational white-sand beach.

comfy little 10-bed YHA cottage in Foster is the closest backpacker hostel to the park. The owners also run the motel next door.

 Eating

The General Store in Tidal River stocks grocery items and some camping equipment, but if you're hiking it's cheaper to stock up in Foster. The **Prom Café** (☉breakfast, lunch & dinner; mains $12-22) is open daily for takeaway food, and serves breakfast, light lunches and bistro-style meals on weekends and holidays.

ⓘ Information

Parks Victoria (☏1800 350 552, 13 19 63; www.parkweb.vic.gov.au; Tidal River; ☉8.30am-4.30pm)

ⓘ Getting There & Away

There's no direct public transport between Melbourne and the Prom, but the Wilsons Promontory Bus Service (Moon's Bus Lines; ☏03-5687 1249) operates from Foster to Tidal River (via Fish Creek) on Friday at 4.30pm, returning on Sunday at 4.30pm ($8). This service connects with the V/Line bus from Melbourne at Fish Creek.

V/Line (☏13 61 96; www.vline.com.au) buses from Melbourne's Southern Cross Station travel direct to Foster ($16.60, three hours, four daily).

Uluru & the Red Centre

From Australia's youngest city, the lively Top End capital of Darwin, the Stuart Hwy tracks south to incredible Kakadu National Park, a tropical wonderland full of Aboriginal rock-art galleries, crocodiles, waterfalls and raucous birdlife.

The famous *Ghan* train continues further south, passing through ancient, little-populated desert lands. In this vast and apparently empty country, locals' wits are as dry as dusty boots, and ancient spirituality rubs up against Western ways.

Darwin looks towards Asia and at the same time celebrates the region's Indigenous culture and amazing natural splendour. Kakadu offers an unsurpassed education in both. The Red Centre of Australia – the sand really is red – offers a different story. Here the harsh climate has shaped a bare beauty and deep spirituality that is lost on few who visit Uluru. The nearby formations of Kata Tjuta are just as mesmerising.

Working on a didgeridoo, Darwin

JAMES BRAUND/LONELY PLANET IMAGES ©

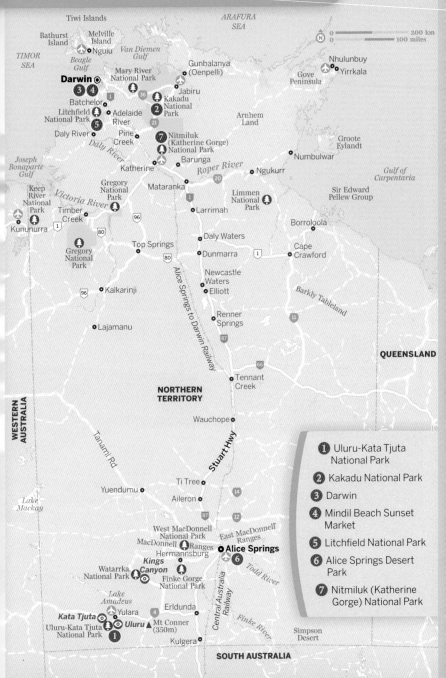

Uluru & the Red Centre

Uluru & the Red Centre Highlights

Uluru-Kata Tjuta National Park

Come and see the sun rising to unveil an ancient and spectacular rock in the middle of the continent, just as it has done every day for more than 3000 million years. Wonder at how this rock has provided water to a resourceful people for tens of thousands of years. Above: Uluru; Top Right: Kata Tjuta; Bottom Right: Aboriginal story-telling, Uluru

Need to Know

BEST BIRDWATCHING TIME From May to September BEST BIRDWATCHING SPOT Along the Valley of the Winds walk or Walpa Gorge at Kata Tjuta For further coverage, see p286.

Uluru-Kata Tjuta National Park Don't Miss List

BY TIM ROGERS, VISITOR SERVICES OFFICER,
ULURU-KATA TJUTA NATIONAL PARK

1 ANANGU TOURS

Make sure you go on a **tour** (p286) with a traditional owner and learn to see the landscape through Anangu eyes. You'll experience a land that's been sung about through story and law for generations, and hear a true Australian language that's been spoken throughout the desert regions for thousands of years. You'll begin to see how everything is interconnected and how this land has always provided everything the people need.

2 ULURU'S CHANGING MOODS

I'm a keen photographer, so here are my tips. Winter months are best for great sunrise shots. If you come in summer, then sunset shots are your best bet. If you're really lucky you'll get a rainbow with sun showers. When the heavens open and rain falls, Uluru suddenly has over 60 waterfalls cascading down – but only one in a hundred visitors gets to see this remarkable event.

3 YOUR OWN CONNECTION

If you want to be on your own at Uluru, slip off to one of the waterholes along the base walk an hour before sunset. While all the other guests are scrabbling for sunset photos, you'll have the whole rock to yourself. If you sit quietly the birds will come in to drink and just on dusk the microbats will come out and snatch insects out of the air.

4 KATA TJUTA

My favourite activity is a sunrise walk at Kata Tjuta (p289). As the sun comes up it casts an array of hues, and you'll see the wildlife among the domes. Or, contrary to the crowd, you can visit the car sunset viewing area at sunrise. It's a nice spot to have breakfast, and you have a fantastic view of the mysterious silhouette of Uluru as dawn awakens.

Kakadu National Park

There's an incredibly broad range of things to see and do in Kakadu: flora, fauna, waterfalls, Indigenous culture, lookouts, walks... The distinct shifts between the Wet and the Dry seasons alter the landscape dramatically – enough to warrant two visits! Below: Gunlom; Top Right: Aboriginal rock art, Nourlangie (p279); Bottom Right: Saltwater crocodile, Yellow Water (p280)

Need to Know

BEST PHOTO OPPORTUNITY Ubirr at sunset. **BEST TIME TO VISIT** Early in the Dry is best (May or June). Waterfalls open up and things are still green. **For further coverage, see p277.**

②

Kakadu National Park Don't Miss List

BY RICK DELANDER, KAKADU TOUR GUIDE, ADVENTURE TOURS AUSTRALIA

1 WILDLIFE

On the way into Kakadu from Darwin, Fogg Dam is a wonderful spot which attracts lots of wildlife and birdlife. Billabongs like Yellow Water are a must if people want to see crocodiles. The jumping crocodile cruises allow you to see crocs up close, but billabong cruises are more natural, with birds and crocodiles in their natural environment.

2 WATERFALLS & SWIMMING HOLES

Wet or Dry season, there are always places you can swim. Signs say 'Swim at Your Own Risk' because of crocodiles, but the park runs an extensive monitoring process so they can be pretty sure crocs aren't there. My favourite out-of-the-way spots are Maguk (Barramundi Gorge), Jim Jim Falls, Gunlom Falls... There's a big plunge pool at the base of Jim Jim that stays fresh all Dry season – it's a wonderful place.

3 WALKS & LOOKOUTS

There are some great long and short walks here, depending on what you're into. On the longer walks you can see waterfalls and have a nice refreshing swim! On the short walks around Ubirr and Nourlangie you can see rock art and some great views. Ubirr has a magnificent 360-degree lookout at the top: that's when people say they really feel they're in Kakadu.

4 INDIGENOUS KAKADU

Aboriginal culture is another big aspect of the park. Ubirr is a great spot to see some rock art and understand some of the culture. There's also a group at Muirella Park who run cultural talks and workshops. The Bowali Visitor Information Centre near Jabiru has a good display, but it's not really a one-on-one experience.

5 SCENIC FLIGHTS

You have to walk for an hour to get to some of the best spots, but if you can't do that scenic flights are a quick option. Fixed-wing and helicopter flights operate out of Jabiru and Cooinda, but you can get them from Darwin as well.

Darwin

Darwin (p266) is a boomtown, but maintains a small-town feel and a relaxed vibe that fits easily with the tropical climate. Boats sail around the harbour, chairs and tables spill out of streetside restaurants and bars, museums reveal the city's absorbing past, and galleries showcase the region's rich Indigenous art. Darwin's cosmopolitan mix is typified by the wonderful Asian markets held throughout the Dry season.

Litchfield National Park

Just 115km south of Darwin via the Stuart Hwy, impressive **Litchfield National Park** (p280) makes a brilliant, compact alternative to Kakadu if you're short on time. The park's waterfalls and swimming holes are as accessible as they are photogenic – and best of all you can take a swim! Crocodiles are less of an issue here than in Kakadu, and sealed roads make for a smooth-riding day trip.

Mindil Beach Sunset Market 4

Just follow your nose (and, seemingly, everyone else from Darwin) to the magical **Mindil Beach Sunset Market** (p267) behind the dunes north of the city at Mindil Beach. Every Thursday and Sunday from May to October, the market plays host to didgeridoo players, cavorting dance troupes, pan-Asian food stalls, souvenir stalls, masseurs, tarot readers, henna tattooists and more dreadlocks than Barbados.

JAMES BRAUND/LONELY PLANET IMAGES ©

ANDREW WATSON/LONELY PLANET IMAGES ©

6 Alice Springs Desert Park

Take a trip beyond the outskirts of Alice to discover this wonderful **wildlife park** (p284), where Australia's desert's creatures shed just enough shyness for you to get a good look at them. Make sure you catch the acrobatic birds of prey show, or come for breakfast or dinner to see either dawn-lit birdlife or spot-lit nocturnal beasties scratching through the sand.

7 Nitmiluk (Katherine Gorge) National Park

A short drive from Katherine (itself a three hour drive or train ride from Darwin), **Nitmiluk National Park** (p283) is a real jaw-dropper! Comprising a series of 13 sheer sandstone canyons, sliced through by the Katherine River, it's a brilliant place for canoeing, bushwalking, swimming or cruising below craggy stone overhangs. If you're time-poor you can take a helicopter flight and see it all from the sky.

Uluru & the Red Centre's Best...

Indigenous Cultural Experiences

○ **Kakadu National Park** (p277) Amazing rock art, ranger talks and tours.

○ **Uluru-Kata Tjuta National Park** (p286) Anangu-led tours reveal the true spirituality of these amazing rock formations.

○ **Museum & Art Gallery of the Northern Territory** (p266) Have a look at the Indigenous art exhibits at this outstanding centre.

○ **Alice Springs** (p281) Explore 'the Alice' and the MacDonnell Ranges with a local Warlpiri guide.

Wildlife Encounters

○ **Kakadu National Park** (p277) Crocodiles, brolgas, lizards, snakes, sea eagles, butterflies, barramundi... Kakadu is a veritable zoo!

○ **Alice Springs Desert Park** (p284) A brilliant place to meet Australia's mostly nocturnal and shy desert wildlife.

○ **Territory Wildlife Park** (p276) A showcase of Top End animals and birds.

○ **Crocosaurus Cove** (p267) Meet a croc in downtown Darwin.

Outdoor Activities

○ **Kata Tjuta hiking** (p289) Wandering through Kata Tjuta's Valley of the Winds is a timeless trip.

○ **Nitmiluk (Katherine Gorge) National Park canoeing** (p283) Head upstream and paddle below Nitmiluk's massive walls.

○ **Litchfield National Park swimming** (p280) Plunge into a refreshing rock pool at the base of a cascading waterfall.

○ **Darwin cycling** (p267) A flat city with good bike tracks and not much traffic: cycling is a great way to get around!

Need to Know

Shopping Opportunities

o **Mindil Beach Sunset Market** (p267) Glorious multicultural food, Asian crafts and buskers.

o **Darwin's Indigenous Galleries** (p267) Darwin's commercial Indigenous galleries stock everything from 'X-ray art' to dot paintings and craft from the Tiwi Islands.

o **Alice Springs Galleries** (p284) Close to the wellspring of Central Desert art, especially hyper-coloured dot paintings.

Left: Black-breasted buzzard, Territory Wildlife Park; **Above** Ubirr, Kakadu National Park

o **One month before** In peak times, book your room at Yulara at least a month before.

o **Two weeks before** Reserve a seat on the *Ghan* railway plus accommodation and a hire car in Darwin.

o **One week before** Book a guided overnight tour of Kakadu National Park or a day-trip to from Darwin.

o **Tourism Top End** (www. tourismtopend.com.au) Darwin-based tourism body.

o **Travel NT** (www.travelnt. com) Official tourism site.

o **Parks & Wildlife Service** (www.nt.gov.au/ nreta/parks) Details on Northern Territory (NT) parks and reserves.

o **Automobile Association of the Northern Territory** (AANT; www.aant.com.au) Driving information and emergency roadside assistance.

o **Road Report** (www.ntlis. nt.gov.au/roadreport) NT road-conditions report.

o **Fly** To Alice Springs or Darwin from the big east-coast cities.

o **Train** From Darwin to Alice Springs on the *Ghan*.

o **Drive** Around Kakadu and Litchfield National Parks.

o **Walk** Around the base of Uluru and through Kata Tjuta.

o **Crocodiles** Crocs move a long way inland – believe the warning signs.

o **Box jellyfish** We know, it's hot, but swimming in the tropical sea between October and May is a bad idea.

o **Yulara** Accommodation here gets mightily stretched in the peak season (winter), so book well in advance.

Uluru & the Red Centre Itineraries

There's an ethereal feel to Australia's red centre and Top End: blue skies collide with the flat desert expanse around Uluru, while Darwin and the tropical north burst with birdlife, wild rivers and untamed wilderness.

3 DAYS

DARWIN TO KAKADU NATIONAL PARK

Top End Taster

Start your tour at the Top End capital of **(1) Darwin**, where you can savour the delights of Asia and other cuisines from around the globe amidst the smoky aisles of Mindil Beach Sunset Market. You'll also come across crocodile, emu, kangaroo (trust us – it's delicious!) and barramundi on the menus at many of the city's relaxed restaurants. Celebrate your culinary bravery over a beer on Mitchell St afterwards.

Head south down the Stuart Hwy and follow the signs to **(2) Litchfield National Park**, which boasts some of the best natural swimming holes in the entire Top End. Nearby Batchelor has a slew of good accommodation options and a busy pub.

Next stop is **(3) Kakadu National Park**, via the boat tours at Adelaide River Crossing. You can catch your own barramundi at Kakadu, or join a bush-tucker Indigenous tour: learn about the hunt, the seasonal migrations of animals and vegetation changes. Watch bush food being prepared, join in and taste the results. Don't miss a hike up Nourlangie or Ubirr to check out ancient Aboriginal rock-art.

Top Left: Gunlom Falls, Kakadu National Park (p277); **Top Right:** Aboriginal performer, Katherine

PHOTOGRAPHERS: (TOP LEFT) RESIDENT MAGAZINE PTY. LTD./LONELY PLANET IMAGES ©; (TOP RIGHT) TIM WIMBORNE/REUTERS/CORBIS ©

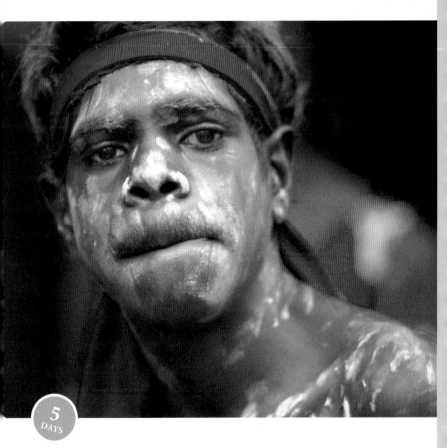

5 DAYS

KAKADU NATIONAL PARK TO ULURU-KATA TJUTA NATIONAL PARK

Journey to the Centre

The celebrated Indigenous cultures of Australia are as varied as the country itself. Begin this journey in the tropical Top End at **(1) Kakadu National Park** where, as the many rock-art galleries attest, Aboriginal people have lived for millennia. The bush-tucker larder here is full: there are few places in Australia with such a rich wild-food bounty.

For a different national park perspective, visit the gorgeous gorges of **(2) Nitmiluk (Katherine Gorge) National Park** near Katherine, or jump on the famous *Ghan* train and head south to **(3) Alice Springs**. While in 'the Alice' you can also experience Central Desert Aboriginal culture and maybe purchase a dot painting. Don't miss a visit to the excellent Alice Springs Desert Park to see how the local wildlife survives the desert heat.

The many colours and moods of **(4) Uluru** change with the hours of the day, and a full appreciation of this amazing region requires a couple of days. A tour with an Anangu guide will reveal the true nature and spirituality of the Rock. Also take some time to converse with the country by yourself – by walking around Uluru and the eerie rust-red domes of **(5) Kata Tjuta**.

Discover Uluru & the Red Centre

At a Glance

○ **Darwin** (p266) Australia's ebullient northern capital.

○ **Kakadu National Park** (p277) Tropical wilds, crocodiles and Indigenous heritage.

○ **Alice Springs** (p281) Central Australia's biggest town.

○ **Uluru-Kata Tjuta National Park** (p286) Iconic Uluru and the less-heralded (but no less impressive) Kata Tjuta.

○ **Litchfield National Park** (p280) A compact Kakadu for Darwin day-trippers.

Driving through Kakadu National Park
PHOTOGRAPHER: RICHARD I'ANSON/LONELY PLANET IMAGES ©

DARWIN

Australia's only tropical capital, Darwin gazes out confidently across the Timor Sea. It's closer to Bali than Bondi, and many from the southern states still see it as some strange outpost or jumping-off point for Kakadu National Park.

But Darwin is a surprisingly affluent, cosmopolitan, youthful and multicultural city, thanks in part to an economic boom fuelled by the mining industry and tourism.

⊙ Sights

MUSEUM & ART GALLERY OF THE NORTHERN TERRITORY Museum (MAGNT; www.nt.gov.au/nreta/museums; Conacher St, Fannie Bay; admission free; ⊙9am-5pm Mon-Fri, 10am-5pm Sat & Sun) This superb museum and gallery boasts beautifully presented Top End–centric exhibits. The **Aboriginal art collection** is a highlight, with carvings from the Tiwi Islands, bark paintings from Arnhem Land and dot paintings from the desert.

An entire room is devoted to **Cyclone Tracy**, in a display that graphically illustrates life before and after the disaster. You can stand in a darkened room and listen to the whirring sound of Tracy at full throttle – a sound you won't forget in a hurry. The cavernous **Maritime Gallery** houses an assortment of weird and wonderful craft from the nearby islands and Indonesia, as well as a pearling lugger and a Vietnamese refugee boat.

Pride of place among the stuffed animals undoubtedly goes to **Sweetheart**: a 5m-long, 780kg saltwater crocodile. It became a Top End personality after attacking several fishing dinghies on the Finniss River south of Darwin.

CROCOSAURUS COVE
Zoo

(www.croccove.com.au; 58 Mitchell St; adult/child $28/16; ⏱9am-8.30pm, last admission 7pm) Right in the middle of Mitchell St, Crocosaurus Cove is as close as you'll ever want to get to these amazing creatures. Six of the largest crocs in captivity can be seen in state-of-the-art aquariums and pools. Other aquariums feature barramundi, turtles and stingrays, plus there's an enormous reptile house (allegedly the largest variety of reptiles on display in the country!).

MINDIL BEACH SUNSET MARKET
Market

(www.mindil.com.au; off Gilruth Ave; ⏱5-10pm Thu, 4-9pm Sun May-Oct) As the sun heads towards the horizon on Thursday and Sunday, half of Darwin turns up to this spot, with their tables, chairs, rugs, grog and kids in tow. **Food** is the main attraction – Thai, Sri Lankan, Indian, Chinese and Malaysian to Brazilian, Greek, Portuguese and more – all at around $5 to $8 a serve. Don't miss a flaming satay stick from Bobby's brazier. Top it off with fresh fruit salad, decadent cakes or luscious crepes. But that's only half the fun: **arts and crafts** stalls bulge with handmade jewellery, fabulous rainbow tie-died clothes, Aboriginal artefacts, and wares from Indonesia and Thailand. Peruse and promenade, stop for a pummelling massage or to listen to rhythmic **live music**. Mindil Beach is about 2km from the city centre. Buses 4 and 6 go past the market area or you can catch a shuttle ($2).

DARWIN WATERFRONT PRECINCT
Neighbourhood

(www.waterfront.nt.gov.au) The bold redevelopment of the old Darwin Waterfront Precinct is well under way. The first stage of the multimillion-dollar project features a cruise-ship terminal, luxury hotels, boutique restaurants and shopping, an access walkway and free elevator at the south end of Smith St, and a **Wave Lagoon** (adult/child half-day $5/3.50, full-day $8/5; ⏱10am-6pm).

The old **Stokes Hill Wharf** (www.darwinport.nt.gov.au) is well worth an afternoon promenade. At the end of the wharf an old warehouse houses a **food centre** that's ideal for an alfresco lunch, cool afternoon beer or a seafood dinner as the sun sets over the harbour.

GALLERIES
Art Galleries

 **Maningrida Arts & Culture** (www.maningrida.com; Shop 1, 32 Mitchell St; ⏱9am-5pm Mon-Fri, 11.30am-4.30pm Sat) Features fibre sculptures, weavings and paintings from the Kunibidji community at Maningrida on the banks of the Liverpool River, Arnhem Land. Fully Aboriginal-owned.

Territory Colours (www.territorycolours.com; 46 Smith St Mall; ⏱10am-5pm) Contemporary paintings and crafts, including glass, porcelain and wood from local artists; features the work of contemporary Indigenous artist Harold Thomas.

Mbantua Fine Art Gallery (www.mbantua.com.au; 2/30 Smith St Mall; ⏱9am-5pm Mon-Sat) Vivid Utopian designs painted on everything from canvasses to ceramics.

EAST POINT RESERVE
Garden

North of Fannie Bay, this spit of land is particularly attractive in the late afternoon when wallabies emerge to feed and you can watch the sun set over the bay.

Lake Alexander, a small, recreational saltwater lake, was created so people could enjoy a swim year-round without having to worry about box jellyfish.

On the point's northern side is a series of WWII gun emplacements and the small but fascinating **Darwin Military Museum** (www.darwinmilitarymuseum.com.au; 5434 Alec Fong Lim Dr; adult/child $12/5; ⏱9.30am-5pm).

🏃 Activities

Cycling

Darwin is great for cycling. Traffic is light and a series of **bike tracks** covers most of the city, with the main one running from the northern end of Cavenagh St to Fannie Bay, Coconut Grove, Nightcliff and Casuarina.

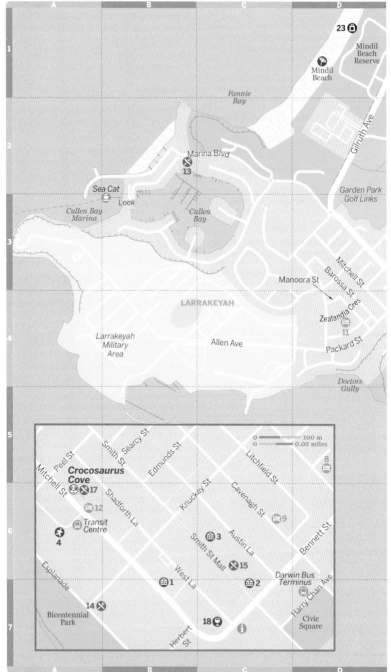

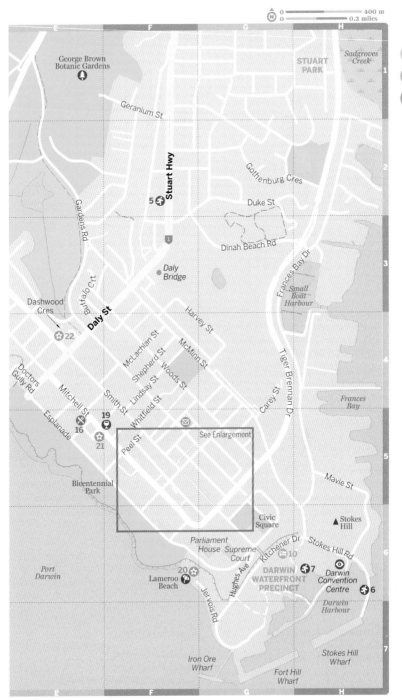

George Brown
Botanic Gardens

STUART
PARK

Sadgroves
Creek

Geranium St

Stuart Hwy

5

Gothenburg Cres

Duke St

Dinah Beach Rd

Frances Bay Dr

Small
Boat
Harbour

Gardens Rd

Daly
Bridge

Harvey St

Dashwood
Cres

Buffalo Crt

Daly St

22

McLachlan St

McMinn St

Tiger Brennan Dr

Frances
Bay

Doctors
Gully Rd

Mitchell St

Smith St

Shepherd St

Lindsay St

Woods St

Carey St

Esplanade

Whitfield St

16

19

21

Peel St

See Enlargement

Mavie St

Bicentennial
Park

Stokes
Hill

Civic
Square

Port
Darwin

20

Lameroo
Beach

Parliament
House Supreme
Court

Kitchener Dr

10

DARWIN
WATERFRONT
PRECINCT

7

Stokes Hill Rd

Darwin
Convention
Centre

6

Jervois Rd

Hughes Ave

Darwin
Harbour

Iron Ore
Wharf

Fort Hill
Wharf

Stokes Hill
Wharf

0 ____ 400 m
0 ____ 0.2 miles

Central Darwin

Darwin Scooter Hire Cycling
(www.esummer.com.au; 9 Daly St; ◷8am-5pm
Mon-Fri, 9am-3pm Sat) Mountain bikes for $20 a
day ($100 deposit required).

Darwin Holiday Shop Cycling
(www.darwinholidayshop.com.au; Shop 2, Mantra
on the Esplanade, 88 The Esplanade; ◷9am-5pm
Mon-Fri, 9am-1pm Sat) Mountain bikes per half/
full day $20/25.

Jetboating

If a harbour cruise is too tame, jump on **Oz
Jet** (☎1300 135 595; www.nt.ozjetboating.com;
30min rides adult/child $55/30) for a white-
knuckle ride around the harbour that'll
test how long it's been since you had
lunch. Departs from Stokes Hill Wharf.

 Tours

City Tours

**▰ Darwin Walking &
Bicycle Tours** Walking, Cycling
(☎08-8942 1022; www.darwinwalkingtours.com.
au) Two-hour guided history walks around the
city for $25 (children free), plus three-hour bike

tours (adult/child $45/35) that take you out to
Fannie Bay and East Point.

Tour Tub Sightseeing
(☎08-8985 6322; www.tourtub.com.au; adult/
child $40/15; ◷9am-4pm Jan-Nov) This open-
sided hop-on, hop-off minibus tours around
Darwin's big-ticket sights throughout the day.
Pay the driver onboard – cash only.

Harbour Cruises

Anniki Pearl Lugger Cruises Sailing
(☎0428 414 000; www.anniki.com.au; tours
adult/child $70/50) Three-hour sunset cruises
on this historical pearling lugger depart at
4.45pm from Cullen Bay Marina and include
sparkling wine and nibbles.

Spirit of Darwin Cruises
(☎0417 381 977; www.spiritofdarwin.net; tours
adult/child $45/20) This fully licensed air-con
motor-catamaran does a two-hour sightseeing
cruise at 2pm and a sunset cruise at 5.30pm
daily from Cullen Bay Marina.

Territory Trips

**Northern Territory
Indigenous Tours** Indigenous
(☎1300 921 188; www.ntindigenoustours.
com) Upmarket Indigenous tours to Litchfield

National Park stopping off at Territory Wildlife Park (adult/child $249/129).

 **Sacred Earth Safaris** Wilderness
(☏08-8981 8420; www.sacredearthsafaris.com. au) Multiday, small-group 4WD camping tours around Kakadu, Katherine and the Kimberley. Two-day Kakadu tour starts at $695; the five-day Top End tour is $1995.

 **Wallaroo Eco Tours** Sightseeing
(☏08-8983 2699; www.litchfielddaytours.com) Small-group tours to Litchfield National Park ($120).

🛏 Sleeping

City Centre

CAVENAGH Hostel, Motel $
(☏1300 851 198, 08-8941 6383; www.the cavenagh.com; 12 Cavenagh St; dm $25-30, d $89-159; ❄@🛜🏊) This converted '80s motel features stylish doubles and decent dorms convening around an enormous central pool. It's an informal, sociable kinda joint with a perpetual pool-party atmosphere and a rowdy on-site bar (even rowdier when the rugby is showing).

MELALEUCA ON MITCHELL Hostel $
(☏1300 723 437; www.momdarwin.com.au; 52 Mitchell St; dm $30, d with/without bathroom $115/95; ❄@🛜🏊) The highlight at this busy backpackers is the rooftop island bar and pool area overlooking Mitchell St – complete with waterfall spa and big-screen TV. Party heaven! The modern hostel is immaculate but a little sterile, with stark white walls and sparse rooms.

ARGUS Apartments $$$
(☏08-8925 5000; www.argusdarwin.com. au; 6 Cardona Ct; 1-/2-/3-bedroom apt from $260/410/495; ❄@🏊) In a corner of town awash with apartment towers, the Argus stands out as a quality option. Apartments are *very* spacious, with lovely bathrooms, generous expanses of cool floor tiles, simple balcony living/dining spaces and snazzy kitchens with all the requisite appliances.

VALUE INN Hotel $$
(☏08-8981 4733; www.valueinn.com.au; 50 Mitchell St; d from $135; ❄@🛜🏊) Right in the rump of the Mitchell St action but quiet and comfortable, Value Inn lives up to its name, especially out of season.

Mindil Beach (p267)

Ensuite rooms are small but sleep up to three and have fridge and TV.

MEDINA VIBE Hotel $$
(☎08-8941 0755; www.medina.com.au; 7 Kitchener Dr; d/studios from $170/180, 1-/2-bedroom apt $425/600; ❄@🛜❄) Two hotels in one building: standard doubles at Vibe, and studios and apartments next door at Medina. Either way, you're in for an upmarket stay with friendly staff and a great location in the Darwin Waterfront Precinct.

City Fringe & Suburbs

FEATHERS SANCTUARY Boutique Hotel $$$
(☎08-8985 2144; www.featherssanctuary.com; 49a Freshwater Rd, Jingili; d incl breakfast $330; ❄❄) A sublime retreat for bird-nerds and nature lovers, Feathers has beautifully designed 'Bali-meets-bush' timber-and-iron cottages with semi-open-air bathrooms and luxurious interiors. The lush gardens have a private aviary breeding some rare birds, and a waterhole – more tropical birds than you're ever likely to see in one place again!

STEELES AT LARRAKEYAH B&B $$
(Darwin City B&B; ☎08-8941 3636; www.darwinbnb.com.au; 4 Zealandia Cres, Larrakeyah; d from $175, 1-/2-bedroom apt $250/270; ❄❄) With a perfect residential location midway between the city centre, Cullen Bay and Mindil Beach, the three rooms in this pleasant Spanish Mission–style home are equipped with fridges, flat-screen TVs and private entrances.

 Eating

City Centre

FOUR BIRDS Cafe $
(Shop 2, Star Village, 32 Smith St Mall; items $4-8; ⏲breakfast & lunch Mon-Fri, plus Sat Jun-Aug) What a hip little cafe! Nooked into the arcade on the site of the old Star Cinema (a '74 cyclone victim), this hole-in-the-wall does simple things very well: bagels,

toasted sandwiches, muffins, paninis and coffee.

HANUMAN   Indian, Thai $$

(08-8941 3500; www.hanuman.com.au; 28 Mitchell St; mains $16-36; lunch Mon-Fri, dinner daily;) Sophisticated but not stuffy or pretentious (you can wear a T-shirt), enticing aromas of innovative Indian and Thai Nonya dishes waft from the kitchen to the stylish open dining room and deck. The signature dish is oysters bathed in lemon grass, chilli and coriander, or the *meen mooli* (reef fish in coconut and curry leaves) but the menu is broad, with exotic vegetarian choices and banquets available.

DUCKS NUTS
BAR & GRILL   Modern Australian $$

(08-8942 2122; www.ducksnuts.com.au; 76 Mitchell St; mains $15-35; breakfast, lunch & dinner) An effervescent bar/bistro delivering a clever fusion of Top End produce with that Asian/Mediterranean blend we like to claim as Modern Australian. Try the red Thai duck shank and banana curry, barra wrap or succulent lamb shanks. Good brekkies and caffeinated brews, too.

CHAR RESTAURANT   Steakhouse $$$

(08-8981 4544; www.charrestaurant.com. au; 70 The Esplanade; mains $31-46; lunch Wed-Fri, dinner daily) The speciality here is chargrilled steaks – aged, grain-fed and cooked to perfection – but there's also a range of seafood, a crab-and-croc lasagne and a thoughtful vegetarian menu.

City Fringe & Suburbs

SAFFRON   Indian $$

(08-8981 2383; www.saffrron.com; Shop 14, 34 Parap Rd, Parap; mains $14-26; lunch & dinner Tue-Sun;) Saffrron is Darwin's newest Indian restaurant, a contemporary but intimate dining experience. The menu spans the subcontinent, from rich butter chicken to Kerala lamb curry or Madras whole Northern Territory (NT) snapper.

273

If You Like…
Markets

If you like Darwin's mesmeric Mindil Beach Sunset Market, we think you'll like these markets too:

1 PARAP VILLAGE MARKET
(www.parapvillage.com.au; Parap Shopping Village, Parap Rd, Parap; ◷8am-2pm Sat) This compact, crowded food-focused market is a Darwin favourite with the full gamut of Southeast Asian cuisine, as well as plenty of ingredients to cook up your own tropical storm.

2 RAPID CREEK MARKET
(www.rapidcreekshoppingcentre.com.au; 48 Trower Rd; ◷6.30am-1.30pm Sun) Darwin's oldest market is another Asian marketplace, with a tremendous range of tropical fruit and vegetables mingled with a heady mixture of spices and swirling satay smoke.

3 NIGHTCLIFF MARKET
(www.marketsonline.com.au; Pavonia Way; ◷8am-2pm Sun) Another popular Darwin community market, north of the city in the Nightcliff Shopping Centre.

4 TODD MALL MARKET
(www.toddmallmarkets.com.au; ◷9am-1pm 2nd Sun, May-Dec) Buskers, craft stalls, sizzling woks, smoky satay stands, Aboriginal art, jewellery and knick-knacks make for a relaxed Alice Springs amble.

BUZZ CAFÉ   Modern Australian **$$**
(☎08-8941 1141; www.darwinhub.com/buzz-cafe; 48 Marina Blvd, Cullen Bay; mains $16-41; ◷lunch & dinner daily, breakfast Sun) This chic bar-restaurant furnished in Indonesian teak and Mt Bromo lava has a super multilevel deck overlooking the marina and makes a seductively sunny spot for a lazy lunch and a few drinks. Meals are Mod Oz, with some zingy salads and dishes to share.

🍷 Drinking

TAP ON MITCHELL   Bar
(www.thetap.com.au; 51 Mitchell St) One of the busiest of the Mitchell St terrace bars, the Tap is always buzzing and there are inexpensive meals (nachos, burgers, calamari) to complement a good range of wine and beers.

DARWIN SKI CLUB   Sports Club
(www.darwinskiclub.com.au; Conacher St, Fannie Bay) Leave Mitchell St behind and head for a sublime sunset at this laid-back (and refreshingly run-down) water-ski club on Vestey's Beach. The view through the palm trees from the beer garden is a winner, and there are often live bands.

DECK BAR   Bar
(www.thedeckbar.com.au; 22 Mitchell St) At the nonpartying parliamentary end of Mitchell St, the Deck Bar still manages to get lively with happy hours, pub trivia and regular live music. Blurring the line between indoors and outdoors brilliantly, the namesake deck is perfect for people-watching.

⭐ Entertainment

Live Music

NIRVANA   Jazz, Blues
(☎08-8981 2025; 6 Dashwood Cres) Behind an imposing dungeonlike doorway, this cosy restaurant-bar has live jazz/blues every Thursday, Friday and Saturday night and an open-mic jam session every Tuesday.

Nightclubs

DISCOVERY & LOST ARC   Nightclub
(www.myspace.com/discovery_nightclub; 89 Mitchell St; ◷9pm-4am Fri & Sat) Discovery is Darwin's biggest, tackiest nightclub and dance venue with three levels playing techno, hip hop and R&B. Lost Arc is the neon-lit chill-out bar opening on to Mitchell St, which starts to thaw after about 10pm.

Cinemas

DECKCHAIR CINEMA Outdoor Cinema
(08-8981 0700; www.deckchaircinema.com;
Jervois Rd, Waterfront Precinct; tickets adult/
child $13/6; box office from 6.30pm Apr-Nov)
During the Dry, the Darwin Film Society
runs this fabulous outdoor cinema below
the southern end of the Esplanade. Watch
a movie under the stars while reclining
in a deckchair – bring a cushion for extra
comfort. There's a licensed bar serving
food from Friday to Wednesday (teriyaki
noodles, pasta bolognese etc) or you can
bring a picnic (no BYO alcohol).

ℹ Information

Medical Services

Royal Darwin Hospital (08-8920 6011; www.
health.nt.gov.au; Rocklands Dr, Tiwi; 24hr)
Accident and emergency.

Travellers Medical & Vaccination Centre
(08-8901 3100; www.traveldoctor.com.au; 1st
fl, 43 Cavenagh St; 8.30am-noon & 1.30-5pm
Mon-Fri) GPs by appointment.

Money

There are 24-hour ATMs dotted around the city
centre, and exchange bureaux on Mitchell St.

Tourist Information

Tourism Top End (1300 138
886, 08-8980 6000; www.
tourismtopend.com.au; 6 Bennett
St; 8.30am-5pm Mon-Fri,
9am-3pm Sat, 10am-3pm Sun)
Stocks hundreds of brochures
and can book tours and
accommodation.

ℹ Getting There & Away

Air

Apart from the following major
carriers arriving at Darwin

International Airport (www.darwinairport.com.
au; Henry Wrigley Dr, Marrara), smaller routes are
flown by local operators; ask a travel agent.

Qantas (www.qantas.com.au) Direct flights to
Perth, Adelaide, Canberra, Sydney, Brisbane,
Alice Springs and Cairns.

Virgin Australia (www.virginaustralia.com)
Direct flights between Darwin and Brisbane,
Melbourne and Perth.

Jetstar (www.jetstar.com) Direct flights to
Melbourne.

Bus

Greyhound Australia (www.greyhound.com.
au) operates long-distance bus services from
the Transit Centre (69 Mitchell St). There's at
least one service per day up/down the Stuart
Hwy, stopping at Pine Creek ($71, three hours),
Katherine ($88, 4½ hours), Mataranka ($125,
seven hours), Tennant Creek ($265, 14½ hours)
and Alice Springs ($367, 22 hours).

For Kakadu, there's a daily return service from
Darwin to Cooinda ($87, 4½ hours) via Jabiru
($62, 3½ hours).

Darwin Ski Club

A Great Train Journey

The famous interstate *Ghan* train is run by Great Southern Rail (www.gsr.com.au), grinding across the long, straight desert tracks between Darwin and Adelaide via Katherine and Alice Springs. It's not the cheapest or fastest way to go, but it's a brilliant way to gain an appreciation of the vast, dry heart of Central Australia.

The Darwin terminus is on Berrimah Rd, 15km/20 minutes from the city centre. A taxi fare into the centre is about $30, though there is a shuttle service to/from the Transit Centre for $10. Darwin or Katherine to Alice Springs seat/sleeper costs $358/668; Darwin to Adelaide costs $716/1372. Trains runs weekly (twice weekly May to July).

Car & Campervan

For driving around Darwin, conventional vehicles are cheap enough, but most companies offer only 100km free, which won't get you very far. Rates start at around $40 per day for a small car with 100km per day. There are also plenty of 4WD vehicles available in Darwin, but you usually have to book ahead and fees/deposits are higher than for 2WD vehicles.

Most rental companies are open every day and have agents in the city centre. Avis, Budget, Hertz and Thrifty all have offices at the airport.

Advance Car Rentals (www.advancecar.com.au; 86 Mitchell St) Small local operator with some good deals (ask about unlimited kilometres).

ℹ️ Getting Around

To/From the Airport

Darwin International Airport (www.darwinairport.com.au) is 12km north of the city centre, and handles both international and domestic flights. Darwin Airport Shuttle (☎1800 358 945, 08-8981 5066; www.darwinairportshuttle.com.au) will pick up or drop off almost anywhere in the centre for $13. When leaving Darwin book a day before departure. A taxi fare into the centre is about $25.

Public Transport

Darwinbus (www.nt.gov.au/transport) runs a comprehensive bus network that departs from the Darwin Bus Terminus (Harry Chan Ave), opposite Brown's Mart.

A $2 adult ticket gives unlimited travel on the bus network for three hours (validate your ticket when you first get on). Daily ($5) and weekly ($15) travel cards are also available from bus interchanges, newsagencies and the visitor information centre.

Alternatively, the privately run Tour Tub (www.tourtub.com.au) is a hop-on, hop-off minibus touring Darwin's sights throughout the day.

Scooter

Darwin Scooter Hire (www.esummer.com.au; 9 Daly St) Rents out mountain bikes/500cc scooters/motorbikes for $20/60/180 per day.

Taxi

Call Darwin Radio Taxis (☎13 10 08; www.131008.com).

AROUND DARWIN

TERRITORY WILDLIFE PARK   Zoo

(www.territorywildlifepark.com.au; 960 Cox Peninsula Rd; adult/child $26/13; ⏰8.30am-6pm, last admission 4pm) Showcases the best of Aussie wildlife in a state-of-the-art open-air zoo. Highlights include the Flight Deck, where birds of prey display their dexterity (free-flying demonstrations at 11am and 2.30pm daily); the nocturnal house, where you can observe nocturnal fauna such as bilbies and bats; 11 habitat aviaries, each representing a different habitat from mangroves to woodland; and a huge walk-through aviary, representing a monsoon rainforest. Pride of place must go to the aquarium, where a clear walk-through tunnel puts you among giant barramundi, stingrays, sawfish and saratogas, while a separate tank holds a 3.8m saltwater crocodile.

The turn-off to the Territory Wildlife Park is 48km down the Track from Darwin; it's then 10km to the park.

KAKADU & ARNHEM LAND
Kakadu National Park

Kakadu is much more than just a national park. It's an adventure into a natural and cultural landscape that almost defies description.

In just a few days you can cruise on billabongs bursting with **wildlife**, examine 25,000-year-old rock paintings with the help of an Indigenous guide, swim in pools at the foot of tumbling **waterfalls** and hike through ancient sandstone escarpment country.

Kakadu has over 60 species of mammals, more than 280 bird species, about 120 types of reptile, 25 species of frog, 55 freshwater fish species and at least 10,000 different kinds of insect.

Tours

Kakadu Animal Tracks   Indigenous
(📞08-8979 0145; www.animaltracks.com.au; tours adult/child $189/129) Based at Cooinda, this outfit runs tours with an Indigenous guide combining a wildlife safari and Aboriginal cultural tour.

Top End Explorer Tours   Sightseeing
(📞1300 556 609, 08-8979 3615; www.kakadutours.net.au; tours adult/child $168/140) 4WD tours to Jim Jim Falls and Twin Falls – not on everyone's hit list.

Kakadu Air   Flights
(📞1800 089 113; www.kakaduair.com.au) Offers 30-minute/one-hour fixed-wing flights for $130/210 per adult. Helicopter tours, though more expensive, give a more dynamic aerial perspective. They cost from $195 (20 minutes) to $495 (70 minutes) per person.

YELLOW WATER CRUISES   Cruises
(📞1800 500 401; www.gagudju-dreaming.com) Cruise the South Alligator River and Yellow Water Billabong spotting wildlife. Purchase tickets from Gagudju Lodge, Cooinda, where a shuttle bus will deliver

Saltwater crocodile, Territory Wildlife Park

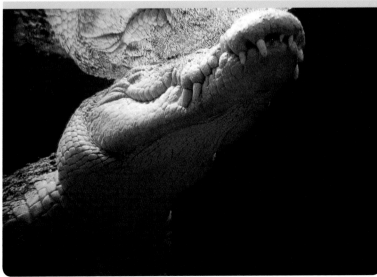

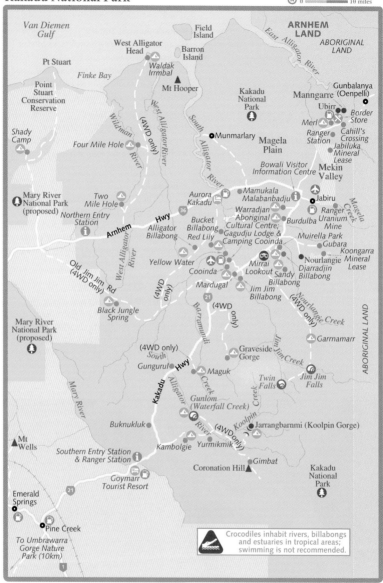

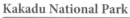

DISCOVER ULURU & THE RED CENTRE KAKADU NATIONAL PARK

Crocodiles inhabit rivers, billabongs and estuaries in tropical areas; swimming is not recommended.

you to the departure point. Two-hour cruises ($95/69 per adult/child) depart at 6.45am, 9am and 4.30pm; 1½-hour cruises ($64/44) leave at 11.30am, 1.15pm and 2.45pm.

Ubirr & Around

It'll take a lot more than the busloads of visitors here to disturb Ubirr's inherent majesty and grace. Layers of **rock-art paintings**, in various styles and from various centuries, command a mesmerising stillness.

The magnificent **Nardab Lookout** is a 250m scramble from the main gallery. Surveying the exotic floodplain and watching the sun set in the west and the moon rise in the east, like they're on an invisible set of scales gradually exchanging weight, is humbling.

Jabiru

It may seem surprising to find a town of Jabiru's size and structure in the midst of a wilderness national park, but it exists solely because of the nearby Ranger uranium mine.

🛏 Sleeping & Eating

LAKEVIEW PARK — Cabins **$$**
(📞08-8979 3144; www.lakeviewkakadu. com.au; 27 Lakeside Dr; en suite powered sites $35, bungalows/d/cabins $115/125/ 225; ❄) Although there are no lake views as such, this beautifully landscaped Aboriginal-owned park is one of Kakadu's best with a range of interesting tropical-design bungalows set in lush gardens.

KAKADU LODGE & CARAVAN PARK — Resort, Caravan Park **$$$**
(📞1800 811 154; www.auroraresorts.com.au; Jabiru Dr; unpowered/powered sites $26/38, cabins from $240; ❄ @ 🏊) A resort and caravan park with shady, grassed sites and a lagoon swimming pool (movie nights by the pool on Fridays). Self-contained cabins sleep up to five people but are booked up well in advance (despite the decor being a little behind the times). There's also a bar and bistro.

Nourlangie

The sight of this looming outlier of the Arnhem Land escarpment makes it easy to understand its ancient importance to Aboriginal people. Its long red-sandstone bulk, striped in places with orange, white and black, slopes up from surrounding woodland to fall away at one end in stepped cliffs. Below is Kakadu's best-known collection of **rock art**.

♥ If You Like…
National Parks

If you like Kakadu National Park, we think you'll get a kick out of these other amazing national parks:

1 LITCHFIELD NATIONAL PARK The waterfalls that pour off the edge of spectacular Tabletop Range are a highlight of the 1500-sq-km Litchfield National Park, feeding crystal-clear cascades and croc-free plunge pools.

2 NITMILUK (KATHERINE GORGE) NATIONAL PARK Eye-popping Katherine Gorge is the highlight of the 2920-sq-km Nitmiluk (Katherine Gorge) National Park, about 30km from Katherine (itself three hours south or Darwin). Take a cruise or paddle a canoe upstream to check out amazing canyon walls and swim-spots.

3 WEST MACDONNELL NATIONAL PARK (www.nt.gov.au/nreta/parks/find/ westmacdonnell.html) This spectacular gorge country west of Alice Springs offers excellent camping and bushwalking, including the renowned Larapinta Trail.

4 WATARRKA (KINGS CANYON) NATIONAL PARK (www.nt.gov.au/nreta/parks/find/watarrka.html) This park is centred on the grand Kings Canyon (north of Uluru) – one of the best short walks in the Territory.

The 2km looped walking track (open 8am to sunset) takes you first to the **Anbangbang Shelter**, used for 20,000 years as a refuge and canvas. Next is the **Anbangbang Gallery**, featuring Dreaming characters repainted in the 1960s. From here it's a short walk to **Gunwarddehwarde Lookout**, with views of the Arnhem Land escarpment.

Jim Jim Falls & Twin Falls

Remote and spectacular, these two falls epitomise the rugged Top End. **Jim Jim Falls**, a sheer 215m drop, is awesome after rain (when it can only be seen from the air), but its waters shrink to a trickle by

279

Detour:
Litchfield National Park

It may not be as well known as Kakadu, but many Territory locals rate Litchfield even higher. In fact, there's a local saying that goes: 'Litchfield-do, Kaka-don't'. We don't entirely agree – we think Kaka-do-too – but this is certainly one of the best places in the Top End for **bushwalking**, **camping** and especially **swimming**, with waterfalls plunging into gorgeous, safe swimming holes.

The two routes to Litchfield (115km south of Darwin) from the Stuart Hwy join up and loop through the park.

About 17km after entering the park from Batchelor you come to what look like tombstones. But only the very tip of these **magnetic termite mounds** is used to bury the dead; at the bottom are the king and queen, with workers in between.

Another 6km further along is the turn-off to **Buley Rockhole** (2km), where water cascades through a series of rock pools big enough to lodge your bod in. This turn-off also takes you to **Florence Falls** (5km), accessed by a 15-minute, 135-step descent to a deep, beautiful pool surrounded by monsoon forest.

About 18km beyond the turn-off to Florence Falls is the turn-off to the spectacular **Tolmer Falls**, which is for looking only. A 1.6km loop track (45 minutes) offers beautiful views of the valley.

It's a further 7km along the main road to the turn-off for Litchfield's big-ticket attraction, **Wangi Falls** (pronounced *Wong*-guy), 1.6km up a side road. The falls flow year-round, spilling either side of a huge orange-rock outcrop and filling an enormous swimming hole bordered by rainforest.

about June. **Twin Falls** flows year-round (no swimming), but half the fun is getting there, involving a little **boat trip** (adult/child $2.50/free, running 7.30am to 5pm) and an over-the-water boardwalk.

Cooinda & Yellow Water

Cooinda is best known for the cruises on the wetland area known as Yellow Water (see p277), and has developed into a slick resort. About 1km from the resort, the **Warradjan Aboriginal Cultural Centre** (www.kakadu-attractions.com/warradjan; Yellow Water Area; ⏰9am-5pm) depicts Creation stories and has a fabulous permanent exhibition that includes clap sticks, sugar-bag holders and rock-art samples.

Gagudju Lodge & Camping Cooinda (☎1800 500 401, 08-8979 0145; www. gagudjulodgecooinda.com.au; unpowered/powered sites $32/40, dm $55, budget/lodge r from $110/208; ❄@☐) is the most popular accommodation resort in the park. The budget air-con units share camping ground facilities and are compact and comfy enough (but for this money should be more than glorified sheds). The lodge rooms are spacious and more comfortable, sleeping up to four people. There's also a grocery shop, tour desk, fuel pump and the excellent open-air **Barra Bar & Bistro** (mains $13-30; ⏰breakfast, lunch & dinner) here too.

ⓘ Information

Admission to the park is via a 14-day Park Pass (adult/child $25/free): pick one up (along with the excellent *Visitor Guide* booklet) from Bowali visitor information centre, Tourism Top End in Darwin, Gagudju Lodge Cooinda or Katherine visitor information centre. Carry it with you at all times, as rangers conduct spot checks (penalties apply for nonpayment).

The excellent Bowali Visitor Information Centre (☎08-8938 1121; www.kakadunational parkaustralia.com/bowali_visitors_center.htm; Kakadu Hwy, Jabiru; ⏰8am-5pm) has walk-through displays that sweep you across the land, explaining Kakadu's ecology from Aboriginal and non-Aboriginal perspectives. The 'What's On' flier details where and when to catch a free and informative park ranger talk.

Getting There & Around

Many people choose to access Kakadu on a tour, which shuffles them around the major sights with the minimum of hassles. But it's just as easy with your own wheels, if you know what kinds of road conditions your trusty steed can handle (Jim Jim Falls and Twin Falls, for example, are 4WD-access only).

Greyhound Australia (www.greyhound.com.au) runs a daily return coach service from Darwin to Cooinda ($87, 4½ hours) via Jabiru ($62, 3½ hours).

ALICE SPRINGS

The iconic outback town of Alice Springs is no longer the lonely frontier settlement of legend, yet the vast surroundings of red desert and burnished ranges still underscore its remoteness.

The town is a natural base for exploring central Australia, with Uluru-Kata Tjuta National Park a relatively close four-hour drive away.

Sights

ARALUEN CULTURAL PRECINCT
Cultural Centre
(www.nt.gov.au/nreta/arts/ascp; cnr Larapinta Dr & Memorial Ave; precinct pass adult/child $10/7) You can wander around freely outside, accessing the cemetery and grounds, but the 'precinct pass' provides entry to the exhibitions and displays.

ARALUEN ARTS CENTRE
Art Gallery
For a small town, Alice Springs has a thriving arts scene and the

Araluen Arts Centre is at its heart. There is a 500-seat theatre and four galleries with a focus on art from the central desert region.

MUSEUM OF CENTRAL AUSTRALIA
Museum
(⏱10am-5pm) The natural history collection at this compact museum recalls the days of megafauna – when hippo-sized wombats and 3m-tall flightless birds roamed the land. There's a free audio tour, narrated by a palaeontologist, which helps bring the exhibition to life.

Tours

DREAMTIME TOURS
Indigenous
(☎08-8955 5095; www.rstours.com.au; adult/child $84/42, self-drive $66/33; ⏱8.30-11.30am) Runs the three-hour Dreamtime & Bushtucker Tour, where you meet Warlpiri Aboriginal people and learn a little about their traditions.

Aboriginal design on stained-glass window at Araluen Cultural Precinct

PHOTOGRAPHER: PAUL DYMOND/LONELY PLANET IMAGES ©

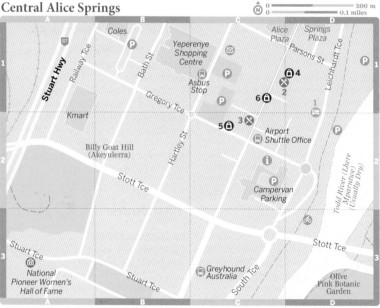

Central Alice Springs

L'Astragale   Town
(☎ 08-8953 6293; eroullet@gmail.com; $35)
Francophone Evelyne Roullet runs a local
walking tour of Alice Springs which leaves from
the visitor centre at 9.30am and 2.30pm.

EMU RUN TOURS   Outback
(☎ 08-8953 7057; www.emurun.com.au)
Operates day tours to Uluru ($199) and
three-day tours to Uluru and Kings Canyon ($390). There are also recommended
small-group day tours through the West
MacDonnell Ranges or Palm Valley
($120), including morning tea, lunch and
entrance fees.

🛏 Sleeping

ALICE STATION BED &
BREAKFAST   B&B $$
(☎ 08-8953 6600; www.alicestation.com; 25 The
Fairway; s/d/ste $175/190/210; ❄ @ ☎) The
host of this lovely B&B, which backs on to
the bush, really does have kangaroos in her
backyard. Made out of old *Ghan* railway
sleepers, the whimsically designed home
has a relaxed atmosphere with a commu-
nal lounge and stylishly decorated rooms
with local Aboriginal art on the walls.

ALICE IN THE TERRITORY   Hotel $
(☎ 08-8952 6100; www.alicent.com.au;
46 Stephens Rd; dm/s/d $25/89/99; ❄ @ ☎)
Formerly the Comfort Inn, this sprawling
hotel has had a $2 million refurbishment
and is now the best bargain stay in town.
Deluxe rooms have tiny bathrooms but
they are bright and comfortable and offer
two free movie channels.

ALICE ON TODD   Apartments $$
(☎ 08-8953 8033; www.aliceontodd.com; cnr
Strehlow St & South Tce; studio $120, 1-/2-bedroom

Detour:
Nitmiluk (Katherine Gorge) National Park

Spectacular **Katherine Gorge** forms the backbone of the 2920-sq-km **Nitmiluk (Katherine Gorge) National Park** (www.nt.gov.au/nreta/parks/find/nitmiluk.html), about 30km from Katherine. A series of 13 deep sandstone **gorges** have been carved out by the **Katherine River** on its journey from Arnhem Land to the Timor Sea.

The park has around 120km of marked walking tracks, ranging from 2km stretches to 66km multinight hikes.

Nitmiluk Tours (1300 146 743, 08-8972 1253; www.nitmiluktours.com.au) hires out single/double canoes for a half-day ($45/67, departing 8am and 12.30pm) or full day ($59/86, departing 8am), including the use of a splash-proof drum for cameras and other gear (it's not fully waterproof), a map and a life jacket.

An easy way to see far into the gorge is on a cruise run by **Nitmiluk Tours** (1300 146 743, 08-8972 1253; www.nitmiluktours.com.au). The **two-hour cruise** (adult/child $60/36) goes to the second gorge and visits a rock-art gallery (including 800m walk).

Nitmiluk Helicopter Tours (1300 146 743; www.airbournesolutions.com.au; flights from $88 per person) has a variety of flights ranging from an eight-minute buzz over the first three gorges ($88 per person) to an 18-minute flight over all 13 gorges ($202).

INFORMATION

The **Nitmiluk Centre** (1300 146 743, 08-8972 1253; www.nitmiluktours.com.au; 7am-6pm) has excellent displays and information on the park's geology, wildlife, the traditional owners (the Jawoyn) and European history.

GETTING THERE & AWAY

It's 30km by sealed road from Katherine to the Nitmiluk Centre, and a few hundred metres further to the car park, where the gorge begins and the cruises start.

Daily transfers between Katherine and the gorge are run by **Nitmiluk Tours** (1300 146 743, 08-8972 1253; www.nitmiluktours.com.au; Shop 2, 27 Katherine Tce; adult/child return $25/18), departing the Nitmiluk Town Booking Office and also picking up at local accommodation places on request.

---

apt $147/184, deluxe 1-/2-bedroom apt $160/198; ❄ @ ≋) This attractive and secure apartment complex on the banks of the Todd River offers one- and two-bedroom self-contained units with kitchen and lounge.

AURORA ALICE SPRINGS　　　Hotel $$
(1800 089 644, 08-8950 6666; www.aurora resorts.com.au; 11 Leichhardt Tce; standard/deluxe/executive d $130/150/230; ❄ @ ≋) Right in the town centre (the 'back' door opens out onto Todd Mall), this modern hotel has a relaxed atmosphere and a good restaurant, the Red Ochre Grill (see p284).

Eating

HANUMAN RESTAURANT　　　Thai $$
(08-8953 7188; Crowne Plaza Alice Springs, Barrett Dr; mains $14-30; lunch Mon-Fri, dinner daily) You won't believe you're in the outback when you try the incredible Thai- and Indian-influenced cuisine at this stylish restaurant. Although the menu is ostensibly Thai, there are enough Indian dishes to satisfy a curry craving.

SOMA　　　Cafe $
(64 Todd Mall; mains $12-15; breakfast & lunch) There's excellent people-watching

MARTIN COHEN/LONELY PLANET IMAGES ©

Don't Miss **Alice Springs Desert Park**

If you haven't managed to glimpse a spangled grunter or a marbled velvet gecko on your travels, head to the **Alice Springs Desert Park** (www.alicespringsdesertpark.com.au; Larapinta Dr; adult/child $20/10; ⊘7.30am-6pm, last entry 4.30pm) to find all the creatures of central Australia.

Try to time your visit with for the **birds of prey show** (⊘10am & 3.30pm), featuring flying Australian kestrels, kites and wedge-tailed eagles. Twitchers will also enjoy the dawn **bird walkabout** (adult/child $50/25; ⊘7.30am Wed & Sat) where you breakfast with the birds.

To catch some of the park's rare and elusive animals like the bilby, visit the excellent **nocturnal house**. If you like what you see, come back at night and spotlight endangered species on the guided **nocturnal tour** (adult/child $20/10; ⊘7.30pm Mon-Fri), which also has a dinner option (adult/child $60/35; ⊘6pm Tue-Thu).

It's an easy 2.5km cycle out to the park. Alternatively, **Desert Park Transfers** (⊘1800 806 641; www.tailormadetours.com.au; adult/child $48/28) operates five times daily during park hours and the cost includes park entry and pick-up and drop-off at your accommodation.

and even better eating to be had at this Todd Mall cafe which offers sophisticated dishes and great coffee. There is a focus on organic ingredients and a number of gluten-free options.

RED OCHRE
GRILL   Modern Australian $$
(Todd Mall; mains $11-31; ⊘6.30am-9.30pm)
Offering innovative fusion dishes with a focus on outback cuisine, the menu fea-

tures locally bred proteins matched with garden natives: lemon myrtle, pepper berries and bush tomatoes.

 **Shopping**

GALLERY GONDWANA   Indigenous Art
(⊘08-8953 1577; www.gallerygondwana.com.au; 43 Todd Mall; ⊘9.30am-6pm Mon-Fri, 10am-5pm Sat & Sun) Gondwana is a well-established

private gallery, recognised for dealing directly with community art centres and artists. Quality works from leading and emerging Central and Western Desert artists include work from Yuendumu and Utopia.

MBANTUA GALLERY   Indigenous Art
(☏ 08-8952 5571; www.mbantua.com.au; 71 Gregory Tce; ◷ 9am-6pm Mon-Fri, 9.30am-5pm Sat) This privately owned gallery, which extends through to Todd Mall, includes a cafe and extensive exhibits of works from the renowned Utopia region, as well as watercolour landscapes from the Namatjira school.

ℹ Information

Medical Services

Alice Springs Hospital (☏ 08-8951 7777; Gap Rd)

Alice Springs Pharmacy (☏ 08-8952 1554; Shop 19, Yeperenye Shopping Centre, 36 Hartley St; ◷ 8.30am-7.30pm)

Money

Major banks with ATMs, such as ANZ, Commonwealth, National Australia and Westpac, are located in and around Todd Mall in the town centre.

Tourist Information

Tourism Central Australia Visitor Information Centre (☏ 1800 645 199, 08-8952 5199; www.centralaustraliantourism.com; 60 Gregory Tce; ◷ 8.30am-5pm Mon-Fri, 9.30am-4pm Sat & Sun) This helpful centre can load you up with stacks of brochures and the free visitors guide. Ask about their unlimited kilometre deals if you are thinking of renting a car.

ℹ Getting There & Away

Air

Alice Springs is well connected, with Qantas (☏ 13 13 13, 08-8950 5211; www.qantas.com.au) and Tiger Airways (☏ 08-9335 3033; www.tigerairways.com.au) operating daily flights to/from capital cities.

Bus

Greyhound Australia (☏ 1300 473 946; www.greyhound.com.au; Shop 3, 113 Todd St; ◷ office 8.30-11.30am & 1.30-4pm Mon-Fri) has regular services from Alice Springs (check website for timetables).

Austour (☏ 1800 335 009; www.austour.com.au) runs the cheapest daily connections between Alice Springs and Yulara ($140/70 per adult/child). AAT Kings (☏ 08-8952 1700; www.aatkings.com) also runs between Alice Springs and Yulara (adult/child $150/75), and between Kings Canyon and Alice Springs ($159/80).

Car & Motorcycle

All the major companies have offices in Alice Springs, and many have counters at the airport. Talk to the visitor centre (☏ 1800 645 199, 08-8952 5199) about its unlimited kilometres deal before you book. A conventional (2WD) vehicle will get you to most sights in the MacDonnell Ranges and out to Uluru and Kings Canyon via sealed roads.

Train

A classic way to enter or leave the Territory is by the *Ghan* which can be booked through Trainways (☏ 13 21 47; www.trainways.com.au) or Travelworld (☏ 08-8953 0488; 40 Todd Mall).

ℹ Getting Around

To/From the Airport

Alice Springs airport is 15km south of the town. It's about $30 by taxi. The airport shuttle (☏ 08-8953 0310; Gregory Tce; 1/2/3-5 persons one-way $18.50/30/46) meets flights and drops off passengers at city accommodation.

Bus

The public bus service, Asbus (☏ 08-8952 5611), departs from outside the Yeperenye Shopping Centre (Hartley St). The visitor information centre has timetables.

The Alice Wanderer (☏ 1800 722 111, 08-8952 2111; www.alicewanderer.com.au; adult/child $40/30; ◷ 9am-4pm) is a hop-on, hop-off sightseeing bus that covers 11 major sites, including the Telegraph Station, School of the Air, Old Ghan Rail Museum and Araluen.

ULURU-KATA TJUTA NATIONAL PARK

For many visitors, Australian and international, a visit to Uluru is high on the list of 'must-sees' and the World Heritage–listed icon has attained the status of a pilgrimage.

There's plenty to see and do: meandering walks, guided tours, desert culture and contemplating the many changing colours and moods of the great monolith itself.

 Tours

Bus Tours

Seit Outback Australia   Bus Tours
(☏0458 107 777; www.seitoutbackaustralia.com.au) This small group operator has sunset tours around Uluru ($120/95 per adult/child); and does sunrise at Kata Tjuta for the same price including breakfast and a walk into Walpa Gorge.

AAT Kings   Bus Tours
(☏08-8956 2171; www.aatkings.com) Operating the biggest range of coach tours you can choose from a range of half- and full-day tours, or buy one of a selection of three-day tour passes (from $279/130 adult/child).

Uluru

Cultural Tours

ANANGU TOURS   Cultural Tours
(☏08-8950 3030; www.ananguwaai.com.au) Owned and operated by Anangu from the Mutitjulu community, this company offers a range of trips to give you an insight into the significance of the Rock through the eyes of the traditional owners.

The daily, five-hour Aboriginal Uluru Tour ($139/95 adult/child) starts with sunrise over Uluru and breakfast at the Cultural Centre, followed by a guided stroll down the Liru Walk (including demonstrations of bush skills such as spear-throwing).

The Kuniya Sunset Tour ($116/75, 4½ hours) departs at 2.30pm (3.30pm between November and February) and includes a visit to Mutitjulu Waterhole and the Cultural Centre, finishing with a sunset viewing of Uluru.

Scenic Flights

Ayers Rock Helicopters   Helicopter Flights
(☏08-8956 2077) A 15-minute buzz of Uluru costs $125; to include Kata Tjuta costs $240.

RICHARD I'ANSON/LONELY PLANET IMAGES ©

Uluru (Ayers Rock)

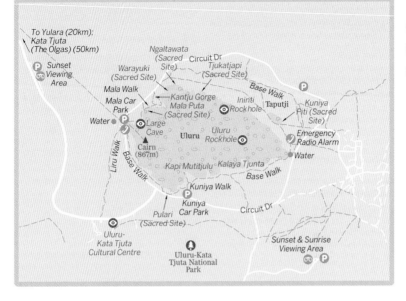

Ayers Rock Scenic Flights Scenic Flights
(✆08-8956 2345; www.ayersrockresort.com.
au/helicopter-flights) Prices start from $95 for a
20-minute flight over Uluru. Include Kata Tjuta
and it's $185.

ℹ Information

The park (www.environment.gov.au/parks/uluru;
adult/child $25/free) is open from half an hour
before sunrise to sunset daily (varying between
5am to 9pm November to March and 6am to
7.30pm April to October). Entry permits are valid
for three days and available at the drive-through
entry station on the road from Yulara.

Uluru-Kata Tjuta Cultural Centre (✆08-8956
1128; ⌚7am-6pm, information desk 7am-6pm)
is 1km before Uluru on the road from Yulara and
should be your first stop. During the week a local
Anangu ranger runs a presentation at 10am each
morning on bush foods and Aboriginal history.

Uluru (Ayers Rock)

No matter how many times you've seen it
on postcards; nothing quite prepares you
for the real thing. The first sight of Uluru
on the horizon will astound even the most
jaded traveller. Closer inspection reveals
a wondrous contoured surface conceal-
ing numerous sacred sites of particular
significance to the Anangu people.

🏃 Activities

Walking

There are walking tracks around Uluru, and
ranger-led walks explain the area's plants,
wildlife, geology and cultural significance.

The excellent *Visitor Guide & Maps*
brochure, which can be picked up at
the Cultural Centre, gives details on the
following self-guided walks (except the
climb).

Base Walk Walking
This track (10.6km, three to four hours)
circumnavigates the rock, passing caves,
paintings, sandstone folds and geological
abrasions along the way.

Liru Walk Walking
Links the Cultural Centre with the start of the
Mala walk and climb, and winds through strands
of mulga before opening up near Uluru (4km
return, 1½).

287

Mala Walk *Walking*

From the base of the climbing point (2km return, one hour), signs explain the tjukurpa of the Mala (hare-wallaby people), which is significant to the Anangu, as well as fine examples of rock art.

Kuniya Walk *Walking*

A short walk (1km return, 45 minutes) from the car park on the southern side leads to the most permanent waterhole, Mutitjulu, home of the ancestral watersnake. Great birdwatching and some excellent rock art are highlights of this walk.

Sunset & Sunrise Viewing Areas

About halfway between Yulara and Uluru, the **sunset viewing area** has plenty of car and coach parking for that familiar post-card view. The **Talnguru Nyakunytjaku sunrise viewing area** is perched on a sand dune and captures both the Rock and Kata Tjuta in all their glory.

Yulara (Ayers Rock Resort)

Yulara is the service village for the national park and has effectively turned one of the world's least hospitable regions into a comfortable place to stay. Lying just outside the national park, 20km from Uluru and 53km from Kata Tjuta, the complex is the closest base for exploring the park. Yulara supplies the only accommodation, food outlets and other services available in the region.

Even though there are almost 5000 beds, it's wise to make a reservation, especially during school holidays.

Bookings can be made through **central reservations** (☎1300 134 044; www.ayersrockresort.com.au).

ⓘ Information

The useful *Welcome to Ayers Rock Resort* flier is available at the visitor information centre and at hotel desks.

Tour & Information Centre (☎08-8957 7324; Resort Shopping Centre; ⊗8am-8pm; @) Most tour operators and car-hire firms have desks at this centre.

Visitor Information Centre (☎08-8957 7377; ⊗9am-4.30pm) Contains displays on the geography, wildlife and history of the region.

ⓘ Getting There & Away

Air

Qantas (☎13 13 13; www.qantas.com.au) has direct flights from Alice Springs, Melbourne, Perth, Adelaide and Sydney. Virgin Australia (☎13 67 89; www.virginaustralia.com) has daily flights from Sydney.

Bus

Daily shuttle connections (listed as mini tours) between Alice Springs and Yulara are run by AAT Kings (☎1300 556 100; www.aatkings.com) and cost adult/child $150/75. Austour (☎1800 335 009; www.austour.com.au) runs the cheapest daily connections between Alice Springs and Uluru ($140/70).

A Question of Climbing

Many visitors consider climbing Uluru to be a highlight (even a rite of passage) of a trip to the Centre. But for the traditional owners, the Anangu, Uluru is a sacred place. When you arrive at Uluru you'll see a sign from the Anangu saying 'We don't climb' and a request that you don't climb either.

The Anangu are the custodians of Uluru and take responsibility for the safety of visitors. Any injuries or deaths that occur (and they do occur – a man died in 2010) are a source of distress and sadness to them. For similar reasons of public safety, Parks Australia would prefer that people didn't climb.

JOHN BANAGAN/LONELY PLANET IMAGES ©

Don't Miss **Kata Tjuta (The Olgas)**

No journey to Uluru is complete without a visit to Kata Tjuta (the Olgas), a striking group of domed rocks huddled together about 35km west of the Rock. There are 36 boulders shoulder to shoulder forming deep valleys and steep-sided gorges. Many visitors find them even more captivating than their prominent neighbour. The tallest rock, **Mt Olga** (546m, 1066m above sea level) is approximately 200m higher than Uluru.

The 7.4km **Valley of the Winds** loop (two to four hours) is one of the most challenging and rewarding bushwalks in the park. It winds through the gorges giving excellent views of the surreal domes and traversing varied terrain.

The short signposted track beneath towering rock walls into pretty **Walpa Gorge** (2.6km return, 45 minutes) is especially beautiful in the afternoon, when sunlight floods the gorge.

Like Uluru, the Olgas are at their glorious, blood-red best at sunset.

Car & Motorcycle

The road from Alice to Yulara is sealed, with regular food and petrol stops along the way. Yulara is 441km from Alice Springs (241km west of Erldunda on the Stuart Hwy), and the direct journey takes four to five hours.

🛈 Getting Around

A free shuttle bus meets all flights and drops off at all accommodation points around the resort; pick-up is 90 minutes before your flight.

Uluru Express (☎08-8956 2152; www. uluruexpress.com.au) falls somewhere between a shuttle-bus service and an organised tour. It provides return transport from the resort to Uluru ($43/30 adult/child, $50/30 for the sunrise and sunset shuttles). Morning shuttles to Kata Tjuta cost $70/40; afternoon shuttles include a stop at Uluru for sunset and cost $75/40.

Hiring a car will give you the flexibility to visit the Rock and the Olgas whenever you want. Hertz (☎08-8956 2244) has a desk at the Tour & Information Centre, which also has direct phones to the Avis (☎08-8956 2266) and Thrifty (☎08-8956 2030) desks at Connellan Airport.

Perth & the West Coast

Western Australia (WA) is seriously big – almost four times the size of Texas! With swaths of gloriously empty outback, a small population hugging the coast and Perth's distinction as the world's most isolated capital city, WA is Australia at its most 'frontier'. Backed by a booming economy fuelled by mining, Western Australians are defiantly independent and happily distinct from that 'other' Australia on the east coast.

To the north of Perth, Shark Bay delivers a watery wildlife spectacle like no other. South of the city is the effervescent port of Fremantle, beyond which you'll find uncrowded beaches, expanses of wildflowers and lush green forests.

Around Margaret River, the fruit of the vine keeps winemakers busy, vineyard restaurants offer the freshest food and artisans of all sorts make inspired craft from the salvaged wood of stunning karri, marri and jarrah trees.

Perth skyline at night

Ningaloo Marine Park (p332)
PETER PTSCHELINZEW/LONELY PLANET IMAGES ©

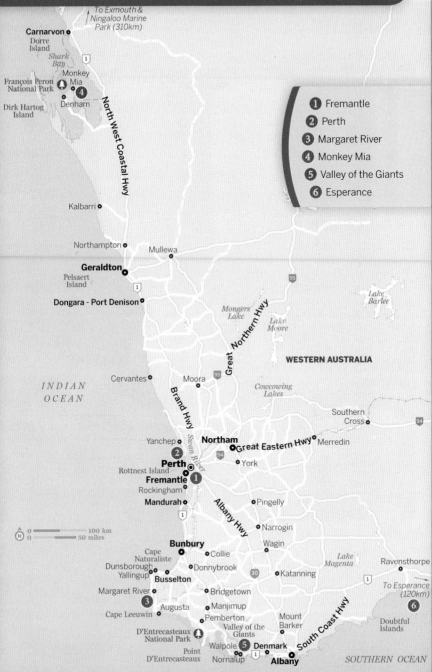

Perth & the West Coast Highlights

1 Fremantle
2 Perth
3 Margaret River
4 Monkey Mia
5 Valley of the Giants
6 Esperance

To Exmouth & Ningaloo Marine Park (310km)

Carnarvon
Dorre Island
Shark Bay
Monkey Mia
François Peron National Park
Dirk Hartog Island
Denham

North West Coastal Hwy

Kalbarri

Northampton
Mullewa

Geraldton
Pelsaert Island
Dongara - Port Denison

Mongers Lake
Lake Moore

Lake Barlee

WESTERN AUSTRALIA

INDIAN OCEAN

Cervantes
Moora
Cowcowing Lakes

Great Northern Hwy

Southern Cross
94

Brand Hwy

Yanchep
Northam
Great Eastern Hwy Merredin
Perth
Rottnest Island
Fremantle
Rockingham
Mandurah

Swan River

York

Albany Hwy

Pingelly

0 ____ 100 km
0 ____ 50 miles

Narrogin
Wagin

Bunbury
Cape Naturaliste
Dunsborough
Yallingup
Busselton
Margaret River
Cape Leeuwin
Augusta

Collie
Donnybrook
Bridgetown
Manjimup
Pemberton
Valley of the Giants

Lake Magenta

Ravensthorpe

To Esperance (120km)
6

Katanning

30

Mount Barker

South Coast Hwy

Doubtful Islands

D'Entrecasteaux National Park
Point D'Entrecasteaux
Walpole
Nornalup
Denmark
Albany

SOUTHERN OCEAN

Perth & the West Coast Highlights

1 Fremantle

Fremantle is the kind of place locals like to come home to. The seaside vibe is eclectic and artistic, with an upbeat pub and cafe scene. There are lots of travellers around, and there's a university here too, which keeps Freo young-at-heart. Above: Little Creatures; Top Right: Fishing Boat Harbour; Bottom Right: Rottnest Island

Need to Know

BEST PHOTO OPPORTUNITY A sunset beer by the harbour. **ONLY TWO HOURS?** Head to Fremantle Market or Little Creatures for a pint. **For further coverage, see p313**.

Fremantle Don't Miss List

BY PHOEBE PHILLIPS, BAR STAFF, LITTLE CREATURES BREWERY

1 LITTLE CREATURES

You never know what you're going to get at **Little Creatures** (p316)! Dress-up days, theme days... The main bar is really buzzy and has wicked views, and the Loft next door is more of a chilled-out lounge bar. The beer brewed here is awesome – I love the Bright Ale, Pale Ale and Pipsqueak Cider – and the food is great, too. We'd get hate mail from the locals if we ever changed the menu!

2 LIVE MUSIC

Live music is the best thing about Fremantle! **Mojos** (p317) in North Freo has gigs or open-mic nights every night: every hippie and his guitar has heard about Mojos! The Basement at the **Norfolk Hotel** (p317) has really good bands, and DJs upstairs on Sunday and Friday. The **Monk** (p317) has live musicians on weekends, and there are heaps of buskers around.

3 EATING & DRINKING

Fremantle does cafe and pub culture really well. **Moore & Moore** (p316) in the West End is a cool little cafe attached to an art gallery. **Harvest** (p316) in North Fremantle is great for an upmarket dinner – it has a really extensive wine list. Pub-wise, on the cafe strip there's the **Monk** (p317), which is another microbrewery, and the **Norfolk Hotel** (p317).

4 FISHING BOAT HARBOUR

There didn't used to be much here, but now there's Little Creatures and a string of fish restaurants along the boardwalk. It's all very laid-back, and it's a nice walk from Creatures along the waterfront, with lots of boatyards and yachts around.

5 ROTTNEST ISLAND

Ferries to **Rottnest Island** (p317) also leave from Perth, but it's a shorter ride from Fremantle. There's good surf, the snorkelling is amazing, or you can take a tour in a glass-bottom boat. There are a couple of cafes on the island, or you can hit the beaches with a BBQ and some beers.

Perth

If you think **Perth** (p302) feels a bit shy and embarrassed about being so isolated, think again! This is a town with spirit, enthusiasm and a progressive go-get-'em attitude. And really, who needs the east coast when the beaches, beer and BBQ weather are so good here? Cap it off with beaut museums, restaurants, bars and clubs and Perth proves to be a real winner.

2

Monkey Mia

4

World-renowned **Monkey Mia** (p330) needs little introduction: the friendly wild dolphins that visit daily have really put it on the map! Dolphins started interacting with humans here when local Aboriginal fishermen Jimmy Poland and Laurie Bellotti began handing them fish after their fishing expeditions. Then, in the 1960s, a visitor called Nin Watts started feeding the dolphins from the beach... And now you can, too!

MICHAEL AW/LONELY PLANET IMAGES ©

Margaret River

Wildly popular **Margaret River** (p320) serves up some of the best surfing in Australia, along with coastal caves, sophisticated restaurants, and internationally acclaimed vineyards scattered throughout richly forested land. The town itself, affectionately known as 'Margs', is an affable enclave of cafes and accommodation that satisfies both surfies and affluent weekend escapees travelling down the coast from Perth.

Valley of the Giants

Giant tingle trees live for up to 400 years, can grow up to 60m tall and 16m around the base, and are unique to this region of southwestern WA. For years folks would come to the **Valley of the Giants** (p323), eager to walk among the stoic 'Ancient Empire' stand of trees. Now you can explore the elevated realm of the canopy on the magical Tree Top Walk.

Esperance

Arriving in welcoming, easy-going **Esperance** (p327) feels a bit like a homely small town... But things have changed! The cafes are turning out top-notch tucker, accommodation is now first-rate, and there seem to be more tourists around these days. And the area's beautiful beaches, islands, lookouts and lakes are just as wonderful as ever.

Perth & the West Coast's Best...

Wildlife & Wilderness

○ **Shark Bay** (p329) Compelling marine wonderland surrounded by starkly beautiful landforms.

○ **Ningaloo Marine Park** (p332) Highly accessible coral reef sustaining abundant marine life.

○ **Valley of the Giants** (p323) Be humbled by the grandeur of mighty tingle trees.

○ **Kings Park & Botanic Garden** (p307) It mightn't be remote, but the indigenous plants and flowers here are wild indeed.

Urban Experiences

○ **Eating out in Perth** (p306) Superb seafood with river views or Indian Ocean sunsets.

○ **Live music in Fremantle** (p316) The sounds of Freo: buskers on the streets and rockin' bands in the pubs.

○ **Indigenous art at the Art Gallery of Western Australia** (p302) Outstanding Indigenous art from across the state.

○ **Drinking in Northbridge** (p309) Sometimes rough, often trashy...but never boring!

Places to Unwind

○ **Margaret River** (p320) Lose the kids and treat yourself to some wining and dining or a quiet country drive.

○ **Esperance** (p327) A long way from anywhere (just how the locals like it).

○ **Denmark** (p324) No, not next to Sweden...WA's version is a beachy, laid-back, alt-lifestyle haven.

○ **Rottnest Island** (p317) The perfect old-fashioned swimmin' and fishin' beach holiday.

Need to Know

Diving & Snorkelling

○ **Ningaloo Marine Park** (p332) One of the world's premier places to dive with whale sharks and manta rays.

○ **Rottnest Island** (p317) Family friendly, with protected reef and wreck snorkelling sites and dive lessons.

○ **Monkey Mia** (p330) Strap on a snorkel and Monkey Mia's famously friendly dolphins may join you.

○ **Aquarium of Western Australia** (p303) Muster some nerve and snorkel or dive with sharks.

ADVANCE PLANNING

○ **One month before** Plan your tour route through Western Australia (WA) and book accommodation and hire vehicles.

○ **Two weeks before** Book regional flights to Denham if you're headed for Shark Bay, and Exmouth if Ningaloo Marine Park is on your agenda.

○ **One week before** Book a diving lesson or whale swim tour, and a table at Harvest restaurant in Fremantle or Balthazar in Perth.

RESOURCES

○ **Tourism Western Australian** (www.westernaustralia.com) The official website for general statewide information. Most country towns have their own helpful visitors centres.

○ **Western Australian Visitor Centre** (www.bestofwa.com.au) Accommodation, tours, events and various deals on all things WA.

○ **Department of Environment & Conservation** (www.dec.wa.gov.au) Government department responsible for WA's national parks.

○ **Royal Automobile Club of Western Australia** (RACWA; www.rac.com.au) Driving info and emergency roadside assistance. Also distributes the useful *Go See Discover Stay – WA* guide, full of accommodation and touring information.

GETTING AROUND

○ **Walk** Beneath giant tingle trees or amid WA's famed wildflower blooms.

○ **Swim** With whale sharks and dolphins.

○ **Train** Across the continent to Sydney.

○ **Fly** To Denham (for Monkey Mia) and Exmouth (for Ningaloo).

○ **Ferry** To Rottnest Island.

BE FOREWARNED

○ **Rottnest Island** Summer and school-holiday accommodation on 'Rotto' gets booked out months in advance.

○ **Ningaloo Marine Park** The whale sharks arrive in May and depart in July.

Left: Osprey fledgling, Shark Bay; **Above:** Valley of the Giants (p323)

Perth & the West Coast Itineraries

Perth and Fremantle offer urban enticements, while Western Australia's southwestern corner is strewn with beaches, vineyards and tall forests. A short hop north you can swim with dolphins at Shark Bay.

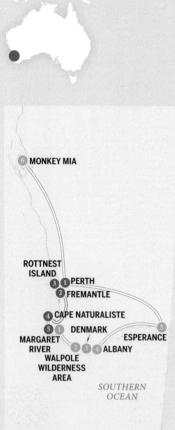

3 DAYS

PERTH TO MARGARET RIVER

City to the Sea

Begin your Western Australian adventure in **(1) Perth** and expend all of your urban urges in the city's great pubs, galleries, bars and restaurants. Don't miss the Indigenous galleries at the Art Gallery of Western Australia, and a dip at Cottesloe Beach. In season you can also take a whale-watching cruise.

Pay a quick visit to happening **(2) Fremantle** for some maritime history, or just to drink a beer with the Fremantle Doctor (the afternoon sea breeze that arrives like clockwork in summer). Alternatively, from Freo you can catch the ferry out to pedal-powered **(3) Rottnest Island** for a car-free, care-free day on the sand.

Back on the mainland, head south to the awesome beaches of **(4) Cape Naturaliste** before rolling into **(5) Margaret River**, a richly forested region with award-winning wineries. Here you can find a cosy restaurant and enjoy some chilled Sauvignon Blanc and marinated marron (freshwater crayfish). The beaches around 'Margs' have some of the country's best surf breaks: hire a long board and a wetsuit and go for a paddle.

Top Left: Art Gallery of Western Australia (p302)
Top Right: Shark Bay (p329)

5 DAYS

MARGARET RIVER TO MONKEY MIA

Whales, Wilderness & Wild Dolphins

Surfing, exploring caves, taste-testing quality wines... It's tempting to hang out in **(1) Margaret River** for weeks, but there's much more to see around here!

Steer east through the Southern Forests and check out the magnificent karri forests of Western Australia (WA). Next stop is **(2) Walpole Wilderness Area**, where you can walk through a lofty canopy of magnificent tingle trees. Alt-lifestyle **(3) Denmark** is a relaxed spot to spend the night: access the cool-climate Great Southern wine region from here.

Next stop is the old whaling port of **(4) Albany**, WA's oldest European settlement. The coastline around here is spectacular: the whales have forgiven and forgotten, and you can usually spot them from the beaches between July and mid-October.

Put your foot down and roll east along Hwy 1 to beachy **(5) Esperance** for a night. From here you can take the long drive back to Perth via the quirky outback outpost of Kalgoorlie, or hop a flight back to Perth.

If you have time, catch another flight north to Denham, the gateway to the astonishing marine splendour of Shark Bay. Here you can take an eye-opening Indigenous cultural tour and splash around with wild dolphins at **(6) Monkey Mia**.

Discover Perth & the West Coast

PERTH

Planted by a river and beneath an almost permanent canopy of blue sky, the city of Perth is a modern-day boomtown, stoking Australia's economy from its glitzy central business district. Yet it remains as relaxed as the sleepy Swan River – black swans bobbing atop – which winds past the sky-scrapers and out to the Indian Ocean.

 Sights

FREE ART GALLERY OF WESTERN AUSTRALIA   Art Gallery
(www.artgallery.wa.gov.au; Perth Cultural Centre, Northbridge; ⊘10am-5pm Wed-Mon) Founded in 1895, this excellent gallery houses the state's pre-eminent art collection, with the Indigenous galleries providing the highlight. Free tours take place daily.

FREE WESTERN AUSTRALIAN MUSEUM – PERTH   Museum
(www.museum.wa.gov.au; Perth Cultural Centre, Northbridge; ⊘9.30am-5pm) This branch of the state's six-headed museum includes dinosaur, mammal, butterfly and bird galleries, a **children's discovery centre**, and an excellent **WA Land and People** display that covers Indigenous and colonial history.

BEACHES   Beaches
When the mercury rises the only sensible decision is to go west to one of Perth's many sandy beaches. Most of them are comparatively undeveloped and there's certainly nothing as glitzy as, say, Sydney's Bondi. The most famous of them, **Cottesloe**, gets by quite well with

Cottesloe Beach
PHOTOGRAPHER: ORIEN HARVEY/LONELY PLANET IMAGES ©

a beachside pavilion, a couple of giant pubs and a scattering of other businesses delineating the edge of suburbia.

AQUARIUM OF WESTERN AUSTRALIA
Aquarium

(AQWA; ☎08-9447 7500; www.aqwa.com.au; Hillarys Boat Harbour, Hillarys; adult/child $28/16; ⊙10am-5pm) AQWA offers the chance to enjoy the state's underwater treasures without getting wet...or eaten, stung or poisoned. You can wander through a 98m underwater tunnel as gargantuan stingrays, turtles, fish and sharks stealthily glide over the top of you. The daring can snorkel or dive with the sharks; book in advance ($159 with your own gear; hire snorkel/dive gear $20/40; 1pm and 3pm).

FREE PERTH INSTITUTE OF CONTEMPORARY ARTS
Art Gallery

(www.pica.org.au; Perth Cultural Centre, Northbridge; ⊙11am-6pm Tue-Sun) PICA may have a traditional wrapping (it's housed in an elegant 1896 school) but inside it's anything but, being one of Australia's principal platforms for cutting-edge contemporary art.

Activities

Whale Watching

Mills Charters Whale Watching

(☎08-9246 5334; www.millscharters.com. au; adult/child $80/55) Departs Hillarys Boat Harbour at 9am on Tuesday, Thursday, Saturday and Sunday.

Oceanic Cruises Whale Watching

(☎08-9325 1191; www.oceaniccruises.com.au; adult/child $70/35) Departs Barrack St Jetty at 9.15am daily and returning at 5.45pm.

Cycling

Kings Park has some good bike tracks and there are cycling routes along the Swan River, running all the way to Fremantle, and along the coast. Bikes can be taken free-of-charge on ferries anytime and on trains outside of weekday peak hours (7am to 9am and 4pm to 6.30pm).

To hire bikes, try:

Cycle Centre Bicycle Hire

(☎08-9325 1176; www.cyclecentre.com.au; 313 Hay St; per day/week $25/$65; ⊙9am-5.30pm Mon-Fri, to 3pm Sat, 1-4pm Sun)

About Bike Hire Bicycle Hire

(☎08-9221 2665; www.aboutbikehire.com.au; Causeway Carpark, 1-7 Riverside Dr; per day/week from $36/80; ⊙9am-5pm) Also hires kayaks (per hour/day $16/65).

Scarborough Beach Cycles Bicycle Hire

(☎08-9245 3887; www.scarboroughbeachcycles. com.au; 10-12 Scarborough Beach Rd, Scarborough; per day/week $40/150; ⊙9am-5pm)

Surf Sail Australia Windsurfing, Kitesurfing

(☎1800 686 089; www.surfsailaustralia.com. au; 260 Railway Pde, West Leederville; ⊙10am-5pm Mon-Sat) When the afternoon sea breeze blusters in, windsurfers take to the Swan River, Leighton and beaches north of Perth. Here's where you can hire or buy your gear.

Funcats Sailing

(☎0408 926 003; Coode St Jetty, South Perth; per hr $35; ⊙Oct-Apr) Rents catamarans on the South Perth foreshore.

Surfschool Surfing

(☎08-9444 5399; www.surfschool.com; 190 Scarborough Beach Road, Mt Hawthorn; adult/child $55/50) Two-hour lessons at Scarborough Beach, including boards and wetsuits.

Tours

INDIGENOUS TOURS WA Indigenous

(www.indigenouswa.com) See Perth through the eyes of the local Wadjuk people. Options include the **Indigenous Heritage Tour** (☎08-9483 1106; adult/child $25/15; ⊙1.30pm), a 90-minute guided walk around Kings Park – and the **Swan River Dreaming Tour** (☎1300 467 688; adult/child $50/25; ⊙10am Tue & Wed), a 90-minute boat ride.

PERTH TRAM City

(☎08-9322 2006; www.perthtram.com.au; adult/child $30/12) This hop-on, hop-off bus masquerading as a historic tram takes you around Perth's main attractions in two interlinking loops.

Central Perth

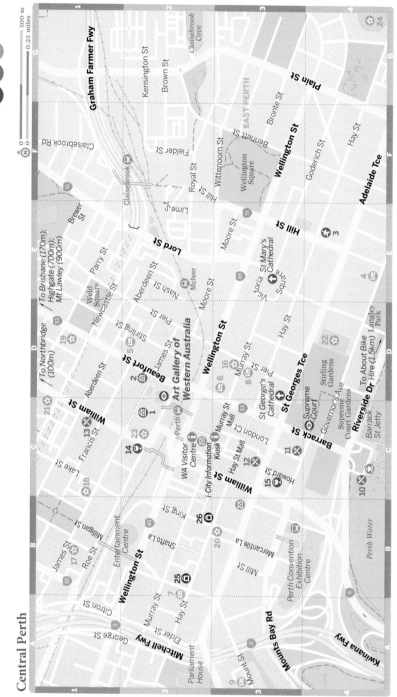

500 m
0.25 miles

Graham Farmer Fwy

Kensington St

Brown St

Claisebrook Cove

Claisebrook Rd

EAST PERTH

Bennett St

Plain St

Wellington St

Bronte St

Goderich St

Hay St

Adelaide Tce

Wittenoom St

Wellington Square

Fielder St

Royal St

Hill St

Lime St

Hill St

Moore St

St Mary's Cathedral

Victoria Sq

To Brisbane (170m);
Highgate (700m);
Mt Lawley (900m)

Brewer St

Parry St

Lord St

McIver

Moore St

Nash St

Aberdeen St

Pier St

Stirling St

Newcastle St

Weld Square

James St

Wellington St

Murray St

Hay St

Pier St

St George's Tce

St Georges Tce

Supreme Court

Governor's Ave

Stirling Gardens

Supreme Court Gardens

Riverside Dr

Langley Park

To About Bike Hire (1.5km)

Barrack St Jetty

Art Gallery of Western Australia

Beaufort St

To Northbridge (100m)

Aberdeen St

William St

Francis St

Lake St

Perth

WA Visitor Centre

i City Information Kiosk

Murray St Mall

London Ct

Hay St Mall

Howard St

William St

Barrack St

Governor's

Court Gardens

Perth Water

James St

Roe St

Milligan St

Entertainment Centre

King St

Shafto La

Mercantile La

Wellington St

Citron St

George St

Parliament House

Mitchell Fwy

Murray St

Elder St

Hay St

Mill St

Perth Convention Exhibition Centre

Mount St

Mounts Bay Rd

Kwinana Fwy

Central Perth

City Sightseeing Perth Tour   City
(🕿 08-9203 8882; www.citysightseeingperth.
com; adult/child $28/10) Hop-on, hop-off
double-decker bus tour. Tickets are valid for two
days. The Kings Park section (adult/child $6/3)
can be purchased separately.

Captain Cook Cruises   Cruises
(🕿 08-9325 3341; www.captaincookcruises.
com.au) Takes the river to the Swan Valley or
Fremantle, with an array of add-ons such as
meals, wine tastings and tram rides.

Swan Valley Tours   Food, Wine
(🕿 08-9274 1199; www.svtours.com.au)

Rottnest Air Taxi   Scenic Flights
(🕿 08-9292 5027; www.rottnest.de; 30min $85)

Sleeping

City Centre
RIVERVIEW ON MOUNT
STREET   Apartments $$
(🕿 08-9321 8963; www.riverviewperth.com.au;
42 Mount St; apt from $140; ❄ @ 🛜) There's
a lot of brash new money up here on
Mount St, but character-filled Riverview

stands out as the best personality on the
block. Its refurbished 1960s bachelor
pads sit neatly atop a modern foyer and
relaxed, minimalist cafe.

MEDINA EXECUTIVE
BARRACK PLAZA   Apartments $$$
(🕿 08-9267 0000; www.medina.com.au; 138 Bar-
rack St; apt from $204; ❄ 🏊) The Medina's
meticulously decorated apartment-sized
hotel rooms are minimalist yet welcoming. All one-bedrooms have balconies, and
rooms on Barrack St tend to have more
natural light (not always easy to obtain in
central Perth).

MELBOURNE   Hotel $$
(🕿 08-9320 3333; www.melbournehotel.com.
au; cnr Hay & Milligan Sts; r $165-290; ❄ 🛜)
Classic country charm wafts through this
heritage-listed hotel. Its deep, corrugat-
ed-iron, wraparound balcony recalls a
mining-town pub perched on the edges of
the red-dust desert. Rooms are unpretentious and comfortable but can be noisy.

MISS MAUD   Hotel $$
(🕿 08-9325 3900; www.missmaud.com.au; 97
Murray St; s/d $169/189; ❄ @ 🛜) Anyone

with a love of Scandinavia, kitsch or *The Sound of Music* will find a few of their favourite things in the alpine murals and dainty rooms. The smorgasbords (lunch/dinner $32/43) are enough to feed a goatherd.

CITY WATERS Motel $$
(☏08-9325 1566; www.citywaters.com.au; 118 Terrace Rd; s/d $105/120; ❄) Apricot-hued City Waters is one of a dying breed of old-fashioned Perth waterfront motels. Rooms are small, simple and face onto the car park, but they're clean and airy and the waterfront location is top-notch.

Northbridge, Highgate & Mt Lawley

EMPEROR'S CROWN Hostel $
(☏08-9227 1400; www.emperorscrown.com.au; 85 Stirling St; dm $32, r with/without bathroom $98/88; ❄@✉) The best of Perth's hostels has a great position (close to the Northbridge scene without being in the thick of it), friendly staff and high house-keeping standards. Granted, it's a bit pricier than most, but it's well worth it.

DURACK HOUSE B&B $$
(☏08-9370 4305; www.durackhouse.com.au; 7 Almondbury Rd, Mt Lawley; s $160, d $175-190; ✉) It's hard to avoid words like 'delight-ful', enunciated in slightly English accent, when describing this cottage, set on a peaceful suburban street behind a white picket fence swathed in climbing roses. The three rooms have plenty of old-world charm, paired with thoroughly modern bathrooms.

PENSION OF PERTH B&B $$
(☏08-9228 9049; www.pensionperth.com.au; 3 Throssell St; s/d from $120/150; ❄@✉❆) Pension of Perth's French belle époque style lays luxury on thick: chaises longues, rich floral rugs, heavy brocade curtains, open fireplaces and gold-framed mirrors. Two doubles with bay windows (and small bathrooms) look out onto the park; the spa room is round the back. And it's across the road from gorgeous Hyde Park.

Subiaco & Kings Park

RICHARDSON Hotel $$$
(☏08-9217 8888; www.therichardson.com.au; 32 Richardson St; r $450-550; ❆) Ship-shaped and ship-shape, the Richardson offers luxurious, thoughtfully designed rooms – some with sliding doors to divide them into pseudo suites. The whole complex has a breezy, summery feel, with pale marble tiles, creamy walls and interesting art.

Beaches

SWANBOURNE GUEST HOUSE Guesthouse $$
(☏08-9383 1981; www.swanbourneguesthouse.com.au; 5 Myera St, Swanbourne; s/d $90/120) Peace and solitude are the key here. Off a leafy residential street, 20 minutes' walk from Swanbourne Beach, you'll hear nothing more than the birds twittering from your sun-filled room.

Eating

City Centre

BALTHAZAR Modern Australian $$$
(☏08-9421 1206; 6 The Esplanade; mains $37-40; ⏲lunch Mon-Fri, dinner Mon-Sat) Low-lit, discreet and sophisticated, Balthazar's informal cool vibe is matched by exquisite food and a famously excellent wine list. The menu here is refreshingly original, combining European and Asian flavours with not-at-all-reckless abandon.

🍃GREENHOUSE Tapas $$
(☏08-9481 8333; www.greenhouseperth.com; 100 St Georges Tce; tapas $10-18; ⏲7am-midnight Mon-Sat) The talk is shifting from the groundbreaking design (straw bales, plywood, corrugated iron and living ex-terior walls covered with 5000 individual pot plants) and onto the excellent food offered at this hip tapas-style eatery.

ANNALAKSHMI Indian $
(☏08-9221 3003; www.annalakshmi.com.au; 1st fl, Western Pavilion; pay by donation; ⏲lunch Tue-Fri & Sun, dinner Tue-Sun; ✐) While the 360-degree views of the

PHILIP GAME/LONELY PLANET IMAGES ©

Don't Miss Kings Park & Botanic Garden

(www.bgpa.wa.gov.au) The 400-hectare bush-filled expanse of Kings Park is where the city's good burghers head for a picnic under the trees or to let the kids off the leash in one of the playgrounds. Its numerous tracks are popular with walkers, while the steep stairs leading up from the river support a steady procession of masochistic middle-aged joggers.

At the park's heart is the 17-hectare Botanic Garden, containing over 2000 indigenous plant species. In spring there's an impressive display of the state's famed wildflowers. A highlight is the **Lotterywest Federation Walkway** (⊙9am-5pm), a 620m path through the gardens that includes a 222m-long, glass-and-steel bridge that passes through the canopy of a stand of eucalypts.

Free **guided walks** (⊙10am & 2pm) leave from **Kings Park Visitor Centre** (Fraser Ave; ⊙9.30am-4pm).

Swan River are worth a million dollars, the food's literally priceless (donate whatever your conscience suggests). The spicy vegetarian curries attract an eclectic mix of hippies, Hindus and the just plain hungry.

Northbridge, Highgate & Mt Lawley

JACKSON'S Modern Australian $$$
(☏08-9328 1177; 483 Beaufort St, Highgate; mains $44, degustation $125; ⊙dinner Mon-Sat) The finest of fine dining is offered in this upmarket dining room, where the staff don white gloves to present you with wonderfully creative treats. In the pampering stakes, it's the foodie equivalent of a day spa, minus the bikini wax.

MUST WINEBAR French $$$
(☏08-9328 8255; www.must.com.au; 519 Beaufort St, Highgate; mains $36-44; ⊙noon-midnight) Not content with being Perth's best wine bar, Must is one of its best restaurants as well. The vibe's hip, slick and a little cheeky, while the menu marries classic bistro dishes with the best local produce.

LITTLE WILLY'S　　　　　Cafe　$
(267 William St, Northbridge; mains $8-12;
⊗breakfast & lunch) It's tiny and it's on William St, so the name's probably got nothing to do with the tall dude driving the
coffee machine who's universally known
as Hot Rob (much to his obvious embar-
rassment). He works that baby like a pro
and the food, while simple, is delicious.

Mt Hawthorn & Leederville

DIVIDO　　　　　Italian　$$
(✆08-9443 7373; www.divido.com.au; 170
Scarborough Beach Rd, Mt Hawthorn; mains $30-
36; ⊗dinner Mon-Sat) Italian but not rigidly
so, this excellent, romantically inclined
restaurant serves handmade pasta dishes
and delicately flavoured mains.

DUENDE　　　　　Tapas　$$
(✆08-9228 0123; www.duende.com.au; 662
Newcastle St, Leederville; tapas $5-17; ⊗6pm-
late Sat-Thu, noon-late Fri) Sleek Duende
occupies a corner site watching the com-
ings and goings of Leederville after dark.

Subiaco & Kings Park

SUBIACO HOTEL　　　　Gastropub　$$
(✆08-9381 3069; www.subiacohotel.com.au;
465 Hay St; mains $19-32; ⊗breakfast, lunch
& dinner) A legendary boozer that's been
given a glitzy makeover, the Subi now has
a buzzy dining room that's the suburb's
main place to see and be seen. The menu
ranges from lighter fare like Caesar salads
and vegetarian risottos to perfectly
cooked steaks and excellent fish dishes.

OLD BREWERY　　　　Steakhouse　$$
(✆08-9211 8910; www.theoldbrewery.com.
au; 173 Mounts Bay Rd, Kings Park; mains
$29-43; ⊗breakfast Sun, lunch & dinner daily)
Perth's the kind of town where even the
steakhouses are glamorous, as evidenced
by this designer joint at the heart of the
historic Swan Brewery building (1838).
There are wonderful views over the river
to the city, but hardcore carnivores can
trade them for views of the beef ageing
gracefully in glass display cabinets.

Left: Must Winebar (p307); **Below:** Luxe

PHOTOGRAPHERS: (LEFT & BELOW) ORIEN HARVEY/LONELY PLANET IMAGES ©

 # Drinking

City Centre

GREENHOUSE
Cocktail Bar

(www.greenhouseperth.com; 100 St Georges Tce; ⏲7am-midnight Mon-Sat) In a city so in love with the great outdoors, it's surprising that nobody's opened a rooftop bar in the central city before now. Hip, eco-conscious Greenhouse is leading the way, mixing up a storm amid the greenery above the award-winning restaurant.

HELVETICA
Bar

(www.helveticabar.com; rear, 101 St Georges Tce; ⏲3pm-midnight Tue-Thu, noon-midnight Fri, 6pm-midnight Sat) Clever artsy types tap their toes to delicious alternative pop in this bar named after a typeface and specialising in whisky and cocktails.

Northbridge, Highgate & Mt Lawley

BRISBANE
Pub

(www.thebrisbanehotel.com.au; 292 Beaufort St, Highgate; ⏲11.30am-late) It was a very clever architect indeed who converted this classic corner pub (1898) into a thoroughly modern venue, where each space seamlessly blends into the next. Best of all is the large courtyard where the palms and ponds provide a balmy holiday feel.

EZRA POUND
Bar

(189 William St, Northbridge; ⏲1pm-midnight Thu-Tue) Down a much graffitied lane leading off William St, Ezra Pound is favoured by Northbridge's bohemian set.

LUXE
Cocktail Bar

(www.luxebar.com; 446 Beaufort St, Highgate; ⏲8pm-late Wed-Sun) With retro wood panelling, big, sexy lounge chairs and velvet curtains, Luxe is knowingly hip.

309

Beaches

ELBA
Bar

(www.elbacottesloe.com.au; 29 Napoleon St; ☺noon-midnight Mon-Sat, to 10pm Sun) Elba has taken its street name as inspiration and produced a slick little Napoleonic bar complete with sparkly chandeliers and a gilt-framed portrait of the little man.

COTTESLOE BEACH HOTEL
Pub

(www.cottesloebeachhotel.com.au; 104 Marine Pde; ☺11am-midnight Mon-Sat, to 10pm Sun) Grab a spot on the lawn in the massive beer garden, or watch the sun set from the balcony. Sunday is big.

 **Entertainment**

Nightclubs

Hip-E Club
Nightclub

(www.hipeclub.com.au; 663 Newcastle St, Leederville; ☺Tue-Sat) Thrust about to *Tainted Love* all night long. Tuesday is backpackers' night.

Ambar
Nightclub

(www.boomtick.com.au/ambar; 104 Murray St) Perth's premier club for breakbeat, drum'n'bass and visiting international DJs.

Live Music

Ellington Jazz Club
Nightclub

(www.theellington.com.au; 191 Beaufort St, Northbridge; standing-only $10; ☺7pm-1am Mon-Thu, to 3am Fri & Sat, 5pm-midnight Sun) There's live jazz nightly in this handsome, intimate venue.

Bakery
Arts Centre

(www.nowbaking.com.au; 233 James St, Northbridge; ☺7pm-1am Thu-Sun) Popular indie gigs almost every weekend.

Moon
Cafe

(www.themoon.com.au; 323 William St, Northbridge; ☺6pm-12.30am Mon & Tue, 11am-1.30am Wed, Thu & Sun, 11am-3.30am Fri & Sat) Late-night cafe with singers on Wednesday, jazz on Thursday and poetry on Saturday afternoon.

Theatre & Classical Music

Check the *West Australian* newspaper for what's on. Most tickets can be booked through **BOCS Ticketing** (☎08-9484 1133; www.bocsticketing.com.au).

STATE THEATRE CENTRE
Theatre

(www.statetheatrecentrewa.com.au; 174 William St, Northbridge) Opened in 2011, this flash new complex includes the 575-seat Heath Ledger Theatre and the 234-seat Studio Underground. It's home to the Black Swan State Theatre Company and Perth Theatre Company.

HIS MAJESTY'S THEATRE
Theatre

(www.hismajestystheatre.com.au; 825 Hay St) The WA Ballet (www.waballet.com.au) and WA Opera (www.waopera.asn.au) are based here.

His Majesty's Theatre

Perth for Children

With a usually clement climate and plenty of open spaces and beaches to run around in, Perth is a great place to bring children. Of the beaches, Cottesloe is the safest. Kings Park has playgrounds and walking tracks.

Many of Perth's big attractions cater well for young audiences, especially AQWA, the WA Museum and the Art Gallery of WA.

Part of the fun of **Perth Zoo** (www.perthzoo.wa.gov.au; 20 Labouchere Rd, South Perth; adult/child $21/11; ⊙9am-5pm) is getting there by ferry. **Scitech** (www.scitech.org.au; City West Centre, Sutherland St, West Perth; adult/child $14/9; ⊙10am-4pm) has over 160 hands-on, large-scale science and technology exhibits.

Adventure World (www.adventureworld.net.au; 179 Progress Dr, Bibra Lake; adult/child $47/39; ⊙10am-5pm Thu-Mon Oct-Apr) has rides, pools, waterslides and a castle. It's open daily during school holidays and through December.

At 26-sq-km, **Whiteman Park** (www.whitemanpark.com; enter from Lord St or Beechboro Rd, West Swan; ⊙8.30am-6pm) is Perth's biggest, with over 30km of walkways and bike paths, and numerous picnic and BBQ spots. Within its ordered grounds are **Caversham Wildlife Park** (www.cavershamwildlife.com.au; adult/child $22/10; ⊙8.30am-5.30pm, last entry 4.30pm), **Bennet Brook Railway** (www.bennettbrookrailway.org; adult/child $8/4; ⊙11am-1pm Wed, Thu, Sat & Sun), **tram rides** (www.pets.org.au; adult/child $5/2.50; ⊙noon-2pm Tue & Fri-Sun) and the **Motor Museum of WA** (www.motormuseumofwa.asn.au; adult/child $8/5; ⊙10am-4pm).

Perth Concert Hall — Concert Hall
(www.perthconcerthall.com.au; 5 St Georges Tce) Home to the WA Symphony Orchestra (WASO; www.waso.com.au).

Cinema

Somerville Auditorium — Outdoor Cinema
(www.perthfestival.com.au; UWA, 35 Stirling Hwy, Crawley; ⊙Dec-Mar) A quintessential Perth experience.

Cinema Paradiso — Cinema
(www.lunapalace.com.au; Galleria complex, 164 James St, Northbridge)

Moonlight Cinema — Outdoor Cinema
(☑1300 551 908; www.moonlight.com.au; Kings Park) Summer only.

🔒 Shopping

Murray St and Hay St Malls are the city's shopping heartland, while King St is the place for swanky boutiques. Leederville's Oxford St is the place for groovy boutiques, eclectic music and bookshops.

Wheels & Doll Baby — Clothing
(www.wheelsanddollbaby.com; 26 King St) Punky rock-chick chic with a bit of baby doll mixed in. Perhaps Perth fashion's coolest export, being worn by the likes of Amy Winehouse and Debbie Harry.

78 Records — Music
(www.78records.com.au; 914 Hay St) Big, independent record shop with a massive range of CDs and lots of specials.

Oxford St Books — Books
(119 Oxford St) Knowledgeable staff, great range of fiction and a travel section.

ℹ Information

Medical Services
Royal Perth Hospital (☑08-9224 2244; www.rph.wa.gov.au; Victoria Sq)

Travel Medicine Centre (08-9321 7888; www.travelmed.com.au; 5 Mill St; 8am-5pm Mon-Fri)

Tourist Information

i-City Information Kiosk (Murray Street Mall; 9.30am-4.30pm Mon-Thu & Sat, to 8pm Fri, 11am-3.30pm Sun) Volunteers answer your questions and run walking tours.

WA Visitor Centre (08-9483 1111; www.wavisitorcentre.com; cnr Forrest Pl & Wellington St; 9am-5.30pm Mon-Fri, 9.30am-4.30pm Sat, 11am-4pm Sun) A good resource for a trip anywhere in WA.

Getting There & Away

The east coast is the most common gateway for international travellers, although if you're coming from Europe, Asia or Africa its more convenient and quicker to take any of the 16 airlines flying directly to **Perth Airport** (08-9478 8888; www.perthairport.com).

The only interstate rail link is the famous Indian Pacific, run by **Great Southern Railway** (08-8213 4592; www.trainways.com.au), which travels 4352km to Perth from Kalgoorlie (10 hours), Adelaide (two days), Broken Hill (2¼ days) and Sydney (three days).

Getting Around

To/From the Airport

The domestic and international terminals of Perth's airport are 10km and 13km east of Perth respectively, near Guildford. Taxi fares to the city are around $25/35 from the domestic/international terminal, and about $60 to Fremantle.

Connect (1300 666 806; www.perthairportconnect.com.au) runs shuttles to and from hotels and hostels in the city centre (one way/return $18/30, every 50 minutes) and in Fremantle (one way/return $33/58, every 2½ hours).

Transperth bus 37 travels to the domestic airport from St Georges Tce, near William St ($3.70, 44 minutes, every 10 to 30 minutes, hourly after 7pm).

Public Transport

Transperth (13 62 13; www.transperth.wa.gov.au) operates Perth's public buses, trains and ferries. There are Transperth information offices at Perth Station (Wellington St), Wellington St Bus Station, Perth Underground Station (off Murray St) and the Esplanade Busport (Mounts Bay Rd). There's also a journey planner on the website.

From the central city, the following fares apply for all public transport:

Free Transit Zone (FTZ) Central commercial area, bounded (roughly) by Fraser Ave, Kings Park Rd, Thomas St, Newcastle St, Parry St, Lord St and the river (including City West and Claisebrook train stations, to the west and east respectively).

Zone 1 City centre and inner suburbs ($2.50).

Zone 2 Fremantle, Guildford and the beaches as far north as Sorrento ($3.70).

DayRider Unlimited travel after 9am weekdays and all day on the weekend in any zone ($9).

FamilyRider Lets two adults and up to five children travel for a total of $9 on weekends, after 6pm weekdays and after 9am on weekdays during school holidays.

BUS

As well as regular buses the FTZ is well covered during the day by the three free CAT (Central Area Transit) services. The Yellow and Red CATs operate east–west routes, Yellow sticking mainly to Wellington St and Red looping roughly east on Murray and west on Hay. The Blue Cat does a figure eight through Northbridge and the south end of the city; this is the only one to run late – until 1am on Friday and Saturday nights only.

The metropolitan area is serviced by a wide network of Transperth buses. Pick up timetables from any of the Transperth information centres or use the 'journey planner' on its website.

FERRY

The only ferry runs every 20 to 30 minutes between Barrack Street Jetty and Mends Street Jetty in South Perth – you'll probably only use it to get to the zoo.

TRAIN

Transperth operates five train lines from around 5.20am to midnight weekdays and until about 2am Saturday and Sunday. Your rail ticket can also be used on Transperth buses and ferries within the ticket's zone. You're free to take your bike on the train in non-peak times.

Taxi

The two main companies are **Swan Taxis** (13 13 30; www.swantaxis.com.au) and **Black & White** (131 008; www.bwtaxi.com.au), both of which have wheelchair-accessible cabs.

FREMANTLE

Perth has sprawled to enfold Fremantle within its suburbs, yet the port city maintains its own distinct personality – proud of its nautical ties, working-class roots, bohemian reputation and, especially, its football team.

There's a lot to enjoy here – fantastic museums, edgy galleries, pubs thrumming with live music and a thriving coffee culture.

 Sights

FREMANTLE PRISON   Historic Building
(☎08-9336 9200; www.fremantleprison.com.au; 1 The Terrace; torchlight tours $25/21; ⏱9am-5.30pm) With its foreboding 5m-high walls enclosing a nearly 6-hectare site, the old convict-era prison still dominates present-day Fremantle.

Entry to the **gatehouse**, including the **Prison Gallery**, **gift shop** (where you can purchase fetching arrow-printed prisoner PJs) and **Convict Cafe** is free. To enter the prison proper, you'll need to take a tour. During the day there are two fascinating 1¼-hour tours on offer (**Doing Time** and **Great Escapes**), timed so that you can take one after the other on a combined ticket (single tour adult/child $19/10, combined $25/17).

Torchlight Tours (90 minutes, adult/child $25/21, Wednesday and Friday evenings) are designed to chill. The 2½-hour **Tunnels Tour** (adult/child over 12 $59/39) takes you 20m underground to tunnels and includes an underground boat ride.

WESTERN AUSTRALIAN MUSEUM – MARITIME   Museum
(www.museum.wa.gov.au; Victoria Quay; museum adult/child $10/3, submarine $8/3, museum & submarine $15/5; ⏱9.30am-5pm) Housed in an intriguing sail-shaped building on the harbour, just west of the city centre, this is a fascinating exploration of WA's relationship with the ocean. Various boats are on display and, if you're not claustrophobic, you can take an hour-long tour of the Australian Navy submarine **HMAS Ovens** (departing every half-hour from 10am to 3.30pm).

Fremantle Markets (p315)

Fremantle

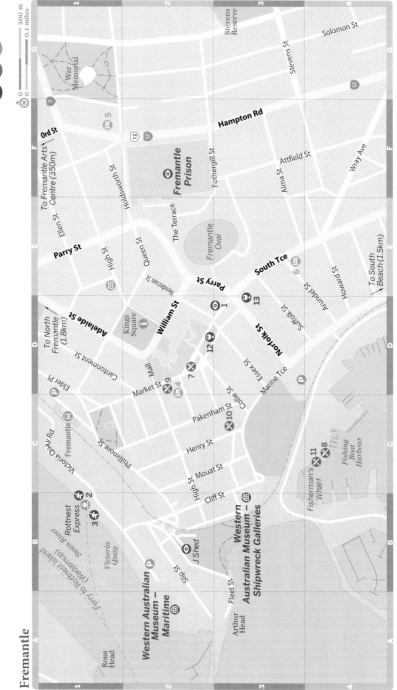

0   200 m
0   0.1 miles

Rous Head

Ferry to Rottnest Island (Wadjemup)
Rottnest Express

Swan River (Steam Ferry)

Western Australian Museum – Maritime

Victoria Quay

Slip St

Fleet St

Arthur Head

J Shed

Western Australian Museum – Shipwreck Galleries

Fishing Boat Harbour

Fisherman's Wharf

Victoria Quay Rd

Elder Pl

Phillimore St

To North Fremantle (1.8km)

Adelaide St

Cantonment St

Market St

Mall

Pakenham St

Henry St

High St

Mouat St

Cliff St

Essex St

Collie St

Marine Tce

Kings Square

William St

Henderson St

Queen St

High St

To Fremantle Arts Centre (350m)

Ord St

Ellen St

Holdsworth St

The Terrace

Fremantle Prison

Fremantle Oval

Parry St

Parry St

South Tce

Norfolk St

Suffolk St

Essex St

Arundel St

Howard St

To South Beach (1.5km)

Hampton Rd

Fothergill St

Attfield St

Alma St

Stevens St

Stevens Reserve

Solomon St

Wray Ave

War Memorial

Fremantle

FREE **WESTERN AUSTRALIAN MUSEUM – SHIPWRECK GALLERIES** Museum

(www.museum.wa.gov.au; Cliff St; ⊗9.30am-5pm) Housed in an 1852 commissariat store, the Shipwreck Galleries are considered the finest display of maritime archaeology in the southern hemisphere. The highlight is the **Batavia Gallery**, where a section of the hull of Dutch merchant ship the *Batavia*, wrecked in 1629, is displayed.

FREE **FREMANTLE ARTS CENTRE** Gallery

(www.fac.org.au; 1 Finnerty St; ⊗9am-5pm) An impressive neo-Gothic building surrounded by lovely elm-shaded gardens, the Fremantle Arts Centre was constructed by convict labourers as a lunatic asylum in the 1860s. Saved from demolition in the late 1960s, it houses a changing roster of interesting exhibitions.

FREMANTLE MARKETS Market

(www.fremantlemarkets.com.au; cnr South Terrace & Henderson St; ⊗8am-8pm Fri, to 5pm Sat & Sun) Originally opened in 1897, these colourful markets were reopened in 1975 and today draw slow-moving crowds combing over souvenirs. The fresh-produce section is a good place to stock up on snacks.

 Tours

Fremantle Tram Tours City

(☎08-9433 6674; www.fremantletrams.com.au; departs Town Hall) Actually a bus that looks like an old-fashioned trolley car, taking an all-day hop-on, hop-off circuit around the city (adult/child $24/5).

Captain Cook Cruises Cruises

(☎08-9325 3341; www.captaincookcruises.com.au; C Shed, Victoria Quay) Cruises between Fremantle and Perth (one way/return $22/41). A three-hour lunch cruise departs at 12.45pm (adult/child $64/41).

 Sleeping

NORFOLK HOTEL Pub $$

(☎08-9335 5405; www.norfolkhotel.com.au; 47 South Tce; s/d without bathroom $80/110, d with bathroom $150; ❄☎) Far above your standard pub digs, the Norfolk's rooms have all been tastefully decorated in muted tones and crisp white linen, and there's a communal sitting room. It can be noisy, but the bar closes at midnight.

FOTHERGILLS OF FREMANTLE B&B $$

(☎08-9335 6784; www.fothergills.net.au; 18-22 Ord St; r $160-255; ☎) Naked bronze women sprout from the front garden, while a life-size floral cow shelters on the verandah of these neighbouring mansions on the hill. Inside, the decor is in keeping with their venerable age (built 1892), aside from the contemporary art scattered about.

TERRACE CENTRAL B&B HOTEL B&B $$
(☎08-9335 6600; www.terracecentral.com. au; 79-85 South Tce; d $165; ❄@🖤) It may be a character-filled B&B at heart, but Terrace Central's larger size gives it the feel of a boutique hotel. The main section is created from an 1888 bakery and an adjoining row of terraces, and there are modern one- and two-bedroom apartments out the back.

BANNISTER SUITES FREMANTLE Hotel $$$
(☎08-9435 1288; www.bannistersuites fremantle.com.au; 22 Bannister St; r from $210; ❄) Modern and fresh, boutiquey Bannisters is a stylish new addition to the central city's accommodation scene. It's worth paying extra for one of the suites with the deep balconies, where you can enjoy views over the rooftops.

Eating

City Centre

MAYA Indian $$
(☎08-9335 2796; www.mayarestaurant.com.au; 77 Market St; mains $17-28; ⊙dinner Tue-Sun, lunch Fri) Maya's white tablecloths and wooden chairs signal classic style without the pomp. Its well-executed meals have earnt it the reputation of WA's best Indian restaurant. Try a Punjabi, Delhi or Bombay banquet.

MOORE & MOORE Cafe $
(46 Henry St; mains $8-22; ⊙8am-4pm; 🖤) An urban-chic cafe that spills into the adjoining art gallery and overflows into a flagstoned courtyard. Great coffee, good cooked breakfasts (including half serves for undersized appetites), pastries and wraps; free wi-fi.

GINO'S Cafe $
(www.ginoscafe.com.au; 1 South Tce; mains $13-17; ⊙breakfast, lunch & dinner; 🖤) Old-school Gino's is Freo's most famous cafe, and while it's become a tourist attraction in its own right, the locals still treat it as their second living room, only with better coffee.

Fishing Boat Harbour

LITTLE CREATURES Pub Fare $$
(www.littlecreatures.com.au; 40 Mews Rd; mains $16-34; ⊙10am-midnight) Little Creatures is classic Freo: harbour views, fantastic brews (made on the premises) and excellent food. In a cavernous converted boatshed overlooking the harbour, it can get chaotic at times, but the wood-fired pizzas and substantial mains are well worth the wait.

MUSSEL BAR Seafood $$
(☎08-9433 1800; www.musselbar.com.au; 42 Mews Rd, Fishing Boat Harbour; mains $26-31; ⊙breakfast Sun, lunch & dinner daily) Mussel Bar's large glass windows afford romantic views of the glittering harbour. Mussels, of course, are the go – or you can knock back fresh oysters with a sunset glass of bubbly.

North Fremantle

HARVEST Modern Australian $$
(☎08-9336 1831; www.harvestrestaurant.net. au; 1 Harvest Rd, North Fremantle; mains $32-39; ⊙breakfast & lunch Fri-Sun, dinner Tue-Sun) Swing through the heavy, fuchsia-painted metal doors and into the dark-wood dining room lined with artworks and curios, then settle down to comforting Mod Oz dishes cooked with a dash of panache.

 Drinking & Entertainment

LITTLE CREATURES Microbrewery
(www.littlecreatures.com.au; 40 Mews Rd, Fishing Boat Harbour; mains $16-34; ⊙10am-midnight) In an old boatshed by the harbour, this brewery churns out beers that are a great source of WA pride. You can admire the brewery vats and spot bald patches from

the mezzanine or almost nuzzle the boats from the boardwalk out back.

NORFOLK HOTEL
Pub

(www.norfolkhotel.com.au; 47 South Tce; ⏱11am-midnight Mon-Sat, to 10pm Sun) Slow down to the Freo pace and take your time over one of the many beers on tap at this 1887 pub. The limestone courtyard, with the sun streaking in through the elms and eucalypts, is downright soporific sometimes.

MONK
Microbrewery

(www.themonk.com.au; 33 South Tce; ⏱11.30am-late) Park yourself at the voyeuristic front terrace or in the chic interior, partly fashioned from recycled railway sleepers, and enjoy the Monk's own brews or a slap-up meal.

MOJOS
Pub, Music

(www.mojosbar.com.au; 237 Queen Victoria St, North Fremantle; ⏱7pm-late) Good old Mojos is one of Freo's longstanding live music pubs – a real stalwart. Local and national bands and DJs play at this small venue, and there's a sociable beer garden out back.

ℹ Information

Visitor Centre (☎08-9431 7878; www.fremantle.wa.com.au; Town Hall, Kings Sq; ⏱9am-5pm Mon-Fri, 10am-3pm Sat, 11.30am-2.30pm Sun) Free maps and brochures.

ℹ Getting There & Around

Fremantle sits within Zone 2 of the Perth public-transport system, Transperth, and is only 30 minutes away by train. There are numerous buses between Perth's city centre and Fremantle, including routes 103, 106, 107, 111 and 158.

Another very pleasant way to get here from Perth is by the 1¼-hour river cruise run by Captain Cook Cruises; see p315 for details.

AROUND PERTH
Rottnest Island (Wadjemup)

'Rotto' has long been the family-holiday playground of choice for Perth locals. Although it's only about 19km offshore from Fremantle, this car-free, off-the-grid slice of paradise, ringed by secluded beaches and bays, feels a million miles from the metropolis.

Cycling round the 11km-long, 4.5km-wide car-free island is a real pleasure; just ride around and pick your own bit of beach to spend the day on.

If you fancy further diversions, snorkelling, fishing, surfing and diving are all excellent on the island.

Rotto is also the site of annual school leavers' and end-of-uni-exams parties, a time when the island is overrun by kids 'getting blotto on Rotto'. Depending on your age, it's either going to be the best time you've ever had or the worst – check the calendar before proceeding.

Longreach Bay, Rottnest Island
PHOTOGRAPHER: PAUL KENNEDY/LONELY PLANET IMAGES ©

Quokkas

Once found throughout the southwest, quokkas are now confined to forest on the mainland and a population of 8000 to 10,000 on Rottnest Island. These cute, docile little marsupials have suffered a number of indignities over the years. First de Vlamingh's crew mistook them for rats. Then the British settlers misheard and mangled their name (the Noongar word was probably *quak-a* or *gwaga*). But worst of all, a cruel trend for 'quokka soccer' by sadistic louts in the 1990s saw many kicked to death before a $10,000 fine was imposed.

◎ Sights

**QUOD & ABORIGINAL
BURIAL GROUND**   Historic Site
(Kitson St) This octagonal 1864 building with a central courtyard was once the Aboriginal prison block but is now part of a hotel. Immediately adjacent to the Quod is a wooded area where hundreds of Aboriginal prisoners were buried in unmarked graves.

ROTTNEST MUSEUM   Museum
(Kitson St; admission by gold coin donation; ⏱11am-3.30pm) Housed in the old hay-store building, this little museum tells the island's natural and human history.

🏃 Activities

REEFS & WRECKS   Snorkelling, Diving
Excellent visibility in the temperate waters, coral reefs and shipwrecks makes Rottnest a top spot for **scuba diving** and **snorkelling**. There are snorkel trails with underwater plaques at **Little Salmon Bay** and **Parker Point**. Rottnest Island Bike Hire rents masks, snorkels and fins, as well as kayaks.

The only wreck which is accessible to snorkellers without using a boat is at **Thomson Bay**.

BREAKS   Surfing
The best breaks are at **Strickland, Salmon** and **Stark Bays**, at the west end

of the island. Boards can be hired at Rottnest Island Bike Hire.

Tours

FREE **Rottnest Voluntary
Guides**   Walking
(☏08-9372 9757; www.rvga.asn.au) Themed walks leave from the Salt Store daily.

Discovery Coach Tour   Coach
(www.rottnestisland.com; adult/child $33/16) Leaves from Thomson Bay three times daily (book at the visitor centre); includes commentary and a stop at West End.

Rottnest Adventure Tour   Boat
(www.rottnestexpress.com.au; adult/child $50/25) Ninety-minute cruises around the coast with a special emphasis on spotting wildlife, including whales in season. Packages available from Perth (adult/child $130/65) and Fremantle ($115/57).

🛏 Sleeping & Eating

**ROTTNEST ISLAND AUTHORITY
COTTAGES**   Rental Houses $$
(☏08-9432 9111; www.rottnestisland.com; cottages $117-214) There are more than 250 villas and cottages for rent around the island. Some have magnificent beach-front positions and are palatial; others are more like beach shacks. Sizes range from four to eight beds.

HOTEL ROTTNEST Pub $$$
(☎08-9292 5011; www.hotelrottnest.com.au; 1 Bedford Ave; r $270-320; ❄) Based around the 1864 summer-holiday pad for the state's governors, the former Quokka Arms has been completely transformed with a glass pavilion grafted onto it, creating an open, inviting space. The whiter-than-white rooms are smart and modern, if a little pricy for what's offered. Bistro-style food (including pizza) is served at quite reasonable rates (mains $18 to $27).

ROTTNEST LODGE Hotel $$
(☎08-9292 5161; www.rottnestlodge.com.au; Kitson St; r $205-310; ❖) It's claimed there are ghosts in this comfortable complex, which is based around the former Quod. If that worries you, ask for one of the cheery rooms with a view in the new section fronting onto a salt lake. The attached **Marlins Restaurant** (mains $26-36; ☯lunch & dinner) does buffet lunches for tour groups, as well as a crowd-pleasing menu of pub-style evening meals.

ARISTOS Seafood $$
(www.aristosrottnest.com.au; Colebatch Ave; mains $16-30; ☯lunch & dinner) An upmarket

option for fish and chips, burgers, ice creams and excellent coffee, right on the waterfront near the main jetty.

ℹ Information

Visitor Centre (www.rottnestisland.com); Thomson Bay (☎08-9372 9732; ☯7.30am-5pm Sat-Thu, to 7pm Fri, extended in summer); Fremantle (☎08-9432 9300; E Shed, Victoria Quay) Handles check-ins for all the island authority's accommodation. There's a bookings counter at the Fremantle office, near where the ferry departs.

ℹ Getting There & Away

Air
Rottnest Air-Taxi (☎08-9292 5027; www.rottnest.de) Flies from Jandakot airport in four-seater (up to three passengers one way/same day return/extended return $220/300/350) or six-seater planes (up to five passengers one way/same day return/extended return $300/400/480).

Boat
Rottnest Express (☎1300 467 688; www.rottnestexpress.com.au); Fremantle (C Shed,

Quokka, Rottnest Island

DENNIS JONES/LONELY PLANET IMAGES ©

Victoria Quay; adult/child $60/36); Northport (1 Emma Pl, Rous Head, North Fremantle; adult/child $60/36); Perth (Pier 2, Barrack St Jetty; adult/child $80/46) The above prices are for return day trips and include the island admission fee; add $9 for an extended return. Schedules are seasonal. Various packages are available, adding on bike hire, snorkelling equipment, meals and tours. Also runs the Mega Blast (adult/child $69/36), a speedboat service for thrill seekers, departing Fremantle daily from September to May.

Rottnest Fast Ferries (☎ 08-9246 1039; www.rottnestfastferries.com.au; adult/child $82/43) Departs from Hillarys Boat Harbour (40 minutes, thrice daily); add $3 for an extended return.

ℹ️ Getting Around

Bike
Bikes can be booked in advance online or on arrival from Rottnest Island Bike Hire (☎ 08-9292 5105; www.rottnestisland.com; cnr Bedford Ave & Welch Way; single speed per 1/2/3/4/5 days $20/31/40/48/56, multi-gear

$27/43/54/65/76; ⏰ 8.30am-4pm, to 5.30pm summer).

Rottnest Express also hires bikes (per 1/2/3 days $28/41/56). It doesn't provide locks and it's not unheard of for an unlocked bike to be grabbed and used by someone else.

Bus
A free shuttle runs between Thomson Bay and the main accommodation areas. The Bayseeker (day pass adult/child $13/5.50) does an hourly loop around the island.

THE SOUTHWEST
The farmland, forests, rivers and coast of the lush south-western corner of WA contrast vividly with the stark, sunburnt terrain of much of the state. On land, world-class wineries beckon and tall trees provide shade for walking trails and scenic drives, while offshore, bottlenose dolphins and whales frolic, and devoted surfers search for – and often find – their perfect break.

Margaret River Wine Region
With its blissful country roads shaded by mature trees, its crashing surf beaches, and, of course, its excellent Chardonnays and Bordeaux-style reds, Margaret River is our favourite Australian wine region and a highlight of any trip to WA.

Yallingup & Around
Beachside Yallingup is as much a mecca for salty-skinned surfers as it is for wine aficionados. You're permitted to let a 'wow' escape when the surf-battered coastline first comes into view.

Wine bottles on display, Wilyabrup

Surfing the Southwest

Known to surfers as 'Yals' (around Yallingup) and 'Margs' (around the mouth of the Margaret River), the beaches between Capes Naturaliste and Leeuwin offer powerful reef breaks, mainly left-handers.

Around Dunsborough, the better locations are between Eagle and Bunker Bays. Near Yallingup there's the Three Bears, Rabbits (a beach break towards the north of Yallingup Beach), Yallingup, Injidup Car Park and Injidup Point. The annual surfer pro is held around Margaret River Mouth and Southside ('Suicides').

Pick up a surfing map ($5.25) from one of the visitor centres on the way through.

Sights & Activities

FREE WARDAN CULTURAL CENTRE
Indigenous Culture

(☎08-9756 6566; www.wardan.com.au; Injidup Springs Rd; adult/child $15/8; Sun, Mon, Wed & Fri, closed 15 Jun-15 Aug) Offers experiences such as stone tool–making, boomerang and spear throwing and guided bushwalks exploring Wardandi spirituality and the uses of plants for food, medicine and shelter.

NGILGI CAVE
Cave

(☎08-9755 2152; www.geographebay.com; Yallingup Caves Rd; adult/child $19/10; 9.30am-4.30pm) Between Dunsborough and Yallingup, this 500,000-year-old cave is known for its limestone formations. Entry is by semiguided tours, which depart every half-hour.

Sleeping

Smiths Beach Resort
Resort $$$

(☎08-9750 1200; www.smithsbeachresort.com.au; Smiths Beach Rd; apt from $220; ❄☃) A large complex of tastefully plush one- to four-bedroom apartments by a very beautiful beach.

Eating & Drinking

Lamont's
Winery, Restaurant $$$

(☎08-9755 2434; www.lamonts.com.au; Gunyulgup Valley Dr; mains $39-41; lunch daily, dinner Sat) Raised on stilts over its own lake, Lamont's is an idyllic spot for lunch or tapas, with a glass of wine, naturally.

Cowaramup & Wilyabrup

Cowaramup is little more than a couple of blocks of shops lining Bussell Hwy. That a significant percentage of those are devoted in one way or another to eating or drinking is testament to its position at the heart of the wine region. The rustic area to the north-west known as Wilyabrup is where, in the 1960s, the Margaret River wine industry was born.

Sleeping

NOBLE GRAPE GUESTHOUSE
B&B $$

(☎08-9755 5538; www.noblegrape.com.au; 29 Bussell Hwy, Cowaramup; s $130-150, d $150-165; ❄) More like an upmarket motel than a traditional B&B, Noble Grape's rooms offer privacy and each has a little courtyard as well as a microwave and a DVD player.

Eating & Drinking

VASSE FELIX
Winery, Restaurant $$$

(☎08-9756 5050; www.vassefelix.com.au; cnr Caves Rd & Harmans Rd South; mains $35-39; lunch) Vasse is considered to have the finest restaurant in the region. The grounds are peppered with sculpture, while the gallery displaying works from the Holmes à Court collection is worth a trip in itself. And, of course, the much-lauded and -awarded wine is magnificent.

KNEE DEEP IN MARGARET RIVER
Winery, Restaurant $$

(📞08-9755 6776; www.kneedeepwines.com.au; 61 Johnson Rd; mains $32-37; ⏱lunch) Only a handful of mains are offered – with locally sourced, seasonal produce to the fore – and the open-sided pavilion among the vines provides a pleasantly intimate setting. The attention to detail is impressive, both in the flavours and in the service.

Margaret River

Although tourists might outnumber locals much of the time, Margaret River still feels like a country town. The advantage of basing yourself here is that after 5pm, once the surrounding wineries shut up shop, it's one of the few places with any vital signs.

🛏 Sleeping

RIVERGLEN CHALETS   Apartments $$

(📞08-9757 2101; www.riverglenchalets.com.au; Carters Rd; chalets $155-280; ❄ 🛜) Just north of town, these good-value and very comfortable timber chalets are spacious and fully self-contained, with verandahs looking out onto bushland; there's wheelchair access to a couple of them.

PRIDEAU'S   Motel $$

(📞0438 587 180; www.prideaus.com.au; 31 Fearn Ave; r $145-185; ❄ 🛜) At this price and in such a central location, you'd expect a fairly middling sort of motel, which is what Prideau's looks like from the outside. But step through the door and you'll find sharp, newly renovated units opening on to little courtyards.

Bridgefield   B&B $$

(📞08-9757 3007; www.bridgefield.com.au; 73 Bussell Hwy; r $130-160; 🛜) A 19th-century coach house, this lovely higgledy-piggledy B&B is all wood panels, high ceilings, tiled floors and ancient claw-foot baths.

🍴 Eating & Drinking

SETTLER'S TAVERN   Pub

(www.settlerstavern.com; 114 Bussell Hwy; ⏱11am-midnight Mon-Sat, to 10pm Sun) There's live entertainment most nights at Settler's, so settle in for the evening with good pub grub and a wine from the extensive list.

MUST   Restaurant, Bar $$

(📞08-9758 8877; www.must.com.au; 107 Bussell Hwy; mains $30-38, 2-/3-course lunch $33/44; ⏱lunch & dinner) The sister property to one of our favourite Perth restaurants, Must doesn't disappoint. The service is excellent and the charcuterie plates are legendary. If you can't bear the thought of leaving, there are four bedrooms upstairs (per night $180).

ℹ Information

Visitor Centre (📞08-9780 5911; www.margaretriver.com; 100 Bussell Hwy; ⏱9am-5pm)

ℹ Getting Around

Margaret River Beach Bus (📞08-9757 9532; www.mrlodge.com.au) Minibus heading between the township and the beaches around Prevelly ($10, thrice daily); summer only, bookings essential.

SOUTH COAST

Standing on the cliffs of the wild south coast as the waves pound below is an elemental experience. And on calm days, when the sea is varied shades of aquamarine and the glorious white-sand beaches lie pristine and welcoming, it's an altogether different type of magnificent.

ℹ Getting There & Away

Skywest (📞1300 66 00 88; www.skywest.com.au) flies daily from Perth to Albany (70 minutes) and Esperance (1¾ hours).

Walpole & Nornalup

The peaceful twin inlets of Walpole and Nornalup make good bases from which to explore the heavily forested Walpole Wilderness Area – an immense wilderness incorporating a rugged coastline, several national parks, marine parks, nature reserves and forest-conservation areas – covering a whopping 3630-sq-km (an area considerably bigger than Samoa and 57 other countries).

TAOLMOR | DREAMSTIME.COM ©

Don't Miss Walpole-Nornalup National Park

The giant trees of this park include red, yellow and Rates tingle trees and, closer to the coast, the red flowering gum. The **Valley of the Giants Tree Top Walk** (adult/child $10/5; ⊗9am-4.15pm) is the main drawcard. A 600m-long ramp rises from the floor of the valley, allowing visitors access high into the tree canopy. At its highest point, the ramp is 40m above the ground. The ramp is an engineering feat in itself, though vertigo sufferers might have a few problems; it's designed to sway gently in the breeze. At ground level, the **Ancient Empire** boardwalk meanders around and through the base of veteran red tingles, some of which are 16m in circumference.

There are numerous good walking tracks around, including a section of the **Bibbulmun Track**, which passes through Walpole to Coalmine Beach. Scenic drives include **Knoll Drive**, 3km east of Walpole; the **Valley of the Giants Rd**; and through pastoral country to **Mt Frankland**. Here you can climb to the summit for panoramic views or walk around the trail at its base. Opposite Knoll Dr, Hilltop Rd leads to a **giant tingle tree**; this road continues to the **Circular Pool** on the Frankland River, a popular canoeing spot.

Midway between Nornalup and Peaceful Bay, check out **Conspicuous Cliffs**. It's a great spot for whale watching from July to November, with a boardwalk, a hilltop lookout and a steep-ish 800m walk to the beach.

Tours

WOW WILDERNESS ECOCRUISES River Cruises
(☏08-9840 1036; www.wowwilderness.com. au; adult/child $40/15) This magnificent landscape and its ecology are brought to life with anecdotes about Aboriginal settlement, salmon fishers and shipwrecked pirates. The 2½-hour cruise through the river systems leaves daily at 10am; book at the visitor centre.

Naturally Walpole Eco Tours 4WD
(08-9840 1019; www.naturallywalpole.com.au)
Half-day tours through the Walpole wilderness
(adult/child $75/40).

Sleeping & Eating

RIVERSIDE RETREAT Chalets $$
(08-9840 1255; www.riversideretreat.com.au;
South Coast Hwy, Nornalup; chalets $140-260)
Set up off the road and on the banks of
the beautiful Frankland River, these
well-equipped chalets are great value,
with pot-bellied stoves for cosy winter
warmth and tennis and canoeing as
outdoor pursuits.

Nornalup Riverside Chalets Chalets $$
(08-9840 1107; www.walpole.org.au/nornalup
riversidechalets; Riverside Dr, Nornalup; chalets
$85-170) Stay a night in sleepy Nornalup in
these comfortable, colourful self-contained
chalets, just a rod's throw from the fish in the
Frankland River.

Thurlby Herb Farm Cafe $
(www.thurlbyherb.com.au; 3 Gardiner Rd; mains
$13-18; 9am-5pm Mon-Fri) Apart from
distilling its own essential oils and making herb-
based products including soap, Thurlby serves
up tasty light lunches and cakes in a pretty cafe
overlooking the garden.

Information

Visitor Centre (08-9840 1111; www.walpole.
com.au; South Coast Hwy, Walpole; 9am-
5pm; @)

Denmark

The first wave of alternative lifestylers
landed in idyllic Denmark about 20 years
ago, attracted by its beaches, river, sheltered inlet, forested backdrop and rolling
hinterland.

The town is located in the cool-
climate Great Southern wine region and
has some notable wineries, including
Howard Park (www.howardparkwines.com.au;
Scotsdale Rd; 10am-4pm) and **Forest Hill**

Left: Elephant Rocks and Greens Pool, Denmark; **Below:** Canoeing, Walpole
PHOTOGRAPHERS: (LEFT) WAYNE WALTON/LONELY PLANET IMAGES ©; (BELOW) MARTIN ROBINSON/LONELY
PLANET IMAGES ©

(www.foresthillwines.com.au;
cnr South Coast Hwy & Myers Rd;
🕙10am-5pm).

🔘 Sights & Activities

Surfers and anglers usually waste no time in heading to ruggedly beautiful **Ocean Beach**. If you're keen to try surfing, accredited local instructor Mike Neunuebel gives **surf lessons** (📞08-9848 2057; 2hr private lessons incl equipment $80).

To get your bearings, walk the **Mokare Heritage Trail** (3km circuit along the Denmark River) or the **Wilson Inlet Trail** (12km return, starting at the river mouth), which forms part of the longer **Nornalup Trail**. Put everything into perspective at **Mt Shadforth Lookout**, with its view of fine coastal scenery.

🛏 Sleeping

**CAPE HOWE
COTTAGES**   Cottages **$$**
(📞08-9845 1295; www.capehowe.com.au; 322 Tennessee Rd South; cottages $160-270; ❄) If you fancy a remote getaway, these five cottages in bushland south-east of Denmark (off Lower Denmark Rd) make the grade. They're all different, but the best is only 1½km from dolphin-favoured Lowlands Beach and is properly plush.

SENSATIONAL HEIGHTS   B&B **$$**
(📞08-9840 9000; www.sensationalheights bandb.com.au; 159 Suttons Rd; r $175-260; ❄🛜) Yep, it's on top of a hill (off Scotsdale Rd) and, yes, the views are sensational. It's a new house, so expect contemporary decor, shiny new fixtures, luxurious linen and very comfy beds.

325

The Road to Mandalay

About 13km west of Walpole, at Crystal Springs, is an 8km gravel road to **Mandalay Beach** where the *Mandalay,* a Norwegian barque, was wrecked in 1911. Every 10 years or so, as the sand gradually erodes with storms, the wreck eerily appears in shallow water that is walkable at low tide. The beach is glorious, often deserted, and accessed by an impressive boardwalk across sand dunes and cliffs.

 ## Eating & Drinking

Denmark Bakery Bakery $
(Strickland St; pies $5-6; ☼7am-5pm) Prize-winning and proud of it; this bakery is an institution because of its pies – and the bread is also good.

Southern End Brewery, Restaurant
(www.denmarkbrewery.com.au; 427 Mt Shadforth Rd; ☼11.30am-4.30pm Thu-Mon) Home to Denmark Brews & Ales ('the brew with a view'), it also serves a wide range of imported beers and local wines on its hilltop terrace.

ⓘ Information

Visitor centre (☎08-9848 2055; www.denmark.com.au; 73 South Coast Hwy; ☼9am-5pm) Houses the 'world's largest barometer' in its own custom-made tower.

Albany

Established shortly before Perth in 1826, the oldest European settlement in the state is now the bustling commercial centre of the southern region. Albany is a mixed bag, comprising a stately and genteelly decaying colonial quarter, a waterfront in the midst of sophisticated redevelopment and a hectic sprawl of malls and fast-food joints. Less ambivalent is its coastline, which is uniformly spectacular.

◉ Sights

MIDDLETON & EMU BEACHES Beaches
Just around the headland east of the town centre, facing King George Sound, these beautiful beaches share one stretch of sand and are perfect for families – both human and cetacean. In winter, you'll often see mother whales and their calves here – sometimes two or three sets at once. Head around Emu Point to Oyster Harbour and there are swimming pontoons and even calmer waters.

WESTERN AUSTRALIAN MUSEUM – ALBANY Museum
(www.museum.wa.gov.au; Residency Rd; admission by donation; ☼10am-4.30pm Thu-Tue) This branch of the state museum has a kids' discovery section, a lighthouse exhibition and a gallery. It incorporates the 1850s home of the resident magistrate, which tells seafaring stories, explains local natural history and has displays on Minang Noongar history.

 ## Activities

WHALE-WATCHING Whale Watching
After whaling ended in 1978, whales slowly began returning to the waters of Albany. You can usually spot them from the beach from July to mid-October, but if you fancy a closer look, **Albany Dolphin & Whale Cruises** (☎0428 429 876; www.whales.com.au; adult/child $80/45) and **Albany Whale Tours** (☎08-9845 1068;

www.albanywhaletours.com.au; adult/child $75/40) both run regular whale-watching trips in season.

DIVING
Diving

Albany's appeal as a top-class diving destination grew after the 2001 scuttling of the **HMAS Perth** (www.hmasperth.com.au). **Dive Locker Albany** (08-9842 6886; www.albanydive.com.au; 114 York St) and **Southcoast Diving Supplies** (08-9841 7176; www.divealbany.com.au; 84b Serpentine Rd) will show you the underwater world.

Information

Visitor Centre (08-9841 9290; www.amazingalbany.com; Proudlove Pde; 9am-5pm)

Around Albany

Sights

WHALE WORLD MUSEUM
Museum

(08-9844 4019; www.whaleworld.org; Frenchman Bay Rd; adult/child $25/10; 9am-5pm) When the Cheynes Beach Whaling Station ceased operations in November 1978, few could have guessed that its gore-covered decks would eventually be covered in tourists, craning to see whales passing within harpoon-shot of the slaughterhouse itself. The museum screens films about marine life and whaling operations, and displays giant skeletons, harpoons, whaleboat models and scrimshaw (etchings on whalebone). Free guided tours depart on the hour from 10am.

FREE TORNDIRRUP NATIONAL PARK
National Park

(Frenchman Bay Rd) Covering much of the peninsula that encloses the southern reaches of King George Sound, this national park is known for its windswept, ocean-bashed cliffs. The **Gap** is a natural cleft in the rock, channelling blistering surf through walls of granite. Close by is the **Natural Bridge**, a self-explanatory landmark. Further east, the **Blowholes** can put on a show when the surf is up, worth the 78 steps down and back up.

Esperance

Esperance sits in solitary splendour on the Bay of Isles, a seascape of aquamarine waters fringed with squeaky white beaches. There's no need to fight for space here, as the town's isolation all but guarantees it.

Out in the bay, the pristine environment of the Recherche Archipelago can be wild and windy, or turn on a calmly charming show; its 105

Twilight Cove (p328), Esperance
PHOTOGRAPHER: ORIEN HARVEY/LONELY PLANET IMAGES ©

Detour:
François Peron National Park

Covering the whole peninsula north of Denham is an area of low scrub, salt lakes and red sandy dunes home to the rare bilby, mallee fowl and woma python. The excellent **Wanamalu Trail** (3km return) follows the cliff top between Cape Peron and Skipjack Point, from where you can spot marine life in the crystal waters below. Park entry is $11 per vehicle. Tours start around $180 from Denham or Monkey Mia, though you can hire your own 4WD from Denham for the same price.

islands are home to colonies of fur seals, penguins and a variety of sea birds.

Sights & Activities

GREAT OCEAN DRIVE — Scenic Drive
Many of Esperance's most dramatic sights can be seen on this well-signposted 40km loop. Starting from the waterfront it heads south-west along a breathtaking stretch of coast that includes popular surfing and swimming spots, including **Blue Haven Beach** and **Twilight Cove**. Stop to enjoy the rollers breaking against the cliffs from **Observatory Point** and the lookout on **Wireless Hill**.

ESPERANCE MUSEUM — Museum
(cnr James & Dempster Sts; adult/child $6/2; ⏱1.30-4.30pm) One of those zany regional museums where glass cabinets are randomly crammed with collections of sea shells, frog ornaments, tennis rackets and bed pans. Bigger items include boats, a train carriage and the remains of US space station Skylab, which made its fiery re-entry at Balladonia, east of Esperance, in 1979.

Tours

Mackenzie's Island Cruises — Boat
(☎08-9071 5757; www.woodyisland.com.au; 71 The Esplanade; ⏱till late daily Sep-May) Tours Esperance Bay and Woody Island in a power catamaran (half-/full day $88/139), getting close to fur seals, sea lions, Cape Barren geese and (with luck) dolphins.

Kepa Kurl Eco Cultural Discovery Tours — Indigenous Culture
(☎08-9072 1688; www.kepakurl.com.au; Museum Village) Explore the country from an Aboriginal perspective: visit rock art and waterholes, sample bush food and hear ancient stories (adult/child $115/80, minimum four).

Sleeping

ESPERANCE B&B BY THE SEA — B&B $$
(☎08-9071 5640; www.esperancebb.com; 34 Stewart St; s/d $110/150) This beach house has a private guest wing, and the views from the deck overlooking Blue Haven Beach are breathtaking, especially at sunset. It's just a stroll from the ocean and a five-minute drive from Dempster St.

CLEARWATER MOTEL APARTMENTS — Motel $$
(☎08-9071 3587; www.clearwatermotel.com.au; 1a William St; s $110, d $140-195; ❄) The bright, spacious rooms and apartments here have balconies and are fully self-contained, and there's a well-equipped shared BBQ area. It's just a short walk from both waterfront and town.

Eating

TAYLOR STREET JETTY Cafe $$
(Taylor St Jetty; lunch $13-19, dinner $24-32;
⊙breakfast & lunch Wed-Mon, dinner Thu-Mon;
🛜) This attractive, sprawling cafe by the
jetty serves cafe fare, tapas, seafood and
salads. Locals hang out at the tables on
the grass or read on the covered terrace.

ℹ Information

Visitor Centre (📞08-9083 1555; www.
visitesperance.com; cnr Kemp & Dempster Sts;
⊙9am-5pm Mon-Fri, to 2pm Sat, to noon Sun)

SHARK BAY

World Heritage–listed Shark Bay,
with more than 1500km of pristine
coastline, barren peninsulas, white-
sand beaches and bountiful marine
life draws tourists from around the
world. The sheltered turquoise waters
and skinny fingers of stunted land at
the westernmost edge of the conti-
nent are one of WA's most biologically
rich habitats.

ℹ Getting There & Away

Air

Shark Bay Airport is located between Denham
and Monkey Mia. Skippers flies regularly to Perth.

Bus

The closest Greyhound approach is the
Overlander roadhouse 128km away on the North
West Coastal Hwy (Rte 1). Shark Bay Car Hire
(📞0427 483 032; www.carhire.net.au) runs a
connecting shuttle ($65 per person; book ahead!).
It also hires cars/4WDs from $40/185 per day.

Denham

Beautiful, laid-back Denham, with its
aquamarine sea and palm-fringed beach-
front, only 26km from world-famous
Monkey Mia, makes a great base for ex-
ploring the surrounding Shark Bay Marine
Park and Peron Peninsula.

♡ If You Like…
Discovering National Parks

If you like Francois Peron National Park,
jutting into Shark Bay, we think you'll also
like these detour-worthy national parks:

1 YALGORUP NATIONAL PARK
This beautiful coastal region of woodlands, lakes
and sand dunes is 50km south of Mandurah, itself
70km south of Perth. The park is an internationally
significant wetland for migrating waterbirds. Rock
hounds will want to see the globular thrombalites at
Lake Clifton.

2 WALPOLE-NORNALUP NATIONAL PARK
On WA's south coast, this is the place to walk
among and above enormous tingle trees on the Valley
of the Giants Tree Top Walk.

3 TORNDIRRUP NATIONAL PARK
Near Albany in the southwest, Torndirrup is a
rocky coastal park studded with amazing canyons,
blowholes, rock bridges, bays and beaches.

4 STIRLING RANGE NATIONAL PARK
Rising abruptly from the plains 80km north of
Albany, this 1156-sq-km national park consists of a
10km-wide, 65km-long chain of peaks pushed up by
plate tectonics. Bluff Knoll (Bular Mai) is the highest
point in the southwest (1095m).

5 FITZGERALD RIVER NATIONAL PARK
Midway between Albany and Esperance,
this gem has been declared a Unesco Biosphere
Reserve. Protected here are 22 mammal species,
200 species of birds and 1700 species of plants
(20% of WA's native species). Wildflowers are
abundant in spring, but bloom year-round.

◎ Sights & Activities

**SHARK BAY WORLD HERITAGE
DISCOVERY CENTRE** Museum
(📞08-9948 1590; www.sharkbayinterpretive
centre.com.au; 53 Knight Tce; adult/child $11/6;

MARTIN COHEN/LONELY PLANET IMAGES ©

Don't Miss Monkey Mia

Watching the wild dolphins each morning in the shallow waters of **Monkey Mia** (adult/child/family $8/3/15), 26km north-east of Denham, is a highlight of every traveller's trip. The first feed is around 7.45am, but the dolphins will normally arrive earlier. The pier's a good vantage point. Hang around after the first session, as the dolphins routinely come back a second and sometimes a third time.

Monkey Mia Visitor Centre (☎08-9948 1366; ☺8am-4pm) has a good range of publications and can book tours.

TOURS

WULA GUDA NYINDA ABORIGINAL CULTURAL TOURS
Indigenous Culture

(☎0429 708 847; www.wulaguda.com.au; adult/child $40/20) Local Aboriginal guide Darren 'Capes' Capewell leads excellent bushwalks where he shows 'how to let the bush talk to you'. You'll learn some local Malgana language, and identify bush tucker and native medicine. The evening 'Didgeridoo Dreaming' walks are magical. There's also a 'Saltwater Dreaming' kayak tour (three hours; adult/child $90/50).

Aristocat II
Cruises

(☎1800 030 427; www.monkey-mia.net; 2½hr tours $75) Cruise in comfort on this large catamaran, and you might see dugongs, dolphins and loggerhead turtles. Also visits the **Blue Lagoon Pearl Farm**.

SLEEPING & EATING

MONKEY MIA DOLPHIN RESORT
Resort $$$

(☎1800 653 611; www.monkeymia.com.au; tent sites per person $15, van sites back/beach $37/50, dm/d $29/89, garden units $238, beachfront villas $320; ❄ @ ☎ ☎) A stunning location, friendly staff and good-value backpackers doubles are the highlights at this resort catering for all markets. Unfortunately, it can get seriously crowded and at times sounds like a continuous party.

⌚**9am-6pm**) One of WA's best museums has engaging, informative displays on Shark Bay's ecosystem and its Indigenous people, early explorers and settlers.

OCEAN PARK Aquarium
(☏08-9948 1765; www.oceanpark.com.au; Shark Bay Rd; adult/child $17/12; ⌚9am-5pm) Superbly located on a headland just before town, this family-run aquaculture farm features an artificial lagoon where you can observe feeding sharks, turtles, stingrays and fish on guided 45-minute tours. The licensed cafe has sensational views. Also on offer are full-day 4WD tours with bushwalks and snorkelling to François Peron National Park ($180) and Steep Point ($350).

 Tours

AUSSIE OFF ROAD TOURS 4WD
(☏0429 929 175; www.aussieoffroad tours.com.au) Culture and history feature strongly in these excellent Indigenous-owned and operated tours including twilight wildlife ($90), a full-day at François Peron National Park ($189), overnight camping in François Peron National Park ($300) and an overnight tour to Steep Point ($390).

SHARK BAY SCENIC
FLIGHTS Scenic Flights
(☏08-9948 1773; www.sharkbayair.com. au) Various scenic flights including 15-minute Monkey Mia flyovers ($55), 40-minute trips over Steep Point and the Zuytdorp Cliffs ($150) and one-way charters to/from the Overlander road-house ($120).

Shark Bay Coaches &
Tours Sightseeing
(☏08-9948 1081; www.sbcoaches.com; bus/quad $80/80) Half-day bus tours to all key sights, and two-hour quad-bike expeditions to various locations.

♥ **If You Like...**
The Underwater World

If you like diving and snorkelling at Ningaloo Marine Park, here are some other beaut places to explore the underwater world:

1 GERALDTON
The Houtman Abrolhos archipelago of 122 coral islands is about 60km off the coast of Geraldton, itself three hours south of Shark Bay. Here *Acropora* genus corals abound and, thanks to the warm Leeuwin Current, a rare and spectacular mix of tropical and temperate fish species thrives.

2 BUSSELTON
Take the plunge into Geographe Bay at Busselton, 230km south of Perth. Don't miss Four Mile Reef (a 40km limestone ledge about 6.5km off the coast) and on the scuttled navy vessel HMAS *Swan* off Dunsborough.

3 ALBANY
Albany has been a top-class diving destination since the warship HMAS *Perth* was scuttled in 2001, creating an artificial reef. Natural reefs here feature temperate corals, home to the bizarre and wonderful leafy and weedy sea dragons.

4 ESPERANCE
In the amazing Recherche Archipelago off Esperance you can bubble beneath the surface to the wreck of the *Sanko Harvest*. Keep an eye out for dolphins.

🛏 **Sleeping & Eating**

DENHAM SEASIDE TOURIST
VILLAGE Caravan Park $
(☏1300 133 733; www.sharkbayfun.com; Knight Tce; sites unpowered/powered/with bathroom $29/34/42, d cabins $80, 1-/2-bedroom chalets $120/130; ✳) This lovely, shady park on the water's edge is the best in town. Ring first if arriving after 6pm.

Detour:
Ningaloo Marine Park

A two-hour flight north of Perth, Ningaloo is Australia's largest fringing reef, in places only 100m offshore, and it's this accessibility and the fact it's home to a staggering array of **marine life** that make it so popular. Sharks, manta rays, humpback whales, turtles, dugongs and dolphins complement more than 500 species of fish.

Over 220 species of hard **coral** have been recorded in Ningaloo, ranging from bulbous brain corals found on bommies to delicate branching staghorns and the slow-growing massive coral. Spawning, where branches of hermaphroditic coral simultaneously eject eggs and sperm into the water, occurs after full and new moons between February and May, but the peak action is usually six to 10 days after the March and April full moons.

It's this spawning that attracts the park's biggest drawcard, the solitary speckled **whale shark** *(Rhiniodon typus)*. Ningaloo is one of the few places in the world where these gentle giants arrive like clockwork each year to feed on plankton and small fish, making it a mecca for marine biologists and visitors alike.

Most travellers visit Ningaloo Marine Park for the **snorkelling**. Stop at **Milyering Visitor Centre** (✆08-9949 2808; Yardie Creek Rd; ◷9am-3.45pm) for maps and information on the best spots and conditions. Check its tide chart and know your limits, as the currents can be dangerous. The shop next door rents equipment ($10 per day).

There is also great **scuba diving** in **Lighthouse Bay** at the Labyrinth and Blizzard Ridge.

OCEANSIDE VILLAGE   Cabins **$$**
(✆1800 680 600; www.oceanside.com.au; 117 Knight Tce; cabins $130-185; ❄🛜🏊) These neat, Dutch-owned, self-catering cottages with sunny balconies are perfectly located directly opposite the beach.

**OLD PEARLER
RESTAURANT**   Seafood **$$$**
(✆08-9948 1373; 71 Knight Tce; meals $26-48; ◷dinner, closed Sun) Avast, mateys! Built from shell bricks, and feeling downright nautical, this atmospheric haven does fantastic seafood. The exceptional platter features local red emperor, whiting, cray, prawns and squid with nary a chip in sight, as it's all grilled, not fried.

. . . .

ℹ️ Information

Shark Bay Visitor Centre (✆08-9948 1590; www.sharkbaywa.com.au; 53 Knight Tce; ◷9am-6pm) In the Discovery Centre foyer. Good parks information and offers accommodation and tour bookings. Issues free bush camping permits for South Peron.

Best of The Rest

Canberra (p334)
'Our nation's capital' is a lot more than just bureaucracy and filing cabinets (...try the museums, for starters).

Adelaide & Kangaroo Island (p336)
Adelaide has dignity, culture, poise...and plenty of pubs to help you forget all that stuff. Offshore, 'KI' is a wildlife spectacular.

Tasmania & Port Arthur (p339)
Australia's island state, 'Tassie' delivers convict sites, photogenic wilderness and a show-stopping art museum.

Top: Baby seal, Kangaroo Island (p338);
Bottom: Port Arthur (p341)

PHOTOGRAPHER: (TOP) CHRISTOPHER GROENHOUT/LONELY PLANET IMAGES ©;
(BOTTOM) KRZYSZTOF DYDYNSKI/LONELY PLANET IMAGES ©

Canberra

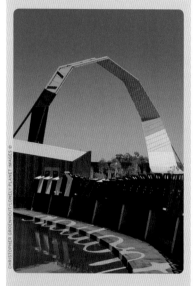

CHRISTOPHER GROENHOUT/LONELY PLANET IMAGES ©

HIGHLIGHTS

1 **National Museum of Australia** (pictured above) Negotiate a network of Australiana.

2 **National Gallery of Australia** Stroll the corridors of creativity.

3 **Australian War Memorial** Pay your respects or silently stand for the last post.

Canberra

The city of Canberra has an urban landscape that is expertly designed to show off the nation's democratic and cultural institutions. It is an excellent destination for museum addicts, with wonderful fine art and historical collections.

💿 Sights

NATIONAL MUSEUM OF AUSTRALIA Museum
(📞 1800 026 132, 02-6208 5000; www.nma. gov.au; Lawson Cres, Acton Peninsula; admission free; 🕘 9am-5pm) Designed by Ashton Raggatt McDougall and Robert Peck von Hartel Trethowan, the National Museum uses creativity, controversy, humour and self-contradiction to dismantle national identity and provoke visitors to come up with ideas of their own. There are lots of attendants on hand to help you navigate exhibitions on environmental change, Indigenous culture, national icons and more, and you can take one-hour **guided tours** (adult/child $7.50/5.50).

NATIONAL GALLERY OF AUSTRALIA Art Gallery
(📞 02-6240 6502; www.nga.gov.au; Parkes Pl, Parkes; permanent collection admission free; 🕘 10am-5pm) The national gallery has a stunning collection of more than 100,000 works of art representing four major areas: Aboriginal and Torres Strait Islander, Australian (from colonial to contemporary), Asian and international. In addition to regular all-inclusive **guided tours** (🕘 11am & 2pm), there's also a **tour** (🕘 11am Thu & Sun) focusing on Aboriginal and Torres Strait Islander art.

AUSTRALIAN WAR MEMORIAL Museum
(📞 02-6243 4211; www.awm.gov.au; Treloar Cres, Campbell; admission free; 🕘 10am-5pm) In a stately position, overlooking Anzac Pde and Lake Burley Griffin, the magnificent war memorial is Australia's most visited museum, and one of the finest in the country. There are free 90-minute guided tours; alternatively, purchase the *Self-Guided Tour* leaflet ($3).

PARLIAMENT HOUSE Notable Building

(📞02-6277 5399; www.aph.gov.au; admission free; ⏰9am-5pm) The symbolic and extravagant Parliament House opened in 1988 after a $1.1 billion construction project. The building is dug into Capital Hill, its roof covered in grass and topped by an 81m-high flagpole with a flag the size of a double-decker bus.

Free 45-minute **guided tours** (⏰every 30min 9am-4pm) are available on non-sitting days and 20-minute tours on sitting days, but you're welcome to self-navigate and watch parliamentary proceedings from the public galleries.

Sleeping

DIAMANT Boutique Hotel $$$

(📞02-6175 2222; www.diamant.com.au; 15 Edinburgh Ave, Civic; r/ste from $180/295; ❄️📶) This hip boutique hotel is tucked away in a quiet corner of Civic, not far from the National Museum. Its 80 rooms have all been decorated with an eye for detail: printed wallpaper on the ceilings, mini fish-scale tiles in the bathrooms and flat-screen TVs.

BRASSEY Hotel $$

(📞02-6273 3766; www.brassey.net.au; Belmore Gardens & Macquarie St, Barton; s $175-192, d $190-207, incl breakfast; ❄️📶) This charming and historic hotel is an easy walk from Parliament House, the National Gallery and other museums. The rooms are spacious and decorated in a stately, mock-1920s style.

Eating

ITALIAN & SONS Italian $$

(📞02-6162 4888; 7 Lonsdale St, Braddon; mains $23-32; ⏰lunch Tue-Fri, dinner Mon-Sat) This friendly new restaurant on the edge of Civic serves sophisticated yet hearty mains along with superlative pastas and wood-fired pizzas, all made from the best ingredients.

ℹ️ Information

Tourist Information

Canberra Visitors Centre (📞1300 554 114, 02-6205 0044; www.visitcanberra.com.au; 330 Northbourne Ave, Dickson; ⏰9am-5.30pm Mon-Fri, to 4pm Sat & Sun)

ℹ️ Getting There & Away

Air

Canberra International Airport (📞02-6275 2236) is serviced by **Qantas** (📞13 13 13, TTY 1800 652 660; www.qantas.com.au; Jolimont Centre, Northbourne Ave, Civic) and **Virgin Australia** (📞13 67 89; www.virginaustralia. com), with direct flights to Adelaide, Brisbane, Melbourne and Sydney.

Bus

The **interstate bus terminal** (Northbourne Ave, Civic) is at the Jolimont Centre.

Train

Kingston train station (Wentworth Ave), is the city's rail terminus. CountryLink trains run to/ from Sydney ($56, 4½ hours, two daily).

Adelaide & Kangaroo Island

DIANA MAYFIELD/LONELY PLANET IMAGES ©

HIGHLIGHTS

① **Central Market** Sniff out the ripest cheese, fullest fruit and strongest coffee.

② **Kangaroo Island (p338)** Watch the little penguins waddle.

③ **National Wine Centre of Australia** (pictured above) Encircled by famous wine regions (Barossa Valley, McLaren Vale, Clare Valley...), Adelaide is the place to try Aussie wines.

Adelaide

Sophisticated, cultured, neat casual – this is the self-image Adelaide projects, a nod to the days of free colonisation without the 'penal colony' taint. Multicultural flavours infuse Adelaide's restaurants; there's a great pub, arts and live-music scene; and the city's festival calendar has vanquished dull Saturday nights.

Sights

CENTRAL MARKET Market
(www.adelaidecentralmarket.com.au; btwn Grote & Gouger Sts; ⊙7am-5.30pm Tue, 9am-5.30pm Wed & Thu, 7am-9pm Fri, 7am-3pm Sat) Satisfy both obvious and obscure culinary cravings at the 250-odd stalls in Adelaide's superb Central Market. A gluten-free snag from the Gourmet Sausage Shop, a sliver of English stilton from the Smelly Cheese Shop, a tub of blueberry yoghurt from the Yoghurt Shop – you name it, it's all here.

FREE **ART GALLERY OF SOUTH AUSTRALIA** Art Gallery
(www.artgallery.sa.gov.au; North Tce; ⊙10am-5pm) Spend a few hushed hours in the vaulted, parquetry-floored gallery, which represents the big names in Australian art. Free audio tours of the Australian collection are insightful, as are the free guided tours (11am and 2pm daily).

FREE **NATIONAL WINE CENTRE OF AUSTRALIA** Winery
(www.wineaustralia.com.au; cnr Botanic & Hackney Rds; tastings from $10; ⊙9am-5pm Mon-Fri, 10am-5pm Sat & Sun) Check out the free self-guided, interactive Wine Discovery Journey exhibition, paired with tastings of Australian wines (extra charge), at this very sexy wine centre. Free 30-minute **tours** run at 11.30am daily.

Sleeping

CLARION HOTEL SOHO Hotel $$
(☎ 08-8412 5600; www.clarionhotelsoho.com.au; 264 Flinders St; d $145-590; ❄ ✷) *Ooh-la-la!*

Don't Miss Flinders Chase National Park

Occupying the western end of the island, **Flinders Chase National Park** (www.environment.sa.gov.au; admission adult/child/concession/family $9/5.50/7/24.50) is one of South Australia's top national parks.

Once a farm, **Rocky River** is a rampant hotbed of wildlife, with kangaroos, wallabies and Cape Barren geese competing for your affections.

From Rocky River, a road runs south to a remote 1906 lighthouse atop wild **Cape du Couedic**. A boardwalk weaves down to **Admirals Arch**, a huge archway ground out by heavy seas, and passes a colony of New Zealand fur seals (sweet smelling they ain't...).

At Kirkpatrick Point, a few kilometres east of Cape du Couedic, the **Remarkable Rocks** are a cluster of hefty, weather-gouged granite boulders atop a rocky dome that arcs 75m down to the sea.

Thirty very plush suites (some with spas, most with balconies) are complimented by sumptuous linen, 24-hour room service, iPod docks, Italian marble bathrooms, jet pool and a fab restaurant.

HOTEL RICHMOND   Hotel   **$$**
(📞08-8223 4444; www.hotelrichmond.com. au; 128 Rundle Mall; d from $165; ❄ 📶) This opulent hotel in a grand 1920s building in the middle of Rundle Mall has mod-minimalist rooms with king-sized beds,

marble bathrooms and American oak and Italian furnishings.

 Eating

MESA LUNGA   Mediterranean   **$$**
(📞08-8410 7617; www.mesalunga.com; cnr Gouger & Morphett Sts; tapas $4-25, mains $17-28; ⏱lunch Fri & Sun, dinner Tue-Sun) In a fishbowl corner room with an amazing dark-wood wine wall, sassy Mesa Lunga serves tapas and quality pizzas. Magic.

ⓘ Information

Tourist Information

South Australian Visitor & Travel Centre (✆1300 764 227; www.southaustralia.com; 18 King William St; ⏰8.30am-5pm Mon-Fri, 9am-2pm Sat & Sun)

ⓘ Getting There & Away

Air

Adelaide Airport (www.aal.com.au; 1 James Schofield Dr, Adelaide Airport) connects flights to all Australian capitals and many regional centres.

Bus

Adelaide Central Station (www.cityofadelaide.com.au; 85 Franklin St) for interstate and statewide buses.

Train

Adelaide's interstate train terminal is **Adelaide Parklands Terminal** (www.gsr.com.au; Railway Tce, Keswick), 1km southwest of the city centre.

Kangaroo Island

Long devoid of tourist trappings, Kangaroo Island these days is a booming destination for wilderness and wildlife fans – it's a veritable zoo of seals, birds, dolphins, echidnas and (of course) kangaroos.

◉ Sights & Activities

The **Kangaroo Island Penguin Centre** (www.kipenguincentre.com.au; Kingscote Wharf; adult/child/family $17/6/40; ⏰tours 8.30pm & 9.30pm Oct-Jan & Mar, 7.30pm & 8.30pm Apr-Oct, closed Feb) runs one-hour tours of their saltwater aquariums and the local penguin colony, plus some stargazing if the sky is clear.

'Observation, not interaction' is the mentality at the **Seal Bay Conservation Park** (✆08-8553 4460; www.environment.sa.gov.au/sealbay; South Coast Rd; tours adult/child/concession/family self-guided $12.50/8/10/35, guided $22.50/16.50/22/75, sunset $50/30/40/136; ⏰tours 9am-4.15pm year-round, plus 5.15pm Dec-Feb), where guided tours stroll along the beach (or boardwalk

on self-guided tours) to a colony of (mostly sleeping) Australian sea lions.

🛏 Sleeping & Eating

AURORA OZONE HOTEL   Hotel $$
(✆1800 083 133, 08-8553 2011; www.auroraresorts.com.au.com; cnr Commercial St & Kingscote Tce, Kingscote; d motel/ste from $139/231, 1-/2-/3-bed apt from $293/505/597; ❄@🛜☒) Opposite the foreshore with killer views, the 100-year-old Ozone has standard motel-style rooms, stylish deluxe suites and apartments in a new wing. The bistro (mains $17 to $30; breakfast, lunch and dinner) serves grills and seafood, with great KI wines at the bar.

KANGAROO ISLAND WILDERNESS RETREAT   Hotel $$
(✆08-8559 7275; www.kiwr.com; South Coast Rd; d $190-530; ❄@) This low-key resort on the Flinders Chase doorstep guarantees guests will see some wildlife: 30 or 40 wallabies graze in the courtyard every evening! There's a restaurant and bar here too, serving breakfast ($13 to $27) and dinner ($28 to $35).

ⓘ Information

Gateway visitor information centre (✆08-8553 1185; www.tourkangarooisland.com.au; Howard Dr, Penneshaw; ⏰9am-5pm Mon-Fri, 10am-4pm Sat & Sun)

ⓘ Getting There & Away

Air

Regional Express (www.regionalexpress.com.au) flies daily between Adelaide and Kingscote.

Bus

Sealink (www.sealink.com.au) operates a morning and afternoon bus service between Adelaide Central Station and Cape Jervis.

Ferry

Sealink (www.sealink.com.au) operates a car ferry between Cape Jervis and Penneshaw on KI, with at least three ferries each way daily.

Tasmania & Port Arthur

HIGHLIGHTS

1 **MONA** (pictured above) Hobart's new Museum of Old and New Art is awesome!

2 **Salamanca Market** Meander lazily through the labyrinth of Saturday-morning stalls.

3 **Port Arthur (p341)** Contemplate the contrast of melancholy silence and beautiful scenery.

Hobart

Australia's second-oldest city and southernmost capital lies at the foothills of Mt Wellington on the banks of the Derwent River. The town's rich colonial heritage and natural charms are accented by a spirited, rootsy atmosphere: festivals, superb restaurants and hip urban bars abound.

Sights

SALAMANCA PLACE   Historic Area

This picturesque row of four-storey sandstone warehouses on Sullivans Cove is a wonderful example of colonial architecture and Australia's best-preserved historic urban precinct. The 1970s saw the dawning of Tasmania's sense of 'heritage', from which flowed a push to revive the warehouses as home to restaurants, cafes, bars and shops. Colourful hippies and craftspeople have been selling their wares at **Salamanca Market** (☺8.30am-3pm Sat) on Saturday mornings since 1972.

MONA   Museum

The $75-million Museum of Old and New Art (MONA; ☎03-6277 9900; www.mona.net. au; over 16 yrs $20; ☺10am-6pm Wed-Mon) is described by owner David Walsh as 'a subversive adult Disneyland'. The extraordinary installation is arrayed across three underground levels concealed inside a sheer rock face. Ancient antiquities are showcased next to more recent works, such as *Snake* by Sir Sidney Nolan and *Untitled* (both pictured, left) by Jannis Kounellis.

Sleeping

ASTOR PRIVATE HOTEL   Hotel **$$**

(☎03-6234 6611; www.astorprivatehotel.com. au; 157 Macquarie St; s from $77, d $93-140, all incl breakfast; 🛜) A rambling, 1920s charmer, the Astor features stained-glass windows, old furniture, ceiling roses and the irrepressible Tildy at the helm.

GRANT DIXON/LONELY PLANET IMAGES ©

Don't Miss Cradle Mountain-Lake St Clair National Park

Tasmania is world famous for the stunning 168,000-hectare World Heritage area of Cradle Mountain-Lake St Clair. It was one of Australia's most heavily glaciated areas, and includes Mt Ossa (1617m) – Tasmania's highest peak – and Lake St Clair, Australia's deepest natural freshwater lake (167m).

The **Cradle Mountain visitor information centre** (☎ 03-6492 1110; www.parks.tas.gov.au; Cradle Mountain Rd; www.parks.tas.gov.au; ⌚ 8am-5pm, reduced hours in winter) provides extensive bushwalking information and informative flora, fauna and park history displays.

HENRY JONES ART HOTEL Boutique Hotel $$$
(☎ 03-6210 7700; www.thehenryjones.com; 25 Hunter St; d $320-420, ste $400-850; @) Since opening in 2004, superswish HJs has become a beacon of sophistication. Absolute waterfront in a restored jam factory, it oozes class but is far from intimidating. Modern art enlivens the walls, while facilities and downstairs distractions (bar, restaurant, cafe) are world class.

Eating

GARAGISTES Modern Australian $$$
(☎ 03-6231 0558; www.garagistes.com.au; 103 Murray St; Sunday lunch $65 & dinner small plates $17-32; ⌚ lunch Sun & dinner Wed-Sat) The very fine Garagistes delivers innovative small plates in a simple, yet dramatic, dining room. Sunday lunch is four highly recommended courses.

ℹ️ Information

Tourist Information

Hobart visitors centre (☎03-6230 8233; www.hobarttravelcentre.com.au; cnr Davey & Elizabeth Sts; ⊙8.30am-5.30pm Mon-Fri, 9am-5pm Sat, Sun & public holidays)

Port Arthur

From 1830 to 1877, 12,500 convicts did hard, brutal prison time at Port Arthur. Although Port Arthur is a hugely popular tourist site – over 300,000 visitors annually – it remains a sombre, confronting and haunting place.

The visitor centre at the **Port Arthur Historic Site** (☎03-6251 2310, 1800 659 101; www.portarthur.org.au; Arthur Hwy, Port Arthur; adult/child/concession/family from $30/15/25/75; ⊙tours & buildings 9am-5pm, grounds 8.30am-dusk) includes an information counter, cafe, restaurant and gift shop.

Worthwhile guided tours (included in admission) leave regularly from the visitor centre. Extremely popular is the 90-minute, lantern-lit **Historic Ghost Tour** (☎1800 659 101; adult/child/family $22/12/60), which leaves from the visitor centre nightly at dusk.

ℹ️ Getting There & Away

Air

Hobart Airport (☎6216 1600; www.hobartairpt.com.au) is at Cambridge, 16km east of town. Airlines flying between Tasmania and mainland Australia:

Jetstar (☎13 15 38; www.jetstar.com.au)

Qantas (☎13 13 13; www.qantas.com.au)

Virgin Australia (☎13 67 89; www.virginaustralia.com)

Boat

The Spirit of Tasmania (☎1800 634 906; www.spiritoftasmania.com.au) operates two car and passenger ferries that cruise nightly between Melbourne and Devonport in both directions.

Australia
In Focus

Road sign, Mornington Peninsula, Victoria
PHOTOGRAPHER: REGIS MARTIN/LONELY PLANET IMAGES ©

Australia Today

Bondi Beach (p75), Sydney

> Travel around the country and you'll invariably hear people talking about climate change and the weather

belief systems
(% of population)

64 — Christian
19 — Agnostic
2 — Buddhist
2 — Muslim
1 — Hindu
12 — Other

if Australia were 100 people

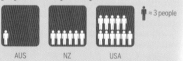

80 would speak English at home
2 would speak Chinese at home
2 would speak Italian at home
2 would speak Vietnamese at home
14 would speak other languages at home

population per sq km

≈ 3 people

AUS
NZ
USA

The Australians

Australia's identity, both geographic and cultural, has been forged by millennia of survival and isolation. Cut from the ancient Gondwanaland continent more than 45 million years ago, this savvy landscape continues to survive voracious fires, desperate droughts and unbelievable floods. You'll find resilience too in the Australian people – it hides behind the larrikin wit and amicable informality that sucks you in before your eyebrows can arch in surprise. National pride is on the up, manifest in urban arts and culinary scenes, as well as the occasional xenophobic outbreak of anti-immigration sentiment. But this country hates the generic: multiculturalism prevails.

Talk of the Town

Travel around the country and you'll invariably hear people talking about climate change and the weather. The latter seems to have gone completely haywire in recent years, with increasing numbers of people pointing the finger of blame at the former. A decade

OLIVER STREWE/LONELY PLANET IMAGES ©

infrastructure is causing ructions. The state Labor government, in power since 1995, was ousted in 2011.

In Victoria the hot issues are environmental. Aside from bushfires and floods, the $3.5 billion desalination plant under construction in Wonthaggi has become controversial now the drought has broken. Also controversial are the Latrobe Valley's coal-fired power stations, which supply 85% of Victoria's electricity but contribute significantly to Australia's greenhouse gas emissions.

Up north, the Northern Territory government is attempting to stem juvenile crime in Alice Springs, creating a youth detention centre and 'safe houses' where young people can go. Substance abuse, domestic violence and shocking health and suicide statistics in Indigenous communities remain a blight on Australia's position as an 'advanced' nation.

Western Australia is enigmatic: still bound by drought, but blessed with phenomenal mineral wealth that continues to put a rocket under the local economy. The average family income here is higher than everyone else's over east – to the tune of a carton of beer per week! Nobody here wants to know about the federal government's mooted mining tax.

South Australia – Australia's driest state – is feeling the flow-on effects from all that rain further north. The mighty River Murray is flowing strongly again after years of salination and habitat degradation.

In Tasmania, green-minded organisations and government logging and hydro-electric authorities have been at each other's necks for decades. Trees or jobs? Jobs or trees? Can we have both? The so-called 2010 'peace deal' between timber company Gunns and forestry conservation groups has resulted in a logging moratorium in Tasmania's native forests.

of drought, the shocking nadir of which were the 2009 'Black Saturday' bushfires in Victoria, came to an end in 2010 with mass flooding across eastern Australia. This continued into 2011 with yet more floods and the sweeping devastation brought by category-five tropical Cyclone Yasi in Queensland (the same intensity as Hurricane Katrina that annihilated New Orleans in 2005). The central deserts are green, the nation's biggest lake, Lake Eyre, is brimming (which only happens once or twice a century) – and yet drought persists across Western Australia. It's little wonder people are scratching their heads.

States of Mind

Of course, state-by-state, local issues dominate. Queensland is still attempting to wring itself dry after extraordinary floods were followed just weeks later by Cyclone Yasi.

In New South Wales the dire state of the economy, transport and general

History
Dr Michael Cathcart

Aboriginal and Australian flags wave during Prime Minister Kevin Rudd's apology to Indigenous Australians (p353)

TIM BARKER/LONELY PLANET IMAGES

By sunrise the storm had passed. Zachary Hicks was keeping sleepy watch on the British ship Endeavour *when suddenly he was wide awake. He summoned his commander, First Lieutenant James Cook, who climbed into the brisk morning air to a miraculous sight. Ahead lay an uncharted country of wooded hills and gentle valleys. It was 19 April 1770. In the coming days Cook began to draw the first European map of Australia's eastern coast. He was mapping the end of Aboriginal supremacy.*

Two weeks later Cook led a party of men onto a narrow beach. As they waded ashore, two Aboriginal men stepped onto the sand, and challenged the intruders with spears. Cook drove the men off with musket fire. For the rest of that week, the Aborigines and the intruders watched each other warily.

Cook's ship *Endeavour* was a floating annexe of London's leading scientific organisation, the Royal Society. The ship's gentlemen passengers included technical

60,000–35,000 BC
The first Australians arrive by sea to northern Australia.

artists, scientists, an astronomer and a wealthy botanist named Joseph Banks. As Banks and his colleagues strode about the Aborigines' territory, they were delighted by the mass of new plants they collected.

The local Aborigines called the place Kurnell, but Cook gave it a foreign name: he called it Stingray Bay and later Botany Bay.

When the *Endeavour* reached the northern tip of Cape York, Cook and his men could smell the sea-route home. And on a small, hilly island (Possession Island), Cook raised the Union Jack. Amid volleys of gunfire, he claimed the eastern half of the continent for King George III.

Cook's intention was not to steal land from the Aborigines. In fact he rather idealised them. 'They are far more happier than we Europeans', he wrote. 'They think themselves provided with all the necessaries of Life and that they have no superfluities.' At most, his patriotic ceremony was intended to contain the territorial ambitions of the French, and of the Dutch, who had visited and mapped much of the western and southern coast over the previous two centuries. Indeed, Cook knew the western half of Australia as New Holland.

Convict Beginnings

Eighteen years after Cook's arrival, in 1788, the English were back to stay. They arrived in a fleet of 11 ships, packed with supplies including weapons, tools, building materials and livestock. The ships also contained 751 convicts and over 250 soldiers, officials and their wives. This motley 'First Fleet' was under the command of a humane and diligent naval captain, Arthur Phillip. As his orders dictated, Phillip dropped anchor at Botany Bay. But the paradise that had so delighted Joseph Banks filled Phillip with dismay. So he left his floating prison and embarked in a small boat to search for a better location. Just a short way up the coast his heart leapt as he sailed into the finest harbour in the world. There, in a small cove, in the idyllic lands of the Eora people, he established a British penal settlement. He renamed the place after the British Home Secretary, Lord Sydney.

Phillip's official instructions urged him to colonise the land without doing violence to the local inhabitants. Among the Aborigines he used as intermediaries was an Eora man named Bennelong, who adopted many of the white people's customs and manners. For many years Bennelong lived in a hut on the finger of land now known as Bennelong Point, the site of the Sydney Opera House. But his people were shattered by the loss of their lands. Hundreds died of smallpox, and many of the survivors, including Bennelong himself, succumbed to alcoholism and despair.

In 1803, English officers established a second convict settlement in Van Diemen's Land (later called Tasmania). Soon, re-offenders filled the grim prison at Port Arthur on the beautiful and wild coast near Hobart.

1606
Dutch Navigator Willem Janszoon makes the first authenticated European landing on Australian soil.

1770
First Lieutenant James Cook claims the entire east coast of Australia for England.

1788
Captain Arthur Phillip and the First Fleet – 11 ships and about 1350 people – arrive at Botany Bay.

The Best...
Convict History

From Shackles To Freedom

At first, Sydney and the smaller colonies depended on supplies brought in by ship. Anxious to develop productive farms, the government granted land to soldiers, officers and settlers. After 30 years of trial and error, the farms began to flourish. The most irascible and ruthless of these new landholders was John Macarthur. Along with his spirited wife, Elizabeth, Macarthur pioneered the breeding of merino sheep on his property near Sydney.

Macarthur was also a leading member of the Rum Corps, a clique of powerful officers who bullied successive governors (including William Bligh of *Bounty* fame) and grew rich by controlling much of Sydney's trade, notably rum. But the Corps' racketeering was ended in 1810 by a tough new governor named Lachlan Macquarie. Macquarie laid out the major roads of modern-day Sydney, built some fine public buildings (many of which were designed by talented convict-architect Francis Greenway) and helped to lay the foundations for a more civil society.

Macquarie also championed the rights of freed convicts, granting them land and appointing several to public office. By now, word was reaching England that Australia offered cheap land and plenty of work, and adventurous migrants took to the oceans in search of their fortunes.

Melbourne & Adelaide

In the cooler grasslands of Tasmania, the sheep farmers were also thriving. In the 1820s they waged a bloody war against the island's Aborigines, driving them to the brink of extinction. Now these settlers were hungry for more land. In 1835 an ambitious young man named John Batman sailed to Port Phillip Bay on the mainland. On the banks of the Yarra River, he chose the location for Melbourne, famously announcing 'This is the place for a village'. Batman persuaded local Aborigines to 'sell' him their traditional lands (a whopping 250,000 hectares) for a crate of blankets, knives and knick-knacks. Back in Sydney, Governor Bourke declared the contract void, not because it was unfair, but because the land officially belonged to the British Crown.

At the same time, a private British company settled Adelaide in South Australia. Proud to have no links with convicts, these God-fearing folk instituted a scheme under which their company sold land to well-heeled settlers, and used the revenue to assist poor British labourers to emigrate. When these worthies earned enough to buy land from the company, that revenue would in turn pay the fare of another shipload of labourers.

1835
John Batman negotiates a land deal with the Kulin nation; Melbourne is settled that same year.

1851
A gold rush in central Victoria brings settlers from across the world. Democracy is introduced in the eastern colonies.

1880
Bushranger Ned Kelly is hanged as a criminal – and remembered as a folk hero. Ned Kelly's armour, Old Melbourne Gaol (p213)

Gold & Rebellion

Transportation of convicts to eastern Australia ceased in the 1840s. This was just as well: in 1851, prospectors discovered gold in New South Wales and central Victoria, including at Ballarat. The news hit the colonies with the force of a cyclone. Young men and some women from every social class headed for the diggings. Soon they were caught up in a great rush of prospectors, publicans and prostitutes. In Victoria the British governor was alarmed – both by the way the Victorian class system had been thrown into disarray, and by the need to finance the imposition of law and order on the goldfields. His solution was to compel all miners to buy an expensive monthly licence.

But the lure of gold was too great and in the reckless excitement of the goldfields, the miners initially endured the thuggish troopers who enforced the government licence. After three years, though, the easy gold at Ballarat was gone, and miners were toiling in deep, water-sodden shafts. They were now infuriated by a corrupt and brutal system of law which held them in contempt. Under the leadership of a charismatic Irishman named Peter Lalor, they raised their own flag, the Southern Cross, and swore to defend their rights and liberties. They armed themselves and gathered inside a rough stockade at Eureka, where they waited for the government to make its move.

In the predawn of Sunday 3 December 1854, a force of troopers attacked the stockade. It was all over in 15 terrifying minutes. The brutal and one-sided battle claimed the lives of 30 miners and five soldiers. But democracy was in the air and public opinion sided with the miners. The eastern colonies were already in the process of establishing democratic parliaments, with the full support of the British authorities.

The Long Walk to Ballarat

During the 1850s gold rush in Victoria, the town of Robe in South Australia came into its own when the Victorian government whacked a $10-per-head tax on Chinese gold miners arriving to work the goldfields. Thousands of Chinese miners dodged the tax by landing at Robe instead, then walking the 400-odd kilometres to Bendigo and Ballarat; 10,000 arrived in 1857 alone. But the flood stalled as quickly as it started when the South Australian government instituted its own tax on the Chinese.

Today, the vibrant and busy Chinatowns in Australia's capital cities and the presence of Chinese restaurants in towns across the country are reminders of the vigorous role of the Chinese in Australia since the 1850s.

1901

The Australian colonies form a federation of states. The federal parliament sits in Melbourne.

1915

On 25 April the Anzacs join a British invasion of Turkey: a military disaster that spawns a nationalist legend.

Meanwhile, in the West...

Western Australia lagged behind the eastern colonies by about 50 years. Though Perth was settled by genteel colonists back in 1829, its material progress was handicapped by isolation, Aboriginal resistance and the arid climate. It was not until the 1880s that the discovery of remote goldfields promised to gild the fortunes of the isolated colony. At the time, the west was just entering its own period of self-government, and its first premier was a forceful, weather-beaten explorer named John Forrest. He saw that the mining industry would fail if the government did not provide a first-class harbour, efficient railways and reliable water supplies. Ignoring the threats of private contractors, he appointed the brilliant engineer CY O'Connor to design and build each of these as government projects.

Nationhood

On 1 January 1901, Australia became a federation. When the members of the new national parliament met in Melbourne, their first aim was to protect the identity and values of a European Australia from an influx of Asians and Pacific Islanders. The solu-

Soldiers at the Shrine of Remembrance, Melbourne
PHOTOGRAPHER: PHIL WEYMOUTH/LONELY PLANET IMAGES ©

1939
Prime Minister Robert Menzies announces that Britain has gone to war; 'as a result, Australia is also at war'.

1942
The Japanese bomb Darwin, the first and most destructive of numerous air strikes on the northern capital.

1945
Australia's new slogan: 'Populate or Perish!'. Over the next 30 years more than two million immigrants arrive.

CY O'Connor's Uphill Battle

The engineer Charles Yelverton O'Connor made all the difference to the survival of the colony in Western Australia. His scheme created a 560km pipeline and a series of mighty pumping stations that would drive water uphill from the coast to the dry goldfields round Kalgoorlie. As the work neared completion, O'Connor was subjected to merciless slander in the press, alleging corruption and the gross mishandling of public funds. In 1902 the tormented man rode a horse into the South Fremantle surf and shot himself. A lonely statue in the waves marks the spot. His great pipeline continues to pump water into the thirsty gold cities of central Western Australia.

tion was a law which became known as the White Australia Policy. It became a racial tenet of faith in Australia for the next 70 years.

For whites who lived inside the charmed circle of citizenship, this was to be a model society, nestled in the skirts of the British Empire. Just one year later, white women won the right to vote in federal elections. In a series of radical innovations, the government introduced a broad social welfare scheme and it protected Australian wage levels with import tariffs. Its radical mixture of capitalist dynamism and socialist compassion became known as the 'Australian settlement'.

Entering The World Stage

Living on the edge of a dry and forbidding land, and isolated from the rest of the world, most Australians took comfort in the knowledge that they were a dominion of the British Empire. When war broke out in Europe in 1914, thousands of Australian men rallied to the Empire's call. They had their first taste of death on 25 April 1915, when the Australian and New Zealand Army Corps (the Anzacs) joined thousands of other British and French troops in an assault on the Gallipoli Peninsula in Turkey. It was eight months before the British commanders acknowledged that the tactic had failed. By then 8141 young Australians were dead. Before long the Australian Imperial Force was fighting in the killing fields of Europe. By the time the war ended, 60,000 Australians had died. Ever since, on 25 April, Australians have gathered at war memorials around the country for the sad and solemn services of Anzac Day.

In the 1920s Australia embarked on a decade of chaotic change. The country careered wildly through the 1920s until it collapsed into the abyss of the Great Depression in 1929. World prices for wheat and wool plunged. Unemployment brought its shame and misery to one in three households.

1956

The Olympic Games are held in Melbourne, where the flame is lit by young running champion Ron Clarke.

1965

Menzies commits Australian troops to the American war in Vietnam, and divides the nation.

1967

In a national referendum, white Australians vote overwhelmingly to give citizenship to Indigenous people.

The Best...
Historic Atmosphere

1 The Rocks, Sydney (p67)

2 Salamanca Place, Hobart (p339)

3 Fremantle, Western Australia (p313)

4 Katoomba, New South Wales (p103)

War With Japan

After 1933, the economy began to recover. Daily life was hardly dampened when Hitler hurled Europe into a new war in 1939. Though Australians had long feared Japan, they took it for granted that the British navy would keep them safe. In December 1941, Japan bombed the US Fleet at Pearl Harbor. Weeks later, the 'impregnable' British naval base in Singapore crumbled, and before long thousands of Australians and Allied troops were enduring the savagery of Japanese prisoner-of-war camps.

As the Japanese swept through Southeast Asia and into Papua New Guinea, the British announced that they could not spare any resources to defend Australia. But US commander General Douglas MacArthur saw that Australia was the perfect base for American operations in the Pacific. In fierce sea and land battles, Allied forces turned back the Japanese advance. Importantly, it was the US, not the British Empire, which saved Australia. The days of the alliance with Britain alone were numbered.

Visionary Peace

When WWII ended, a new slogan rang out: 'Populate or Perish!'. The Australian government embarked on a scheme to attract thousands of immigrants. People flocked from Britain and non-English-speaking countries. They included Greeks, Italians, Serbs, Croatians and Dutch, followed by Turks and many others.

In addition to growing world demand for Australia's primary products (wool, meat and wheat), there were jobs in manufacturing and on major public works, notably the mighty Snowy Mountains Hydro-Electric Scheme in the mountains near Canberra.

Sticky Wicket

The year 1932 saw accusations of treachery on the cricket field. The English team, under captain Douglas Jardine, employed a violent new bowling tactic known as 'bodyline'. The aim was to unnerve Australia's star batsman, the devastatingly efficient Donald Bradman. The bitterness of the tour provoked a diplomatic crisis with Britain and became part of Australian legend. Bradman batted on. When he retired in 1948 he had an unsurpassed career average of 99.94 runs.

1975
Against a background of radical reform and inflation, Governor General Sir John Kerr sacks the Whitlam government.

1992
The High Court of Australia recognises the principle of native title in the Mabo decision.

2000
The Sydney Olympic Games are a triumph of spectacle and goodwill.
Cathy Freeman wins a gold medal for the 400m sprint

This era of growth and prosperity was dominated by Robert Menzies, the founder of the Liberal Party of Australia, and Australia's longest-serving prime minister. Menzies was steeped in British tradition, and was also a vigilant opponent of communism. As Asia succumbed to the chill of the Cold War, Australia and New Zealand entered a formal military alliance with the US – the 1951 Anzus security pact. When the US jumped into a civil war in Vietnam, Menzies committed Australian forces to battle. The following year Menzies retired, leaving his successors a bitter legacy.

In an atmosphere of youthful rebellion and new-found nationalism, the Labor Party was elected to power in 1972 under an idealistic lawyer named Gough Whitlam. In four short years his government transformed the country, ending conscription and abolishing university fees. He introduced a free universal health scheme, no-fault divorce, the principle of Indigenous land rights and equal pay for women. By now, around one million migrants had arrived from non-English speaking countries, filling Australia with new languages, cultures, food and ideas.

By 1975, the Whitlam government was rocked by inflation and scandal. At the end of 1975 his government was dismissed from office by the governor general.

The Best...
History
Museums

1 Rocks Discovery Museum (p68)

2 Melbourne Museum (p221)

3 Western Australian Museum – Perth (p302)

4 Queensland Museum (p133)

Today

Today Australia faces new challenges. After two centuries of development, the strains on the environment are starting to show – on water supplies, forests, soil and the oceans.

Under John Howard, Australia's second-longest serving prime minister (1996–2007), the country grew closer to the US, joining the Americans in their war in Iraq. The government's harsh treatment of asylum seekers, its refusal to acknowledge the reality of climate change, its anti-union reforms and the prime minister's lack of empathy with Aboriginal people dismayed more liberal-minded Australians. But Howard presided over a period of economic growth and won continuing support in middle Australia.

In 2007, Howard was defeated by the Labor Party's Kevin Rudd, an ex-diplomat who immediately issued a formal apology to the Indigenous Australians for the injustices they had suffered over the past two centuries. Though it promised sweeping reforms in environment and education, the Rudd government found itself faced with a crisis when the world economy crashed in 2008; by June 2010 it had cost Rudd his position. New prime minister Julia Gillard, along with other world leaders, now faced three related challenges – climate change, a diminishing oil supply and a shrinking economy.

2007
Kevin Rudd is elected prime minister and says 'Sorry' to Australia's Indigenous people.

2010
Kevin Rudd is ousted as prime minister, replaced by Julia Gillard.

© INTERFOTO / ALAMY

Family Travel

Wet 'n' Wild (p130), Gold Coast

RICHARD I'ANSON/LONELY PLANET IMAGES ©

Are we there yet? The key to hassle-minimised travel with kids is good planning. Don't underestimate distances if planning a road trip. The wide yonder may be just the tonic for stressed-out parents, but it is probably not numero uno on the kids' menu. The big cities and the populated east coast, however, abound with attractions and distractions designed for bright young minds and bodies of limitless energy.

Lonely Planet's *Travel with Children* contains plenty of useful information. All cities and most major towns have centrally located public rooms where mothers (and usually fathers) can go to nurse their baby or change its nappy; check with the local tourist office or city council for details. While most Australians have a relaxed attitude about breastfeeding or nappy changing in public, some do frown on it.

Top-end hotels and many (but not all) midrange hotels are well versed in the needs of guests with children. B&Bs, on the other hand, often market themselves as sanctuaries from all things child related. Many cafes and restaurants have a specialised kids' menu or will provide small serves from the main menu.

If you want to leave Junior behind for a few hours, some of Australia's numerous licensed childcare agencies offer casual care. Check under 'Baby Sitters' and 'Child Care Centres' in the *Yellow Pages* telephone directory, or phone the local council for a list.

Child concessions (and family rates) often apply to accommodation, tours, admission fees and transport, with some discounts as high as 50% of the adult rate. However, the definition of 'child' varies from under 12 to under 18 years. Accommodation concessions generally apply to children under 12 years sharing the same room as adults. On the major airlines, infants travel free provided they don't occupy a seat – child fares usually apply between the ages of two and 11 years.

Australia has high-standard medical services and facilities, and items such as baby formula and disposable nappies are widely available in urban and regional centres. Major hire-car companies will supply and fit booster seats, charging around $18 for up to three days' use, with an additional daily fee for longer periods.

Sights & Activities

There's no shortage of active, interesting or amusing things for children to focus on in Australia. Plenty of museums, zoos, aquariums, interactive technology centres and pioneer villages have historical, natural or science-based exhibits to get kids thinking. And of course outdoor destinations are always a winner. This guide has hot tips for keeping kids occupied in Sydney (p80), Melbourne (p226), Perth (p311) and Brisbane (p139).

The Best... For Kids

1 Gold Coast theme parks (p130)

2 Sydney Aquarium (p71)

3 AFL footy at the MCG (p217)

4 Territory Wildlife Park (p276)

5 Australia Zoo (p155)

6 Sydney Harbour ferries (p80)

Need to Know

- **Change Facilities** Found in most towns and large shopping malls in cities
- **Cots** Available in midrange and top-end establishments
- **Health** See the general health section (p376)
- **Highchairs** Widely available in restaurants, as are booster seats
- **Nappies (diapers)** Widely available
- **Strollers** Even on public transport you will get a helping hand
- **Transport** All public transport caters for young passengers

Female eastern grey kangaroo with joey in pouch

MITCH REARDON/LONELY PLANET IMAGES ©

Australia's plants and animals are just about the closest things to alien life you are likely to encounter on earth. That's because Australia has been isolated from the other continents for a very long time – at least 45 million years.

Other habitable continents have been able to exchange species at different times because they've been linked by land bridges. Just 15,000 years ago it was possible to walk from Africa right through Asia and the Americas to Tierra del Fuego. Not Australia, however. Its birds, mammals, reptiles and plants have taken their own separate and very different evolutionary journey, and the result is the world's most distinct natural realm.

If you are visiting Australia for a short time, you might need to go out of your way to experience some of the richness of the environment. Places like Sydney, however, have preserved extraordinary fragments of the original environment that are relatively easy to access. Before you enjoy them though, it's worthwhile understanding the basics about how nature operates in Australia.

Fundamentally Different

There are two really big factors that go a long way towards explaining nature in Australia: its soils and its climate. Both are unique. It may not be obvious but Australian soils have been fundamental in shaping life here. On other continents in recent geological times, processes such as volcanism, mountain building and glacial activity have been busy creating new soil.

All of these soil-forming processes have been almost absent from Australia in more recent times. Only volcanoes have made a contribution, and they cover less than 2% of the continent's land area. In fact, for the last 90 million years, beginning deep in the age of dinosaurs, Australia has been geologically comatose. It was too flat, warm and dry to attract glaciers, and its crust too ancient and thick to be punctured by volcanoes or folded into mountains.

Under such conditions no new soil is created and the old soil is leached of all its goodness by the rain, and is blown and washed away. Almost all of Australia's mountain ranges are more than 90 million years old, so you will see a lot of sand, and a lot of country where the rocky 'bones' of the land stick up through the soil. It is an old, infertile landscape, and life in Australia has been adapting to these conditions for aeons.

Australia's misfortune in respect to soils is echoed in its climate. In most parts of the world outside the wet tropics, life responds to the rhythm of the seasons – summer to winter, or wet to dry. Most of Australia experiences seasons – sometimes very severe ones – yet life does not respond solely to them. This can clearly be seen by the fact that although there's plenty of snow and cold country in Australia, there are almost no trees that shed their leaves in winter, nor do any Australian animals hibernate. Instead there is a far more potent climatic force that Australian life must obey: El Niño.

The cycle of flood and drought that El Niño brings is profound. Australia's rivers – even the mighty Murray River, the nation's largest river, which runs through the southeast – can be miles wide one year, yet you can literally step over its flow the next. This is the power of El Niño, and its effect, when combined with Australia's poor soils, manifests itself compellingly. As you might expect from this, relatively few of Australia's birds are seasonal breeders, and few migrate. Instead, they breed when the rain comes, and a large percentage are nomads, following the rain across the breadth of the continent.

The Best... Sydney Wilderness

1 Sydney Harbour National Park (p64)

2 Bondi to Coogee Clifftop Walk (p75)

3 Royal National Park (p98)

4 Ku-ring-gai Chase National Park (p77)

In Bloom

Win friends and influence people with your nerdy knowledge of Australia's official state and territory floral emblems: Waratah (NSW), Royal Bluebell (ACT), Cooktown Orchid (Queensland), Common Heath (Victoria), Tasmanian Blue Gum (Tasmania), Sturt's Desert Pea (South Australia), Sturt's Desert Rose (Northern Territory) and Red and Green Kangaroo Paw (Western Australia).

Sharky

Shark-o-phobia getting you down? Despite media hype, Australia has averaged just one shark-attack fatality per year since 1791 – a remarkably low number considering how many beaches there are around the coastline (and how many Australians are on them). Sydney in particular has a bad rep. Attacks here peaked between 1920 and 1940, but since shark net installation began in 1937 there's only been one fatality (1963), and dorsal-fin sightings are rare enough to make the nightly news. Realistically, you're more likely to get hit by a bus, so get wet and enjoy yourself!

Fuel-efficient Fauna

Australia is, of course, famous as the home of the kangaroo (roo) and other marsupials. Have you ever wondered why kangaroos, alone among the world's larger mammals, hop? It turns out that hopping is the most efficient way of getting about at medium speeds. This is because the energy of the bounce is stored in the tendons of the legs – much like in a pogo stick – while the intestines bounce up and down like a piston, emptying and filling the lungs without needing to activate the chest muscles.

Marsupials are so energy-efficient that they need to eat one-fifth less food than equivalent-sized placental mammals (everything from bats to rats, whales and ourselves). But some marsupials have taken energy efficiency much further. If you visit a wildlife park or zoo you might notice that faraway look in a koala's eyes. It seems as if nobody is home – and this is near the truth. Several years ago biologists announced that koalas are the only living creatures that have brains that don't fit their skulls. Instead they have a shrivelled walnut of a brain that rattles around in a fluid-filled cranium. Other researchers have contested this finding, pointing out that the brains of the koalas examined for the study may have shrunk because these organs are so soft. Whether soft-brained or empty-headed, there is no doubt that the koala is not the Einstein of the animal world, and we now believe that it has sacrificed its brain to energy efficiency. Brains cost a lot to run – our brains typically weigh 2% of our body weight, but use 20% of the energy we consume. Koalas eat gum leaves, which are so toxic that koalas use 20% of their energy just detoxifying this food, leaving little energy for the brain.

The peculiar constraints of the Australian environment have not made everything dumb. The koala's nearest relative, the wombat (of which there are three species), has a large brain for a marsupial. These creatures live in complex burrows and can weigh up to 35kg, making them the largest herbivorous burrowers on Earth. Wombats can remain underground for a week at a time, and can get by on just a third of the food needed by a sheep of equivalent size.

Two unique monotremes (egg-laying mammals) live in Australia: the bumbling echidna, something akin to a hedgehog but bigger and spikier; and the platypus, a bit like an otter, with webbed feet and a duck-like bill. Echidnas are common along bushland trails, but platypuses are elusive, seen at dawn and dusk in quiet rivers and streams.

Aboriginal Art

Aboriginal dot painting, Northern Territory

OLIVER STREWE/LONELY PLANET IMAGES ©

There's a huge range of Aboriginal art produced across Australia, including paintings, batik and wood carvings from Central Australia; bark paintings from Arnhem Land; and carvings and silk-screen printing from the Tiwi Islands. A common theme is the ancient connection Indigenous people have with their land, mixed with a sense of loss occasioned by the horrors since white settlement. Ultimately, however, the viewer is left with a sense of Indigenous cultural strength and renewal.

Rock Art

In Australia's tropical north, Arnhem Land is an area of rich artistic heritage. Recent finds suggest that rock paintings were being produced here as early as 60,000 years ago.

Paintings here range from hand prints to paintings of animals, people, mythological beings and European ships, constituting one of the world's most important and fascinating rock-art collections – a record of changing environments and lifestyles over the millennia. In some places they are concentrated in large galleries, with paintings from more recent eras sometimes superimposed over older paintings. Some sites are kept secret – not only to protect them from damage but also because they are private or sacred to their Aboriginal owners.

Buying Aboriginal Art

Taking home a piece of Aboriginal art can create an enduring connection with Australia. For Aboriginal artists, painting is an important cultural and economic enterprise. To ensure you're not perpetuating non-Indigenous cash-in on Aboriginal art's popularity, avoid buying cheap imported fridge magnets, stubbie holders, boomerangs or didgeridoos. Make sure you're buying from an authentic dealer selling original art, and if the gallery doesn't pay their artists up front, ask exactly how much of your money will make it back to the artist or community.

A good test is to request some biographical information on the artists – if the vendor can't produce it, keep walking. An authentic piece will come with a certificate indicating the artist's name, language group and community, and the work's title, its story and when it was made.

You may also check that the selling gallery is associated with a regulatory body, such as the **Australian Commercial Galleries Association** (www.acga.com.au). Where possible, buy direct from Aboriginal arts centres or their city outlets (see www.ankaaa.org.au or www.aboriginalart.org); this is generally cheaper and ensures authenticity. You also get to view the works in the context in which they were created.

Rock art in Western Australia's Kimberley district is known for its images of the Wandjina, ancestral beings who came from the sky and sea and were associated with fertility. Wandjina controlled the elements and were responsible for the formation of the country's natural features.

In Queensland the superb Quinkan rock galleries at Laura on the Cape York Peninsula are justifiably famous. Among the many creatures depicted on the walls are the Quinkan spirits, which are shown in two forms – the long and stick-like Timara, and the crocodile-like Imjim with their knobbed, club-like tails.

It's also possible to see rock art in urban Sydney, on the cliffs north and south of Bondi Beach.

Painting

In Central Australia, painting has flourished to such a degree that it's now an important source of community income. It has also been an important educational tool for children, through which they can learn different aspects of religion and ceremony.

Western Desert painting, also known as dot painting, partly evolved from 'ground paintings', which formed the centrepiece of dances and songs. 'Paints' were made from pulped plant material, and designs were made on the ground using dots. Dots also outline objects in rock paintings, and highlight geographical features or vegetation.

Dot paintings depict Dreaming stories. The Dreaming is a complex concept that forms the basis of Aboriginal spirituality, incorporating the creation of the world and the spiritual energies operating around us. A story is a tale from the Dreaming that taps into concepts of legend, myth, tradition and law.

Symbology is widely used, but the meaning within each painting is known only to the artist and people closely associated with him or her – either by clan or by the Dreaming – and different clans apply different interpretations to each painting. In this way sacred stories can be publicly portrayed, yet the deeper meaning is not revealed to uninitiated viewers.

Bark Painting

Bark painting is integral to the cultural heritage of Arnhem Land Indigenous people. It's difficult to establish when bark was first used, partly because it's perishable, so very old pieces don't exist. The paintings were never intended to be permanent records.

The bark used is from the stringy-bark tree (*Eucalyptus tetradonta*). The pigments used in bark paintings are mainly red and yellow (ochres), white (kaolin) and black (charcoal). These natural pigments give the paintings their superb soft and earthy finish.

One of the main features of Arnhem Land bark paintings is the use of *rarrk* (crosshatching) designs. These designs identify the particular clans, and are based on body paintings handed down through generations. The paintings can also be broadly categorised by their regional styles: naturalistic images and plain backgrounds in the west, and geometric, abstract designs in the east.

Contemporary Painting

The work of contemporary Indigenous metropolitan and rural artists is at times deeply confronting. Content often focuses on the terrible injustices of the past 200-plus years while raising issues of dispossession; access to language, cultural practices and land; contemporary Indigenous culture; and the artist in the modern post-colonial world.

In the late 1980s artists from the Utopia community northeast of Alice Springs, and Ngukurr, a settlement near Roper Bar in southeastern Arnhem Land, started producing vibrant works using acrylic paints on canvas – media now commonplace in heavily touristed areas such as Alice Springs and in big-city shops and galleries.

Contemporary art in the eastern Kimberley sometimes features elements of the works of the Indigenous people of Central Australia, a legacy of the forced relocation of people during the 1970s.

Artefacts & Crafts

Objects traditionally made for practical or ceremonial uses, such as weapons and musical instruments, often featured intricate symbolic decoration.

The most widespread craft objects seen for sale these days are didgeridoos – originally ceremonial musical instruments by Indigenous people in Arnhem Land – and boomerangs, curved wooden throwing sticks used for hunting. Although they all follow the same fundamental design, boomerangs come in a huge range of shapes, sizes and decorative styles, and are made from a number of different wood types.

Fibre craft and weaving are major art forms among women, although in some regions men also made woven objects as hunting tools. String or twine was traditionally made from bark, grass, leaves, roots and other materials, hand-spun and dyed with natural pigments, then woven to make dilly bags, baskets, garments, fishing nets and other items.

The Best... Indigenous Art Encounters

1 Rock art at Ubirr and Nourlangie, Kakadu National Park (p277)

2 Ian Potter Centre: National Gallery of Victoria Australia (p212)

3 Art Gallery of Western Australia (p302)

4 Art Gallery of New South Wales (p70)

5 Darwin's commercial art galleries (p267)

Food & Wine

Modern Australian 'Mod Oz' cuisine

Modern Australian 'Mod Oz' cuisine

GREG ELMS/LONELY PLANET IMAGES ©

Once upon a time in a decade not so far away, Australians proudly survived and thrived on a diet of 'meat and three veg'. Fine fare was a Sunday roast cooked to carcinogenic stages and lasagne was considered exotic. Fortunately, the country's culinary sophistication has evolved and, mirroring the population's cheeky and disobedient disposition, contemporary Australian cuisine now thrives on breaking rules and conventions.

Australian cuisine may not have a high international profile, but visitors will find a huge range and wealth of food available in city restaurants, markets, delicatessens and cafes. Competition for the custom of savvy tastebud-owners is increasingly high and so too are standards. This is most evident in Sydney and Melbourne, but also in all large urban areas and tourist destinations. In regional areas, variety diminishes along with the population.

Mod Oz?

The Australian propensity to absorb global influences is spurred by an inquisitive public willing to give anything new a go. The result is dynamic and constantly surprising cuisine, and what's hot this morning may be dated by tomorrow – or reinvented and improved.

Immigration has been the key to Australia's culinary rise. A significant influx of migrants in the last 60 years, from Europe, Asia, the Middle East and Africa, has introduced new ingredients and new ways to use existing staples. Anything another country does, Australia does too. Vietnamese, Japanese, Fijian – no matter where it's from, there's an expat community and interested locals desperate to cook and eat it. Dig deep enough and you'll find Jamaicans using scotch-bonnet peppers and Tunisians making tajine.

With this wealth of inspiration, urban Australians have become culinary snobs. In order to wow the socks off diners, restaurants must succeed in fusing contrasting ingredients and traditions into ever more innovative fare. The phrase Modern Australian (Mod Oz) has been coined to classify this unclassifiable technique: a melange of East and West; a swirl of Atlantic and Pacific Rim; a night flight from authentic French or Italian.

If this sounds overwhelming, fear not. Dishes are characterised by bold and interesting flavours, and fresh ingredients rather than fuss or clutter. Spicing ranges from gentle to extreme, coffee is great (it still reaches its heights in cities), wine is world renowned, seafood is plentiful and meats are tender and full flavoured. The range of food in Australia is its greatest culinary asset – all palates, timid or brave, shy or inquisitive, are well catered for.

The Best...
Wine Tasting

1 National Wine Centre of Australia, Adelaide, South Australia (p336)

2 Hunter Valley, New South Wales (p100)

3 Margaret River, Western Australia (p320)

4 Yarra Valley, Victoria (p241)

Cheers!
No matter what your poison, you're in the right country if you're after a drink.

Wine
Long recognised as some of the finest in the world, wine is now one of Australia's top exports. In fact, if you're in the country's southern climes, you're probably not far from a wine region. Some regions have been producing wines from the early days of settlement more than 220 years ago. Most wineries have small cellar door sales where you can taste for a minimal fee, or free. Although plenty of good wine comes from big producers with economies of scale on their side, the most interesting wines are usually made by smaller, family-run wineries.

Beer
As the public develops a more demanding palate, local beers are rising to the occasion, with a growing wealth of flavours and varieties available. Most beers have an alcohol content between 3.5% and 5.5%. That's less than many European beers but more than most in North America. Light beers contain under 3% alcohol and are finding favour with people observing Australia's stringent drink-driving laws.

The terminology used when ordering beer varies state by state. In New South Wales you ask for a 'schooner' (425mL) if you're thirsty and a 'middy' (285mL) if you're not quite so dry. In Victoria it's a 'pot' and in Tasmania a '10 ounce' (285mL) – and in most of the country you can just ask for a beer and wait to see what turns up. Pints (425mL or 568mL, depending on where you are) tend to warm quickly on a summer's day but are still popular with an 'upsize' generation.

Your shout!

At the bar, 'shouting' is a revered custom, where people take turns to pay for a round of drinks. Leaving before it's your turn to buy won't win you many friends! Once the drinks are distributed, a toast of 'Cheers!' is standard practice: everyone should touch glasses and look each other in the eye as they clink – failure to do so is reported to end in seven years' bad sex.

Coffee

Coffee has become an Australian addiction; there are Italian-style espresso machines in virtually every cafe, boutique roasters are all the rage and, in urban areas, the qualified barista (coffee-maker) is virtually the norm. Sydney and Melbourne have borne a whole generation of coffee snobs, but Melbourne easily takes top billing as Australia's coffee-obsessed capital. The cafe scene there rivals the most vibrant in the world – the best way to immerse yourself is by wandering the city centre's cafe-lined lanes.

Sport

Sydney Swans football fans, Melbourne Cricket Ground (p217)

TIM BARKER/LONELY PLANET IMAGES ©

Although Australia is relatively small population-wise (around 22 million), its inhabitants constantly vie for kudos by challenging formidable and well-established sporting opponents around the globe in just about any event they can attempt. This has resulted in some extraordinary successes on the world stage. But it's the local football codes that really excite Aussies and tap into primal passions.

Australian Rules Football

Australia's number-one-watched sport is Australian Rules football. Originally exclusive to Victoria, the **Australian Football League** (AFL; www.afl.com.au) has expanded into South Australia, New South Wales, Western Australia and Queensland. Long kicks, high marks and brutal collisions whip crowds into fevered frenzies: the roar of 50,000-plus fans yelling 'Carn the [insert team nickname]' and '*Baaalll!!!*' upsets dogs in suburban backyards for kilometres around.

Rugby

The **National Rugby League** (NRL; www.nrl.com.au) is the most popular football code north of the Murray River, with the season highlight the annual State of Origin series between New South Wales and Queensland. To witness an NRL game is to acquire a grim appreciation of Newton's laws of motion: a

The Best... Sporting Experiences

1 AFL football at the MCG (p217)

2 Learning to surf at Byron Bay (p123)

3 Cricket at the Sydney Cricket Ground (p92)

4 Watching the Melbourne Cup in a pub (p47)

force travelling in one direction can only be stopped with the application of an equal and opposite force. Bone-crunching!

Meanwhile, the national rugby union team, the Wallabies, won the Rugby World Cup in 1991 and 1999 and were runners-up in 2003, but couldn't make the semi-finals in 2007. By the time you read this, the 2011 event will have delivered either tears or glory...

Soccer

Australia's star-studded national soccer team, the Socceroos, qualified for the 2006 and 2010 World Cups after a long history of almost-but-not-quite getting there. Results were mixed, but national pride in the team remains undiminished. The national **A-League** (www.a-league.com .au) has enjoyed increased popularity in recent years, effectively developing home-grown talent for the home-grown competition.

Cricket

The Aussies dominated both test and one-day cricket for much of the naughties, holding the number-one world ranking for most of the decade. But things aren't looking so rosy these days. The retirements of once-in-a-lifetime players like Shane Warne, Glenn McGrath and Adam Gilchrist exposed a leaky pool of second-tier talent, and recent test series losses to archrivals England have caused nationwide misery.

Tennis

Every January, tennis shoes melt in the Melbourne heat at the **Australian Open** (www. ausopen.com.au), one of tennis's four Grand Slam tournaments, which attracts more people to Australia than any other sporting event. In the men's competition, last won by an Australian back in 1976, Lleyton Hewitt has been Australia's great hope in recent years, but the former world No 1's best days are behind him. In the women's game, the athletic Sam Stosur has been steadily climbing the ranks.

Horse Racing

On the first Tuesday in November the nation stops for a horse race, the **Melbourne Cup** (www.racingvictoria.net.au). In Victoria it's cause to have a day off. Australia's most famous cup winner was Phar Lap, who won in 1930, then died of a mystery illness in the USA. Makybe Diva is the event's most recent star, winning three in a row before retiring in 2005. Check out the Victorian Racing Club website (www.vrc.net.au) for a full calendar of horse-racing events.

Australia
Outdoors

Larapinta Trail, West MacDonnell National Park (p279), Northern Territory

TONY WHEELER/LONELY PLANET IMAGES ©

Australia is a natural adventure playground and its sheer size means there is an incredible range of outdoor activities. The easy-on-the-eye landscape, so much of it still refreshingly free from the pressures of overpopulation, lends itself to any number of energetic pursuits and pure natural fun, whether you're on a wilderness trail or ski slope, under the sea beside a coral reef, or catching a wave.

Bushwalking

Bushwalking is supremely popular in Australia and vast tracts of untouched scrub and forest provide ample opportunity. The best time to go varies significantly from state to state, but a general rule is that the further north you go, the more tropical and humid the climate gets: June to August are the best walking months up north; in the south, summer (December to March) is better.

You can follow fantastic trails through many national parks. Notable walks include the Overland Track and the South Coast Track in Tasmania, and the Australian Alps Walking Track, Great Ocean Walk, Great South West Walk in Victoria. The Bibbulmun Track in Western Australia is fabulous, as are the Thorsborne Trail across Hinchinbrook Island and the Gold Coast Hinterland's Great Walk in Queensland.

The Best...
Surf Spots

1 Byron Bay, New South Wales (p122)

2 Bells Beach, Victoria (p244)

3 Burleigh Heads, Queensland (p129)

4 Margaret River, Western Australia (p320)

5 Sydney's Northern Beaches, New South Wales (p77)

In New South Wales you can trek between Sydney and Newcastle on the Great North Walk, tackle the Royal National Park's coastal walking trail, the 42km Six Foot Track or trek Mt Kosciuszko. In Sydney, it's worth picking up *Sydney's Best Harbour & Coastal Walks*. It includes the 6km Bondi to Coogee Coastal Walk and the 10km Manly Scenic Walkway, in addition to wilder walks.

In South Australia there's the epic 1200km Heysen Trail and in the Northern Territory the majestic, 233.5km Larapinta Trail and beautifully remote tracks in Nitmiluk (Katherine Gorge) National Park.

Outdoor stockists are good sources of bushwalking information. For national park information and detailed descriptions of national park trails, visit the websites of the various state government national parks departments. *Walking in Australia* by Lonely Planet provides detailed information and trail notes for Australia's best bushwalks.

Cycling

Avid cyclists have access to great routes and can tour the country for days, weekends or even on multiweek trips.

Victoria is a great state for on- and off-road cycling and mountain biking. Standout routes for longer rides in this state include the Murray to the Mountains Rail Trail and the East Gippsland Rail Trail. There is a whole network of routes that follow disused railway lines; **Railtrails Australia** (www.railtrails.org.au) describes these and other routes.

In Western Australia, the Munda Biddi Mountain Bike Trail offers 900km of pedal power; you can tackle the same distance on the Mawson Trail in South Australia.

Rates charged by most bike-hire companies for renting road or mountain bikes are usually around $20 per hour and $40 per day. Security deposits can range from $50 to $200, depending on the rental period.

The **Bicycles Network Australia** (www.bicycles.net.au) website is useful, as is Lonely Planet's *Cycling Australia*.

Safety Guidelines For Bushwalking

Before embarking on a walking trip, consider the following points to ensure a safe and enjoyable experience:

○ Pay any fees and possess any permits required by local authorities.

○ Obtain reliable information about physical and environmental conditions along your intended route (eg from park authorities).

○ Be aware of local laws, regulations and etiquette about wildlife and the environment.

○ Walk only in regions, and on tracks, within your realm of experience.

○ Be aware that weather conditions and terrain vary significantly from one region, or even from one track, to another. Seasonal changes can significantly alter any track. These differences influence the way walkers dress and the equipment they carry.

Diving & Snorkelling

Professional Association of Diving Instructors (PADI) dive courses are offered throughout the country; on the east coast you don't have to travel far before stumbling across one. Learning here is fairly inexpensive: PADI courses range from two to five days and cost anything between $300 and $800. Also, don't forget you can enjoy the marine life by snorkelling; hiring a mask, snorkel and fins is cheap.

North of Sydney try Broughton Island near Port Stephens, and further north, Fish Rock Cave off South West Rocks is renowned for its excellent diving, with shells, schools of clownfish and humpback whales. Swim with grey nurse sharks at the Pinnacles near Forster, and leopard sharks at Julian Rocks Marine Reserve off Byron Bay. On the south coast popular diving spots include Jervis Bay, Montague Island and Merimbula.

The Great Barrier Reef has more dazzling dive sites than you can poke a fin at. There are coral reefs off some mainland beaches and around several of the islands, and many day trips to the Great Barrier Reef provide snorkelling gear free.

In Western Australia, Ningaloo Reef is every bit as interesting as the east-coast coral reefs, without the tourist numbers.

Skiing & Snowboarding

Australia has a small but enthusiastic skiing industry, with snowfields straddling the New South Wales–Victoria border. The season is relatively short, however, running from about mid-June to early September, and snowfalls can be unpredictable. The top places to ski are within Kosciuszko National Park in the Snowy Mountains in New South Wales, and Mt Buller, Falls Creek and Mt Hotham in Victoria's High Country. Cross-country skiing is popular and most resorts offer lessons and equipment.

Skiing Australia (www.skiingaustralia.org.au) has links to the major resorts and race clubs.

Apollo Bay (p246), Great Ocean Road, Victoria
PHOTOGRAPHER: WILL SALTER/LONELY PLANET IMAGES ©

A Whale of a Time

A driving economic force across much of southern Australia from the time of colonisation, whaling was finally banned in Australia in 1979. The main species on the end of the harpoon were humpback, blue, southern right and sperm whales, which were culled in huge numbers for their oil and bone.

Over recent years, whales have made cautious returns to both Sydney Harbour and Hobart's Derwent River. Whale watching has emerged as a lucrative tourist activity in migratory hot-spots like Victor Harbor and Head of Bight in South Australia, Warrnambool in Victoria and out on the ocean beyond Sydney Harbour. If you're lucky enough to be out on the water with one of them, give them a wide berth – humanity owes them a little peace and quiet.

Surfing

World-class waves can be found all around Australia, from Queensland's subtropical Gold Coast, along the entire New South Wales coast and at beaches in Victoria and Tasmania. Surf shops in these areas generally offer board hire and have information on surf schools. If you've never hit the surf before, it's a good idea to have a lesson or two.

New South Wales has 2137km of coastline and 721 ocean beaches. Sydney is strewn with ocean beaches with decent breaks. Crescent Head is the longboard capital of Australia and further north you can surf at Lennox Head and Byron Bay. The New South Wales south coast has great surf beaches (try Wollongong and Merimbula).

There are some great breaks along Queensland's southeastern coast, most notably at Coolangatta, Burleigh Heads, Surfers Paradise, North Stradbroke Island and Noosa.

Victoria's Southern Ocean coastline has great surf. Local and international surfers head to Torquay, while Bells Beach hosts the Rip Curl Pro comp. For the less experienced, there are surf schools in Victoria at Anglesea, Lorne and Phillip Island. Elsewhere, southern Western Australia is a surfing mecca, and Margaret River is the heartland.

Wildlife Watching

Wildlife is one of Australia's top selling points. Most national parks are home to native fauna, although much of it is nocturnal so you may need good flashlight skills to spot it.

Australia is a twitcher's haven, with a wide variety birdlife, particularly water birds. Canberra has the richest birdlife of any Australian capital city.

In the Northern Territory, the best parks to spot wildlife are in the tropical north, especially Kakadu National Park, where birdlife is abundant and you can spot crocodiles.

In New South Wales, there are platypuses and gliders in New England National Park, and 120 bird species in Dorrigo National Park. The Border Ranges National Park is home to a quarter of all of Australia's bird species. Willandra National Park is World Heritage–listed and has dense temperate wetlands and wildlife, and koalas are everywhere around Port Macquarie. Western Australia also has ample birdwatching hotspots.

In Victoria, Wilsons Promontory National Park teems with wildlife – in fact, wombats seem to have right of way.

In South Australia, make a beeline for Flinders Chase National Park. In Queensland, head to Malanda for birdlife, turtles and pademelons, Cape Tribulation for even better birdlife, Magnetic Island for koala spotting, Fraser Island for dingoes and the Daintree for cassowaries. In Tasmania, Maria Island is another twitcher's paradise, while Mt William and Mt Field National Parks and Bruny Island teem with native fauna.

Survival
Guide

Dangerous jellyfish with venomous tentacles (p377)
PHOTOGRAPHER: LEONARD ZELL/LONELY PLANET IMAGES ©

A-Z

Directory

●●●

Accommodation

Australia offers everything from the tent-pegged confines of camping grounds and the communal space of hostels to gourmet breakfasts in guesthouses, chaperoned farmstays and everything-at-your-fingertips resorts, plus the full gamut of hotel and motel lodgings.

Accommodation listings in this book have price range indicators (budget, midrange and top-end, see table below). Within each Sleeping section, listings are in order of author preference, based on our assessment of atmosphere, cleanliness, facilities, location and bang for your buck.

PRICE RANGES

Budget ($)	Up to $100
Midrange ($$)	$100 to $200
Top end ($$$)	More than $200

In most areas you'll find seasonal price variations. During the high season over summer (December to February) and at other peak times, particularly school and public holidays, prices are usually at their highest, whereas outside these times you will find useful discounts and lower walk-in rates. Three notable exceptions are central Australia, the Top End and Australia's ski resorts, where summer is the low season and prices drop substantially.

Normal summer-season prices (as opposed to peak-season prices that apply Christmas to New Year, Easter and school holidays – see p381) are quoted in this guidebook unless otherwise indicated. Note that accommodation from Friday night through to Sunday can be in greater demand (and pricier) in major holiday areas.

B&BS

The local 'bed and breakfast' (guesthouse) industry is thriving. Options include everything from restored miners' cottages, converted barns, rambling old houses, upmarket country manors and beachside bungalows to a simple bedroom in a family home. In areas that tend to attract weekenders – quaint historic towns, wine regions, accessible forest regions such as the Blue Mountains in New South Wales and the Dandenongs in Victoria – B&Bs are often upmarket, charging small fortunes for weekend stays in high season. Tariffs are typically in the midrange bracket, but can be higher. Local tourist offices can usually provide a list of places.

Online resources:

Bed & Breakfast Accommodation in Australia (BABS; www.babs. com.au)

Bed & Breakfast Farmstay and Accommodation Australia (www. australianbedandbreakfast. com.au)

OZ Bed & Breakfast (www. ozbedandbreakfast.com)

HOTELS & MOTELS

Except for pubs, hotels in Australian cities or well-touristed places are generally of the business or luxury-chain variety: comfortable, anonymous, mod-con-filled rooms in multistorey blocks. For these hotels we quote 'rack rates' (official advertised rates), though significant discounts can be offered when business is quiet.

Motels (or motor inns) offer comfortable budget to midrange accommodation and are found all over Australia. There's rarely a cheaper rate for singles, so they're better value for couples or groups of three. Most motels are modern, low rise, and have similar facilities (tea- and coffee-making,

Book Your Stay Online

For more accommodation reviews by Lonely Planet authors, check out hotels.lonelyplanet. com/australia. You'll find independent reviews, as well as recommendations on the best places to stay. Best of all, you can book online.

fridge, TV, air-con, bathroom) but the price will indicate the standard. You'll mostly pay between $80 and $150 for a room.

Useful booking agencies:

Last Minute (www. lastminute.com.au)

Quickbeds (www.quickbeds. com.au)

Wotif (www.wotif.com.au)

PUBS

Hotels in Australia – the ones that serve beer – are commonly known as pubs (from the term 'public house'). Many were built during boom times, so they're often among the largest, most extravagant buildings in town. Some have been restored, but generally, rooms remain small and weathered, with a long amble down the hall to the bathroom. They're usually cheap and central, but if you're a light sleeper, avoid booking a room above the bar and check whether a band is playing downstairs that night.

Pubs have singles/ doubles with shared facilities starting at around $50/80, more if you want a private bathroom.

Business Hours

Business hours do vary from state to state, but use the following as a guide. Note that nearly all attractions across Australia are closed on Christmas Day; many also close on New Years Day and Good Friday.

ℹ Practicalities

○ Newspapers: leaf through the daily *Sydney Morning Herald*, Melbourne's *Age* or the national *Australian* broadsheets.

○ Radio: tune-in to ABC radio; see www.abc.net.au/radio.

○ TV: free-to-air channels include the ad-free, government-sponsored ABC, multicultural SBS, and three commercial TV stations – Seven, Nine and Ten – plus additional digital channels.

○ DVDs: Australian DVDs are encoded for Region 4, which includes Mexico, South America, Central America, New Zealand, the Pacific and the Caribbean.

○ Electrical: Australia uses three-pin adaptors (different from British three-pin adaptors) to plug into the electricity supply (240V AC, 50Hz). See p375.

○ Australia uses the metric system for weights and measures.

Banks
Open 9.30am to 4.30pm Monday to Friday; sometimes to 5pm on Friday. Some large city branches open 8am to 6pm weekdays; a few also to 9pm on Friday.

Post offices
Open 9am to 5pm Monday to Friday; often to noon on Saturdays. Stamps are also available from newsagencies and Australia Post shops.

Restaurants
Breakfast 8am to 10.30am; lunch noon to 3pm; dinner from 6pm or 7pm to 10pm. Most dinner bookings are made for between 7pm and 8pm.

Shops & businesses
Open 9am to 5pm Monday to Friday; 9am to noon or 5pm Saturday. Sunday trading operates in major cities, urban areas and tourist towns. There is late-night shopping to 9pm in major towns (usually Thursday or Friday night). Most supermarkets open to 8pm; some are 24-hour. Milk bars (aka delis, corner shops or convenience stores) open till late.

Customs Regulations

For information on customs regulations, contact the **Australian Customs Service** (☏ 1300 363 263, 02-6275 6666; www.customs. gov.au).

When entering Australia you can bring most articles in free of duty provided that customs is satisfied they are for personal use and that you'll be taking them with you when you leave.

Climate

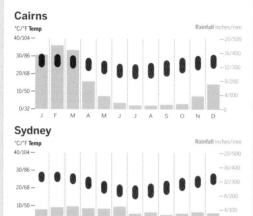

Cairns

Sydney

Melbourne

DUTY-FREE QUOTAS PER PERSON

Alcohol	2.25L (over the age of 18)
Cigarettes	250 cigarettes (over the age of 18)
Dutiable goods	Up to the value of $900 ($450 for people under 18)

Australia takes quarantine very seriously. All luggage is screened or X-rayed – if you fail to declare quarantine items on arrival and are caught, you risk a hefty on-the-spot fine or prosecution, which may result in much more significant fines and up to 10 years' imprisonment.

For more information on quarantine regulations contact the **Australian Quarantine and Inspection Service** (AQIS; ☎ 1800 020 504, 02-6272 3933; www.aqis.gov.au).

When arriving or departing the country, declare all animal and plant material (wooden spoons, straw hats, the lot) and show them to a quarantine officer. If you bring in a souvenir, such as a drum with animal hide for a skin, or a wooden article (though these items are not strictly prohibited, they are subject to inspection) that shows signs of insect damage, it won't get through. Some

items may require treatment to make them safe before they are allowed in. Food and flowers are also prohibited, plus there are restrictions on taking fruit and vegetables between states.

You also need to declare currency in excess of $10,000 (including foreign currency) and prescription medicines. Bring medications in their original, clearly labelled containers. A signed and dated letter from your physician describing your medical conditions and medications, including generic names, is also a good idea. If carrying syringes or needles, be sure to have a physician's letter documenting their medical necessity.

Don't bring illegal drugs in with you. Customs authorities are adept at searching for them and sniffer dogs are permanent fixtures in arrival and baggage halls.

There are strong restrictions on the possession and use of weapons in Australia. If you plan to travel with weapons of any sort contact the customs service or consult its website well before departure – permits may be required.

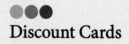

Discount Cards

SENIOR CARDS

Senior travellers with some form of identification are often eligible for concession prices. Overseas pensioners are entitled to discounts of at least 10% on most express-bus fares with Greyhound.

STUDENT & YOUTH CARDS

The **International Student Travel Confederation** (ISTC; www.istc.org) is the controlling body behind the internationally recognised International Student Identity Card (ISIC). Full-time students aged 12 and over are eligible. The card gives the bearer discounts on accommodation, transport and admission to various attractions.

The ISTC also produces the International Youth Travel Card (IYTC), issued to people under 26 years of age and not full-time students, and has benefits equivalent to the ISIC. A similar ISTC brainchild is the International Teacher Identity Card (ITIC), available to teaching professionals. All three cards are chiefly available from student travel companies.

Electricity

240V/50Hz

Interstate Quarantine

When travelling within Australia, whether by land or air, you'll come across signs (mainly in airports, in interstate train stations and at state borders) warning of the possible dangers of carrying fruit, vegetables and plants (which may be infected with a disease or pest) from one area to another. Certain pests and diseases – such as fruit fly, cucurbit thrips, grape phylloxera and potato cyst nematodes, just to name a few – are prevalent in some areas but not in others, and so for obvious reasons authorities would like to limit them spreading.

There are quarantine inspection posts that are located on some state borders and occasionally elsewhere. While quarantine control often relies on honesty, many posts are staffed and officers are entitled to search your car for items that are undeclared. Generally they will confiscate all fresh fruit and vegetables, so it's best to leave shopping for these items until the first town past the inspection point.

Gay & Lesbian Travellers

Australia is a very popular destination for gay and lesbian travellers, with the so-called 'pink tourism' appeal of Sydney that is especially big, thanks largely to the city's high-profile and spectacular Sydney Gay & Lesbian Mardi Gras, which is held annually. Throughout the country, but particularly on the east coast, there are tour operators, travel agents and accommodation places that make a point of welcoming gay men and lesbians.

In general, Australians are open-minded about homosexuality, but the further into the country you get, the more likely you are to run into overt homophobia. Having said that, you will find active gay communities in places such as Alice Springs and Darwin. Even Tasmania, once a bastion of sexual conservatism, now actively encourages gay and lesbian tourism. Same-sex acts are legal in all states but the age of consent varies.

Major gay and lesbian events held thoughout the country:

Midsumma Festival (www.midsumma.org.au) Melbourne; mid-January to mid-February.

Sydney Gay & Lesbian Mardi Gras (www.mardigras.org.au) Annually; February and March.

Pride March & Perth Pride (www.pridewa.asn.au) Both in October in Perth.

Feast (www.feast.org.au) November in Adelaide.

PUBLICATIONS & CONTACTS

All major cities have gay newspapers, available from gay and lesbian venues, and from newsagents in popular gay and lesbian residential areas. Gay lifestyle magazines include *DNA*, *Lesbians on the Loose*, the monthly *Queensland Pride* and the bimonthly *Blue*. Perth has the free *Out in Perth* and Adelaide has *Blaze*.

Useful websites with general information:

Gay and Lesbian Counselling & Community Services of Australia (GLCCS; www.glccs.org.au) Telephone counselling.

Gay and Lesbian Tourism Australia (Galta; www.galta.com.au)

Pinkboard (www.pinkboard.com.au)

Health

Healthwise, Australia is a remarkably safe country in which to travel, considering that such a large portion of it lies in the tropics. Tropical diseases such as malaria and yellow fever are unknown; diseases of insanitation such as cholera and typhoid are unheard of. Thanks to Australia's isolation and quarantine standards, even some animal diseases such as rabies and foot-and-mouth disease have yet to be recorded.

Few travellers to Australia will experience anything worse than an upset stomach or a bad hangover, and, if you do fall ill, the standard of hospitals and health care is high.

VACCINATIONS

Since most vaccines don't produce immunity until at least two weeks after they're given, visit a physician four to eight weeks before departure. Ask your doctor for an International Certificate of Vaccination (otherwise known as 'the yellow booklet'), which will list all the vaccinations you've received.

If you're entering Australia within six days of having stayed overnight or longer in a yellow-fever-infected country, you'll need proof of yellow-fever vaccination. For a full list of these countries visit:

Centers for Disease Control & Prevention (www.cdc.gov/travel).

World Health Organization (WHO; www.who.int/wer) The WHO recommends that all travellers should be covered for diphtheria, tetanus, measles, mumps, rubella, chickenpox and polio, as well as hepatitis B, regardless of their destination. The consequences of these diseases can be severe, and while Australia has high levels of childhood vaccination coverage, outbreaks of these diseases do occur.

HEALTH INSURANCE

Health insurance is essential for all travellers. While health care in Australia is of a high standard and not overly expensive by international standards, considerable costs can build up and repatriation is extremely expensive. Make sure your existing health insurance will cover you – if not, organise extra insurance.

Check lonelyplanet.com for more information.

Find out in advance if your insurance plan will make payments directly to providers or if it will reimburse you later for overseas health expenditures. In Australia, as in many countries, doctors expect payment at the time of consultation. Make sure you get an itemised receipt detailing the service and keep the contact details of the health provider. See p377 for details of health care in Australia.

INTERNET RESOURCES

There is a wealth of travel health advice on the internet: **Lonely Planet** (www.lonelyplanet.com) is a good place to start. The **World Health Organisation** (WHO; www.who.int/ith) publishes a superb book called *International Travel and Health,* which is revised annually and is available online at no cost. Another website of general interest is **MD Travel Health** (www.mdtravelhealth.com), which provides complete travel health recommendations for every country and is updated daily.

It's usually a good idea to consult your government's travel health website before departure, if one is available:

Australia (www.dfat.gov.au/travel)

Canada (www.travelhealth.gc.ca)

UK (www.nhs.uk/livewell/travelhealth)

USA (www.cdc.gov/travel)

AVAILABILITY & COST OF HEALTH CARE

Australia has an excellent health-care system. It's a mixture of privately run medical clinics and hospitals alongside a system of public hospitals funded by the Australian government. There are excellent specialised, public health facilities for women and children in Australia's major centres.

The Medicare system covers Australian residents for some of their health-care costs. Visitors from countries with which Australia has a reciprocal health-care agreement are eligible for benefits specified under the Medicare program. There are agreements currently in place with Finland, Ireland, Italy, Malta, the Netherlands, New Zealand, Norway, Sweden and the UK – check the details before departing from these countries. In general, the agreements provide for any episode of ill-health that requires prompt medical attention. For further information, visit www.medicareaustralia.gov.au/public/migrants/visitors.

Over-the-counter medications are widely available at privately owned chemists throughout Australia. These include painkillers, antihistamines for allergies, and skin-care products.

You may find that medications readily available over the counter in some countries are only available in Australia by prescription. These include the oral contraceptive pill, most medications for asthma and all antibiotics. If you take

Where the Wild Things Are

Australia's profusion of dangerous creatures is legendary. Snakes, spiders, sharks, crocodiles, jellyfish...Travellers needn't be alarmed, however – you're unlikely to see many of these creatures in the wild, much less be attacked by one.

CROCODILES

Around the northern Australian coastline, saltwater crocodiles ('salties') are a real danger. They also inhabit estuaries, creeks and rivers, sometimes a long way inland. Observe safety signs or ask locals whether that inviting-looking waterhole or river is croc-free before plunging in.

JELLYFISH

With venomous tentacles up to 3m long, box jellyfish (aka sea wasps or stingers) inhabit Australia's tropical waters. You can be stung during any month, but they're most common during the wet season (October to March) when you should stay out of the sea. Stinger nets are in place at some beaches, but never swim unless you've checked. If you are stung, wash the skin with vinegar then get to hospital.

SHARKS

Despite extensive media coverage, the risk of shark attack in Australia is no greater than in other countries with extensive coastlines. Check with surf life-saving groups about local risks.

SNAKES

There's no denying it: Australia has plenty of venomous snakes. Most common are brown and tiger snakes, but few species are aggressive. Unless you're messing around with or accidentally standing on one, it's extremely unlikely that you'll get bitten. If you are bitten, prevent the spread of venom by applying pressure to the wound and immobilising the area with a splint or sling before seeking medical attention.

SPIDERS

Australia has several poisonous spiders, bites from which are usually treatable with antivenins. The deadly funnel-web spider lives in NSW (including Sydney) – bites are treated as per snake bites (pressure and immobilisation before transferring to a hospital.). Redback spiders live throughout Australia. Bites cause pain, sweating and nausea: apply ice or cold packs, then transfer to hospital.

medication on a regular basis, bring an adequate supply and ensure you have details of the generic name, as brand names may differ between countries.

Insurance

A good travel insurance policy covering theft, loss and medical problems is essential. Most policies offer lower and higher medical-expense options; the higher ones are chiefly for countries that have extremely high medical costs, such as the USA. There is a wide variety of policies available, so compare the small print.

Some policies specifically exclude designated 'dangerous activities' such as scuba diving, bungee jumping, motorcycling, skiing and even bushwalking. Make sure the policy you choose fully covers you for your activity of choice.

You may prefer a policy that pays doctors or hospitals directly rather than requiring you to pay on the spot and claim later. If you have to claim later make sure you keep all documentation. Check that the policy covers ambulances and emergency medical evacuations by air.

See also Health Insurance (p376). For information on insurance matters relating to cars that are rented, see p389.

Worldwide travel insurance is available at www.lonelyplanet.com /travel_services. You can buy, extend and claim online anytime – even if you're already on the road.

Internet Access

Internet addicts will find it easy to get connected throughout Australia.

GETTING CONNECTED

Australia uses RJ-45 telephone plugs and Telstra EXI-160 four-pin plugs, but neither is universal – electronics shops such as Tandy and Dick Smith should be able to help. You'll also need a plug adaptor, and a universal AC adaptor will enable you to plug in without frying the innards of your machine.

Keep in mind that your PC-card modem may not work in Australia. The safest option is to buy a reputable 'global' modem before you leave home or buy a local PC-card modem once you get to Australia.

INTERNET CAFES

Most internet cafes in Australia have broadband access, but prices vary significantly depending on where you are. Most public libraries also have internet access, but this is provided primarily for research needs, not for travellers to check their email, so head for an internet cafe first. You'll find these in cities, sizable towns and pretty much anywhere else that travellers congregate. The cost ranges from $3 per hour in cut-throat places in Sydney's King's Cross to $10 per hour in more remote locations. The average is about $6 per hour, usually with a minimum of 10 minutes' access.

INTERNET SERVICE PROVIDERS

If you've brought your palm-top or notebook computer and want to get connected to a local Internet Service Provider (ISP), there are plenty of options – some ISPs do limit their dial-up areas to major cities or particular regions. Whatever enticements a particular ISP offers, make sure it has local dial-up numbers for the places where you intend to use it – the last thing you want is to be making timed long-distance calls every time you connect to the internet. Another useful tip when dialling up from a hotel room is to put 0 in front of your number to enable your modem to dial an outside line. Some major ISPs:

Australia On Line (☎ 1300 650 661; www.ozonline.com.au)

Dodo (☎ 13 36 36; www.dodo. com.au)

iinet (☎ 13 19 17; www.iinet. net.au)

iPrimus (☎ 13 17 89; www. iprimus.com.au)

Optus (☎ 1800 780 219; www. optus.com.au)

Telstra BigPond (☎ 13 76 63; www.bigpond.com)

WIRELESS

An increasing number of hotels, cafes and bars in cities offer wi-fi (wireless) access. Some charge a fee so make sure you ask the price before connecting. These locations are most prevalent in Sydney and Melbourne but they're on the rise elsewhere. The following websites are helpful for sourcing locations:

Azure Wireless (www.azure.com.au)

Free WiFi (www.freewifi.com.au)

Wi-Fi HotSpotList (www.wi-fihotspotlist.com/browse/au)

Money

ATMS & EFTPOS

Branches of the ANZ, Commonwealth, National Australia, Westpac and affiliated banks are found all over Australia, and many provide 24-hour automated teller machines (ATMs). But don't expect to find ATMs *everywhere*, certainly not off the beaten track or in very small towns. Most ATMs accept cards issued by other banks and are linked to international networks.

Eftpos (Electronic Funds Transfer at Point of Sale) is a convenient service that most Australian businesses have embraced. It means you can use your bank card (credit or debit) to pay for services or purchases directly, and often withdraw cash as well. Eftpos is available practically everywhere these days, even in outback roadhouses where it's a long way between banks. Just like using an ATM, you need to know your Personal Identification Number (PIN) to use Eftpos.

Bear in mind that withdrawing cash via ATMs or Eftpos may attract significant fees – check the associated costs with your bank first.

CREDIT & DEBIT CARDS

Credit Cards

Arguably the best way to carry most of your money around is in the form of a plastic card. Australia is well and truly a card-carrying society; it's unusual to line up at a supermarket checkout, petrol station or department store and see someone actually paying with cash these days. Credit cards such as Visa and MasterCard are widely accepted for everything from a hostel bed or a restaurant meal to an adventure tour, and are pretty much essential (in lieu of a large deposit) for hiring a car. They can also be used to get cash advances over the counter at banks and from many ATMs, depending on the card, though these transactions incur immediate interest. Charge cards such as Diners Club and American Express (Amex) are not as widely accepted.

Lost credit-card contact numbers:

American Express
(☏ 1300 132 639)

Diners Club
(☏ 1300 360 060)

MasterCard
(☏ 1800 120 113)

Visa
(☏ 1800 450 346)

Debit Cards

Apart from losing them, the obvious danger with credit cards is maxing out your limit and going home to a steaming pile of debt. A safer option is a debit card with which you can draw money directly from your home bank account using ATMs, banks or Eftpos machines. Any card connected to the international banking network (Cirrus, Maestro, Visa Plus and Eurocard) should work, provided you know your PIN. Fees for using your card at a foreign bank or ATM vary depending on your home bank; ask before you leave. Companies such as Travelex offer debit cards (Travelex calls them Cash Passport cards) with set withdrawal fees and a balance you can top up from your personal bank account while on the road – nice one!

CURRENCY

Australia's currency is the Australian dollar, made up of 100 cents. There are 5c, 10c, 20c, 50c, $1 and $2 coins, and $5, $10, $20, $50 and $100 notes. Although the smallest coin in circulation is 5c, prices are often still marked in single cents and then rounded to the nearest 5c when you come to pay.

Cash amounts equal to or in excess of the equivalent of $10,000 (in any currency) must be declared on arrival or departure.

In this book, unless otherwise stated, all prices given in dollars refer to Australian dollars.

EXCHANGING MONEY

Changing foreign currency or travellers cheques is usually no problem at banks throughout Australia or at licensed moneychangers such as Travelex or Amex in cities and major towns.

TAXES & REFUNDS

Goods and services tax (GST) is a flat 10% tax on all goods and services – accommodation, eating out, transport, electrical and other goods, books, furniture, clothing etc. There are exceptions, however, such as basic foods (milk, bread, fruits and vegetables etc). By law the tax is included in the quoted or shelf prices, so all prices in this book are GST-inclusive. International air and sea travel to/from Australia is GST-free, as is domestic air travel when purchased outside Australia by nonresidents.

If you purchase new or secondhand goods with a total minimum value of $300 from any one supplier no more than 30 days before you leave Australia, you are entitled under the Tourist Refund Scheme (TRS) to a refund of any GST or WET (wine equalisation tax) paid. The scheme doesn't apply to all goods, and those that do qualify you must be able to wear or take as hand luggage onto the plane or ship. Also note that the refund is valid for goods bought from more than one supplier, but only if at least $300 is spent in each. For more details, contact the **Australian Customs Service** (☑ 1300 363 263, 02-6275 6666; www.customs.gov.au).

TRAVELLERS CHEQUES

The ubiquity and convenience of internationally linked credit and debit card facilities in Australia means that travellers cheques are virtually redundant. However, Amex and Travelex will exchange their associated travellers cheques, and major banks will change travellers cheques also. In all instances you'll need to present your passport for identification when you are cashing them.

There are no notable restrictions on importing or exporting travellers cheques.

● ● ●
Public Holidays

The following is a list of the main national and state public holidays (* indicates holidays that are only observed locally). As the timing can varybetween states, check locally for precise dates.

NATIONAL

New Year's Day 1 January

Australia Day 26 January

Easter (Good Friday to Easter Monday inclusive) March/April

Anzac Day 25 April

Queen's Birthday (except WA) Second Monday in June

Queen's Birthday (WA) Last Monday in September

Christmas Day 25 December

Boxing Day 26 December

AUSTRALIAN CAPITAL TERRITORY

Canberra Day Second Monday in March

Bank Holiday First Monday in August

Labour Day First Monday in October

NEW SOUTH WALES

Bank Holiday First Monday in August

Labour Day First Monday in October

NORTHERN TERRITORY

May Day First Monday in May

Show Day* (Alice Springs) First Friday in July; (Tennant Creek) second Friday in July; (Katherine) third Friday in July; (Darwin) fourth Friday in July

Picnic Day First Monday in August

QUEENSLAND

Labour Day First Monday in May

RNA Show Day* (Brisbane) Second or third Wednesday in August

SOUTH AUSTRALIA

Adelaide Cup Day Third Monday in May

Labour Day First Monday in October

Proclamation Day Last Monday or Tuesday in December

TASMANIA

Regatta Day* (Hobart) 14 February

Launceston Cup Day* Last Wednesday in February

Eight Hours Day First Monday in March

Bank Holiday Tuesday following Easter Monday

King Island Show* First Tuesday in March

Launceston Show Day* Thursday preceding second Saturday in October

Hobart Show Day* Thursday preceding fourth Saturday in October

Recreation Day* (Northern Tasmania) First Monday in November

VICTORIA

Labour Day Second Monday in March

Melbourne Cup Day First Tuesday in November

WESTERN AUSTRALIA

Labour Day First Monday in March

Foundation Day First Monday in June

SCHOOL HOLIDAYS

The Christmas holiday season, from mid-December to late January, is part of the summer school holidays – it's also the time you are most likely to find transport and accommodation booked out, and long, restless queues at tourist attractions.

There are three shorter school holiday periods during the year, but they vary by a week or two from state to state. They fall roughly from early to mid-April, late June to mid-July, and late September to early October.

Even though the holidays don't coincide nationwide,

Important Numbers

Regular Australian phone numbers have a two-digit area code followed by an eight-digit number. Drop the initial 0 if calling from abroad.

Country code	☏ 61
International access code	☏ 0011
Emergency (ambulance, fire, police)	☏ 000
Road conditions	☏ 13 27 01
Directory assistance	☏ 1223

accommodation in tourist hot spots like the north and south coasts of New South Wales (NSW), and Queensland's Gold and Sunshine Coasts will still be booked out.

Safe Travel

Australia is a relatively safe place to travel by world standards (crime- and war-wise at any rate) but natural disasters have been wreaking havoc of late. Bushfires, floods, and cyclones decimated parts of Queensland, NSW, Victoria and WA in early 2011, but if you pay attention to warnings from local authorities and don't venture into affected areas, you should be fine.

Sexual harassment is an ongoing problem, be it via an aggressive metropolitan male or a rural bloke living a less-than-enlightened pro forma bush existence. Stereotypically, the further you get from 'civilisation' (ie the big cities), the less enlightened your average Aussie male is probably going to be about women's issues.

Lone female hitchhikers are tempting fate – hitching with a male companion is safer.

Telephone

Australia's main telecommunication companies:

Telstra (www.telstra.com.au) The main player – landline and mobile phone services.

Optus (www.optus.com.au) Telstra's main rival – landline and mobile phone services.

Vodafone (www.vodafone.com.au) Mobile phone services.

Virgin (www.virginmobile.com.au) Mobile phone services.

3 (www.three.com.au) Mobile phone services.

INFORMATION & TOLL-FREE CALLS

Numbers starting with ☏ 190 are usually recorded information services, charged at anything from 35c to $5 or more per minute (more from mobiles and payphones). To make a reverse-charge (collect) call from any public or private phone, dial ☏ 1800 738 3773, or ☏ 12 550.

Toll-free numbers (prefix ☏ 1800) can be called free of charge from almost anywhere in Australia – they may not be accessible from certain areas or from mobile phones. Calls to numbers beginning with ☎13 or ☎1300 are charged at the rate of a local call – the numbers can usually be dialled Australia-wide, but may be applicable only to a specific state or STD district. Telephone numbers beginning with either ☎1800, ☎13 or ☎1300 cannot be dialled from outside Australia.

INTERNATIONAL CALLS

Most payphones allow International Subscriber Dialling (ISD) calls, the cost and international dialling code of which will vary depending on which international phonecard provider you are using. International phone cards are readily available from internet cafes and convenience stores. Check the fine print on your phonecard to ensure you aren't paying a hefty trunk charge every time you make a call.

International calls from landlines in Australia are also relatively cheap and subject to special deals, so if you're paying for residential phone rental it's worth shopping around – look in the *Yellow Pages* for a list of telephone service providers and compare their international rates.

The **Country Direct service** (☎ 1800 801 800) connects callers in Australia with operators in nearly 60 countries to make reverse-charge (collect) or credit-card calls.

When calling overseas you will need to dial the international access code

from Australia (☎0011 or ☎0018), the country code and then the area code (without the initial 0). So for a London telephone number you'll need to dial ☎0011-44-20, then the number. In addition, certain operators will have you dial a special code to access their service.

Some country codes:

COUNTRY	CODES
France	☎33
Germany	☎49
Ireland	☎353
Japan	☎81
Netherlands	☎31
New Zealand	☎64
UK	☎44
USA & Canada	☎1

If dialling Australia from overseas, the country code is ☎61 and you need to drop the 0 in state/territory area codes.

LOCAL CALLS

Calls from private phones cost 15c to 30c, while local calls from public phones cost 50c; both involve unlimited talk time. Calls to mobile phones attract higher rates and are timed.

LONG-DISTANCE CALLS & AREA CODES

Long-distance calls (over around 50km) are timed. Australia uses four Subscriber Trunk Dialling (STD) area codes. These STD calls can be made from any public phone and are cheaper during off-peak hours – generally between 7pm and 7am and on weekends. Broadly, the main area codes are as follows.

STATE/ TERRITORY	AREA CODE
ACT	☎02
NSW	☎02
NT	☎08
QLD	☎07
SA	☎08
TAS	☎03
VIC	☎03
WA	☎08

Area code boundaries don't necessarily coincide with state borders; for example some parts of NSW use neighbouring codes.

MOBILE (CELL) PHONES

Local numbers with the prefixes ☎04xx belong to mobile phones. Australia's GSM and 3G mobile networks service more than 90% of the population but leaves vast tracts of the country uncovered. The east coast, southeast and southwest get good reception, but elsewhere (apart from major towns) it can be haphazard or nonexistent. It is improving, however.

Australia's digital network is compatible with GSM 900 and 1800 (used in Europe), but generally not with the systems used in the USA or Japan. It's easy and cheap enough to get connected short-term, as prepaid mobile systems are offered by the main providers:

Telstra (www.telstra.com.au)

Optus (www.optus.com.au)

Vodafone (www.vodafone.com.au)

Virgin (www.virginmobile.com.au)

3 (www.three.com.au)

PHONECARDS & PUBLIC PHONES

A variety of phonecards can be bought at newsagents, hostels and post offices for a fixed dollar value (usually $10, $20 etc) and can be used with any public or private phone by dialling a toll-free access number and then the PIN number on the card. Some public phones also accept credit cards, but old-fashioned coin-operated public phones are becoming increasingly rare (and if you do find one, chances are the coin slot will be gummed up or vandalised beyond function).

Time

Australia is divided into three time zones: Western Standard Time (GMT/UTC plus eight hours) covering WA; Central Standard Time (plus 9½ hours) covering the Northern Territory (NT) and South Australia (SA); and Eastern Standard Time (plus 10 hours) covering Tasmania, Victoria, NSW, the Australian Capital Territory (ACT) and Queensland. There are minor exceptions – Broken Hill (NSW), for example, is on Central Standard Time. For international times, see www.timeanddate.com/worldclock.

Daylight saving, for which clocks are put forward an hour, operates in some states for the warmer months (October to April). However, things can get confusing, with Western Australia (WA), the NT and Queensland staying on standard time, while in Tasmania daylight saving starts a month earlier than in SA, Victoria, the ACT and NSW.

Tipping

It's common but by no means obligatory to tip in restaurants and upmarket cafes if the service warrants it – a gratuity of between 5% and 10% of the bill is the norm. Taxi drivers will also appreciate you rounding up the fare.

Tourist Information

Australia's highly self-conscious tourism infrastruc-ture means that when you head out looking for informa-tion, you can easily end up being buried neck deep in brochures, booklets, maps and leaflets, or that you can get utterly swamped with detail during an online surf.

The **Australian Tourist Commission** (www.australia.com) is the national government tourist body, and has a good website for pretrip research.

LOCAL TOURIST OFFICES

Within Australia, tourist information is disseminated by various regional and local offices. In this book, the main state and territory tourism authorities are listed in the introductory information section of each destination chapter. Almost every major town in Australia seems to maintain a tourist office of some type and in many cases they are very good, with friendly staff (often retiree volunteers) providing local info not readily available from the state offices. If booking accommodation or tours from local offices, bear in mind that they often only promote businesses that are paying members of the local tourist association. Details of local tourism offices are given in the relevant city and town sections throughout this book.

TOURIST OFFICES ABROAD

The federal government body charged with improving relationships with foreign tourists is **Tourism Australia** (www.tourism.australia.com). A good place to start some pretrip research is on its website, which provides information about many aspects of visit-ing Australia in 10 languages (including French, German, Japanese and Spanish).

Some countries with Tourism Australia offices:

Canada (☎ 416-572 7708; Suite 272, 1920 Yonge St, Toronto M4S 3E2)

China (☎ 21-6887 8129; Unit 1501, 15/F, Citigroup Tower, 33 Hua Yuan Shi Qiao Rd, PuDong, Shanghai 200120)

Germany (☎ 069-274 00622; Neue Mainzer Strasse 22, Frankfurt D 60311)

Japan (☎ 13-5218 2560; 12F Marunouchi Trust Tower North, 1-8-1 Marunouchi, Chiyoda-ku, Tokyo 100-0005)

New Zealand (☎ 09-915 2826; Level 3, 125 The Strand, Parnell, Auckland)

Singapore (☏ 6255 4555; 101 Thomson Rd, United Sq 08-03, Singapore 307591)

UK (☏ 020-7438 4601; 6th fl, Australia House, Melbourne Place/Strand, London WC2B 4LG)

USA (☏ 310-695 3200; Suite 1150, 6100 Center Dr, Los Angeles CA 90045)

Travellers with Disabilities

Disability awareness in Australia is pretty high and getting higher. Legislation requires that new accommodation meets accessibility standards for mobility-impaired travellers, and discrimination by tourism operators is illegal. Many of Australia's key attractions, including many national parks, provide access for those with limited mobility and a number of sites also address the needs of visitors with visual or aural impairments; contact attractions in advance to confirm the facilities. Tour operators with vehicles catering to mobility-impaired travellers operate from most capital cities. Facilities for wheelchairs are improving in accommodation, but there are still far too many older (particularly 'historic') establishments where the necessary upgrades haven't been done.

RESOURCES

Online resources and useful contacts:

Access Travel Australia (www.ebility.com/travel) Lots of info on accessible holidays in Australia, including listings of tour operators and accommodation.

Deaf Australia (www.deafau.org.au)

Easy Access Australia (www.easyaccessaustralia.com.au) A publication by Bruce Cameron available from various bookshops. Provides details on easily accessible transport, accommodation and attraction options.

National Information Communication & Awareness Network (Nican; www.nican.com.au) Australia-wide directory providing information on access issues, accessible accommodation, sporting and recreational activities, transport and specialist tour operators.

National Public Toilet Map (www.toiletmap.gov.au) Lists over 14,000 public toilets around Australia, including those with wheelchair access.

Spinal Chord Injuries Australia (www.spinalcordinjuries.com.au)

Vision Australia (www.visionaustralia.org.au)

AIR TRAVEL

Qantas (☏ 13 13 13; www.qantas.com.au) entitles a disabled person and the carer travelling with them to a discount on full economy fares; contact Nican for eligibility and an application form. Guide dogs travel for free on **Qantas**, **Jetstar** (☏ 13 15 38; www.jetstar.com.au) and **Virgin Australia** (☏ 13 67 89; www.virginaustralia.com.au), and their affiliated carriers. All of Australia's major airports have dedicated parking spaces, wheelchair access to terminals, accessible toilets, and skychairs to convey passengers onto planes via airbridges.

TRAIN TRAVEL

In NSW, CountryLink's XPT trains have at least one carriage (usually the buffet car) with a seat removed for a wheelchair, and an accessible toilet. Queensland Rail's *Tilt Train* from Brisbane to Cairns has a wheelchair-accessible carriage.

Melbourne's suburban rail network is accessible and guide dogs and hearing dogs are permitted on all public transport in Victoria. **Metlink** (☏ 13 16 38; www.metlinkmelbourne.com.au) also offers a free travel pass to visually impaired people for transport in Melbourne.

Visas

All visitors to Australia need a visa – only New Zealand nationals are exempt, and even they receive a 'special category' visa on arrival. Application forms for the several types of visa are available from Australian diplomatic missions overseas, travel agents or the website of the **Department of Immigration & Citizenship** (☏ 13 18 81; www.immi.gov.au).

EVISITOR

Many European passport holders are eligible for an eVisitor visa, which is free and allows visitors to stay in Australia for up to three months within a 12-month period. eVisitor visas must be applied for online at www.immi.gov.au/e_visa/evisitor.htm, and they are electronically stored and linked to individual passport numbers, so no stamp in your passport is required. It's advisable to apply at least 14 days prior to the proposed date of arrival in Australia.

ELECTRONIC TRAVEL AUTHORITY (ETA)

Passport holders from eight countries that aren't part of the eVisitor scheme – Brunei, Canada, Hong Kong, Japan, Malaysia, Singapore, South Korea and the USA – can apply for either a visitor or business ETA. ETAs are valid for 12 months, with stays of up to three months on each visit. You can apply for the ETA online at www.eta.immi.gov.au, which attracts a nonrefundable service charge of $20.

TOURIST VISAS (676)

Short-term tourist visas have largely been replaced by the eVisitor and ETA. However, if you are from a country not covered by either, or you want to stay longer than three months, you'll need to apply for a Tourist Visa. Standard Tourist Visas (which cost $105) allow one (in some cases multiple) entry, for a stay of up to 12 months, and are valid for use within 12 months of issue. For online applications see www.immi.gov.au/e_visa/e676.htm.

Transport

●●●●

Getting There & Away

They don't call Australia the land 'down under' for nothing. It's a long way from just about everywhere, and getting here is usually going to mean a long-haul flight. That 'over the horizon' feeling doesn't stop once you're here, either – the distances between key cities (let alone opposing coastlines) can be vast, requiring a minimum of an hour or two of air time but up to several days of highway cruising or dirt-road jostling to traverse. So if you're short on time, consider an internal flight – they're affordable (compared with petrol and car-hire costs) and will save you some *looong* days in the saddle. Flights, tours and rail tickets can be booked online at lonelyplanet.com/bookings.

ENTERING THE COUNTRY

Disembarkation in Australia is a straightforward affair, with only the usual customs declarations (p373) and the fight to be first to the luggage carousel to endure.

Passports

There are no restrictions when it comes to citizens of foreign countries entering Australia. If you have a current passport and visa (p384), you should be fine.

✈ AIR

The high season for flights into Australia is roughly over the country's summer (December to February), with slightly less of a premium on fares over the shoulder months (October/November and March/April). The low season generally tallies with the winter months (June to August), though this is actually the peak tourist season in central Australia and the Top End.

Airports

Australia has several international gateways, with Sydney and Melbourne being the busiest.

Adelaide (☏ 08-8308 9211; www.adelaideairport.com.au)

Brisbane (☏ 07-3406 3000; www.bne.com.au)

Cairns (☏ 07-4080 6703; www.cairnsairport.com)

Darwin (☏ 08-8920 1811; www.ntapl.com.au)

Melbourne (☏ 03-9297 1600; www.melbourneairport.com.au) Tullamarine.

Perth (☏ 08-9478 8888; www.perthairport.net.au)

Sydney (Kingsford Smith; ☏ 02-9667 9111; www.sydneyairport.com.au)

Climate Change & Travel

Every form of transport that relies on carbon-based fuel generates CO_2, the main cause of human-induced climate change. Modern travel is dependent on aeroplanes, which might use less fuel per kilometre per person than most cars but travel much greater distances. The altitude at which aircraft emit gases (including CO_2) and particles also contributes to their climate change impact. Many websites offer 'carbon calculators' that allow people to estimate the carbon emissions generated by their journey and, for those who wish to do so, to offset the impact of the greenhouse gases emitted with contributions to portfolios of climate-friendly initiatives throughout the world. Lonely Planet offsets the carbon footprint of all staff and author travel.

Getting Around

✈ AIR

Time pressures combined with the vastness of the Australian continent may lead you to consider taking to the skies at some point in your trip. Both **STA Travel** (☏ 13 47 82; www.statravel.com.au) and **Flight Centre** (☏ 13 31 33; www.flightcentre.com.au) have offices throughout Australia, or you can book directly with the airlines listed below, or try www.travel.com.au.

Airlines in Australia

Australia's main (and highly safe and professional) domestic airlines are **Qantas** (☏ 13 13 13; www.qantas.com.au) and **Virgin Australia** (☏ 13 67 89; www.virginaustralia.com), servicing all the main centres with regular flights. **Jetstar** (☏ 13 15 38; www.jetstar.com.au) and **Tiger Airways** (☏ 03-9999 2888; www.tigerairways.com) are the budget subsidiaries of Qantas and Singapore Airlines respectively, flying between most Australian capital cities.

See regional chapters for info on smaller operators flying regional routes.

⚲ BICYCLE

Australia has much to offer cyclists, from leisurely bike paths winding through most major cities to thousands of kilometres of good country roads where you can wear out your sprockets. There's lots of flat countryside and gently rolling hills to explore and, although Australia is not as mountainous as, say, Switzerland or France, mountain bikers can find plenty of forestry trails and high country.

Hire Bike hire in cities is easy (see Activities headings in destination chapters), but if you're riding for more than a few hours or even a day, it's more economical to invest in your own wheels.

Legalities Bike helmets are compulsory in all states and territories, as are white front lights and red rear lights for riding at night.

Maps You can get by with standard road maps, but if you want to avoid highways and low-grade unsealed roads, the government series is best. The 1:250,000 scale is suitable, though you'll need a lot of maps if you're going far. The next scale up is 1:1,000,000 – adequate and widely available in map shops.

Weather In summer carry plenty of water. Wear a helmet with a peak (or a cap under your helmet), use sunscreen and avoid cycling in the middle of the day. Beware summer northerlies that can make a north-bound cyclist's life hell. South-easterly trade winds blow in April, when you can have (theoretically) tail winds all the way to Darwin. It can get very cold in the mountains, so pack appropriate clothing.

Transport If you're bringing in your own bike, check with your airline for costs and the degree of dismantling or packing required. Within Australia, bus companies require you to dismantle your bike and some don't guarantee that it will travel on the same bus as you.

Information

The national cycling body is the **Bicycle Federation of Australia** (☏ 02-6249 6761; www.bicycles.net.au). Each state and territory has a touring organisation that can also help with cycling information and put you in touch with touring clubs.

Principal Bus Routes & Railways

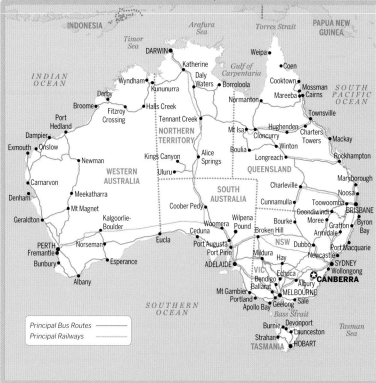

Bicycle New South Wales
(☎ 02-9704 0800; www.
bicyclensw.org.au)

Bicycle Queensland (☎ 07-
3844 1144; www.bq.org.au)

Bicycle SA (☎ 08-8168
9999; www.bikesa.asn.au)

Bicycle Tasmania (www.
biketas.org.au)

**Bicycle Transportation
Alliance** (☎ 08-9420 7210;
www.btawa.org.au) In WA.

Bicycle Victoria (☎ 03-
8636 8888; www.bv.com.au)

**Northern Territory
Cycling Association** (www.
nt.cycling.org.au)

Pedal Power ACT (☎ 02-
6248 7995; www.pedalpower.
org.au)

🚌 BUS

Australia's extensive bus
network is a relatively cheap
and reliable way to get
around, though it can be
tedious over huge distances.
Most buses are equipped with
air-con, toilets and videos; all
are smoke-free. Small towns
eschew formal bus terminals
for a single drop-off/pick-up

point (post office, newsagent,
corner shop etc).

Greyhound Australia
(☎ 1300 473 946; www.
greyhound.com.au) runs a
national network (notably not
across the Nullarbor Plain
between Adelaide and Perth).
Fares purchased online are
roughly 5% cheaper than
over-the-counter tickets;
phone-purchased fares incur
a $4 booking fee.

Other interstate operators:

Firefly Express (☎ 1300 730
740; www.fireflyexpress.com.
au) Runs between Sydney,
Canberra, Melbourne and
Adelaide.

Premier Motor Service

(☎ 13 34 10; www.premierms.
com.au) Runs along the east
coast between Cairns and
Melbourne.

V/Line (☎ 13 61 96; www.
vline.com.au) Connects Victoria
with NSW, SA and the ACT.

Backpacker Buses

Companies offering budget
backpacker transport are
pretty much organised-tour
operators, but they do get you
from A to B (sometimes with
hop-on, hop-off services).
Discounts for members of
hostel organisations are usually available.

Adventure Tours Australia

(☎ 1800 068 886; www.
adventuretours.com.au)
Budget tours in all states.
A two-day Red Centre tour
starting/finishing in Alice
Springs via Uluru, Kata Tjuta
and Kings Canyon costs
$490. Ten days Perth to
Broome costs $1545.

Autopia Tours (☎ 03-9419

8878; www.autopiatours.com.
au) Three-day trips along
the Great Ocean Road from
Melbourne to Adelaide, or
from Melbourne to Sydney
for $395.

Groovy Grape Getaways Australia

(☎ 1800 661
177; www.groovygrape.com.
au) Small-group, SA-based
operator. Tours include three
days Melbourne to Adelaide
via the Great Ocean Road
($355), and seven days
Adelaide to Alice Springs via
Uluru ($895).

Nullarbor Traveller

(☎ 1800 816 858; www.
the-traveller.com.au) Small,
eco-certified company
running relaxed minibus
trips across the Nullarbor.
Ten days Adelaide to Perth
costs $1495, including
bushwalking, surfing,
whale watching, meals and
national-park entry fees.

Oz Experience (☎ 1800

555 287; www.ozexperience.
com) Sociable hop-on, hop-off
services covering eastern
Australia. Travel is one-
directional and passes are
valid for up to six months with
unlimited stops. A Sydney–
Cairns pass is $495; the 'Fish
Hook' pass from Sydney or
Melbourne to Darwin is $1475.

Bus Passes

Greyhound offers a slew of
passes geared towards various types and routes of travel:
see www.greyhound.com.au/
australia-bus-pass for details.
Many offer a 10% discount
for members of YHA, VIP,
Nomads and other approved
organisations.

EXPLORER PASSES

Hop-on, hop-off passes
that are matched to popular
itineraries. You don't have the
backtracking flexibility of the
Kilometre Pass, but if you can
find a route that suits you it
generally works out cheaper.

The Aussie Highlights
Pass ($1864) allows you to
loop around the eastern half
of Australia from Sydney to
Melbourne, Adelaide, Coober
Pedy, Alice Springs, Darwin,
Cairns, Townsville, the
Whitsundays, Brisbane and
Surfers Paradise. Or there
are one-way passes, such

as the Best of the Outback
($976): Sydney to Darwin via
Melbourne, Adelaide and Alice
Springs.

KILOMETRE PASS

This is the simplest pass and
gives you a specified amount
of travel, starting at 500km
($105) and going up in incre-
ments of 1000km to 2000km
($2239), with a maximum
of 25,000km ($2585). It's
valid for 12 months and you
can travel where and in what
direction you please, and stop
as many times as you like. Use
the online kilometre chart to
figure out which one suits you.
Phone at least a day ahead to
reserve your seat.

Classes

There are no class divisions
on Australian buses (very
democratic), and the vehicles
of the different companies
all look pretty similar and
are equipped with air-con,
toilets and videos. Smoking is
a no-no.

Costs

Following are the average,
non-discounted, one-way bus
fares on some well-travelled
routes.

ROUTE	ADULT/ CHILD/ CONCESSION
Adelaide- Darwin	$595/540/560
Adelaide- Melbourne	$70/60/65
Brisbane- Cairns	$260/220/250
Cairns- Sydney	$410/350/370
Sydney- Brisbane	$140/110/115
Sydney- Melbourne	$65/60/60

🚗 CAR & MOTORCYCLE

With its vast distances, endless stretches of bitumen and off-the-beaten-track sights, exploring Australia by road is an experience unlike any other.

Driving Licence

To drive in Australia you'll need to hold a current driving licence issued in English from your home country. If the licence isn't in English, you'll also need to carry an International Driving Permit, issued in your home country.

Hire

Larger car-rental companies have drop-offs in major cities and towns. Most companies require drivers to be over the age of 21, though in some cases it's 18 and in others 25.

Suggestions to assist in the process:

o Read the contract cover to cover.

o Bond: some companies may require a signed credit-card slip, others may actually charge your credit card; if this is the case, find out when you'll get a refund.

o Ask if unlimited kilometres are included and, if not, what the extra charge per kilometre is.

o Find out what excess you'll pay if you have a prang, and if it can be lowered by an extra charge per day. Check if your personal travel insurance covers you for vehicle accidents and excess.

o Check for exclusions (hitting a kangaroo, damage on unsealed roads etc) and whether you're covered on unavoidable unsealed roads (eg accessing campgrounds). Some companies also exclude parts of the car from cover, such as the underbelly, tyres and windscreen.

o At pick-up inspect the vehicle for any damage. Make a note of anything on the contract before you sign.

o Ask about breakdown and accident procedures.

o If you can, return the vehicle during business hours and insist on an inspection in your presence.

There are a huge number of rental companies. Useful sites offering last-minute discounts:

Carhire.com (www.carhire.com.au)

Drive Now (www.drivenow.com.au)

Webjet (www.webjet.com.au)

4WD & Campervan Hire

A small 4WD such as a Suzuki Vitara or Toyota Rav4 costs between $85 and $100 a day. A Toyota Landcruiser is at least $100, which should include insurance and some free kilometres (100km to 200km a day, or sometimes unlimited).

Check conditions carefully, especially the excess, as it can be onerous – in the NT $5000 is typical, but this can often be reduced to around $1000 (or even to nil) by paying an extra daily charge (around $50). Even for a 4WD, insurance offered by most companies may not cover damage caused travelling 'off-road', meaning anywhere that isn't a maintained bitumen or dirt road.

Hertz, Budget and Avis have 4WD rentals, with one-way rentals possible between the eastern states and the NT. Other companies for campervan hire – with rates from around $70 (two-berth) or $100 (four-berth) per day, usually with minimum five-day hire and unlimited kilometres:

Apollo (☎ 1800 777 779; www.apollocamper.com)

Backpacker Campervans (☎ 1800 670 232; www.backpackercampervans.com)

Britz (☎ 1800 331 454; www.britz.com.au)

Maui (☎ 1300 363 800; www.maui.com.au)

Wicked Campers (☎ 1800 246 869; www.wickedcampers.com.au)

Insurance

When it comes to hire cars, understand your liability in the event of an accident. Rather than risk paying out thousands of dollars, take out comprehensive car insurance or pay an additional daily amount to the rental company for excess reduction. This reduces the excess payable in the event of an accident from between $2000 and $5000 to a few hundred dollars.

Be aware that if travelling on dirt roads you will not be covered by insurance unless you have a 4WD. Also, most companies' insurance won't cover the cost of damage to glass (including the windscreen) or tyres.

Auto Clubs

Automobile clubs in each state are handy when it comes to insurance, regulations, maps and roadside assistance. Club membership (around $100 to $150) can save you a lot of trouble if things go wrong mechanically. If you're a member of an auto club in your home country, check if reciprocal rights are offered in Australia. The Australian auto clubs listed below generally offer reciprocal rights in other states and territories:

AAA (Australian Automobile Association; ☎ 02-6247 7311; www.aaa.asn.au)

AANT (Automobile Association of the Northern Territory; ☎ 08-8925 5901; www.aant.com.au)

NRMA (☎ 13 11 22; www.mynrma.com.au) NSW and the ACT.

RAC (Royal Automobile Club of WA; ☎ 13 17 03; www.rac.com.au)

RACQ (Royal Automobile Club of Queensland; ☎ 13 19 05; www.racq.com.au)

RACT (Royal Automobile Club of Tasmania; ☎ 13 27 22; www.ract.com.au)

RACV (Royal Automobile Club of Victoria; ☎ 13 72 28; www.racv.com.au)

Road Rules

Australians drive on the left-hand side of the road and all cars are right-hand drive.

Give way An important road rule is 'give way to the right' – if an intersection is unmarked (unusual), you must give way to vehicles entering the intersection from your right.

Speed limits The general speed limit in built-up and residential areas is 50km/h (or sometimes 40km/h). Near schools, the limit is usually 25km/h in the morning and afternoon. On the highway it's usually 100km/h or 110km/h; in the NT it's either 110km/h or 130km/h. Police have speed radar guns and cameras and are fond of using them in strategic locations.

Seatbelts It's the law to wear seatbelts front and back; you're likely to get a fine if you don't. Small children must be belted into an approved safety seat.

Drink-driving Random breath-tests are common. If you're caught with a blood-alcohol level of more than 0.05% expect a fine and the loss of your licence. Police can also randomly pull any driver over for a breathalyser or drug test.

Mobile phones Talking on a mobile phone while driving is illegal in Australia (excluding hands-free technology).

Parking

A real big-city headache (also occurring in tourist towns like Byron Bay) is finding somewhere to park. When you do find a spot, there's likely to be a time restriction, meter (or ticket machine) or both. Overstaying your welcome (even by a few minutes) in a parking space may cost you anywhere from $50 to $120. If you park in a 'clearway' your car will be towed away or clamped – look for signs. In the cities there are large multistorey car parks where you can park all day for between $10 and $25.

Road Conditions

Australia has few multilane highways, although there are some stretches of divided road (four or six lanes) in busy areas, including the Princes Hwy from Murray Bridge to Adelaide, most of the Pacific Hwy from Sydney to Brisbane, and the Hume Hwy and Princes and Calder Fwys in Victoria. Elsewhere major roads are all sealed two-laners. Anybody who wants to see the country in reasonable detail should expect some dirt-road travelling.

Australian drivers are generally courteous, but risks can be posed by rural petrolheads, inner-city speedsters and, particularly, drunk drivers. Driving on dirt roads can also be tricky if you're not used to them.

Hazards & Precautions

BEHIND THE WHEEL

Be wary of driver fatigue; driving long distances (particularly in hot weather) can be utterly exhausting. Falling asleep at the wheel is not uncommon. On a long haul, stop and rest every two hours or so – do some exercise, change drivers or have a coffee. Carry a mobile phone if possible, but be aware that there isn't always coverage in country areas. Be careful overtaking road trains; you'll need distance and plenty of speed. On single-lane roads get right off the road when one approaches.

ON YOUR BIKE

Motorcyclists should be aware of dehydration in the dry, hot air – carry at least 5L of water on remote roads in central Australia and drink plenty of it, even if you don't feel thirsty. In Tasmania and Victoria, be prepared for cold winters and rain at any time of year. It's worth carrying some spares and tools even if you don't know how to use them, because someone else often does. Carry a workshop manual for your bike and spare elastic (octopus) straps for securing your gear.

ANIMAL HAZARDS

The road kill that you see alongside roads around the country is usually the result of cars and trucks hitting animals at night. It's a huge problem in Australia, particularly in the NT, Queensland, NSW, SA and Tasmania. Many Australians avoid travelling altogether once the sun drops because of the risks posed by animals on the roads.

Kangaroos are common on country roads, as are cows and sheep in the unfenced outback – hitting an animal of this size will make a mess of your car. Kangaroos are most active around dawn and dusk and often travel in groups. If you see one hopping across the road, slow right down, as its friends may be just behind it.

If you hit and kill an animal while driving, pull it off the road, preventing the next car from having a potential accident. If the animal is only injured and is small, perhaps an orphaned joey (baby kangaroo), wrap it in a towel or blanket and call the relevant wildlife rescue line:

Fauna Rescue of South Australia (☏ 08-8289 0896; www.faunarescue.org.au)

NSW Wildlife Information, Rescue & Education Service (WIRES; ☏ 1300 094 737; www.wires.org.au)

Northern Territory Wildlife Rescue hotline Darwin (☏ 0409 090 840); Katherine (☏ 0412 955 336); Alice Springs (☏ 0419 221 128)

Queensland Department of Environment & Resource Management (☏ 1300 130 372; www.derm.qld.gov.au)

Tasmania Parks & Wildlife Service Tasmania (☏ 1300 135 513; www.parks.tas.gov.au)

Western Australia Department of Environment & Conservation (☏ 08-9474 9055, marine emergencies 08-9483 6462; www.dec.wa.gov.au)

Wildlife Victoria (☏ 1300 094 535; www.wildlifevictoria.org.au)

Fuel

Fuel (predominantly unleaded and diesel) is available from service stations sporting well-known international brand names. LPG (liquefied petroleum gas) is not always stocked at more remote roadhouses; if you're on gas it's safer to have dual-fuel capacity.

Prices vary from place to place, but at the time of writing unleaded was hovering between $1.25 and $1.55 in the cities. Out in the country, prices soar – in outback NT and Queensland you can pay as much as $2.20 a litre. Distances between fill-ups can be long in the outback, but there are only a handful of tracks where you'll require a long-range fuel tank. On main roads there'll be a small town or roadhouse roughly every 150km to 200km. Many petrol stations, but not all, are open 24 hours.

Resources

Australian Bureau of Meteorology (www.bom.gov.au)

Motorcycle Riders Association of Australia (MRAA; www.mraa.org.au)

NT Road Conditions Hotline (☏ 1800 246 199; www.roadreport.nt.gov.au)

South Australia Road Conditions (☏ 1300 361 033; www.transport.sa.gov.au)

Queensland Traffic & Travel Information (☏ 13 19 40; http://highload.131940.qld.gov.au)

WA Road Conditions Hotline (☏ 13 81 38; www.mainroads.wa.gov.au)

CARBON OFFSETS

Various organisations use 'carbon calculators' that allow travellers to offset the greenhouse gases they are responsible for with financial contributions. Some Australian-based organisations:

Carbon Neutral (www.carbonneutral.com.au)

Carbon Planet (www.carbonplanet.com)

Elementree (www.elementree.com.au)

Greenfleet (www.greenfleet.com.au)

🚃 TRAIN

Long-distance rail travel in Australia is something you do because you really want to – not because it's cheap, convenient or fast. That said, trains are more comfortable than buses, and there's a certain long-distance 'romance of the rails' that's alive and kicking. Shorter-distance rail services within each state are run by that state's rail body, either government or private – see state and territory transport sections for details.

The three major interstate services in Australia are operated by **Great Southern Rail** (☎ 13 21 47; www.gsr.com.au), namely the *Indian Pacific* between Sydney and Perth, the *Overland* between Melbourne and Adelaide, and the *Ghan* between Adelaide and Darwin via Alice Springs. There's also the *Sunlander* service between Brisbane and Cairns operated by **Queensland Rail** (☎ 1800 872 467; www.queenslandrail.com.au). Trains from Sydney to Brisbane, Melbourne and Canberra are operated by **CountryLink** (☎ 13 22 32; www.countrylink.info).

Costs

Following are standard internet-booked one-way train fares. Note that cheaper seat fares are readily available but are generally nonrefundable with no changes permitted. Backpacker discounts are also available. Discounted tickets work on a first-come, first-served quota basis, so it pays to book in advance.

Adelaide–Darwin Adult/child seated $716/331; from $1372/876 in a cabin.

Adelaide–Melbourne Adult/child seated $90/45.

Adelaide–Perth Adult/child seated $716/286; from $1402/913 in a cabin.

Brisbane–Cairns Adult/child seated $214/157; from $420/252 in a cabin.

Sydney–Canberra Adult/child seated $40/18.

Sydney–Brisbane Adult/child seated $91/65.

Sydney–Melbourne Adult/child seated $91/65.

Sydney–Perth Adult/child seated $751/251, from $2008/1158 in a cabin.

Train Passes

The Ausrail Pass offered by **Great Southern Rail** (☎ 13 21 47; www.gsr.com.au) permits unlimited travel on the interstate rail network (including CountryLink and *Sunlander* services) over a six-month period (seated, not in cabins). The pass costs $990/890 per adult when purchased inside/outside Australia – inexpensive considering the amount of ground you could cover in six months.

Great Southern Rail also offers the Rail Explorer Pass for international visitors (you'll need to prove it!), costing $690 per adult, permitting six months' travel on the *Ghan*, the *Overland* and the *Indian Pacific* (again, seated, not in cabins).

CountryLink (☎ 13 22 32; www.countrylink.info) offers two passes. The East Coast Discovery Pass allows one-way economy travel between Melbourne and Cairns (in either direction) with unlimited stopovers, and is valid for six months – the full trip costs $450, while Sydney to Cairns is $370 and Brisbane to Cairns is $280. The Backtracker Pass, available only to international visitors, permits travel on the entire CountryLink network and has four versions: a 14-day/one-/three-/six-month pass costing $232/275/298/420 respectively.

Behind the Scenes

Author Thanks

CHARLES RAWLINGS-WAY

Huge thanks to Maryanne for the gig, and to my curvaceous co-pilot Meg, with whom I covered a helluva lot of kilometres in search of the perfect review. Thanks to my dedicated co-authors – an expert crew of wandering wordsmiths – and to the all-star in-house Lonely Planet production staff. Thank goodness for that piece of wire that held my exhaust together in the South Australian outback, and for my two daughters who provided countless laughs and unscheduled pit-stops along the way.

Acknowledgments

Climate map data adapted from Peel MC, Finlayson BL & McMahon TA (2007) 'Updated World Map of the Köppen-Geiger Climate Classification', *Hydrology and Earth System Sciences*, 11, 163344.

Image p134: artwork courtesy of the artist Shirana Shahbazi and Galerie Bob van Orsouw, Zurich; image p339: image courtesy of MONA Museum of Old and New Art.

Cover photographs
Front: Uluru (Ayers Rock), Northern Territory, Paul Sinclair
Back: Sydney Opera House and harbour, Glenn van der Knijff

Many of the images in this guide are available for licensing from Lonely Planet Images: www.lonelyplanetimages.com.

Our Readers

Katrina Anlezark, Edward J Burgess, Mirelle Huijskens, Alvin Prima, Maria Rapetskaya

This Book

The 2nd edition of *Discover Australia* was coordinated by Charles Rawlings-Way, and draws on the on-the-ground research and writing of Brett Atkinson, Jayne D'Arcy, Peter Dragicevich, Sarah Gilbert, Paul Harding, Catherine Le Nevez, Virginia Maxwell, Miriam Raphael, Regis St Louis, Steve Waters, Penny Watson and Meg Worby. We'd also like to thank the following people for their contributions to this guide: Dr Michael Cathcart, Hugh Finlay (on whose original text the Aboriginal Art chapter is based), Dr Tim Flannery, Gabi Mocatta and Olivia Pozzan. The first edition was coordinated by Lindsay Brown. This guidebook was commissioned in Lonely Planet's Melbourne office, and produced by the following:

Commissioning Editor Maryanne Netto
Coordinating Editors Nigel Chin, Alison Ridgway
Coordinating Cartographer Hunor Csutoros
Coordinating Layout Designer Lauren Egan
Managing Editors Anna Metcalfe, Kirsten Rawlings
Managing Cartographer David Connolly
Managing Layout Designers Chris Girdler, Jane Hart
Assisting Editors Carly Hall, Elizabeth Swan
Assisting Cartographer Corey Hutchison
Assisting Layout Designers Frank Deim, Paul Iacono
Cover Research Naomi Parker
Internal Image Research Rebecca Skinner
Thanks to Melanie Dankel, Ryan Evans, Liz Heynes, Yvonne Kirk, Trent Paton, Gerard Walker

NOTES

394

NOTES

Index

000 Map pages

How to Use This Book

These symbols will help you find the listings you want:

- 🐬 Beaches
- ◎ Sights
- 🏃 Activities
- 🌀 Courses
- 🍸 Tours
- 🎉 Festivals & Events
- 🛏 Sleeping
- 🍴 Eating
- 🍷 Drinking
- ☆ Entertainment
- 🛍 Shopping
- ⓘ Information/Transport

Look out for these icons:

- **FREE** No payment required
- 🌿 A green or sustainable option

Our authors have nominated these places as demonstrating a strong commitment to sustainability – for example by supporting local communities and producers, operating in an environmentally friendly way, or supporting conservation projects.

These symbols give you the vital information for each listing:

- ♪ Telephone Numbers
- ⊙ Opening Hours
- Ⓟ Parking
- ⊖ Nonsmoking
- ✳ Air-Conditioning
- @ Internet Access
- ☎ Wi-Fi Access
- ⊠ Swimming Pool
- ✐ Vegetarian Selection
- 0 English-Language Menu
- ♣ Family-Friendly
- 🐾 Pet-Friendly
- 🚌 Bus
- ⛴ Ferry
- Ⓜ Metro
- Ⓢ Subway
- ⊖ London Tube
- 🚋 Tram
- 🚆 Train

Reviews are organised by author preference.

Map Legend

Sights
- 🐬 Beach
- 🕉 Buddhist
- 🏰 Castle
- ✝ Christian
- 🕉 Hindu
- ☪ Islamic
- ✡ Jewish
- ❶ Monument
- 🏛 Museum/Gallery
- ⊗ Ruin
- 🍷 Winery/Vineyard
- 🐾 Zoo
- ◉ Other Sight

Activities, Courses & Tours
- 🤿 Diving/Snorkelling
- 🛶 Canoeing/Kayaking
- ⛷ Skiing
- 🏄 Surfing
- 🏊 Swimming/Pool
- 🚶 Walking
- 🏄 Windsurfing
- ✦ Other Activity/Course/Tour

Sleeping
- 🛏 Sleeping
- ⛺ Camping

Eating
- 🍴 Eating

Drinking
- 🍸 Drinking
- ☕ Cafe

Entertainment
- ☆ Entertainment

Shopping
- 🛍 Shopping

Information
- ✉ Post Office
- ⓘ Tourist Information

Transport
- ✈ Airport
- ⊗ Border Crossing
- 🚌 Bus
- 🚠 Cable Car/Funicular
- 🚲 Cycling
- ⛴ Ferry
- Ⓜ Metro
- 🚝 Monorail
- Ⓟ Parking
- Ⓢ S-Bahn
- 🚕 Taxi
- 🚉 Train/Railway
- 🚊 Tram
- Ⓣ Tube Station
- Ⓤ U-Bahn
- ● Other Transport

Routes
- Tollway
- Freeway
- Primary
- Secondary
- Tertiary
- Lane
- Unsealed Road
- Plaza/Mall
- Steps
-)=(Tunnel
- Pedestrian Overpass
- Walking Tour
- Walking Tour Detour
- Path

Boundaries
- International
- State/Province
- Disputed
- Regional/Suburb
- Marine Park
- Cliff
- Wall

Population
- 🟊 Capital (National)
- ◉ Capital (State/Province)
- ● City/Large Town
- ● Town/Village

Geographic
- 🏠 Hut/Shelter
- 🔦 Lighthouse
- 👁 Lookout
- ▲ Mountain/Volcano
- 🌴 Oasis
- 🌳 Park
-)(Pass
- 🍴 Picnic Area
- 💧 Waterfall

Hydrography
- River/Creek
- Intermittent River
- Swamp/Mangrove
- Reef
- Canal
- Water
- Dry/Salt/Intermittent Lake
- Glacier

Areas
- Beach/Desert
- Cemetery (Christian)
- Cemetery (Other)
- Park/Forest
- Sportsground
- Sight (Building)
- Top Sight (Building)

REGIS ST LOUIS

Brisbane & the East Coast Beaches, Tropical North Queensland Regis' love of Australia has taken him all across the country, from rugged Western Australia to tropical Queensland. On his most recent trip, he explored the bohemian side of Brisbane, visited Granite Belt wineries and introduced his daughters to cuddly koalas at Lone Pine Koala Sanctuary. Regis has contributed to over 30 Lonely Planet titles, including *Queensland & the Great Barrier Reef*. When not travelling, he splits his time between New York City and Sydney.

Read more about Regis at:
lonelyplanet.com/members/regisstlouis

STEVE WATERS

Perth & the West Coast It's been sixteen years since Steve first travelled through Western Australia in a battered Torana, and he's been a regular visitor ever since. This trip covered 17,600kms, five blown tyres, four lost hats, three pairs of wrecked sunglasses and a close shave with an emu as he traversed the state from Kalumburu to Cervantes. Steve has also authored the West Sumatra chapter of *Indonesia*, and while not on the road, plays with databases in Lonely Planet's Melbourne office.

PENNY WATSON

Brisbane & the East Coast Beaches Penny Watson is a trained journalist and full-time professional travel writer. She grew up in regional New South Wales and has since become an expert on its varied landscapes. This is her third Australia guide and her fourth title covering this exceptionally unique and diverse chunk of her home country. As a Hong Kong resident, the opportunity to return to Australia and explore some more is always too tempting to ignore. Visit www.pennywatson.com.au for more of Penny's travel stories.

MEG WORBY

Uluru & the Red Centre, Best of the Rest An Adelaide girl who went away and was inexorably drawn back, Meg thinks South Australia is like everywhere else was 10 years ago – yet the best bits of the Festival State (the wine regions, the Adelaide Hills, city parking) are definitely 10 years ahead. Which makes them very 'now'. Darwin and the magnificent Northern Territory, on the other hand, are from the future, when nature takes over... A former member of Lonely Planet's languages, editorial and publishing teams, this is Meg's sixth Australian guidebook.

CONTRIBUTING AUTHORS

Dr Michael Cathcart wrote the History chapter. Michael teaches history at the Australian Centre, the University of Melbourne. He is well known as a broadcaster on ABC Radio National and has presented history programs on ABC TV. His most recent book is *The Water Dreamers* (2009), a history of how water shaped the history of Australia.

Dr Tim Flannery wrote the Environment chapter. Tim is a scientist, explorer and writer. He has written several award-winning books, including *The Future Eaters*, *Throwim Way Leg* and *The Weather Makers*. He lives in Sydney where he is a professor in the faculty of science at Macquarie University.

PETER DRAGICEVICH

Perth & the West Coast If his great-grandfather hadn't died in mysterious circumstances beneath a train in Kalgoorlie, Peter may have been born Western Australian. Instead the family continued on to New Zealand, where Peter lived until his newspaper career took him to Australia in the late 1990s. He has subsequently worked on more than 20 Lonely Planet titles, including *Sydney* and *East Coast Australia*. Co-authoring *Perth & West Coast Australia* took him one step closer to his goal of circumnavigating the continent, one book at a time.

Read more about Peter at:
lonelyplanet.com/members/peterdragicevich

SARAH GILBERT

Brisbane & the East Coast Beaches, Best of the Rest Sarah grew up in Sydney, studied at the Australian National University in Canberra and has since lived in Amsterdam, New York and Buenos Aires. She cut her teeth on the Big Apple's tabloids, took up travel writing in Argentina and has contributed to several Lonely Planet guides. Based in Sydney and Buenos Aires, she makes her living as a freelance writer and a researcher for film and television. She is currently writing her first book of nonfiction.

PAUL HARDING

Melbourne & the Great Ocean Road Melbourne-born but country-raised, Paul spent childhood summers in the Gippsland Lakes, and later many fishing and camping trips along the Murray River and ski trips to Mt Hotham. He's since seen (and written about) a good part of the world, but still calls this part of Australia home. For this edition, Paul travelled around most of regional Victoria and discovered – yet again – what a beautiful state this is. A freelance writer and photographer, Paul has contributed to more than 30 Lonely Planet guides.

CATHERINE LE NEVEZ

Tropical North Queensland Catherine's first writing for Lonely Planet was about Queensland while completing her Doctorate of Creative Arts in Writing, during a 65,000km lap-and-a-half of the continent, driving through two cyclones. Since then, Catherine has authored more than two dozen guidebooks worldwide, including Lonely Planet's *Queensland & the Great Barrier Reef* and *East Coast Australia* guides (and relived one of those cyclone-pounded drives for a Lonely Planet feature).

VIRGINIA MAXWELL

Sydney & the Blue Mountains Despite being born, bred and based in Melbourne, Virginia knows Sydney well and loves it to bits. Having lived there in the past and visited frequently ever since, she has a good grasp of where to swim, sleep and generally swan about. When not writing about the Harbour City, Virginia covers Turkey and Italy for Lonely Planet and produces a well-known Australian book industry catalogue.

Read more about Virginia at:
lonelyplanet.com/members/virginiamaxwell

MIRIAM RAPHAEL

Uluru & the Red Centre Miriam has lived in the Northern Territory since 2009, first in Alice Springs as a reporter for the local paper and now in tropical Darwin where she works as a writer and radio producer. Miriam makes the most of the famous 'territory lifestyle', heading out bush with her ol' Nissan Patrol Dot, jumping into waterholes and drinking beer like water. This is her eighth guidebook for Lonely Planet.

Our Story

A beat-up old car, a few dollars in the pocket and a sense of adventure. In 1972 that's all Tony and Maureen Wheeler needed for the trip of a lifetime – across Europe and Asia overland to Australia. It took several months, and at the end – broke but inspired – they sat at their kitchen table writing and stapling together their first travel guide, *Across Asia on the Cheap*. Within a week they'd sold 1500 copies. Lonely Planet was born.

Today, Lonely Planet has offices in Melbourne, London and Oakland, with more than 600 staff and writers. We share Tony's belief that 'a great guidebook should do three things: inform, educate and amuse'.

Our Writers

CHARLES RAWLINGS-WAY

Coordinating Author, Uluru & the Red Centre, Best of the Rest As a likely lad, Charles suffered in shorts through Tasmanian winters, and in summer counted the days till he visited his grandparents in Adelaide. With desert-hot days, cool swimming pools and *four* TV stations, this flat city held paradisiacal status. He's since broadened his horizons across all of Autsralia's states and territories, developing soft spots for Fremantle, Byron Bay, Fitzroy and the Great Ocean Road. These days Charles lives in the Adelaide Hills and has acquired an unnatural appreciation for Coopers Pale Ale. An underrated rock guitarist and sleepy new dad, this is Charles' 22nd book for Lonely Planet.

BRETT ATKINSON

Best of the Rest Brett Atkinson loves Tasmania's spectacular scenery, the laid-back locals, and the island's superb food and wine. During extended research around his favourite Australian state, he most enjoyed rugged Bruny Island, the stunning Tasman Peninsula, and conducting diligent investigation of the local craft beer scene in Hobart's pubs. Based in Auckland, Brett combines working for Lonely Planet with exploring the world as a freelance food and travel writer. See www.brett-atkinson.net to see what he's been eating and where he's headed next.

JAYNE D'ARCY

Melbourne & the Great Ocean Road Growing up in the Victorian seaside suburb of Frankston had its advantages for Jayne; it motivated her to catch the Met through all three zones to hang out in Prahran's Greville St, Fitzroy's Brunswick St, St Kilda and the Queen Vic market. She eventually switched sides and hung out on the Great Ocean Road while studying journalism. After a longish spell working in community radio in East Timor, she finally settled with her family in Melbourne's vibrant north (in zone 1, just).

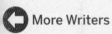 **More Writers** ....

Published by Lonely Planet Publications Pty Ltd
ABN 36 005 607 983
2nd edition – Jan 2012
ISBN 978 1 74220 111 5
© Lonely Planet 2012   Photographs © as indicated 2012
10 9 8 7 6 5 4 3 2 1
Printed in China